STRANGE MYSTERIES OF TIME AND SPACE

HAROLD T. WILKINS

PREFACE

AFTER half a century of travels by train, ship, and air, or on shank's mare, into out-of-the-way parts of the world, the author has found that it is essential, where possible, to visit in person the location of a mystery. And he has been forced to recognize that, in trying to solve *one* mystery, he has often unearthed another mystery which, at first seeming to hold the clue to the first, yet, in the end, may prove either to be a false trail or merely to heighten the *first* mystery that he has been investigating. It is a truism—but one by no means generally recognized—that there is nothing stranger than the mind of man. When men and women lose the sense of mystery, life will prove to be a gray and dreary business, only with difficulty to be endured. But that *any* fool can entertain was, alas, a silly saying of the late Bernard Shaw! If the reader finds entertainment in this book, the author will have achieved his main purpose.

HAROLD T. WILKINS

ISBN-13: 978-1532831126
ISBN-10: 1532831129

PRINTING HISTORY
Ace edition published 1958
Citadel edition published 1959
Saucerian Press edition published 1979
New Saucerian Press edition published 2017

©2017 New Saucerian, LLC

CONTENTS

Preface   6

PART ONE
LEGAL MYSTERIES

Chapter	1	Solving the Great Tichborne Mystery	7
	2	What Happened to Elizabeth Canning?	32

PART TWO
THE EERIE, THE MACABRE AND THE LOST

Chapter	3	Ambrose Bierce "Goes into the Darkness"	53
	4	Walled-up for Twenty-one Years in Modern Times	68
	5	The Monster of Bruges	83
	6	The Mystery of Lord Kitchener's Corpse	85
	7	Missing Persons Mysteries	118

PART THREE
WAR AND POST-WAR MYSTERIES

Chapter	8	The Vanishing Aeroplanes	132
	9	How Did They Get There?	156

PART FOUR
MYSTERIES OF SPACE-TIME

Chapter	10	Tales of Creatures and People Out of This World	178
	11	The Shepton Mallet Mystery	209

PART FIVE
THE QUEER AND THE BIZARRE IN THE TWENTIETH CENTURY

Chapter	12	What Killed Harry Dean?	217
	13	The Strange Piltdown Man Puzzle	230

PART SIX
RIDDLES OF THE SEA

Chapter	14	The Fate of the *Grosvenor*	237
	15	New Light on the *Mary Celeste*	271

PART ONE

LEGAL MYSTERIES

Chapter 1

SOLVING THE GREAT TICHBORNE MYSTERY

Few of the present generation, exclusive of legal historians—and indeed, not many of them—know the inside of this mystery, famous or notorious, of more than eighty years ago. For more than three quarters of a century, a pretty ghastly skeleton has been grinning behind the oak and mahogany panels of the ancestral cupboards of one of the oldest and wealthiest of English aristocratic houses.

Its ancient manor house of Tichborne, in the Selborne country, still stands today, in a romantic corner of Hampshire, with the flighty rooks cawing in a congress dance round and round the tops of its immemorial trees. All round it are the greenest of fields, fragrant with cowslips and oxlips in springtime, where, as a forgotten Victorian poetess said: "Solemn and sweet the churchbells' chime floats through the woods at morn, all other sounds in that still time of leaf and breeze are born." It is, even today, free from the racket of the passing jet and the roar of aero engines warming up on a distant aerodrome. The countryside indeed, is not very different from what it was in 1829, when Roger Tichborne was born in that stately old manor house.

He was educated at the famous Jesuit seminary at Stonyhurst, Lancashire, in the 1840s, became an officer in a regiment of Carabineers, in Ireland, led the usual dissipated life of the *jeunesse dorée* of his age, and, in despair at having been refused the hand of his cousin, Kate Doughty, left England in 1851, to set out on his travels into a part of the world, which, even today, seems almost as remote from Europe as the planet Mars. That is, South America. Our legal historians say that her hand was refused him, because, as good Catholics, neither could marry a first cousin. Alternatively they say that Kate's mamma, Lady Doughty, had been told about Roger's boozing, dissipation, and the sowing of wild oats while he was in the Carabineers, that she became horrified at the prospect of her daughter's union with such a man, and forbade it. We shall see, later, why neither of these pathetic fables is true. The secrets of some of these early and mid-Victorian houses were, sometimes, quite as queer as they were startling.

I well remember an old Victorian maid-servant who, when I was a somewhat scoffing youth, too frequently, as I thought, hinted to me about a dreadful secret of a big country house in Worcestershire, where she was in service in the 1880s. She had the irritating habit of shutting up like a clam when it came to spilling the beans, good and proper—or improper. Indeed, I had grave difficulty in refraining from saying: "What the h—— *was* it?" However, having one day taken the precaution of lacing a black-currant posset, to which she was rather partial, with some very old cognac, "unbeknownst" to her, I extracted the secret: to wit, that the Hon. Miss Bella Marmaduke, who was bed-ridden, had, one very early morning, been seen by the housemaid to be trailing a very *long and simian tail* along the panelled corridor and into the garden-conservatory, where she sampled some very choice, black hothouse grapes before the head-gardener was around.

Now, after travelling up and down the Chilian and Peruvian coasts—what a pity he never told of the adventures he must have had, in those romantic days!—and trailing inland towards the cordilleras of the Andes, Roger Tichborne eventually pulled up, stony-broke, in the port of Rio de Janeiro. This heir to great estates of a very ancient aristocratic family, famed long before the days when King Henry VI, founded "Eton College by Wyndsore" for the poor and and needy scholars who never have been seen there—and you will find the Tichbornes mentioned in the deeds and terriers of Eton College and its endowments—had not enough money to pay his passage out of Brazil, in what were the yellow fever days.

Down in the harbour, moored to the blistering, sun-smitten bollards on the wharves, was a full-rigged British barque of 500 tons, the *Bella*, clipper-built and not long off the stocks. Her captain was named Burkett. Roger Tichborne came aboard her, one April morning, in 1854, when she was busy loading up coffee and logwood, and the bucko mates were blaspheming the sweating greasers and the lazy, Brazilian Negroes, lumping huge bales and casks up the planking from the wharves, and down into the *Bella*'s holds.

He was clad in a half-nautical costume of pea-jacket, round, hard hat, and white trousers. His face and hands had been reddened and burnt by the tropical sun and the winds of the cordilleras and pampas across which he had travelled from Santiago, in Chile, to Buenos Aires. What he looked like, by the time he pulled up in Rio de Janeiro, was a man who had been knocking about for a long time in uncivilized lands, and having a very good time of it, in the process. One would have guessed that he had kept himself out of very few *bodegas, tascas,* and *locandas* (hectic, low-life booze and wine shops) around and in the red-light quarters, and on the odorous and picturesque wharves of Rio Bay, in the 1850s.

Roger told the captain a story of having brought so many curios, jewels, artifacts from Peruvian *huacas* (ancient tombcaches), pictures, and so forth; and spent so much money on boats, rafts, canoes, launches, in his travels, that he could not raise the wind to pay hotel bills, passage by ship, or even the fee for a passport to the Brazilian authorities. No doubt his air of being a gentleman down on his luck, and his accent, impressed the captain as being that of a man who had well-to-do relatives, likely to see that his owners lost nothing, in the end.

The evidence is conflicting about his embarkation from Rio. One story is that he went on board the *Bella* "blind drunk," "lost to the world," after a long spell of boozing the clock round, in this city of lovely and leafy *avenidas,* beautiful *señoritas,* brilliantly star-lit skies, and all the imperial panoply and panache of Dom Pedro II. Anyhow, those were hard-drinking days, even in old England, where Non-conformist chapels *had* to be built almost next door to village taverns, then open for twelve hours; so that, on the Sunday, or any other days for that matter, the local preacher could refresh himself with ale and bread and cheese, after a rousing two-hour Sabbath morning preaching, and fortify his inner man for the two-hour evening preaching, to follow. The old English Puritan was no more teetotaller than was the old English aristocrat—and the author's grandfather preached in this fashion, in russet apple villages, with Methodist chapels, along the Severnside, near Gloucester.

The first story has it that no one was sober aboard the *Bella,* when she cast off from Rio.

The second story is that Roger went on board the ship more sober than many English judges were apt to be, in those days, off the bench. He was smuggled into the lazarette of the ship while a table was set and laid over his head, on a grating, where the Brazilian *alfandegários* (customs officers) drank to the ship and her voyage. If so, he must have skipped from Brazil without a passport. When, on the morning of 20 April, 1854, the *Bella* was fairly out to sea, the grating was removed, and the chuckling captain let out Roger to the light of day. Six days after the *Bella* had left Rio, bound for Jamaica, where, in the port of Kingston, Roger is said to have planned to step ashore, and board a Curaçao barque for Vera Cruz, Mexico, another ship, crossing the *Bella*'s presumed course, saw signs of a wreck, while straw bedding, a water-breaker, and a chest of drawers were floating past on the swell. This ship also sighted a ship's long boat, bottom upwards, on the stern of which the mate read the name: "*Bella*, Liverpool." This flotsam was brought into Rio de Janeiro, and the Brazilian authorities sent out steam-vessels to search for any survivors; but none were found. The British admiral on the South American station also made unsuccessful searches.

There is some reason to suppose that the *Bella* may have turned top-turtle, when hit by a sudden squall or *pampero*, in the South Atlantic. She seems to have been a good way off her proper course, to the southwards. Moreover, she was overladen, to beyond the Plimsoll marks, if one may use an anachronism of the 1850s. It is said that cabin furniture had been placed on her decks to make room for freight. Whatever happened in the South Atlantic is, however, matter for mere conjecture. It is known that the night before the passing ship found this flotsam and jetsam, the weather had been gusty, but there had been nothing worth calling a storm, in those latitudes. This suggests a question: how far had this wreckage drifted, in three or four days?

Meantime, in faraway England, Sir James Tichborne, Roger's father, succeeded to the estates, some years passed, and then he died. Time passed, no news came of any survivors from the *Bella,* and the English High Court at last gave leave to presume Roger's death. But, very much alive, in England, was an old lady of very remarkable appearance, deep-dark eyes, and elfin countenance. She was the natural daughter of a Frenchwoman and an English aristocrat, named Seymour. Her name was Felicité, and she was the Dowager Lady Tichborne, Roger Tichborne's mother, and she had her reasons for disliking the Tichborne family, and the new heir, who was a waster and a rake. He had dissipated much of the Tichborne fortune.

Now, in the *Home News,* of 1862, which was published and read in Australia, there appeared an advertisement, announcing the death and mentioning the will of Sir James Tichborne, father of the missing Roger. It also stated that the next heir was Alfred Tichborne. A year later, the Dowager Lady Tichborne advertised in *The Times,* still seeking news of the missing Roger. Presently, we shall see why she did so. She had probably *heard something!*

In that year, 1863, there was living at a "backblock" place in New South Wales, called Wagga-Wagga, a man named Thomas Castro. He had been there a year, and had married an illiterate domestic servant. The minister, solemnizing the marriage, was a Methodist, whether or no Castro had ever been a member of his flock. Castro was a butcher, fat as if he had lavishly fed on his own joints, and by a curious coincidence—only one of many in, this strangest of all cases of impersonation—he had been in Chile since the year 1849, when he deserted at Valparaiso from his ship, the *Ocean.* He had lodged with one, Don Felipe Tomás Castro, of Melipilla, Chile, and several times had told his host, and people generally, that he, the English sailor, was really a member of the English aristocracy. "The name I bear is not my own," he would say, impressively. (That name was Arthur Orton).

As we have seen, the *real* Roger Tichborne was also travelling in Chile, in the years 1853 and 1854, and sent home letters to England, and to the Dowager Lady Tichborne, at the Dower House at Tichborne Park, Hants. Whether Orton ever met Roger, in Chile, or knew that he was there, does not seem to be known. But there also arose another singular coincidence. The name Castro, which Orton adopted from his *patrón,* Don Felipe, and without any authorization for it, was borne by one, *Rebecca de Castro,* who, as a will shows, had married Roger Robert Tichborne in 1786. Again, one may suspect that Orton knew enough of the family history to recognize the peculiar fitness, from his standpoint, of his adopting the name of Castro. Who can now say? Roger Robert Tichborne had, by this lady, six daughters, the number six bearing a mystic relation to a curse, imposed by a Lady Tichborne, of the thirteenth century, on whomsoever of her posterity should fail, in any one year, to give the famous Tichborne dole to old, labouring men and women on the Tichborne estates. (The dole is still religiously given, today, the modern Tichborne attitude being, presumably: "I do not believe in it; but I will not fail to observe the custom, lest worse befall.")

According to the story told in the famous 102-day Tichborne *versus* Lushington case, heard and tried in the Court of Common Pleas, the claimant, Orton *alias* Castro, read the *Home News* advertisement, and approached an attorney named Gibbes, at Wagga-Wagga. Gibbes behaved with such very unlawyerlike and childish credulity that he unwittingly gave Orton the cue to impersonate the long-lost Roger Tichborne.

Here, at this point, one is giving the conventional and authorized legal version of this strange story. It may well seem hardly credible to the ordinary reader that about two-thirds of the population of Britain, in the 1860s to the 1890s, and even later, firmly believed that Orton was the real Simon Pure, the long-lost Roger Tichborne.

Orton, when calling on Gibbes, smoked a pipe, very carefully and, of course, *artlessly*—it is hoped that the reader will not misinterpret the irony!—inscribed, on the bowl, with the letter, "R.C.T." He put some inquiries about the advertisement, having, at the back of his mind, the possibility of how "to raise the wind and come ashore" in hard times. Gibbes, perhaps, might be lured into becoming his grubstaker, just as if Orton alleged that he had found a lode of gold at Ballarat. Orton uttered certain words of the tendency of what our legal gentlemen call "leading questions": whereupon Gibbes reacted most enthusiastically by acclaiming the "naïve" Orton as the "missing baronet" of the advertisement. Thereupon Orton, with quite artistic casualness, asked if the initials on the pipe he was then, by the most admirable and singular chance, smoking, might by any possibility relate to the long lost Roger Tichborne. And, doubtless, to his immense "surprise", Gibbes at once said: "Good God, man, you must be the very man!"

Not very long after this felicitous meeting with the acute attorney, lo, Castro, who had been married by a Methodist minister, became a Roman Catholic! Whether he ever, in subsequent confession, told the priest, under the secret and sacred seal, that his "memory" of past events had, perhaps, a *little* misled him, we do not know—but we *do* know that Orton had been looking all round the horizon for whatever he could clap his eyes on, and had not failed to recall that no member of the Tichborne family had ever belonged to the Methodist connexion, and that rather awkward questions might, subsequently, be put were it known that the claimant had had, if not a change of heart, at least a change of faith, at a very late, but convenient date in his chequered life. Better late than *never*, he reasoned.

In the year 1863, surely enough, that very point was raised in court, and a witness stated that he thought, when he first saw Orton, that there was as much likeness as between him and the missing Roger as, in torso at any rate, between a dray-horse and a thoroughbred. Of course, Orton lived in the days when the formation and function of ductless and adrenal glands were unknown; or, he would, no doubt, or his expert advisers would, have advanced that as the explanation for the rolling corpulence which the years had brought him. In due time, backed with funds, Orton took ship for Europe.

In Paris, he saw "his mamma," as he called her—the remarkable old Frenchwoman, Felicité, the Dowager Lady Tichborne. Strangely enough, she was convinced that he was the missing Roger, her son! Her conviction was largely based on the result of a physical examination which she—like a Catalan, she was not easily overborne with too much delicacy—*had actually herself* made of the claimant, in a bedroom of a hotel!

That examination showed that Orton, *alias* Castro, possessed a very rare physical malformation, euphemistically referred to, among the Tichbornes, "as the withered leaf." Surgeons and anatomists explain it as the "retractable penis," and say that the statistical rarity is so high that only one man in a million would possess it!

Now, the bar—or at least the bench—affected to pooh-pooh that technical evidence in the eighteen-seventies. Any experienced newspaper man knows that, between doctors and lawyers, there has always existed a very long-standing feud. For example, the law, as regards insanity and some other aspects of medical jurisprudence, is hopelessly out-of-date. Left to some of the judges, it is more than probable that no man who committed murder would, on the plea of insanity or paranoia—and if he were sane in nine points and insane *only* in one—thereby escape the hangman! A psychiatrist, on the *one* point alone, would pronounce him insane; but the judge, regarding the other nine points, probably would say *sane*. We are not here concerned whether it might be better, in the long run, and from the standpoint of communal welfare, to allow judges, unhampered by juries, dealing with fact only, to rid the world of dangerous beasts such as child-rapers and sadistic killers from motives of vanity, all incurables, rather than confine them in criminal lunatic asylums, from which, at any time, they may break out and revert to their former incurable bestialities; or let them free at the end of twenty or thirty years, after very large public expense, to revert to their former unnatural crimes. All one wishes is to try to show that High Court judges, and, perhaps some barristers may evince a natural antagonism—often quite unconscious—in relation to medical men's expertise, as well as to psychiatrists.

In the famous trial, *The Queen V. Thomas Castro*, one mid-Victorian judge, Sir Alexander Cockburn, derided the possibility that a woman of title could, as his judicial innocence averred, "commit such monstrous indelicacy as to strip and examine her own child." But the Dowager Lady Tichborne was no ordinary woman. She was Gallic, realist, and no fool, and she knew the great importance of this rare peculiarity, in relation to the establishment of identity . . . . *And yet*, as "His Highness, the Lord Protector," Oliver Cromwell, said in a very different connotation, one might have repeated to her his words: "Ye say ye are right? I say that, by the bowels of Christ, ye may be mistaken!" But such a retort could *not* have been made to her, as we shall see later, save by the claimant, or a Tichborne Park attorney, or by one of the Tichborne estates trustees. And not one of these would make it—*and say why he made it*!

Arabella Kenealy, daughter of the advocate at the bar, Dr. Kenealy, who defended the man, Orton, *alias* Castro, on trial at the Old Bailey, charged with perjury, in 1873, was alive as late as March, 1936, when she wrote a letter to a London Sunday newspaper. She *rightly contended*, as against the statements made by a former Lord Chancellor, the late Lord Maugham, brother of Somerset Maugham (Miss Kenealy was defending her father's memory), that:

"The Dowager Lady Tichborne's recognition of the claimant, as her long-lost son, was no such cursory affair as it had been described. . . . A clever and astute old Frenchwoman, she was, for a while, in close association with him, and camouflaged as he was by the mountain of flesh, which contributed a note of the phenomenal and monstrous to his personality, and remarkable story, the passing of every day only further convinced her of his identity. A specific malformation had led to her child, Roger, having been dressed, for a period, in girl's clothes. After personally assuring herself that this rare malformation was present in the claimant, further doubt of his identity was beyond question for her."

We shall, later on, return to that point—a very important point in relation to the thesis of this chapter.

Meantime, it is to be noted that the characteristic bias of the law against medicine was seen plainly at work, when the Lord Chief Justice, Sir Alexander Cockburn, flew in the face of the medical evidence, in his summing-up for the jury; and, in order to dispose of what he called Kenealy's innuendo, roundly and stupidly asserted that the "withered leaf" reference, in the correspondence with Lady Doughty, mother of Kate Doughty, whose hand had been refused to

Roger Tichborne, and which was certainly one of the causes persuading him to leave England, had "only a sentimental meaning." Comment on this inanity had best be left to some of Her Majesty's judges, conscious of each other's shortcomings!

Before the civil trial came on, the Dowager Lady Tichborne died, so there is no means of knowing what the nature of her evidence would have been. But, one may here comment, that not the least remarkable feature of this strange affair of personal identity is the fact that, despite the amazing physical resemblances between the lost Roger and the "pretender," Castro, her maternal intuitions, reinforced by differences in "air," breeding, education, accents, social distinctions, and other imponderables, between Castro *alias* Orton, and her own son, Roger, apparently failed to act and inhibit her from going astray. Surely, if it be a wise mother that knows her own child, *something* ought to have warned her that this man was not the missing Roger! Yet, it clearly did *not*.

However, had she lived and appeared in the witness-box, one may doubt whether the testy and pompous old Cockburn, Lord Chief Justice, would have been so asinine and ignorantly dogmatic about this "sentimental" matter of the "withered leaf." He would certainly not have found it so easy to brush away that fact, and confuse the jury, as he did in summing-up at the *second*, or criminal trial, which would follow the civil case. Cockburn would then have a jury to deal with, whose function was to judge of facts; but it is not hard to see that, to have placed this peculiar physical fact fairly before a jury, would hardly have conduced to what Cockburn as head of the Queen's judiciary, had in mind: to end a case that had already lasted a prodigious time and cost much public money, and to secure a unanimous verdict and a conviction.

We may have no brief for Kenealy, or his social, or political views. He was a spell-binder and very much of a charlatan, and there is little doubt that his conduct of the case gravely injured his client, the defendant Orton, or Castro. Yet, Kenealy was a *fighter*, as many of these Victorian advocates of popular, or unpopular causes were; and it may be to some extent true, as the German philosopher, Friedrich Nietzsche once said: "I tell you that a good fight justifies *any* cause."

Kenealy also belonged to the party then hated and loathed and feared by the English governing class and aristocracy, the Radical-Liberal party. He was a friend of John Bright. Bar and Bench, almost to a man, "had it in" for him, on both social and political grounds. His strong point about this malformation was, therefore, scoffed and jeered at by the Bench, and went unmarked by the jury, who were hardly prejudiced in his favour by his eccentric and time-wasting conduct. Be it noted, too, this was a common jury on a criminal case: unpaid, and with not a ha'penny of compensation for lost time and wages. Who might wonder, therefore, if the jury desired to get the case over and done with? We may also, as hinted above, bear in mind that death had removed a very important witness: the Dowager Lady Tichborne.

We have now to revert to the first, *civil* trial, known in the Law Reports as the civil cause of *Tichborne* v. *Lushington*. (Major Lushington was the tenant of the Tichborne estates). This famous trial lasted for 102 days, until March, 1872. The claimant, Orton-Castro, called the "witness," deposed, on 7 November, 1871, that he had been picked up at sea, a castaway, after the sinking of the *Bella*. The ship by which he was rescued was the *Osprey*, and, said the claimant, the *Osprey* arrived at Melbourne, Victoria, Australia, in the summer of 1854, at the height of a gold boom, when ships' crews were deserting wholesale, to join the gold fossickers and sundowners, on the way to the new goldfields, up-country. He added that other passengers, survivors of the *Bella*, had also been rescued in mid-ocean. He produced a witness, named Sharplin, who, from memory, alleged that the claimant had been with him in the *Osprey*.

On inquiry, it appeared that no entry had been made at the Customs House, at Melbourne, about the docking of the *Osprey*. Of course, in a such a time of general confusion there, that might not have been surprising. At the civil trial, none of the owners of the *Bella*, were called, nor any evidence sought from the owners of the *Osprey*, in whose possession was the *Osprey's* log.

As day by day wore on, some very damaging evidence was adduced against the claimant. Someone in Australia had found a pocket-book, in which it was noted that Orton, the claimant, had been practising the writing of the signature of Roger Tichborne: "R. C. Tichborne, Bart., Sir Roger Tichborne," and, in it, he had cited from memory a passage of a mid-Victorian, forgotten novel, in which appeared the famous picaresque aphorism:

"Some men has (*sic*) plenty money and no brains, and some men has plenty brains and no money. Surely men with plenty money and no brains were made for men with plenty brains and no money."

It was, of course, the old crook's philosophy of life in a nutshell; the "faith," with "no damned Socialism about it," of the rogue who desires to live "the life of a perfect gentleman," and never "do a stroke of work."

Then, in the note-book, there followed the rude drawing of a three-masted ship, and the "affidavit" following:

"I, Thos. Castro, do hereby certify that my name is not Thos. Castro at all, therefore, those that say it is don't know nothing about it. . . . R. C. T., R. C. Tichborne, Tichborne Park. . . . I hope some day . . ."

Of course, the claimant's literary style was that of a rather coarsely illiterate man in the street; but, it was rightly pointed out by a witness at the trial—who might fairly have claimed the weight of the testimony of Sir John Fielding, Goldsmith, and nearly all our eighteenth and nineteenth-century novelists and essayists—that the education and manners of many of the best-born English gentlemen, of the 1870s, were not a bit better than those of a common pig-jobber. Nevertheless, the cleverest of advocates could not have removed from the minds of any reasonably *instructed* jurymen the very pronounced dissimilarity between the epistolary style of the *real* Roger Tichborne and the claimant, Orton, assuming that the twelve unfortunates were not mere common garden traders to whom A., the bull's foot, and the beauties of the *Sporting Times* were all one with the poems of Keats, Burns, Shelley, William Shakespeare, Coleridge and Alfred Lord Tennyson.

At last, the trial drew to an end. It had been, like a needless Alexandrine, dragging its slow length along . . . and, ladies and gentlemen of the 1870s well knew *how* it had fleshed the bellies, and stuffed the wallets and pocketbooks of *some* of the legal vultures! Surely, these ingrates of the law and the bar might have wished the claimant better than the very vindictive sentence that the English law—never, at that time, too tender towards low or ill-born men and women—would award to Orton *alias* Castro, at the next forthcoming *criminal* trial of *The Queen* v. *Thomas Castro*, to be staged at the Old Bailey.

The first, or civil trial, cost the defendants, the Tichborne trustees, about £96,000. Their taxed costs, which, of course, Orton, being a bankrupt, could not pay, amounted to no less than £40,000! So, in May 1872, the trustees of the Tichborne estates, to save them from being further wasted by new claimants, or the vultures of the law, applied to the Court of Common Pleas for an order staying all further proceedings in the ejectment action for the recovery of the estates, unless the costs were paid by the defeated claimant, within months—which, of course, was impossible.

This meant that, even had the original Roger Tichborne turned up and claimed his property and patrimony, he would not have been able to start an action, or take over, short of securing the passage of a special Act of Parliament! *But*, no member of the Tichborne family, or the trustees wanted him to turn up, like the devil come to prayers. For, all this time, as we shall later show, *the real, original Roger was actually alive, and both the pretender, Orton, and the trustees of the Tichborne estates KNEW it!* All these tremendous legal charges had to be borne by the Tichborne rent roll of about £30,000 a year. Never, surely, had there been such pickings for the legal fraternity, by which one means the section of it employed by the trustees and the Tichborne family.

Now began the second, *criminal* trial, in the court of Queen's Bench. It was to cost the British taxpayer more than £50,000, even before the 118 days had run their course, on 28 February, 1874.

Today, you may see as the author did in the wet summer of 1954, old engravings of some of the legal lights of the famous civil action, in the saloon bar of the Tichborne Arms, with its ornate and very heraldic sign-board, almost in sight of the umbrageous Tichborne Park in which Orton probably expected to end his days, hunting the nimble fox, and shooting the red deer and the fat pheasants, like a perfect, old English gentleman. But do not, of course, expect that the landlord will be able to unveil any secrets of the family for you. All he knows is, naturally, merely the accepted version. Who could expect him to know more? It all happened long before even his father's day.

At the second trial-at-bar, before three judges, there appeared among the host of witnesses, one, Richard Telfer, second mate of the *Osprey*, which Orton, *alias* Castro alleged had picked him up, after the going-down of the *Bella*, in the South Atlantic. Telfer was also second mate in the *Osprey* on her voyage from Glasgow to Melbourne, Victoria, in 1854. He denied that she had picked up *any* shipwrecked persons in the South Atlantic. One, Stephenson, superintendent of Lloyd's Shipping Corporation of the old Royal Exchange, swore that the long boat of the lost *Bella* was picked up in the South Atlantic, and that wreckage was found on the very day when the *Osprey* anchored in Table Bay, South Africa, which was twenty days' sail, farther south.

Then, the owners of the *Bella* were called into the witness-box. They said, that, from the time she went down, in April 1854, they had never received tidings of her, or her captain, or crew. (This date of April 1854, could not have been more than surmise on the owners' part.) They added that no claim had ever been made by anyone on board, and that insurance on total loss had been settled by the underwriters. An Australian shipping correspondent (he was a member of the staff of the Melbourne *Argus*), said that he had been present when the *Osprey* docked at Geelong, and had heard *no* story of castaways having been picked up on the high seas.

Remarkable evidence was given, too, by Lord Bellew, who had been a schoolfellow of Roger Tichborne, at the Jesuit college of Stonyhurst, England. Both he and Roger had been tattooed, in 1847–8. The marks of a cross, heart, and anchor had been stippled on Roger's arm by himself, Bellew, while Roger had done the like to him. The designs were in China ink, and half an inch long. These marks had been distinctly seen, just before Roger left England to set out on his travels. The marks were indelible. To prove it, Lord Bellew peeled off his coat and showed the marks to the judges and jury. (As doctors know, tattoo marks remain indelible through life.)

The defendant, Orton *alias* Castro, had never been tattooed, and he denied that he had ever had any such desire. This evidence of tattooing was very important in establishing identity. It was, naturally, scouted by the fanatical adherents of Orton; but it was firmly cited by the other side who had ignored the brushed-away and equally incontrovertible evidence of the "withered leaf malformation." Indeed, all the host of lawyers, barristers, or judges who have written memoirs, in which the Tichborne case had been featured, or articles for the lay or legal press, have either paid little or slighting attention to it, or used the wile of judicial, or legal ignorance, or innocence.

Between the two sides, truth has had a very raw deal. Kenealy, the defendant's advocate, seems to have brushed aside this evidence, making the entirely unwarrantable assumption, or innuendo, that the marks were of such trumpery and temporary nature that they vanished almost as soon as they were pricked in Roger's skin. Then came the evidence that has been suppressed, ridiculed, or pooh-poohed by lawyers.

The late Lord Maugham, who was Lord Chancellor, in 1934, wrote a book of 390 pages on the Tichborne case and trials; but, although he tells us he had access to manuscript notes and briefs in the Bar Library of the Middle Temple, he throws no light on the very matter that *is* of interest to the modern reader, and that is, not so much the forensic brilliance of the barristers, the acumen of the Bench, or the perspicuity of old Cockburn, the Lord Chief Justice, but the real and carefully concealed incentive the claimant had for impersonating Roger Tichborne.

Lord Maugham, considering that we are well into the middle of the twentieth century, was singularly old-maidenish in his delicate reticence about the "withered leaf" aspect of the case. After all, he was writing, not merely for lawyers, but for the general public, and that, too, on a very interesting aspect of curious social history and manners. He says:

"There was even a peculiarity in the conformation of the claimant, which the jury investigated, *in corpore vili*, in a private room; for what useful purpose I cannot imagine."

Observations on that prudery had best be left to members of the Bench who are aware of each other's imperfections. We will show that the jury were not such fools as Lord Maugham, and other social-legal historians would have us suppose. Maugham, also, never makes one word of reference to a most attractive "Negress in the woodpile" of this Tichborne affair, and whose portrait, with handsome, middle-age brunette's eyes, long train of straight, and curled black locks, on each side of a pretty and plump face, framed in lace cap and collar, is, or was, easily accessible to Lord Maugham, when he wrote his book.

On 24 October, 1873, the Lord Chief Justice, sitting in the Court of Queen's Bench, heard the evidence of a physician, Dr. David Wilson. This witness said that he had examined the claimant, Orton, and had found a malformation. It took the form he said, of a retracted penis, so that, he went on, when the claimant (now the defendant) passed water, the organ was withdrawn from sight. Witness could not tell whether the malformation would effect sexual potency. (This evidence was, of course, given after the court had been cleared). He said that he agreed with the Lord Chief Justice that, as far as sexual powers were concerned, a man, with this very rare and peculiar malformation, might be as good as anyone else. He had never met such a case before, and he had examined thousands of people.

Other evidence, in court, showed that the real Roger Tichborne, had been kept by his mother, later the Dowager

Lady Tichborne, in a girl's frock, until he was between 11 and 12 years old. Sir William Ferguson, a surgeon well known in the 1870s, confirmed the fact of the malformation. Then came some very curious testimony about Roger Tichborne's correspondence.

At one time, his mother had written to him:

"My dear melancholy Boy,
If you ever want to communicate anything PRIVATE, if you put *private* on top of a separate sheet, I will not show it to anyone."

In 1851, before he left England, Roger wrote the following remarkably significant words:

"I might be the cause of misery to the person whom I married."

To his aunt, Lady Doughty, who had refused her consent to the match between pretty Kate, her daughter, and Roger—although, matrimonially, Roger was a first-rate "capture"—he wrote:

"I told you at Tichborne that I intended to go abroad, and you said it was my duty to remain in England; but, if I died, I have a brother that would take my place."

In another letter, he wrote:

"Shall I ever be worth anything? Suppose I were the head of a family, I could not fulfil the duties of that station as I should do."

It would take much more than the perorations of Scottish Lord Chief Justices to explain away poignant facts like these.

The court was further told that Roger Tichborne had kept his trousers on when bathing at Stonyhurst, and that his brother officers, in the Carabineers, in Ireland, fastened a street woman down in his bed, and tied a donkey up in his room. Two other witnesses, Mr. Gibbes and Major Bott, testified that, to their knowledge, Roger had this malformation. Bott said that his brother officers, in the Carabineers, brought into Roger's bedroom no fewer than ten prostitutes, at one time.

One's reason for entering at this length into a delicate and unpleasant matter is to prove to the unprejudiced reader, whose wits have not been addled by briefs, law-books, affidavits and the conventional accounts, that it is impossible to conceal or dismiss this part of the evidence as moonshine, fantasy or lies, if we are to arrive at the truth, which is the duty of a social historian. The *whole* facts must be given. However, if the other legal side went astray, like sheep, so did the claimant's friends and the advocate, Kenealy, when they urged that the "withered leaf" malformation proved that Arthur Orton was Roger Tichborne.

But *they* could not be blamed—as they never knew it—for not looking to another hypothesis: the "attractive Negress in the Tichborne woodpile." *But,* on the other hand, the Tichborne trustees, in 1870, and their attorneys, or, if not them, then the Tichbornes alive in the 1870s and even earlier, *knew the real reason* for the identity of malformation, so *very* rare, in the cases of Orton and Roger Tichborne. Indeed, some if not, indeed, all the them, *knew a great deal more than that*!

(In February, 1878, three members of the Orton family swore, before a commissioner of oaths, that Arthur Orton, *alias* Castro, had no physical malformation of the genital organs. Mrs. Elizabeth Jury, Orton's sister, said that, as she had been in the habit of washing him all over, when he was an infant, she knew the facts. It is evident that all of them were committing perjury, and whether they had any extraneous inducement to do so, and by whom it was offered, cannot now be said.)

One test advanced by the claimant's friends, in his favour, was the striking facial resemblance between Arthur Orton and Roger Tichborne. If one compares the daguerreotypes of Roger Tichborne, taken in Chile, in 1853, with a photograph of Arthur Orton, taken at Birmingham, England, in 1874, it must be admitted that the similarities in the shape of the eyes, mouth and nose are remarkable. The one difference between the physiognomies of the two men lies in the marked dissimilarity in the angles the eyes make with the bridge of the nose. In Roger's case, there is a pronounced slant downwards; in Orton's case, they were almost horizontal.

The criminal trial ended in the defendant being sentenced to fourteen years' penal servitude, on the consecutive charges of forgery and perjury. The trial cost the public the enormous sum of £55,315. One may *not* agree with Lord Maugham that this sentence was not a savage and vindictive one. It is still the unfortunate fact that we, in Britain, punish even the graver offences against the person less severely than we do those against property—and, in the main, the offence of

Orton was committed against property. It is, however, unlikely, today, that our criminal courts—and in 1870, there was no Court of Criminal Appeal—would award so savage a sentence as this, for the crimes of perjury and forgery.

Not so very long ago, there might have been seen, in the West End of London, the daughter of Arthur Orton—he died on 1 April, 1898, "All Fools' Day!"—selling flowers to passers-by, and advertising her pitch with a placard, whereon her deceased father was called:

"The late Sir Roger Tichborne, victim of a wicked miscarriage of justice."

And the Tichbornes, have their right, if they wish to exercise it, to ride on a horse right into Westminster Abbey, on the day of the King's, or Queen's Coronation! *

Now, we come to the revelation of the skeleton in the Tichborne family cupboard, and the reader will see the meaning of my allusion to the "Negress"—albeit, she was *not* black in skin—in this old family's woodpile.

Many years ago, a certain country magistrate, named Llewellyn, bought from the Tichborne family the estate of Upton, near Poole, Dorset, which was referred to by the claimant, Orton, at the trial. Llewellyn heard from the family lawyer what one may fitly describe, in American slang, as the "low down," the *very* "low down," on what was hidden behind the two trials. But it was not until 1929, that an anonymous writer, in the *Cornhill Magazine,* revealed what the Tichborne family lawyer had said, *sub rosa*, to Llewellyn. I may, however, point out that, although this anonymous writer is inaccurate on many points of the story of Roger Tichborne—for example, he says that the *Bella* sailed from Valparaiso, Chile, bound in April, 1854, for Kingston, Jamaica—from my own private and confidential sources, I have reason to believe that his story is very substantially true in what it discloses of the secret history of this strange legal case.

We see that George Orton, the supposed father, but actual foster-father of the claimant, Arthur Orton, was a well-to-do butcher, in Wapping, close to the old pirate Execution Dock, where they hanged another man, who had good reason to complain of the law and justice of *his* day—I refer to

---

* In High Holborn, London, the observant may note, when going along that busy thoroughfare, a Tichborne Court, which must be one of the ground-rents of the family.

Captain William Kidd of the *Adventure Galley*, in May, 1701. About the year 1840, George Orton's business fell away, and, with a large Victorian family, he had to look out for some means of tempering the cold wind to shorn lambs and skinned cows. He had a wife, a very pretty woman and she had to go out to domestic service, which she found in a good county family. She became housekeeper at Upton House, near Poole, Dorset. The place was then owned by Sir Edward Doughty, and the year was 1833. Pretty Mrs. Orton had married very young, and she proved that the gentlemen also like *brunettes*, as well as blondes. She already had a very fair quiverful; but this is no wise lessened her attractions for James Tichborne, near relative of the Doughtys, and father of the future Roger Tichborne, when he, James, visited the manor-house at Upton. Roger, it may be recalled, was born in 1829, and was probably about five years older than the claimant, Arthur Orton.

Whether Mrs. Orton was a woman of easy-going virtue, or whether she was, as is likely, dazzled by the aristocratic descent and the social advantages of James Tichborne, we cannot say. But we may ask the reader to remember that Mrs. Orton, a member of the British lower middle class, who had "fallen" to the ranks of the working-class, belonged to a country of which William Godwin had written, only a few years earlier: "The very poor, starved labourer in the village pot-house has become a champion of the aristocracy." We *may* say, however, that James Tichborne was never greatly troubled by what the late sardonic Irishman, George Bernard Shaw, has called "British middle-class morality."

Mrs. Orton "fell" for James Tichborne's charms, rank, and blandishments, and, of course, his possession of the thing that "most-mattered"—money. In due time, a child was born of this affair, and packed off along with the mother. It is probable that Mrs. Orton went "for a holiday," at James Tichborne's expense, and before the accouchement took place. But whether the Doughtys knew anything about the amours of James and the fascinating and attractive housekeeper, one has never been told. However, as a woman's eye is *very* keen in matters like these, one would not like to say that Lady Doughty had not observed "something." One has *heard* that Sir Edward Doughty, *né* Tichborne, had suspected what was afoot between James and the pretty brunette of a married housekeeper, and had seen things happening in the bedrooms, woods and parterres of the manor at Upton, and, at last, had been forced to acquaint his wife, when the housekeeper's "interesting condition" became *too* evident.

Needless to say that the child of this amour was the illegitimate son, Arthur Orton, natural son, but not heir, to the presumptive heir to the vast Tichborne estates. We are told that, very many years afterwards—long after the famous trials—a new owner of Upton House was looking through some old papers, that he had found in an attic, when his startled eyes popped out as he observed that, among the deeds, and dockets, and old legal parchments was a letter from fascinating Mrs. Orton, who had returned to hide her shame, or whatever she may have had of it, at Wapping. In this letter, she "thanked dearest Mr. James Tichborne" for a nice sum of money he had sent her, to help her over her confinement. Surely, we *never* heard that the Wapping butcher, George Orton did, in the words of the old Victorian ballad, tear his grey hairs in sorrow and forbid his wife ever to enter the house, or darken doors that might see *him* brought in dishonour to a premature grave. Mr. George Orton seems never to have been *that* sort of man and husband.

Anyway, the child was christened with *his* name, and it is believed that, from his earliest years, his mother had told him, when the rest of the large family were out: "Arthur, you are of noble birth, and you must never forget it. My child, if you had your rights, you would be heir to one of the oldest baronetcies in England. Yes, you are different from the rest of the family. Never forget it for, some time, your day may come."

We say blood will out; so we may fairly imagine young Arthur Orton, in the back streets of old Wapping, or on the wharfside by the old pirates' Execution Dock, repeating to scoffing and ribald youths, against whom he was "peeved," the tale of his noble birth. Naturally, the more they laughed and kicked his fat buttocks—and even then he had begun to develop that mountain of adipose tissue which had such a monstrous effect on the imagination of those who saw him in court, in 1872 and 1874—the more little Arthur fancied his high-born origin.

Indeed, it is but just to say that Orton *alias* Castro was a fine figure of a man, and possessed a more striking face than that of not a few high-born squires, baronets, peers and country gentlemen of the 1870s, in old England. One has a photograph taken of him, in a Midland town, in 1873, that fully attests as much.

He was fourteen years of age, when he went to South America, as a seaman aboard a windjammer, called the *Ocean*, which, as was stated earlier, he promptly deserted in the port of Valparaiso, Chile, and, up-country, tacked himself on to a *patrón* named Castro, whose name, undoubtedly for reasons connected with the Tichborne family history, had inspired him to tell the tale of "his own" aristocractic descent. Whether, by the way, Orton had been coached in the Tichborne family history by that fascinating and vivacious brunette, his mother, or had made his own independent studies, one does not know.

Eight years after the loss of the *Bella*, there began to drift to old England, and into the ears of the family at Tichborne Park, strange, and strong rumours, to the effect that Roger Tichborne was not lying at the bottom of the South Atlantic, but was alive—in Van Diemen's Land, as Australia was usually called, in those days, by the English "lower orders", who had very lively memories of Botany Bay, and the old and infamous convict ships. That would be about the year 1863. Oddly enough, the Tichbornes and the trustees of the vast estates did not seem much rejoiced at these tidings. In this sad connexion, one may recall the storm that Anthony Trollope raised about his ears, in the eighteen-seventies, or a little earlier, when he bluntly and cynically asked the sentimental Victorians: "Despite all your waxen flowers and funeral dirges, your granite obelisks and pious tombstones epitaphs, which of you really *would* wish that your beloved mother or father, brother or sister, aunt or uncle, grandfather or grandmother could, today, return, like Lazarus, from the grave?"

These rumours came to the ears of Madame Felicité, that very vigorous shrewd and realistic old Frenchwoman, the Dowager Lady Tichborne, who was Roger's mother. She had not failed to note the Tichbornian distaste for this "good news," anent a long-lost and dearly loved relative, and she had, too, not failed to mark the manner in which the younger brother of Roger was wasting his patrimony, after succeeding to the estates, on the death of Sir James Tichborne, his father. He was well on the way to making ducks and drakes of what he could touch of the rent-roll. She set inquiries on foot and began to question every sailor she could meet, and who had recently returned from a voyage to Australia.

It may be said here that, despite the false pathos and judicial sympathy of some legal commentators, with a "poor, too affectionate, sentimental, but doddering old lady," as some of them have kindly called her, it is by no means proved that Felicité, the Dowager Lady Tichborne, Roger's mother, was *quite* such a pathetic old fool as these legal gentlemen would have us suppose!

And what were those rumours, to which some judicially "ignorant" ears have not been disposed to listen?

These, we may summarize from various sources:

That, in the interior of New South Wales, not very far from the coast where he must have been landed, about 1855, was a poor, harmless, doddering imbecile who had seen better days. He had neither the toil-worn hands of a working-man, nor the accent. It was said that he had been picked up on the high seas, and brought to Sydney, New South Wales. He was crazed by his sufferings, and committed to an asylum for the insane. The country was sparsely populated and a gold rush was on; so it was no wonder if mention of him had not appeared in any Australian newspaper. The poor lunatic could not say who he was; but, from his talk and manners, it was surmised that he was, or had been a man of good breeding and birth.

The Dowager Lady Tichborne decided to insert an advertisement in *The Times,* and one in a colonial newspaper. She hoped that someone might see it and induce the mystery man to come forward, when it might be seen whether or no he was the long-lost Roger Tichborne. Her agent in Australia was a man named Cubitt, and *his* sub-agent was one Gibbes, the attorney mentioned earlier in this chapter, and who, by a very singular coincidence, had his domicile at Wagga-Wagga, the very place honoured by the residence of Castro *alias* Orton! As we have seen, Castro artlessly turned up at the office of Gibbes with that pipe, carelessly carved with the letters, "R. C. T."

It appeared that what had happened was this: poor Roger Tichborne had been picked up, clinging to wreckage, and crazed with sufferings, thirst, and exhaustion, induced by long exposure to a burning sun and the sea. His mind and memory had gone. Amnesia was total. He could remember neither his name, nor how he had come to be afloat on the high seas, apparently the sole survivor of a ship whose name he could not recall, nor where she was wrecked. The unfortunate castaway was landed at Sydney, rambled up country, and was eventually, and for a time, confined in a lunatic asylum at Parramatta, having been sent there from the "backblocks," far inland. Parramatta, it may be noted, stands at the head of the creek on which is Port Jackson, and is not more than twenty miles from Sydney, at whose Heads he had been landed.

After some time, the man without name or memory, recovered physically, but *not* mentally. He was quite harmless, and, to ease the charge on public funds, he was let out to work on odd jobs. He wandered from place to place in New South Wales. On his wanderings, he must have met one Thomas Castro, *alias* Orton, whose trade as a butcher would bring him into contact with sheep and cattle ranches, where this poor, crazed "sundowner" would be given casual jobs. No one can say with certainty whether, when in England, Roger Tichborne knew that, on the family escutcheon, there was *not* borne a bar sinister, in relation to a young gentleman, at Wapping, who had not come into *his* rights. No one knows whether a righteous woman in the parish of Tichborne, or in some village on the estate at Upton, Dorset, had ever whispered the scandalous story of amours, with a fascinating brunette of a housekeeper, into the ears of Felicité, who married James Tichborne. The Dowager Lady Tichborne was far from a narrow-minded, strait-laced woman, and she was, herself, the natural daughter of an English aristocrat, named Seymour, and a French lady, as we have already said.

Anyway, Castro *alias* Orton struck up a fine friendship with the poor imbecile, and he found that Roger had, occasionally, vague memories of the past that shot across the fog of amnesia, which very soon closed down again on his mind. At one time, Roger would be almost loquacious, then he would shut up like a clam, and not a word could be got from him. But he had said enough to make Castro *alias* Orton suspect that Roger was, indeed, his natural brother, born on the *right* side—not the wrong, as in Castro *alias* Orton's case—of the blanket. When the advertisement appeared in the Australian *Home News*, offering a reward for tidings of the lost Roger Tichborne, Castro *alias* Orton was in two minds about what to do.

If he, Castro *alias* Orton, informed the advertiser and took Roger Tichborne home, he might, in all likelihood, look forward, if not to living on the fat of the land for the rest of his life, or to an annuity, at least to some temporary reward. But he had always to remember the English governing classes' tendency *not* to demoralize any member of the "lower orders," as Castro would certainly be deemed, by handing out to him a *large* sum of money for virtue. Moreover, how if the Tichborne trustees made it conditional that, for the sake of the family's honourable name, he, Castro *alias* Orton, should, if given "hush money," forever put the wide and roaring seas between himself and old England, and never, never come tattling, in the bars of the Tichborne Arms, about ("an he had *his* rights"), he would be lord of that park and the old manor house, that could be seen above the wild dog-rose hedges, at the turn of the lane, outside the inn? There were lawyers around, and they might draw up documents for him to sign, carrying penalties in case of violation.

Here, he hesitated. Suppose the poor imbecile was too far gone ever to recognize anyone, or be recognized by them, then, what should he, Castro *alias* Orton gain by taking home to old England—or seeing some agent doing so—out of Parramatta lunatic asylum, a poor imbecile, whom his friends at home, would place in an English *private* asylum, or under some permanent form of restraint?

When the devil comes to prayers, unwanted, the welcome is rather apt to be too charitable and Christian for his liking. And which was, or would be the *devil*, in this case, Castro *alias* Orton had some doubts, remembering the aspirations he had committed to that pocket-book: "*Me*—of Tichborne Park, some day, I hope!"

So, we see, that when Castro called on the attorney, Gibbes, he had well primed himself with all the reminiscences and scraps he had collected—maybe, from his mother, at Wapping—about the Tichborne history, and what he had himself assembled from what had been let drop by the poor imbecile. This *real*, Roger Tichborne, who, most annoyingly for the peace of mind and comfort of some distinguished folk, in the shires of old England, had had the bad taste to rise from the dead, was not wanted at home. Why did he not stay put in the depths of the South Atlantic? Like the ghost in the well-known gramophone record: "He was dead, but he wunt li-i-i-e down!"

The simple attorney, Gibbes (Lord Maugham says he was too innocent ever to have made a *good* attorney), acclaimed the impersonator, who, until then, had been undecided whether to try for a nice sum down, or to have a good go for the whole of the Tichborne estates, with their £30,000 a year rent-roll. Gibbes's exclamation: "Good God, *you* must be the man!" made up his mind for him. After all, was *he* not as good as any other Tichborne? Nay, an he had his rights, he was; for was he not own father's son to the late Sir James Tichborne?

From sources of my own, I think that the anonymous writer in the *Cornhill Magazine*, in 1929, was quite correct in his assertion that, right through the two trials, in 1872 —4, the claimant, and the defendant, Orton *knew* that the real Roger Tichborne was alive in Australia; and, what is more heinous still, was that the Tichborne trustees and their attorneys, and also the Doughty-Tichborne families were aware that Roger was alive!

The *Cornhill Magazine* writer also tells us that Mr. Llewellyn, who bought the Upton estate, actually knew the name under which Roger Tichborne was known in New South Wales. (He does *not* say so, but it *may* have been "Creswell".) This obviously means that the lawyers and trustees of the Tichborne estates, in the 1870s, knew it, too: and it is more than likely that the Doughtys and Tichbornes, of that day, knew it; and, among other reasons, that secret knowledge caused them to apply to the High Court for an order to make sure that, even if the unfortunate Roger recovered his sanity, he could only very hardly come into his birthright, in face of the order to prevent any ejectment actions. We have seen *why they said they did so*, but it was not *all* the truth. Thus, for very different reasons, fate had so arranged matters that both sides engaged in a conspiracy of silence! It is unlikely that Dr. Kenealy had any part in this conspiracy; or that his client, Orton, had taken him into *his* confidence about the poor imbecile, the *real* Sir Roger Tichborne.

The same Mr. Lewellyn also said that he had seen the passenger list of the unnamed ship that brought the castaway Roger Tichborne into Sydney Heads. But this, of course, was not the *Bella*, in which Roger had sailed in his own name. Here, again, is another small skeleton in the cupboard: that ship, registered at Lloyd's, had owners in England. Why did not *they* not speak out, but keep silent as the grave, about what they *must* have known? The cynic may suggest that "someone squared them." Who, after nearly a century, can now say? But the silence was most certainly *not* attributable to any ignorance of facts that rang throughout Great Britain, and were raised in the House of Commons. To use a homely old English metaphor: "The more it be stirred, the more it stinketh!"

The famous old Tichborne curse had worked itself out in a very peculiar way; or, as the Victorian poet, Matthew Arnold, had said about our own Henry VIII: "He had a desire, so characteristically English, to enjoy forbidden fruits with the utmost legality." It was written in the book of fate that never would Roger Tichborne, or his heirs, ride on horseback into church on Coronation Day at Westminster Abbey!

Meantime, in the records of the lunatic aslyum at Parramatta, New South Wales, Mr. E. H. Statham being then the superintendent, there was registered the entry, under an assumed name, on a date between 1874 and 1884—and the date of the death, the latter being uncertain—of poor, crazed Roger Tichborne. Presumably, there would be also recorded the circumstances in which he reached Sydney. That account may also include the name of the ship which picked him up on the high seas; but it would *not* be the *Osprey*. Also, it would not explain the singular silence of the Parramatta asylum authorities, in 1872 and 1874, when Australia, just as England, must have been ringing with his name.

A Commission was sent out to Australia to collect evidence about the claimant, Orton; but nothing was reported about Roger Tichborne, who, of course, was still alive in New South Wales. In spring 1938, I wrote to the authorities of the Parramatta asylum, asking if they could possibly tell me whether their archives, in the late 1850s or 1860s, or 1870s, contained anything about this mystery. I had little hope that, at so long a time as half a century after the protagonists in the story had gone the way of all flesh, I should have much success.

In the summer of 1938, I received a striking letter from Dr. B. Moore Sampson, medical superintendent of the Mental Hospital at Parramatta, N. S. W.

He says that the particulars are not complete enough for the New South Wales authorities to trace the mysterious patient met by Castro *alias* Orton, on the roads or tracks, in the back blocks of New South Wales . . .

> "But we had a patient here whose name was William Creswell. He was admitted to the Mental Hospital of Gladesville, in August 1871, and transferred to this hospital in April 1872. His case created a stir, at the time—in fact, was mentioned in Parliament, as it was suspected he was the original Sir Roger Tichborne, but nothing could be proved, and the patient himself was averse to discussing the case. He died here on 11 December, 1904. I am sorry we cannot help you further than this."

A careful search of all the House of Commons debates, between the years 1871 and 1874, has failed to reveal any reference to this mystery man, William Creswell. If he were the real "Simon Pure," he would have been 75, when he died, in 1904. But it is to be noted that Creswell comes into the picture only at the date of the famous trial; whereas, ten years earlier, the Dowager Lady Tichborne, Roger's mother, had heard about the existence of a crazed man wandering in the woods and tracks of New South Wales. Had Creswell been admitted to an asylum in New South Wales, in or about the year 1854, it seems rather odd that the remarkable circumstances of a castaway, picked up clinging to a spar in the South Atlantic, would not have been entered on the records of the asylum which received him, and must surely have singled him out from all others, no matter whether the man was known or unknown. Who shall say whether William Creswell had not let drop hints of grandeur of the sort known as megalomaniac?

It is curious that no mention of any such man in an Australian asylum was made in the British House of Commons, either then, in the 1870s, or at any much later date. Apparently, only one source might clear up this mystery of the name by which Roger Tichborne was known in Australia, and the date of his death, and that would be the document found by Mr. Llewellyn in the attic at Upton Manor House, Dorset. We do not know, today, whether that, or any of the other documents, found there, are still in existence. It is unlikely that a lumber-room trunk at Tichborne Park, or some old tin deed-box of a discreet lawyer, will reveal an old scandal which neither can wish to re-open eighty-three years after all concerned are dead.

Some London dailies carried the story following, in their issues of 1 November, 1896:

THE TICHBORNE CASE:

"Mr. Edward Priestman, solicitor, acting on behalf of the Rev. Mr. William, of Devon, an old friend of the Dowager Lady Tichborne, has applied to the Colonial Secretary for the delivery to him of the person of William Creswell, an inmate of the Parramatta Lunatic Asylum, who is alleged to be Sir Roger Tichborne."

Chapter 2

WHAT HAPPENED TO ELIZABETH CANNING?

ONE dark January night, in the year 1753, when Dr. Samuel Johnson, up in a garret, was drudging with his Dictionary, or, with tears and sobs, was inditing that melancholy apostrophe to the Deity, concerning the recent death of his "dear Tetty," a curious incident, taking place some five miles away, as the crow flies, was being witnessed by one, Robert Beals, a turnpike man at Stamford Hill, "in Tottenham road towards Enfield, betwixt Tottenham and London." The night was calm and cold, with a tendency towards rain, and for belated wayfarers the times were very dangerous—too dangerous for honest men, unarmed and unguided, to be abroad.

Most respectable citizens had shot bolts and bars, put up

the shutters two hours and more since, and retired to snuff, or light guttering candles, to read in the *Postboy* how, the day before, the mailbags from the Western counties had come into the "Golden Cross," soaked with the blood of the gallant guards. To the cry of "Who goes home?" in the lobbies of the House of Commons, a party of M.P.s had belted on their swords, or grasped loaded canes of Malacca, and, in the light of the linkboys' flaring torches, had set out from Westminster for the Whittington stone at the foot of old Highgate Hill. Only two nights before, the great Johnson himself had come down from his garret in the Temple, a poker in his hand, and clad only in his shirt, with a little black wig on the top of his head, to answer the violent knocking of Beauclerk and Langton, who were inclined to a night ramble in the purlieus of Covent Garden.

"Oh, what is't you want, you dogs?" said he, as his features relaxed into a smile. "I thought I might have to serve you as I did the four ruffians whom I held at bay in the street, some years ago, until the watch came and carried both them and me to the round-house."

Which remark shows that honest men in that day were not too quick at championing males or females in distress.

Robert Beals had just lit a big candle and was standing at the door of his turnpike, listening to a distant church clock chiming the half hour (after ten), when he thought he could hear the sound of a woman sobbing, about three hundred yards up the road. It came from Newington, going towards Tottenham. Not a glimmer of light, except from his candle, and the road dark as pitch. Beals strained his gaze into the night, shading his eyes under his hands. The sound came nearer. He stood still, and, presently, he perceived the forms of a young person—a girl, by her voice—and of two men, one taller than the other.

"My turnpike lies seven miles from Enfield, and three from Moorfields," he said afterwards; and the reader will recall that these are the eighteenth-century miles, so well known to hikers and push-bikers on the Dover road, or Ermine Street, and rather longer than the modern statute miles:

"I had a large candle burning, and the stile is at the end of the turnpike over the way. As they got up to the light, I heard the one man say: 'Come along you bitch, you are drunk!' That was when the candle shone on them. I put myself a little farther out without-side the posts, that they might see me. The woman seemed not willing to go along with them, by her crying and sobbing, but never spoke a word. The man behind her made a sort of laugh, and said: 'Damn the bitch, how drunk she is!' When they came up to the stile, the tall one got over first, and the hindmost lifted her over, either by one leg or both legs. She came down upright on the other side, then she hung back and fell on her breech upon the step and cried bitterly. I thought she would go no farther. She did not speak a word to me, though I thought they could see me. He before plucked her by the hands at full length, and said: 'Damn you, you bitch, come along, you are drunk!' The other came on the other side of her, and they went away together . . . one of them never letting go of her hand all the time I saw them. She burst out afresh with sobbing, and they were out of my sight, presently. I can't say I saw her face. She had light-coloured clothes on, and did not seem tall; for both men stood over her. I can't say whether they had great coats. I did not attempt to help her; because there were two men and we are fearful in our business and never meddle with such."

Such was the story which Beals was to tell in the court of our Sovereign Lord the King (George II) holden at the Old Bailey, on 29 April, 1754, present Sir Crispe Gascoyne, Lord Mayor of London, and the judges of His Majesty's Court of Oyer and Terminer.

Now, on 1 January, 1753—the year and month in which Robert Beals saw a sobbing girl hoisted like a sack of coals over the stile of his turnpike, a decent servant girl, Elizabeth Canning, aged eighteen, and daughter of a respectable, poor, pious and patriotic widow—she dated one occurrence as happening on the eve of the "Martyrdom of King Charles I"—living in a house in Aldermanbury, London, had been given permission by her mistress, Mrs. Pollie Lyon, to spend the holiday with her uncle, Colley, who lived at Saltpetre bank, near Wellclose square, back of the London Dock. Bet Canning left home in holiday dress—of purple masquerade stuff gown, a white handkerchief, a black, quilted petticoat, a green undercoat, black shoes, blue stockings, a white shaving hat with green ribbons, and a very ruddy colour. These details are here given because of their remarkable contrast to the woebegone state and clothes in which she returned home. She took with her a gold half-guinea in a little box, and three shillings, a few coppers and a farthing, as well as a mince-pie she intended for a young brother.

Bet reached her uncle's house, spent the day there, and he and his wife took leave of her in Houndsditch, at 9 p.m. that night. What happened to her after that is a mystery which would baffle the combined efforts of a clairvoyant, a "wise woman" seer, and a modern psychopathist, or psychiatrist, with a few members of the C.I.D. of Scotland Yard, thrown in as make-weight. It is enough to say that she reached home neither that night, nor for the succeeding twenty-eight nights. Bet was a poor and respectable girl, with not a breath of scandal to "blow upon her" (in the eighteenth-century slang); and the cheap suggestion that she sought the nefarious aid of some eighteenth-century contemporary of Burns's Dr. Hornbrook, in order to hide her shame and subsequently deposit the fruits thereof outside Mr. Coram's celebrated Foundling Hospital in Bloomsbury, is something wide of the mark. As a matter of fact, the midwife's examination of Bet's shift (mentioned to the learned judge at the Old Bailey), satisfied her that the girl had not been ravished by some coach-riding gallant in a perfumed wig and silken clothes, or some base fellow in a tricorne hat and powdered pigtail, lurking in the rear of a press gang.

At nine that January New Year night, her master, Mr. Lyon, called at Mrs. Canning's house and said he wondered she stayed so late. The frightened mother, almost out of her wits, sent her children into the fields to see after Bet, and dispatched an apprentice to Colley, the uncle. All to no purpose! The neighbours shook their heads and wondered, and then did something more helpful—put their hands down and subscribed a small sum to induce Mrs. Canning to advertise for Bet in the *Postboy* and the *Chronicle*. A report had come that a damsel in distress had been heard shrieking from a hackney-coach in Bishopsgate in the small hours of the night of Bet's disappearance; but whether the screams had their origin in a drunken frolic, or were in the nature of passion at the crossroads on a dark and dirty night, could never be clearly ascertained. The hackney-coachman could not be found.

Mrs. Canning advertised thrice in the newspapers:

"the first time out of my own head, and when neighbours gave me a little money, I again advertised."

Nothing coming of it, Mrs. Canning, in desperation, put on her hat and went to a conjuror, or astrologer, who had a black wig over his face. The conjuror shut the door, lighted his candles:

"And look so frightful I was glad to get out of the door again. He asked me some questions and bade me advertise, and wrote and scribbled, scribbled along. He said she *was in the hands of an old woman.* I prayed, and put bills in the churches at Aldermanbury and Cripplegate, and at Mr. Wesley's chapel. I did not leave a meeting or a place where I could put up a bill in. . . ."

The conjuror was right on the mark!

On 29 January, 1753, about 10.15 p.m., when the apprentice at Mrs. Canning's was fastening the shutters, and the family were thinking of retiring to bed, the latch of the door in Aldermanbury was raised, and a woebegone figure entered, pale, tottering and emaciated, bent almost double, with no clothes on save a wretched shift, a miserable petticoat, a filthy bed-gown, and a rag tied round her head, which was bleeding from a cut.

" 'Twas the day before King Charles's Martyrdom," said Mrs. Canning, who, one sees, had not been brought up in a Republican and shovel-hatted, or "dog of a Whig's," household. . . .

"It was a quarter after ten o'clock. I thought she was an apparition . . . my little girl ran screaming to the chimney. I said: 'Feel her, feel her!' She came in almost double, walking sideways, holding her hands before her. She was so ill, she could not even swallow some mulled wine brought by her mistress, Pollie Lyon."

Mrs. Canning then went into a faint in the style of Victorian ladies in novels of the time. When the drumming of her heels had subsided, and her nose had been tickled with a burnt feather, or stung with hartshorn, she came to and found her house full of excited and inquisitive neighbours who had flocked in like cackling geese. At this point arises one of the most puzzling features of a case which is packed with hard-swearers and counter-perjurers.

A certain Robert Scarrat, who was then in Mrs. Canning's house, listened to Bet Canning's strange story, which was that, when she was passing through Moorfield's, by the backside of the Bedlam hospital, after leaving Uncle and Aunt Colley, two lusty fellows, in great coats, attacked her, robbed her of her money, stripped her of her gown, knocked her insensible, and that when she came to she found she was being dragged along a road outside London, in the country, and, at about 4 a.m., was carried into a house on the Hertfordshire road. She told Wintlebury, a neighbour, and former employer, that she recognized the road by looking through a crack in a window and seeing a coachman, who used to drive her mistress to Hertfordshire, pass by.

Mrs. Myers, another neighbour, said that Bet Canning was in very low spirits, and told her:

> "An elderly woman (a gypsy) and two young ones were in the house. The old woman took hold of Bet's arm and said: 'Will you go our way?' (That is, become a bawd). She answered 'No,' whereupon the old woman took a knife out of a drawer, cut the lacing off Bet's stays, took them off, gave her a great slap in the face and said: 'You shall suffer in the flesh.' Then she shoved her through a door into a room, damned her, and said if she moved or made any resistance, she would come and cut her throat. In the room there was hay, a pitcher of water, a fireplace and pieces of bread. Bet took a bedgown and rug out of the grate. The bread was so hard, she had to dip it in the water. The two young women, one with black hair, the other fair, stood by laughing while her stays were being cut. The room was longish and darkish, and she saw the coachman through a crack in the boards nailed over the window. The window did not front the road. She got out at the window by the end, pulling down two boards, put out her head and shoulders, took out some part of the window, pulled out her legs, and, so, dropped down and tore her ear in doing so. The ear was dripping with blood, 'while I (Mrs. Myers) was in Mrs. Canning's house.' Bet said the house was ten miles off, a staircase lay close to the room, and she heard people running up and down o' nights, and the name of Mother Wills or Wells."

Scarrat put some leading questions to Bet Canning, who answered that she remembered crossing a ploughed field, with the road on her right hand coming to London, and that she went over a brook out of the fields and passed a tan-house. Here, Scarrat broke in:

> "There is a tanner nearby at Enfield Wash. I'll lay a guinea to a farthing she has been at Mother Wells: for 'tis as noted a house as any. An old bawdy house."

Bet Canning: "Her name *is Mother Wells or Wills.*"

Scarrat, badgered by an old Bailey prosecuting counsel, admitted that Bet Canning did not say this till *after* he had mentioned the name of Mother Wells; but Mrs. Canning was positive that her daughter Bet spoke the name *first*:

"No soul ever spoke the name of Wells till her own self (Bet) mentioned it."

The newspapers were all full of the strange story of Bet Canning and the gypsy, and there started one of those wars of pamphleteers, broadsheeters and lampooners, which were so very popular in the eighteenth century. It is, of course, a most evil wind that blows nobody a bit of good, and the controversy, hashed and rehashed in the press, warmed many a poor devil's shins, in garrets where they starved and perished for want of a fire, or a tankard of Thrale's beer with a nice bit of ox-cheek, all piping hot. The advocates of the *Postboy*, in the city alehouses were all for Mother Wells and the gypsy; while P. P., clerk of the parish, Amos Turner, collar-maker, Thomas White, wheelwright, George Pilcocks, late exciseman, and especially Robert Jenkins, farrier—he was a man of bright Tory parts who never, in his shrewd conceit, shoed the horse of a Whig, or a fanatic, but he lamed him sorely—and all chosen spirits, who met weekly at the "Rose and Crown" to decide the affairs of the realm, as well as foreign parts, were all for Bet Canning, who came home woebegone on the eve of the Martyrdom of King Charles I.

Two days later, on 31 January, 1753, a certain snuffy and dear old alderman, named Chitty—he had no doubt known something of the affair from the pother the newspapers were making—was not exactly gratified to find Bet Canning and other folk waiting on his doorstep, near the Mansion House. Chitty, not being able to shove the case onto another alderman who refused to take it on out of his turn, was forced to listen while the story was poured into his ears, and then to make an affidavit of it. Chitty, it is to be suspected, was inclined to fancy all was not as it sounded, and that there was a piccaninny lurking in the background, somewhere; or, at any rate, some tale of hidden shame, which would not come out to the delight of many grave women of the parish of Cripplegate and Aldermanbury.

"I can't believe you," he said to poor Bet, when he had heard her story, in the Justice Room at the Guildhall. He took down a statement in which Bet Canning said, or was alleged to have said:

"There were two windows in the room in which she had been confined, an old table, an old stool or two, an old picture over the chimney, three-quarters of a gallon of water in a pitcher, and about a quarter-peck loaf in pieces. Two windows in the room were fastened up, one with boards, and the other, part boards and part glass, in which latter she made a hole by removing a pane, and got out on a small shed of boards or penthouse, and so slid down and jumped on the side of a bank, or the backside of the house."

This statement was not signed by Bet Canning, or by the foggy Chitty, and when this dear old alderman of the type commemorated in "Barnaby Rudge," was called on at the Old Bailey, he actually produced in court *not* the original statement, but only notes taken from it, or from some other statement (?); and offered a perfectly unintelligible explanation, which, it is significant, was not questioned or examined by either side. We will leave legal historians and whitewashers to explain this trifling shortcoming of legal and judicial procedure.

"I did not think there would have been such a pother about this matter," he lamely offered as excuse.

Having taken the affidavit, Chitty, despite his scepticism, and, perhaps, even influenced by the newspaper clamour, issued a warrant for the arrest of Mother Wells and the gypsy; and the two gentlemen, friends of Bet Canning, at their own cost, hired a coach, and went down to Enfield, to hand the warrant to the local constable. Poor Bet and her excitement-seeking friends, jammed themselves into another coach, and took the same road past the turnpike of our old friend Robert Beals of Stamford Hill. When she entered the house of Mother Wells, she saw a gypsy woman sitting on the right side of the chimney, leaning over the fire, bent almost double, smoking a pipe. . . .The Old Bailey barrister's version was:

"Elizabeth Canning, in a moment, without seeing her face, said: 'This is the woman who robbed me of my stays.' The gypsy went on smoking: whereupon, one of her daughters said: 'Lord, mother, the young woman says you robbed her!' Immediately the gypsy started up, showed her hideous face covered with a clout: 'I, rob you? Take care what you say! If you have once seen my face, you cannot mistake it; for God never made such another! I never saw you in my life before. For God Almighty's sake, don't swear my precious life away! I was 120 miles from this place when you say I robbed you.'"

The gypsy's son, by name George Squires, corroborated, and asserted that he and his mother were at Abbotsford, in Dorset, in the early weeks of January, 1753.

Virtue Hall, a young woman in Mother Wells's house, was taken before the famous "Tom Jones" Fielding, then a London police magistrate, who, annoyed with her shuffling and prevarication, threatened to commit her as a felon if she did not tell all she knew about the affair. Later, when Susannah Wells—a "hempen widow" whose husband, unfortunately had been, hanged—by trade a landlady and keeper of a bawdy house, and Mary Squires, the gypsy, were tried for robbery and assault, at the Old Bailey, on 26 February, 1753, Virtue Hall, who was the wife of a gypsy named Fortune Natus, said:

"The gypsies had been at Mother Wells two weeks before Elizabeth Canning came. John Squires was one of the men that brought her, the other went off after that night and I never saw him again. I never saw him before, either. I was a lodger, almost a prisoner in the house, and was forced to do as they would have me. Mary Squires had been there seven or eight weeks."

Virtue Hall subsequently recanted and withdrew this statement.

On the other hand, two witnesses from Abbotsbury, Dorset, alleged that Mary Squires was at their house from 1 to 9 January, 1753.

Elizabeth Canning, at the trial of Wells and Squires, said:

"I set out from home at 11 in the forenoon and stayed till about nine at night on 1 January. I was then alone and came down Houndsditch, and two lusty men, both in greatcoats, laid hold of me, one on each side. They said nothing to me, at first, but took half-a-guinea in my little box out of my pocket, and three shillings that were loose. They took my gown, apron and hat, and folded them up and put them in each great-coat pocket. I screamed out, then the man that took my gown, put a handkerchief to my mouth. They tied my hands behind me, after which one of them gave me a blow on the temple, and said: 'Damn you, you bitch, we'll do for you by and by!' The blow stunned me, and threw me into a fit. I have been subject to convulsion fits these four years. The first thing I remember I found myself by a large road where was water, with the two men that robbed me. I had no discourse with the two men. I had recovered from my fit half an hour before I came to the house, as near as I can remember, about 4 a.m. They lugged me along, and said: 'You bitch, why don't you walk faster?' One had hold of my right arm, and the other my left, and so pulled me along. I think they dragged me along by my petticoats, they being so dirty. I think it was daylight about three hours after I came to the house. I can't say whether my fits were attended with struggling. I escaped from the loft by breaking a board nailed up on the inside, and about 8 to 10 feet from the ground. In the hayloft was a barrel, a saddle, a bason, a tobacco-mould to do up one penny-worth of tobacco. The men were in Moorfields half an hour with me. A lamp was near the place where I was attacked . . . I thought the people in the house might have let me out; so I never tried to get out till I had been four weeks confined in the loft. I jumped out of the window on to soft clayey ground and did not hurt myself. On the Wednesday before I came away, I saw someone peep at me through a crack in the door, which was fast. In the daytime the house was very quiet."

It will be noted that the statement differs, in some respects, from that which Chitty said she made before him, and, in particular, she made no mention of jumping onto a penthouse out of the window.

To the full-throated roars of "the many-headed" out for blood—whose, they cared not very greatly—the wretched Widow Susannah Mother Wells was burnt in the hand; but, luckily for pox-marked, gypsy Mary Squires, while she was in Newgate jail, waiting execution morning, the Lord Mayor of London, Sir Crispe Gascoyne, president of the court, doubted the justice of the verdict. He examined witnesses, found that Hall retracted her evidence, and put the matter before the Law Officers of the Crown, with an earnest recommendation for a reprieve. The Attorney-General and the Solicitor-General reported that the weight of the evidence was in the favour of Mary Squires. Elizabeth Canning's friends complained that they were not allowed to see the memorial sent by the Lord Mayor to the Crown officers, and when they went to the Attorney-General with affidavits about the presence of the gypsy Squires at Enfield, that officer, on purely technical grounds, declined to examine the documents.

One point about the affidavits in favour of the gypsy, and of the Squires' evidence, is the confusion between Old and New Christmas Day, 25 December and 7 January.

The upshot was that Mary Squires was pardoned. The war of pamphleteers recommenced, Fielding took the side of Elizabeth Canning in his "Statement of a Clear Case," and the newspapers and magazines championed either the "Egyptian, or Canning." Then the tables turned with a vengeance! Poor Bet Canning was arrested and tried for perjury, at the sessions of the Old Bailey, held on 29 April, 1754, when thirty-six witnesses from Dorset proved an alibi for the gypsies. All the town, gentle and simple, ladies of quality and men of fashion, gamblers, rakes, libertines and respectable citizens and their wives were agog to see Elizabeth and, if it could be done, get to the bottom of the strange mystery.

Eagle-eyed and hawk-nosed hounds and limbs of the law had detected discrepancies in Elizabeth's statements made at three separate times before various justices. She had told Chitty—or, so that luminary affirmed—that she jumped down on a penthouse on the backside of Mother Well's house. There was no penthouse to be seen; she had said she was confined in a square, darkish and little room; whereas one, Gawen Nash, who kept a coffee-house in Gutter Lane, E. C., and, who as a friend of Lyons, Bet's employer, went to Mother Wells's place, testified to the contrary. Nash, however, said that, although he was present at Chitty's examination, he did *not* remember that Elizabeth said she slid down onto a penthouse:

> "The girl gave an account of the place she had been in to Mr. Alderman Chitty who asked her—how it might slip his memory I cannot tell—what sort of a room she had been confined in. Her answer was that it was a little, square, darkish or dark room, with boards nailed up before the windows . . . I went to Mother Wells's house with the warrant. I saw that the room was a large one. Lyon said these 'things may have been put there since'. The two windows were nailed up with boards. The room was not square, dark, or little. It was 35 feet 3½ inches long by 9 feet 8 inches wide. It is light, from windows and the roof of pantiles. There is not the least sign of a grate or chimney. The whole chimney is full of cobwebs not recently disturbed. A large chest of drawers is by the wall of which Canning said nothing. There is no penthouse under the window and the walls on both sides are perpendicular, the windows being eight feet from the ground at the outside."

If there is one thing this witness succeeded in doing, it was in proving the unreliability of Chitty and his statement, that was derived, as the eighteenth-century critics said: "From the Lord knows who and He won't split." Yet, it cannot be gainsaid that we are struck with a curious air of illusion and unreality, recalling the story of the gentleman who told of a ghostly adventure in a house at Malta, where, it was later seen that a cobwebbed room had not been entered for years, and there were no footmarks in the dust laid down in half a century.

Mr. (afterwards Serjeant) Davy, the prosecuting counsel, pointed out another of the strange circumstances of a strange affair: a lane was under the window of the loft, and was used every night and morning, by farmers and servants taking cattle to the marshes. There was a pond eight yards away, where townsmen watered their horses, and where, in frosty weather, children slid on the ice. Had Elizabeth Canning made the least alarm, men would have come to her assistance:

"But we hear of no endeavours of this kind. May be the gypsy had put a spell upon her!"

Of course, there is to be said in Bet Canning's favour, that the well-known character of this establishment, might not have predisposed outsiders to pay much attention to a young woman calling for assistance. Also, she lay under the fear of having her throat cut, or of being violently assaulted by someone in the house if she shouted and no one came to her help. It is uncertain if Davy were merely jesting; but it may be said that it was not unlikely that Romany Mother Wells *had* hypnotized Bet!

Then the thirty-six witnesses from Dorset came forward into the witness-box and swore that Mary Squires and her family were far away from Enfield at the critical dates. It is noteworthy that that very alert gentleman, Mr. Davy, did not make *too* much of the fact that the Squires were known to be allied with smugglers in the western counties:

"Mary Squires and George, the gypsy's son, travelled about at the latter end of 1752, into the West of England, with smuggled goods of seaport towns to sell to people in the country." (*Davy*).

It is much more noteworthy that poor Bet's counsel did not make very much more of it! One document, put in as evidence, of Squires' *alibi*, took the form of a love-letter—very odd, this, in the case of a Romany *chai!*—written by Mrs. Mary Morris, landlady of the "Spreadeagle" at Basingstoke, for Lucy Squires, from which letter the last cypher of the date "18 January, 175—" was torn off. (Very fine evidence,

Mr. Davy, and your serjeant's eye must have been blinder than Nelson's!)

For Bet Canning, there were a number of as reputable—probably more reputable—Enfield witnesses, who swore that the gypsy Squires *were* in Mother Susannah Wells's house, on 12 January and 19 January, 1753. Samuel Story, of Enfield, saw Mary Squires there, on 22 December, 1752. Another man swore she was in a cowhouse at Enfield, where he saw her on 15 December, 1752. James Pratt saw her before Christmas, 1752, when she asked him about a lost pony, and said her name was on the "clog." Mary Squires had a man with her, said Pratt, and when the witness was asked to look round the court and see if he could identify the man, it was certainly curious that George Squires should duck his head, and draw down the comments of an observant juryman and even the rebuke of Mr. Davy, who said: "It does not look well!" Pratt, however, could not swear to George Squires.

Sniggering hounds of the law went off on another trail. "Far be it from me, my lords and gentlemen of the jury to say anything against the character of Elizabeth Canning—*but*. . . ." and he spoke of the gay life of which there might be more than one consequence—just what he meant, we do not propose to inquire, but his intention was clear. Other delicate physiological matters excited the attention of the sceptical gentlemen of the law—and those not being squeamish days, no judge thought of clearing the court. In our excellent and indispensable eighteenth century of prose and reason, women were as habitually constipated as they often are today . . . "but here, my lords and gentlemen of the jury, is a young woman penned up for four weeks in a room she never leaves—*haw*—and *haw!*"

Mrs. Canning said her daughter had often gone for two weeks without a stool. More, the family were very poor in this world's goods, and "when things have gone hard with me I have known her to live upon half a roll a day." Yes, *them* were the days!—for English *gentry!*

Again, there was that "old picture over the chimney": but there was under a wretched bed, a picture on wood of a crown, used by Mother Wells as a sign for her house of call, or brothel.

A more puzzling circumstance arose in what had happened to her between the time of her abduction, after 9 p.m., and when she found herself between the two men on the Enfield road (?). Chitty, in 1753, had said she was forced along Bishopsgate street, between the two men who were each holding her under the arms; but added "that how she came there she could not tell; that she was not so far stunned but that she knew a little as she went along that part of London; but how she went afterwards, she did not know. She said she might have been put in some house for all she knew; but she could not tell."

Mr. Davy, the prosecuting counsel, asked if it was possible that a person could be dragged along, as Canning suggested, for six hours, a distance of eight or nine miles, and be utterly unconscious of what took place? (A modern alienist, or psychopathist, might not find it easy to answer Davy's perfectly sensible question).

It will be recalled that the girl whom Beals, the turnpike man, saw on the Tottenham—Enfield road, sobbing and crying, was being forced into rapid walk by two men holding her arms; but Elizabeth Canning did not mention that she met anyone. Yet would it not be a remarkable coincidence that two different girls should have been lugged along in this way by two different men on that January night in 1753? Epileptics and somnambulists do queer things; but who has ever heard of a girl, sobbing and crying, and rudely slung over a stile by two men in the dead of night, and still oblivious of what was going forward? Had she suffered from loss of memory since her confinement in the strange house? It is easier to ask than answer these questions.

Beals, again, believed the girl he saw had an apron on, and wore light-coloured clothes—she had something on her head—but he emphasized that the night was dark, very still, and there was no moon, and that it rained a little, so that he could not be positive. Davy pointed out that Stamford-hill turnpike was about four miles from Moorfields; so that, after she was robbed, between 9 and 10 p.m., she must have been carried eleven miles to Mother Wells's house, in six hours, at which rate of travelling, she could not have reached the turnpike till almost twelve.

"Is it possible that the two men could have carried her in such a condition, four miles in one hour?" (*Davy*).

This, of course, begs the very question we ask: How could anyone know that she was carried in that manner until she recovered consciousness?

Mrs. Canning said, in Court:

"When she came back, I fell into a fit directly. My daughter is subject to fits. There was a garret ceiling fell in upon her head, which first occasioned them, and at times, when anyone speaks hastily to her, or at any surprise, she is liable to fall into one. She has sometimes continued in one seven to eight hours; she is not sensible during the time she is in one, no more than a newborn babe."

What one would like to have known was whether Bet Canning could walk like a sleepwalker, when such fits were on her?

There was evidence of witnesses in favour of Elizabeth Canning to which Davy, as Crown prosecutor, paid scant heed.

Mary Cobb, of Edmonton, was walking in Duck's field on a Monday evening 29 January, 1753, when she saw a young person with a handkerchief pinned on her head, almost hiding her face, and wearing an old bedgown worked with flowers that seemed faded:

"She was getting over a stile, and we both looked at each other. I was afraid, and moved on slowly. I thought she would have asked me for charity, and I had no halfpence in my pocket. I saw she had a young face. She appeared in a very wretched and miserable condition, as ever I saw a person in in my life. She walked, creeping along. I could not tell what to make of it, whether she was frightened of me or not. I only saw the tip of her nose. . . .The size answers. (This refers to her scrutiny of Bet Canning in Court). I firmly believe this to be the same person, by the tip of her nose, that bears some resemblance to the person I saw."

David Dyer (a naughty man), of Enfield Wash, against the ten-mile stone a quarter-of-a-mile Londonwards, saw, at 4 a.m. a poor distressed creature come out of the common fields, from Mother Wells's direction, and make towards London:

"I looked at her face as she came by, and I said: 'Sweetheart do you want a husband?' She did not speak to me."

This witness identified the person he saw as Bet Canning, whom he had seen three evenings before Mother Wells was taken up.

Thomas Bennet, of Enfield, at the tenmile stone, saw a poor wretched creature, dressed similarly to Bet Canning, between 4 and 5 in the afternoon of 29 January, 1753.

She asked and he told her the way to London. Later, when he heard that Wells had been taken up, he said to a neighbour;

"I'll be hanged if I did not meet that young woman near this place and told her the way to London!"

Joseph Adamson said that when Elizabeth Canning went into the loft in Mother Wells's place, she said, in answer to his question: "What had you seen out of the window?" "I saw a hill, and houses on the other side of the lane." The hill was Chingford hill, and he found that she spoke truly. He also saw the windows nailed up with boards. Before Elizabeth Canning came to Mother Wells's house, Adamson noticed that some of the plaster had been broken off the outside. The windows were one storey high.

Then came some remarkable testimony which suggests that evidence, in favour of the girl, had been destroyed by someone acting for the gypsies or Mother Wells. William Headland, who said his father's house was located a lane and two fields from Mother Wells, asserted on oath, that:

"The window-front the girl got out by is by the corner of the lane, where you can see into a yard. *I found a piece of lead, just at the corner of the window that joins to the house.* It looked as if it came out of some window. It was a yard from the house under the window that fronts the road. I doubled it up as soon as I found it, because I thought I would carry it home. *It was bloody and I heard that Bet Canning had torn her ear.* I told my mother why I had taken it home. I saw Mary Squires on Tuesday (market day at Waltham), being 9 January, 1753, and I saw her under Loomworth Dame's (an Enfield witness) back wall, telling a young man's fortune."

Elizabeth Headland, the mother of William said:

"I wrapped the piece of lead, all bloody, in a piece of paper and put it on a shelf. I brought it to London with me at Michaelmas time, and carried it down again before Christmas. I laid it in a table-drawer, and when I went to look for it, last Friday, was a week, I could not find it, but I found the paper it was wrapped in."

The only answer made by Mr. Davy, and Mr. Wills (afterwards Solicitor-General), the prosecuting counsel and counsel for the Crown respectively, was to badger subsequent witnesses until they admitted that Mrs. Elizabeth Headland had not as good a character as the neighbours might have wished—the usual dodge common to the logic of barristers-at-law before and since 1754. Here, as frequently in this case, one has a vivid glimpse of the appalling inefficiency of legal practitioners, from the red-robed judge in ermine on the bench, down to the fledgling barrister bluffing his way to briefs and fees in the foetid atmosphere of the Old Bailey of the eighteenth century.

By a majority, the judges agreed to transport the luckless Elizabeth Canning to the New England plantations, for the term of seven years, menacing her with death as a felon if she were found in his happy land of England at any time during the seven years. One very "humane" judge remarked that on no account should she be sent to Newgate for six months; since, so great was the public sympathy, that she would have too pleasant a time there—great sums having been collected on her behalf, and there being a prospect of assemblies outside the gaol, if she were incarcerated there. The *Annual Register,* 1761 tells us that:

"Elizabeth Canning arrived in England in November 1761, and received a legacy of £500, left her, three years before, by an old lady of Newington-green."

(£500 would be worth at least £8,000 in our own depreciated money.)

Other stories are that she married a well-to-do Quaker of the old pirate-broking town of Weathersfield, Connecticut:

"Died at Weathersfield, Connecticut, E. Canning who had resided there ever since she was transported. She became a schoolmistress and married a wealthy Quaker. Notwithstanding the many strange circumstances of her story none is so strange as that it should not be discovered, in so many years, where she had concealed herself, during the time she had invariably declared she was at the house of Mother Wells." (*Gentleman's Magazine*: 22 July, 1773).

Thus, she lived for only twenty years after this farce of a trial, and, no doubt, the comment, above, fairly sums up contemporary opinion on the mystery. But, on the essential question of the identity of the hovel, or bawdy house, wherein Elizabeth Canning was forcibly confined, we propose to attach more weight than did Serjeant Davy to the testimony of one, John Ward, given at her trial, in 1754:

John Ward: a horse-keeper and breeches-maker, whom a jocose friend in a London alehouse, in 1753 or 1745, had slandered with the trifling imputation that he, the said John Ward, did, on sundry occasions, apply to Madame Susannah Wells to procure for him the company of certain light and joyful ladies at the Enfield bagnio-public-house, said:

"I visited Mother Wells in the Clerkenwell Bridewell, and asked her how she came to keep the girl there a fortnight? Wells said: 'She was there twenty-eight days.' I asked her in what room she kept her in. She said: 'You know the room very well!' I had known Wells for about twelve or thirteen years, and had been all over the house. I did not understand what room she meant. She did not, as I know of, form her answer on what had been in the newspapers. I took the newspaper words to mean that she was kept there a fortnight. *Mother Wells did not tell me she was innocent of the charge.*"

Mr. Davy (cross-examining): "Did not she, before the trial, say she was innocent of it?"

John Ward: "No, sir, *what I told you is all truth.*"

Nor did all the barristerial badgering at the Old Bailey, in that year 1754, alter John Ward's testimony, in one jot or tittle.

The late Andrew Lang, perhaps with a recollection of his Psychical Research Society adventures, averred, with truth, that Elizabeth Canning was a victim of the common sense of the eighteenth century, who thought her strange tale could not be true. He might also have added, with equal truth, that poor Bet Canning was a victim of the inefficiency of legal advocacy, the stupid prejudice and inhumanity of eighteenth-century judges, the consistent neglect of opportunities for skilled and impartial cross-examination and of the ruling-out, on the flimsiest of technical objections by the Crown legal authorities, of affidavits supporting her case. A certain amount of London city civic politics was also imported into the Canning case by men who were anxious to discredit one side or the other in what had become a polemical war of newspapers and pamphleteers.

Fielding, whose "Tom Jones" had delighted the town just five years before the Canning trial, had to apologize to that by-word for fussy imbecility, the Duke of Newcastle, George

II's Secretary of State. Newcastle complained that affidavits promised had not been submitted to him by the prosecuting counsel and attorneys, acting for Elizabeth Canning, in the trial of Mother Wells. The multitude of counsellors had certainly darkened the waters of the well of truth by stirring up the mud of prejudice and controversy:

> "I received an order from the Lord Chancellor immediately before the breaking up of the Council, to send your Grace the affidavits; but they were in the possession of attorneys in the city. I have long had no concern in this affair, nor have I seen any of the parties lately, unless once when I was desired to send for the girl to my house, that a great number of noblemen and gentlemen might see her to ask her what questions they pleased." (*Dom. State Papers, Public Record Office,* To the Duke of Newcastle from Mr. Fielding, at Ealing, 14 April, 1753).

He writes again, on 27 April, 1753, to express his concern to hear from the Duke that the prosecution had not laid the affidavits before him:

> ". . . I have long disliked (their behaviour) and have long ago declined giving them any advice; nor would I, unless in obedience to your Grace, have anything to say to a set of the most obstinate fools I ever saw, and who seem to me rather to act from a spleen against my Lord Mayor, than from any motive of protecting innocence; though that was certainly their motive at first. In truth, if I am not deceived, I suspect they desire that the gypsy should be pardoned, and then to convince the world she was guilty, in order to cast greater reflection on him who was principally instrumental in obtaining such pardon." (*Dom. State Papers:* P. R. O.).

It seems to have escaped the notice of those who have written on the subject of this famous and intriguing mystery, that other evidence, not called by Elizabeth Canning's legal advisers, might have helped her. A certain Elizabeth Knot (later, found guilty, at the Old Bailey, of gown-stealing) was urgent to appear as witness, on behalf of Canning, who had been told, by Virtue Hall, in the Gate-house, a circumstantial story of the affair. Knot told the story—what it was cannot now be discovered—to a friend of Canning. It was urged that Knot's testimony was of importance; but she was not subpoenaed, although anxious to give evidence.

(*Vide*: "A collection of several papers relating to E. C.," 1754. *Brit. Museum*).

Why was there no stern cross-examination of the gypsy George Squires, who ducked his head in Court, when a witness was asked to identify a man seen with the Romany *chie*, Mother Squires at Enfield, at a time when Mother Squires swore she was in Hampshire? George Borrow, in his chapter on "The English Gypsies," in "Romano-Lavo-Lil" had no doubt what the solution of the Canning mystery was . . . "the idea of Romanies running away with other people's children . . . as devoid of reason as the suspicion" (in the late sixteenth and early seventeenth centuries) "that they harboured disguised Roman Catholic priests . . ."

> "Now the idea of Gypsy women running away with wenches! Where were they to stow them . . . what were they to do with them? Two Gypsy women were burnt in the hand in the most cruel and frightful manner, about the middle of the eighteenth century, and two Gypsy men, their relatives, sentenced to be hanged for running away with a certain horrible wench of the name of Elizabeth Canning, who, to get rid of a disgraceful burden, had left her service and gone into concealment for a month, and on her return, in order to account for her absence, said she had been run away with by Gypsies . . . but suspicions being entertained about the truth of the wench's story, they were reprieved and, after a little time, the atrocious creature, this wench, who had charged people with doing what they neither did nor dreamt of doing, was tried for perjury, convicted, and sentenced to transportation. Yet, so great is English infatuation that this Canning, this Elizabeth, had a host of friends who . . . swore by her to the last, and almost freighted the ship which carried her away with goods, the sale of which enabled her to purchase her freedom of the planter to whom she was consigned, to establish herself in business, and to live in comfort, and almost in luxury, in the New World, during the remainder of her life."

As is seen, George Borrow shared the views of the snuffy old Alderman Chitty, on one point, but on two other—and legal—points, Borrow was a bit off the track. It was not running away with a wench, but trying to recruit one for a bawdy house that was alleged against Mary Squires; also, Miss Canning was not in the same position as the girl who consulted Burns' "Doctor Hornbook," and was given by that gentleman a "drow" or "draught," which sent her to her "long home" to "hide the shame there." However, George Borrow had no doubt that Romany females "live in almost continual violation of the laws intended for the protection of society; and it may be added, that in this illegal way of life the women have invariably played a more important part than the men . . . being the most accomplished swindlers in the world . . . practising on the superstition of their own sex . . . suddenly vanishing with all the money of an aged gentlewoman on pretence of making decoctions from herbs that would restore all her youthful vigour." In passing it may be said that, in 1952, one gypsy woman was prosecuted in the police court at Gloucester, for playing off a *hokkano* of this sort on a silly woman at whose door she had called and promised to interest the planets, on condition of receiving various not inconsiderable sums of money.

Andrew Lang quotes a curiously similar case to that of Elizabeth Canning happening about 1904, in which a young woman in Cheshire—by occupation, a daily governess—went off alone to skate on a lonely pond, while the family were at church, in the morning. She was never heard of again; until, in the dusk of the following Thursday her hat was found outside the door of her father's farmyard. Her friends found her, farther away, weak, emaciated and with a fractured skull. She said a man had seized her, as she was leaving the pond, and had dragged her across the fields and shut her up in a house, from which she escaped and came to her father's house. When she found she could go no farther, she tossed her hat towards the farm door. Neither man nor house was ever found. The girl's character was excellent, and there was nothing to indicate that she had had "a night out." Lang's theory was that the girl had had a concussion on the ice, and had suffered from hallucinations as she lay in an outhouse on the farm. Here, one might say that Lang's theory was almost as mysterious as the affair itself!

PART TWO

THE EERIE, THE MACABRE AND THE LOST

Chapter 3

AMBROSE BIERCE "GOES INTO THE DARKNESS"

"To know that a man is dead should be enough."
(*Ambrose Bierce*)

NOT even the most hardened sceptic, even if he have in him something of the dry wit and sardonic spirit of Ambrose Bierce, who preferred sense to sentiment, wit to humour, dry wines to sweet, can find it in his heart to agree with the acrid and pungent humour and the bitter mood of the quotation at the head of this chapter. For the sceptic, who so often has a soft spot in his head or heart for a mystery, or the riddles of the unseen or unknown, can never agree that it is enough to know that a man is dead.

In the case of a man of action and a genius, such as was Ambrose Gwinett Bierce, he will want to *know how he died*, and when and where. One can never read the often macabre and always vivid and powerful stories of this prince of short story writers, without wondering how it was he never returned to the land he left, one night, when he clandestinely slipped across the Rio Grande into war-torn and revolution-ridden Mexico. His mysterious ending has all the flavour of his own stories of the rotted corpse of some Confederate soldier, who grappled with the sword arm of some Yankee officer who strayed, at midnight, from the outpost into the shadows of a sinister and whispering glade; of strange murders and coroners' inquests; of the invisible terror that moved out of the wilderness to slay lone ranchers in remote shacks in Arizona; or of that dreadful "march" of mangled thirst-racked soldiers, in the dead of night, over moor and waste, to the already blood-red waters of a river, who were followed by the ethereal lost little boy, who returned to his farmhouse to find it a blackened ruin and his brained mother lying in her blood across the threshold, and himself to become a raving idiot. The horrors of the war that the fierce and stern General Sherman himself called hell!

Ambrose Bierce had a remarkable career, one typical of the eccentrics and strange men, touched with madness and genius, who were the very reverse of the conventional notion of smug, pious and pompous, spade-bearded and Dundreary-whiskered acquisitive and prosperous men, with the Bible in one hand, and the bank book and share warrant in the other, who, many people deem, are *all* that the Victorian Age connotes. Men and ideals of a roaring century of progress that was to go down in the boom of guns and amid the miasma of the poisoned and plague-generating earth of France and Flanders, Galicia and western Russia. Bierce came of old frontier stock of the pioneering and leatherstocking days, when railroads did not exist beyond the littorals of New York and Massachusetts and Pennsylvania, and when Indian braves still flourished their tomahawks and muskets, and rode their cayuses towards small settlements and isolated log cabins, where they disputed the lordship of the "Barcan wilderness" with men who were as ready with the rifle as with the axe, set to the roof of some umbrageous monarch of the vast forests. They were the days when his father heard only the sound of the rivers rushing over rocks shut up in by gloomy *cañons,* wooded to the very tops of their craggy cliffs.

"Bitter Bierce," as he came to be called, was born in a log cabin in Horse Cave Creek, Meigs County, Ohio, in 1842, about seven years before the lawless gold-miners headed in their Conestoga waggons, or aboard windjammers round Cape Horn, for the rich placer deposits of the gold gulches of the Sierra Nevada and the California ranges. His ancestors were poor and obscure farmers who had migrated from Connecticut to Ohio. Bierce told no one about his family origins, or the harsh struggles of his childhood. But his father must have been an intelligent man, much above the ruck of rude frontier settlers. So far as is known, Ambrose Bierce never went to school. It is doubtful if any school, or wandering hedge-schoolmaster, was to be found in many miles of Horse Cave Creek. What education he had he gave himself from the books, in his father's small library.

When he was nineteen he enlisted in the 9th Indiana Infantry Regiment, and fought on the Federal, or Yankee side, in the Civil War of the North and South. He distinguished himself as a soldier in many hard-fought and bloody battles of the Western armies; rescued fallen comrades on the field, at risk of his own life; and, in 1864, was severely wounded at the battle of Kenesaw Mountain, in Georgia. At the end of the war, he was made custodian at Selma, Alabama, of captured and abandoned property; but that job did not appeal to him, and he resigned to accompany General W. B. Hazen on a tour of inspection of Army posts in north-western U.S. He could see no future in army life, and his genius called him in a very different direction. At San Francisco, his brother, Albert Bierce was a newspaper man, and Ambrose joined him in free-lancing.

He wrote "pieces and pars" for the *Argonaut* and a *News Letter*. Already he was "lashing the fool and the knave," and his hardhitting style, and caustic wit, and sardonic fearlessness were becoming recognized. More, certain mystical traits and a flair for the supernatural came out in his first short story, titled "The Haunted Valley," which he wrote for the *Overland Monthly*, in 1871. On Christmas Day, 1871, when he was twenty-nine, he married pretty Mary Day, of San Francisco. It was not to be a happy union. About March 1872, he and his wife sailed for England, where, in London, for the next four years, he wrote for Tom Hood's "Comic Annual," joined the staff of *Fun* and became one of the most striking members of a Bohemian group, which included W. S. Gilbert and George Augustus Sala, whose vast collection of newspaper cuttings are in the *Daily Telegraph's* newspaper library. Sala was the hero of a *bon mot* which would certainly have appealed to Bierce. On the eve of the honours list, in which a well-known watchmaker of Cheapside had been knighted, Sala went to his house, late at night, knocked him up, and called up to his bedroom window: "Watchman, what of the night?"

The ex-Empress Eugénie was then living in exile, with the ex-Emperor Napoleon, at Chislehurst in Kent. The echoes of the crash of the Second Empire and the surrender at Sedan had not died away. Eugénie (Marie de Montijo de Guzman) was the daughter of a grandee of old Spain, and an ironic fate had decided that Ambrose Bierce should undertake to edit for her ex-Imperial Highness a journal called *The Lantern*, which was to be run in opposition to a rival French journal, *La Lanterne,* of which the editor was Victor Henri Rochefort, le marquis de Rochefort-Luçay* a violent nationalist and opponent of all that the Second French Empire stood for. Bierce edited only two numbers of *The Lantern*. He was certainly *not* the man to run in harness with the ideas of grandeur and imperial greatness, or misery, entertained by the ex-Empress Eugénie, nor to take autocratic orders from a woman who was not for noth-

---

*It is a coincidence that Henri Rochefort died in 1913, the year of the mysterious disappearance of Ambrose Bierce.

ing the daughter of an old Spanish hidalgo. Bierce and she, or certainly Bierce, parted company with no regrets. Whatever he was, Ambrose Bierce was no American tuft-hunter of the sort described by Daisy, Princess of Pless, thirty-two years later, as "tumbling over each other to be the first to glow, and swell, under the smile of royalty" or, for that matter, of ex-royalty!

His genius, at this period, took a peculiar and sardonic and savagely jocose form. Under the pseudonym of "Dod Grile," he wrote the "Fiends' Delight," of which he said: "In writing and compiling this cold collation of diabolisms, I have been ably assisted by my scholarly friend, Mr. Satan, and to this worthy gent. must be attributed most of the views set forth in 'Fiends' Delight.' *Palmam qui meruit ferat* (let him wear the palm who deserves it), I shall be content with the profit." Bierce also published a collection of the pungent and mordant sketches that he had written in California. But Bierce was unlucky both in his publishers and editors. In London, he met a rascally editor and publisher named Hotten to whom George Augustus Sala referred, after Hotten's sudden death, as "Hotten, Rotten, and Forgotten!" Hotten paid Bierce with a post-dated cheque, and, on his way to the bank to cash it, Bierce stopped to have a drink in a pub with some journalistic friends. He arrived at the bank late, and the manager would not cash the cheque. Hotten had suddenly died.

In passing, it is interesting to note that publisher Hotten's manager was Chatto, who succeeded to Hotten's business and founded the well-known firm of Chatto and Windus. It seems to have been one of Bierce's friends, an author and a very polite man of an old-fashioned Victorian type, who called at the offices of Chatto and Windus to make a complaint. Not being sure of the identity of the man he saw there, he said—and how it would have delighted Bierce—"Look here, if you are Chatto, damn Windus, and if you are Windus, damn Chatto!"

Bierce wrote a fine sonnet, about this time, and it is an apt summation of his own genius and temperament:

"Fardels of heart-ache, burdens of old sins, luggage sent down from dim ancestral inns. And bales of fantasy from No-Man's Land."

Before quitting London, he published another volume, titled: "Cobwebs from an Empty Skull," containing sketches of his, reprinted from *Fun*. In 1875, he shook the dust of London from his feet and sailed back for California, *via* New

York. Back in San Francisco, he wrote for the *Wisp* and the *Argonaut*, and in 1897, when William Randolph Hearst took over the *San Francisco Examiner*, Bierce conducted a weekly column he called "Prattle." "Prattle" had, in fact, started in 1887, and also appeared in the editorial page of Hearst's *Sunday Examiner*. In it, the sardonic Bierce again "exposed the fool and lashed the knave." By this time, he was regarded as the literary dictator of the Pacific coast; but this stormy phase of his career ended in a disgust for journalism. "It is a frankly low and rotten means of livelihood," he told a friend. But, indeed, literature did not appear, for him, a much better means of livelihood, at least financially.

Not one publishing house in the U.S.A. would issue his splendid short stories—grim, vivid, macabre, but with little or no humour, and no sentiment in them. As he said: "My first volume of short stories was denied existence by the chief publishing houses in this country. Indeed, I could get them published only in 1891, when a merchant-friend, E. L. G. Steele, put up the money." It says nothing in praise or to the credit of the American book publishers of that time—and it was when a New York publisher told Bart Kennedy, whose capital autobiographical novel, "Sailor Tramp" found no takers among U. S. book publishers, "Go to London, Mr. Kennedy. We, here, are under its shadow," that there came out the volume containing the magnificently grim, powerful and sombre and vivid stories: "Tales of Soldiers and Civilians." It is the very cream and essence of his powerful genius. But they had not what the publishers called "human sentiment," and, when published, they attracted very little attention. In 1892, Bierce re-wrote G. A. Danziger's "The Monk and the Hangman's Daughter," a title with a Horace Walpole "Gothick" flavour, its sub-title being: "A medieval romance." As has been said, this is his longest work of sustained narrative, and reveals his deep sympathy and exquisite feeling for beauty, and a power of subjective analysis. But again, it returned him very little indeed, in the way of money; and for years, his genius as an artist in the short story or novel form went unrecognized.

No doubt, he paid the penalty for his life-long satire on fools and knaves, whom he lashed with a bitter and mordant pen. He wearied of the world of everyday men, and loathed shams, commercialism, log-rolling, back-scratching literary coteries, socialists and "mobocrats," against whom, and Catholics, priests and dogmatic theologians, he shot some poisonous shafts. His spirit, however, did not take the secular turn that might have been expected. He turned to the world of mysteries and the supernatural, the kingdom of shadows, masques, and the weird and supernormal, to which he gave vivid and macabre expression in his "Can such things be?" (1893).

Hearst sent him east to Washington, D.C., and, in 1896 and 1897, Bierce was Washington correspondent for the *New York American*. His relations with Hearst would probably make some very piquant reading, seeing his expressed loathing for the "low and rotten trade of journalism." It was an incongrous job for a man, who, as he said of himself, "preferred dry wines to sweet, sense to sentiment, clear English to slang." At the peak of his powers, in 1908, he wrote "The Devil's Dictionary;" but, as always, financial disaster was at his heels and none of his publishers were successful. His married life was unfortunate. By his wife, the San Francisco "socialite," Mary, or Molly Day, he had two sons and two daughters. He parted from his wife, for good, by judicial separation. One son was killed in a brawl over a woman, in North California; the other died in New York, in 1901. Bierce was becoming "Bitter Bierce;" but his genius was becoming recognized, while fate added the often usual drop of gall and anguish as if to remind him that everything in life has to be paid for, even success. No doubt, he would have agreed with the old Greek philosopher, who said: "Happiness? What *is* happiness? Call no man happy till he is dead!" Fate ironically gave him long days; but that guerdon merely made him long for the "good, kind darkness."

Moreover, the evil aura was extended even to his friends. His most brilliant pupil, Emma Francis Dawson, died of starvation at Palo Alto, California, in 1926. George Sterling, his faithful friend, secretary and biographer—he was also a well known American poet—whom, in a last letter from Texas, Bierce called "Great Poet and Damned Scoundrel!" —committed suicide, in the Bohemian Club, in San Francisco, on 17 November, 1926. The police found on a wall in Sterling's flat a fine picture of Ambrose Bierce. Another of his pupils, Hermann Scheffauer, killed himself in Berlin, in 1927.

To be lionized and treated as a celebrity was as little to the taste of Bierce, this lonely and bitter genius on whom life had soured, as was the back-scratching and log-rolling of the coteries that infest the walks and by-ways of literature. He told this story of himself:

"A man heard me give an order to a mail clerk at a hotel desk in New York. He hurried across the lobby and caught me up. 'Do you know Ambrose Bierce?' he asked. I turned and looked solemnly at him, and gently answered: 'No sir!' "

Bierce, who was telling this story to a woman friend, Ruth Guthrie Hardy, lifted an eye and chuckled. She said severely to him: "You should be ashamed of yourself!"
Bierce: "Well, I don't know me, now. Do I?"
In 1913, when 71 years old, he was at the height of his fame. His earnings were high. He was a man of striking appearance. His blue and piercing eyes were as steady and undimmed as they had been in the terrible battlefields of the American Civil War of the 1860s, and his hands were as steady at seventy-one as when he held a rifle or musket in Georgia or Alabama, in that day, His upright carriage and height of six feet attracted as much attention as his snow-white hair. But he was tired of the world and longed for the "good kind darkness." Yet there is no evidence whatever that he had any desire to make away with himself. It is known that he detested undertakers, or what Americans call "morticians," and he hated the idea that his body, after death, should be handled by them. To *some* people, this by no means unnatural phobia might suggest a motive for his slipping out of the world of what we deem to be civilized men.
It may be noted, too, that he was then suffering from asthma; and, *if* it be true that this respiratory disease has a mental origin, as some psycho-medicoes contend, then, those who accept this theory may contend that Bierce, in vanishing as he did, might have been seeking a cure for it. Yet, *if* so, it would have been in vain; since no man can escape from himself. In any case, the flat alkali plains of Mexico, as one of his friends and biographers, Walter Neale, pointed out, are very bad for sufferers from asthma.
Before he vanished to the unknown bourne of the port of missing men, Bierce had spoken to some of his friends of going on foot and by burro over the cordilleras of the southern Andes, starting out from Santiago de Chile, entering western Argentina, and ending up at Buenos Aires. He had no map, would take no one with him, and had no knowledge of the partly unexplored country over which he proposed to trail. He renewed mordant memories of the day when "far flashed the red artillery" over southern swamps and plains, and wooded mountains, by going round all the battlefields of the War of the North and South. It looked as if he were trying to turn the clock back in his life. He wrote to someone:

"I shall try to take a trip diagonally across from northeast to south-west, and then take ship for South America, go over the Andes and come back to the U.S.A. again."

If he really meant this, it did not indicate a desire to abandon old haunts and never more return. About these plans, whether or not they were vague or hazy, there was much, as there was in his strange personality, that aligned him with a man he never met, or, so far as one knows, heard of: the late "Don Roberto," or R. B. Cunninghame Graham. They both went on strange trails that ended in Latin America, were contemporaries and literary artists, and both had the comtempt for what is called success, allied with the spirit of *el gran caballero*. Both, too, were fundamentally aristocratic, the one by instinct, the other by hidalgo birth. Both had the same revulsion from so-called Socialist politicians; but their trails never crossed. Both passed beyond the sunset *in Latin America*.

Writing in September, 1913, from New York, to Walter Neale, Bierce, it was evident, was still playing with the idea of "getting away from it all" by going to South America. Bierce said: "I mean to go there." Neale replied: "Leave off that talk! *You* know what is your purpose. Are you about to depart for the Grand Cañon?" (This deep valley of the Rio Colorado, in Cocomino and Mohave counties, in Arizona, is 217 miles long, eight to 15 miles wide, and over three miles deep. It has remarkable and wild scenery, and strange erosion effects; and, in it, a man who wished not to return, would have little difficulty in forever losing himself without trace).

Bierce gave a characteristic reply, as if he were motivated by a perverse desire to mystify: "I have never been able to solve this question. Is silence always an affirmative? May it not be either negation or affirmation?"

Either at this time, or later, he also said that, at his age, he did not like travel by train. As late as 10 September, 1913, he was still playing with the idea of a solitary trip to South America; but, at *that* time, *via* Mexico. He wrote to Mrs. J. McCracken:

"I have no notion when I shall return. I expect to go to, perhaps across South America, possibly *via* Mexico, if I can get through without being stood up against a wall and shot as a gringo. But this is better than dying in bed, is it not?"

Again, on 13 September, 1913, he wrote to his daughter:

"Yes, I shall go into Mexico with a pretty definite purpose, *not at present disclosable*. . . . You must forgive my obstinacy in not perishing where I am. I want to be where something worth while is going on, or where nothing whatever is going on. . . . Pray for me? Why, yes, dear . . . that will not harm either of us. I loathe religions, and a Catholic sets my teeth on edge . . . but, pray for me, just the same . . . I am pretty fond of you, I guess. May you live as long as you want to, and then pass smiling into the darkness—the good, good darkness. . . ."

"Pray for me, just the same. It will do neither of us harm!" Bierce, here, reminds us of "Tiger" Georges Clemenceau, dying at his home in La Vendée, sixteen years later. *He* was, all his life, a bitter hater of clericals, Catholics and Jesuits. While he was on his deathbed, a Roman Catholic nun called on him with the idea of soothing his dying hours. Someone suggested that the nun be asked to go without entering the dying man's room. "*Mais non*," said Clemenceau. "Let her stay. She means well, and she can do no harm to an old man like myself. You need not send her away."

On 10 September, 1913, Bierce wrote to "dear Lora," from Washington, D.C.:

"I am going away, probably to South America; but if we have a row in Mexico, before I start, I shall go there first. I want to see something going on. I've no notion how long I shall be away."

About the beginning of November 1913, he reached Laredo, on the Texas side of the Rio Grande del Norte, and, on 6 November he again wrote to "Lora:"

"This is my only chance to pay up," (that is, write a letter), "for a long time. For more than a month I have been visiting my old battlefields . . . passing a few days in New Orleans. I turned up here this morning. There is a good deal of fighting going on over the Mexican side of the Rio Grande; but I hold to my intention to go into Mexico, if I can. In the character of an innocent bystander, I ought to be fairly safe, if I don't have too much money on me, don't you think? My eventual destination is South America; but probably I shall not get there this year. . . . *P.S.* You need not believe *all* that these newspapers say of me and my purposes. I had to tell them *something!*"

He seems to have written a second letter to "Lora," on 6 November, 1913:

"... Nuevo Laredo, opposite (on the Mexican side), is held by the Huertistas,* and Americans don't go over there. In fact, a guard on the bridge will not let them. So those that sneak across have to wade (it can be done almost anywhere), and go at night. ... I don't know where I shall be next. Guess it don't matter much.
Adiós. AMBROSE."

Bierce is known to have written letters, about this time, from Galveston, Texas, San Antonio, and Laredo, and apparently had discarded a vague notion of going to the Grand Cañon, where Neale supposed he had vanished. Among these letters is the famous one, in which he wrote:

"Forgive me for not perishing where I am. Goodbye! if you hear of my being stood up against a Mexican stone wall, and shot to rags, please know that I think it a pretty good way to depart this life. It beats old age, or falling down the cellar stairs. To be a gringo in Mexico. ... ah, that is euthanasia!"

As one has noted above, mystery still hung over his intentions, which, he said, "could not, at present, be disclosed." He must have slipped across the Rio Grande at night, at some unguarded point, and not over the bridge from Laredo. What happened to him on the other side of the bridge, in anarchic and revolution-ridden Mexico, is *the* mystery. Not one of his friends, or his near relatives, believed that he had any intention to commit suicide. He was said to have carried with him "3,000 gold dollars," and, when he stole from Laredo, he had credentials passing him through the Constitutionalist lines, and, also was said to be accredited to Pancho Villa. But, on the other hand, his friend and biographer, Walter Neale, says that Bierce had always roundly denounced Villa as a bandit, the Villistas as a rabble of bandits. "He entirely sympathized

---

*Partisans of General Victoriano Huerta, who, in 1913, had overthrown and assassinated the patriot idealist, Francisco Madero. The bandit, Pancho Villa, had been a partisan of Francisco Madero.

with the Carranzistas, who were in arms against the Huertistas, or supporters of the then President of the Mexican Republic, General Huerta."

One may, perhaps, infer from these conflicting stories that Ambrose Bierce had, to some extent, bamboozled his friends as to his real intentions, and had realized that, in order to create an aura of mystery, there is no better way than telling one friend one thing and another something different. All we *know* is that Bierce never returned, and no word ever came from him out of Mexico. The First World War had broken out, in 1914, and with thousands of men dying on the battlefields of France and Flanders, and the whole semi-civilized world in chaos, the mystery of the fate of one man, even were he Ambrose Bierce, was as a drop of water in an ocean, in relation to the world catastrophe on the other side of the Atlantic, and on every sea in the world.

It was on 3 April, 1915, some seventeen months after Bierce had vanished, that, at the home of Mrs. Helen Cowden, Bierce's daughter, at Bloomington, Ill., a mysterious letter arrived, that, said the *New York Sun*, had been written by Ambrose Bierce, who then would have been seventy-three. This letter, it was alleged, said that Bierce was on the staff of Lord Kitchener, and had seen actual service at the front in France! (It will be recalled that the Commander-in-Chief of the British forces, in France at that time, was Field Marshal Sir John French, who was then aged sixty-three.)

Bierce was further alleged to have written:

"I left Mexico for Europe, early in the fall of 1914, fought on the Allied front in France, and am in good health and not wounded."

The *Washington Post*, on 4 April, 1915, got on the trail of Mrs. Cowden and asked her to publish a facsimile of this letter, with further details of her father's movements, since he had vanished into Mexico. Mrs. Cowden *refused*, and replied merely that her father "was on the staff of Lord Kitchener's Army in France," which might or might not have meant on the staff of the army raised by Kitchener in 1915, called "Kitchener's Army," prior to the introduction of conscription, in 1916. On 2 December, 1916, Mrs. Cowden wrote to Neale, stating what, no doubt, was, in once sense, true: "How my father would have enjoyed this European War!" *Enjoyment* was a very strange word, however, to have used in connexion with the most terrible war in history!

Neale said: "I have never been able to discover that she showed or gave a copy of this letter to anyone."

Was this letter merely a hoax on the part of someone feeling the urge to get into the limelight? If so, who was it? If anyone knew, it *must* have been Mrs. Cowden. Why did she refuse to give out the letter, or let anyone see it?

The *Washington Post* also sought out Miss Carrie Christiansen, Ambrose Bierce's former secretary, who had last heard him from Chihuahua, North Mexico, and more than 400 miles north by west from Nuevo Laredo. She said: "Mr. Bierce did not go to Mexico for local colour, but for a rest!"

It seems odd that a man of his advanced age, should, *pace* Miss Christiansen, have looked for "rest," in Mexico, rent in two by a bloody revolution. Also, in that wild region at his age in his state of health, it is rather unlikely that he could have endured the rigours of the life of a war correspondent. Miss Christiansen also added: "Mr. Bierce' relatives always believed that he died in Mexico, and was not in France."

At this point, one may comment that it seems somewhat difficult to say how many daughters Ambrose Bierce had. One account says he had three children, only one of whom was a daughter, but other accounts of his biographers and American newspapers imply that he had three daughters, if not four!

As so often happens in these mysteries of vanished men other rumours and stories began to float around. Ambrose Bierce was alleged to have spent his last days in a lunatic asylum at Napa, a manufacturing township in West California, attended by his faithful secretary, George Sterling—the "great poet and damned scoundrel" of one of Bierce's last letters, from New Orleans. But this myth seems to rest merely on the fact that Miss Christiansen, his secretary, had lived at Napa, a few years before Bierce had vanished. The American War Department, in 1914 and 1915, refused to send a mission to search for Bierce in war-torn Mexico. True, at a later date, the Department questioned all American consuls, and American visitors, and even prospectors, in Mexico, about his fate.

There are eight stories, some of them quite circumstantial, about what befell Ambrose Bierce, in Mexico; but not a bone of him has ever been found or produced; nor any of his possessions that he took with him into Mexico. It has been alleged that scraps of an envelope, bearing an Oakland, Calif., postmark, were found but those scraps were never produced. Let us set out these stories below:

(1) George F. Weeks, a correspondent in the Mexican

revolution, said that he had talked with Dr. Edmundo Melero, in Mexico City, who said that he knew Bierce very well, and that Bierce had deserted to the Constitutionalists from Pancho Villa's bandit and guerila army, and had, later, been captured by General Urbina, a Villista, near Icamole, along with an ammunition train. The only other person was a Mexican *peón*, or peasant. Bierce refused to answer questions, and was shot and buried in the village. His grave was a shallow trench, which he shared with the *peón*. Dr. Melero was later said to have brought a lieutenant of Urbina to Weeks, who confirmed the story, and positively identified Bierce, when shown his photograph. George Sterling, who thought this story was authentic, and that Bierce died in spring 1914, said that the American War Department had heard and told Sterling that Villa's savage and bloodthirsty bandit guerillas had shot Bierce. Sterling relates an alleged incident at Tierra Blanca, where, in the noontide glare of Chihuahua, on 16 December, 1913, Bierce had casually shot one of Carranza's soldiers. Bierce had accompanied the army, and someone asked who was the gringo who was with that army. To allay suspicion, Bierce, it was alleged, took a rifle, calmly walked to the top of a ridge, took careful aim, and killed the soldier. "Poor devil!" said Bierce, later. "I wonder who he was?"

All one may comment is that this casual shedding of blood, for such a reason, is entirely out of character, for about the last man to curry favour, in this way, with either constitutionalists, or bandits, would have been Ambrose Bierce!

Sterling, in his *Memoirs of Ambrose Bierce* (New York, 1922), thought that, carrying so much gold about his person, Bierce might have been captured by a squad, condemned to death as a spy, shot, and the gold kept. "The matter has never been reported."

(2) Dr. Adolphe de Castro Danziger, in Mexico from 1922–9, put out a theory that Bierce had joined the army of the revolution against Huerta, and was in the battle of Ojinaga, along with "his armour-bearer," Pedrito, a *peón*, who spoke some English and had lived for a long time in San Antonio, Texas. De Castro Danziger says that the photograph shown to Urbina's officer, and "found on the body of Bierce," was really that of General Viljeon. He alleged that he talked with the revolutionist-bandit, Pancho Villa, in 1923, and that Villa was annoyed when Bierce's name was brought up. De Castro Danziger says he obtained Villa's own story of Bierce's end, and the conclusion of the tragic episode from Villa's closest associates. Bierce, he said,

was in Chihuahua when Villa captured that place. Bored with the inaction that followed, Bierce got drunk, criticized Villa, and pointed out the superior merits of Carranza and his army. In a rage, Villa ordered Bierce to quit Chihuahua at once.

"*Lo hemos hecho fuera,*" he said. (We chucked him out, bag and baggage). It is added that Villa arranged that Bierce be ambushed, and shot down when he got outside the township. Bierce's corpse was thrown to the *urubus,* or vultures.

R. H. Davis, in the *New York Sun,* accepted this story, and said: "I knew a great deal about Ambrose Bierce, and more than most people."

(3) The story of Tex O'Reilly, a soldier of fortune in Mexico, said that Bierce met his end at the hands of treacherous Mexican associates, but "that the mystery was never solved." O'Reilly says, too, that he discovered the grave of Ambrose Bierce in Sierra Majada.

O'Reilly is said to have been a staff officer of Pancho Villa, in 1914, and said that, when he was in Sierra Majada, in 1914, with General Torivo Ortega, he heard rumours of "an old man who had drifted into the town, searching for Villa, and had been shot by some local soldiers." O'Reilly also referred to scraps of an envelope with an Oakland, Calif., postmark, that were said to have been found. (This is an unconfirmed rumour.)

(4) An unproved story that Bierce was shot and killed during the fighting at Torreon, three hundred miles south of Chihuahua.

(5) *El Corenel Señor* C. J. Velardi of the Mexican Army, wrote to Mrs. Helena Isgrigg, daughter of Ambrose Bierce, and living in Hollywood, Calif., on 17 May, 1928: "I am having a measure of success in clearing up the mystery of your father." (This mission, however, failed.)

(6) An Associated Press dispatch, on 18 May, 1928, says that Ambrose Bierce's daughter (Mrs. Isgrigg?), started an investigation to find out what befell her father "who disappeared in 1913, when the Southern Republic was in the grip of the revolutionary bandit-leader, Pancho Villa." (Result *nil.*)

(7) James H. Wilkins, a California newspaper man, gives a slight variation of No. 1 story. In the *San Francisco Bulletin,* on 4 March, 1920, he said that Bierce had been shot by a firing squad of Villista banditti soldiery, at Icamole, about 110 miles east of Torreon, and some 300 miles southeast of Chihuahua. He gives the date of the execution as in 1915, but is not certain. He speaks of a "mysterious man"

sent by Villa to capture an ammunition train on its way to the forces of Carranza, who was fighting against Huerta for the stakes of the Presidency of the Mexican Republic. The train was captured and two men with it, who were shot by Villistas. The "mysterious man" said that one of the men captured and shot was Ambrose Bierce.

It will be noted that two of the stories (above) and the American War Department concur that Bierce was shot by Villistas. It may be said that while Ambrose Bierce probably had no desire to commit suicide, *if* it be true that he died as stated, destiny did that for him by involving him with the savage guerillas of Pancho Villa, who, himself was characterized by all the bloodthirsty savagery which marks South and Central American revolutions in which *miscegenated* ruffians take part. Bierce might seem to have had a premonition of his fate when he wrote, in 1913, just before clandestinely crossing the Rio Grande del Norte: "If you hear of me being stood against a wall in Mexico and shot to rags, I think that is a pretty good way to depart this life!"

All the same, there were many people in America who did not believe that Ambrose Bierce met his end in this way. Some believed that he had mysteriously entered South America; but no one *knew* why, or *if* he had gone to South America. He never revealed his purpose in going there, as he certainly appears to have planned to do.

As late as April 1932, the story that he was actually in that mysterious continent was revived, when an adventurer in Buenos Aires told a local newspaper that one, named Johnson, a member of "a Government expedition into Brazil," told the adventurer:

"I met in the unexplored jungles of the Matto Grosso of western Brazil, with a strange white man who has long, flowing white hair, and who is clad in jaguar skins. He is being held as a prisoner by a tribe of Indians who look on him as a god, and have mounted a guard to see that he does not escape to Cuyaba. This strange man gave me letters which we lost in our wanderings in the forests. I think he is the lost American writer, Ambrose Bierce."

Apart from the hearsay style of this report, it is in the highest degree improbable that a man who, *if* he were Bierce, would then have been *ninety years of age*, could have lived to that extreme age in a terrible land of unpacified and even unpacifiable Indians, pathogenic insects, and a climate that is calculated to devitalize and reduce to skin and bone a wild buffalo, let alone a white man! This, of course, is the type of story that has so often been told of Colonel P. H. Fawcett.

Bierce must long ago have died, and we may say of him as was said of Sir Francis Drake who was buried at sea off Nombre de Diós:

"Bierce: none thy body will ungrave again!"

Beneath the cloudless Mexican sky, with the *urubu* far aloft in the blue, his bones may have found their sepulture, undefiled by the touch of the undertaker whom his fastidious soul loathed, in some wild *matorral*, or by some *adobe* wall, in a place unknown, where the cicada whistles his threnody. It would be a grave as unknown as that of one of the missing Federal or Confederate soldiers long ago rotted to dust, in some eerie forest beyond the bivouac and camp fires of one of the bloody battles in Kentucky or Georgia. And the *real* purpose of "Bitter Bierce's" odyssey in Latin America is never likely to be known.

Chapter 4

WALLED-UP FOR TWENTY-ONE YEARS
IN MODERN TIMES

SOME 210 miles, north-east of Vienna, as the crow flies, is the ancient city of Krakow, or Cracow, spanning the River Vistula, in Polish Galicia. It has a history of strange vicissitudes, going back as far as the year A.D. 700, when it was founded by Prince Krak, of Poland. The second oldest university in Europe is here, along with a fine library and national museum, parks and a botanical garden, leafy and picturesque suburbs, ruins of a massive castle, and, in 1900, when it was still part of the former Austro-Hungarian empire, a population of 21,000 Jews alone. Krakow is known for two macabre and sadistic historical mysteries, both connected with young women. One of them is linked with some weird caverns, called the "Dorothaeum," and at one time used as grim prisons. These subterraneans lie behind certain apartments of the ancient and royal castle standing on Mount Wavel, right in the centre of the city.

As long ago as 7195, the Dorothaeum contained certain rich treasures, and seven jewelled crowns of the old kings of Poland. Someone unknown stole from the old castle these crowns, the castle itself being built in the fourteenth century by a powerful family of Polish nobles, the Tenczyns. Penned up in these queer caverns for years was a mysterious young girl, of the Tenczyn family, whose name was Dorothea. What crime she had committed, if indeed she had committed any crime, no one knows; but she died in these caverns, and her ghost is traditionally said to haunt the labyrinthine tunnels, in the rocks on which the castle was built. She left her name to the caverns and tunnels, and, in the seventeenth century, the Tenczyn family died out.

Not far away from this sinister and frowning pile, now half in ruins, is a suburb of Krakow, called Wesola, which stands in the middle of pleasant leafy promenades, fringed by a fine park, and a botanical garden, much frequented by the citizens, in the year 1869, when the second mystery came to light. It was associated with a grim and grey walled convent of the order of the barefooted Carmelite nuns, which adjoined the male priory of the same order. This nunnery lay in its own grounds, at the eastern end of the Ulica Kopernika in the suburb of Wesola, from which and two other roads, it was cut off by high stone walls and a massive door.

By a strange freak of history, this convent, unknown to the citizens of Krakow, had, for twenty-one years, concealed a horrible secret, singularly recalling that of the Dorothaeum, which is almost in sight of this nunnery. It was a secret more fit for the middle ages than the middle of the nineteenth century of roaring progress and mechanical transport. There was then sitting on the dual thrones of Austria and Hungary, the Hapsburg potentate, Emperor Franz-Josef, a devout and fanatical son of the Holy Roman Catholic Church, and pillar of the Vatican, who was doomed to live for long years and die, a msierable old man in the year 1916 of the First World War. Nemesis worked slowly.

On 20 June, 1896, there arrived, out of the blue at the stately stone offices of the Criminal Tribunal of Krakow, an anonymous denunciation, to the effect that, in the nunnery of the discalced Carmelites, in Wesola, there had been immured *for twenty-one years,* and still was, penned up in a filthy hole, an unfortunate young nun, now insane, starved and rotted for long years, lying on stinking straw, in appalling and savage conditions. Her prolonged sufferings, sadistic tortures, and the fetid and dreadful horror of her surroundings, had driven her insane; whereas, in earlier years, she had been young and beautiful. The Vice-President of the Tribunal pulled at his beard, narrowed his eyes and gazed at the letter. One account says that the letter was in the handwriting of an anonymous woman, another that it had been penned by a man.

The legal officer was perplexed. He would like to have dismissed it as an anonymous hoax, especially as the power of the clerical orders and the Vatican might be involved; and, if it *were* a hoax, they would want, if not to roll his head in the dust, certainly to move earth, if not heaven to have the Emperor, and the Court in Vienna, sack him from his job. On the other hand, there were also powerful liberal forces and men, not only in Austria, but far outside her frontiers, who hated Vaticanism, monkery and fanatic ultramontanism. They were forces of the modern world. True, it *might* be a hoax—but, suppose there *was* a horrible scandal—who knew? —the Tribunal in Krakow dare not ignore the denunciation; for there was England, country of that dreadful Lord Palmerston, dead not long since, and the Protestant Queen Victoria.

Certainly, the officer knew what sort of help he would get from the Emperor in Vienna, at the Schönbrunn Palace. Yet, there were liberal forces in France and Germany—and much more: the electric telegraph, the instrument of a worldwide press with foreign correspondents in Vienna! On the balance, it would seem less unwise to attempt an investigation than to ignore what this letter said. And, like bureaucrats in every age he could "pass the buck" to a subordinate. Well, he would! He shrugged his shoulders, rang his bell, and bade the usher take the letter to Dr. Sigmund Gebhardt, *der Kriminal-Untersucher-Magistrate* (investigating-magistrate, or *juge d'instruction*).

Gebhardt read the letter, and decided that action was imperative. No humble man or woman, he knew, dared risk the wrath of the controllers of monastic orders, in the clerical stronghold of Krakow, by signing his or her name to a document of *this* sort. He entered the office of the State prosecutor, Keudzierski, or Kinsirski, who read the letter, and then, along with Gebhardt and a beadle, called on Bishop Galewski. In so clerical a country as Austria, no lay or legal authority dared try to enter a monastery or nunnery without an order from the local prelate or bishop. Galewski heard what the law officers had to say, fingered his gold pectoral cross, and smiled gently and blandly.

"You know, gentlemen, this may be merely an invention? In fact, I feel sure it is!"

Keudzierski: "Your paternal lordship, you may be right. Nonetheless, the Vice-president of the tribunal thinks the denunciation should be investigated."

Galewski (shrugging his portly shoulders): "Well, gentlemen, if you insist, I will give you an order to visit this nunnery, and to accompany you I will send Father Spithal, the papal prelate, a very worthy man in whom you may have full confidence. He is very discreet."

So, armed with the bishop's order, the director of justice, *Herr* Stanislaus Grawelewski, a barrister, *Herr* Theophilus Parvi, a legal official, and Dr. Gebhardt, the examining magistrate, got into a coach and rode to the convent, along with the prelate, Spithal. They knocked at the massive door. No answer! They knocked again, and again. Still no answer! The beadle raised his voice and woke the echoes of the suburb. "In the name of the law, open, you within!"

Dusk had come, but the commotion attracted citizens who were taking the air in the nearby park. They were witnesses of the curious scene that followed, and they sped the news all over Krakow. A light appeared inside the door, and a hard-featured woman porteress opened a guichet, and, in the tones of a virago, demanded to know who was disturbing the privacy of a holy convent, at that hour, in so scandalous a manner. Behind this janitress was standing a very ill-favoured elderly nun, who had a strong suspicion of a moustache. It seemed to Gebhardt really as if this convent's controllers had had an inkling of this visit, or why did one light show anywhere in the grim building except at the gate-house?

Spithal pushed in front and showed the bishop's order to the porteress. There was a whispered colloquy between her and the nun standing behind her. Gebhardt, in no indecisive fashion, came forward.

"You have here imprisoned, a nun, named Barbara Ubrik. I wish to see and speak to her."

"Impossible!" barked the porteress. "No such nun is here. The Mother Superior is asleep. Besides, she would never allow such a thing."

She turned on her floppy boots, whisked aside her voluminous skirts, and, along with the elderly nun, was on the point of banging the grille of the guichet in the face of the officers, and retreating inside the convent.

Gebhardt (sternly): "Stand where you are, woman! Move an inch, and I will have you put under arrest. Where is the Prioress? You, too," (to the nun who was trying to steal away), "remain here. How dare you defy the law? Open the door at once!"

The porteress, mumbling: "I told you she was asleep. No one dare disturb her!" By this time, the commotion at the gate-house must have penetrated the convent, for two nuns appeared. Spithal shoved the bishop's order under their noses, and bade them lead him and the officers of the law to the cell of the nun. The commission of the Tribunal had been informed that this nun has been shut up from 1848 to 1869—completely *incommunicada!*

The investigators ascended a long stairway to a very long and gloomy corridor, at the farthest end of which, between a pantry and a latrine over a drain, and a sewer, was what looked like a walled-up back hole of ancient Krakow! Around were other cells, untenanted. In the wall of this den, whose stone exuded dank and noisome moisture, was a massive double-door of oak, banded with iron. By the door was a completely walled-up window. In the door was a very narrow guichet, just big enough for the insertion of a dirty wooden platter. Not a ray of light into the den! Nothing to light up the utter darkness of this medieval *cachot. What lay behind it!*

Gebhardt (sternly): "One of you fetch the key of this door!"

An elderly nun: "But, *mein Herr,*" (her eyes narrowed with malevolence), "if you *had* a key you could not open the door. It would not turn in that long disused lock."

Gebhardt (angrily): "In the name of the law, bring the key, or we will have the door broken down by force."

At last it was opened, and the beadle nearly broke his wrist in manipulating the massive key in the rusted lock. An appalling spectacle met the eyes of the astounded officers. An equally appalling stench nearly drove them back. At sight and stench of the den, Gebhardt bade Spithal send for the Bishop Galewski. This horrible hole was only *3 foot 11 inches long by 1 foot 11 inches wide!* In the darkness, under a foul heap of stinking straw, lay a shapeless mass of repulsive character. As the light came in through the door, which had not been opened *for twenty-one years,* the mass moved. It was seen to be the form of a naked woman, almost literally a skeleton, her emaciated body covered with filth and human excrement. In fact, heaps of the horrible excrement lay all around the cell, as if it had been a dungstable. The commission found, later, that the poor woman had not had even the decency of a chamber-pot! She was crouching; but, at the sight of men whom she had not seen for close on twenty-five years, she heaved herself up on her elbows, caked with the filth of unwashed years, and rubbed her dazzled eyes and forehead, as if in a daze. She was half-mad and wasted away worse than a Hindu ryot, in time of famine. She spoke.

"Why did you not bring me the coffee you promised me

two years ago? Give me something to eat. I am dying of hunger!"

She clasped her hands together and wept.

"Oh, give me food and I will be obedient!"

Frenzy seized her. She burst into a torrent of maledictions, against the Prioress and the senior nuns, and a scoundrel of a father confessor. Her language was so horrible that, it is said, the Commission did not record it. In the filth of the stone floor of the den lay a dirty platter with dirty, cold fragments of potatoes. Not even a morsel of bread. Not a chair in the hole; not even a stool; no stove to heat it in the coldest winter—and they are cold in Krakow! Only the foul straw and the omnipresent effluvia.

Gebhardt (in pity and rage): "Why have you been treated in this unspeakable manner?"

The demented nun: "They said I broke my vows of chastity! . . . But these nuns," she leapt into the air and waved her arms, "*they* are not pure; *they* are not angels!"

At this moment there entered the father confessor, a certain Piant Kiewicz—a Frenchman would have said that this horrible Polish fellow's name should have been *"Puant"*. Kiewicz must have had a hide like that of a rhinoceros, or he would never have dared to show himself before the Commission, in this foul hole. He was the creature and tool of the Prioress, Maria Wenzyk, and her even worse and more sadistic predecessor, the Carmelite Prioress, Teresa Kosiwikiewicz; she who had, years before, ordered the immurement and starvation of this nun, Barbara Ubrik. Kosiwikiewicz was the daughter of a very aristocratic Polish family, in whose strain there must surely have been pure sadists and very beastly hypocrites. Like the equally scoundrelly General of the Carmelite Order in Rome at that time, this confessor and tool of sadistic Prioresses had, it was established, long known about this poor wretch of a nun, but had done nothing, and said nothing, about it, except to grin about it to the Prioress. We shall say a little more of the General of the Carmelite Order later, and give his name, which should not be forgotten. He would have figured admirably as a chaplain at Auschwitz gas chambers, which were situated not very far from Krakow.

At the sight of this crony of the criminal Prioresses, the naked woman sprang towards him and shouted: "Thou beast!"

Gebhardt ordered some of the nuns to take the poor wretch to another cell and feed and clothe her nakedness. As she went out she spoke some unintelligible words, and then cried out, in distress: "Am I to be led back to my grave again?"

Gebhardt: "We are here, my poor woman, to liberate you."

At long last, there arrived the singularly shy and discreet Bishop Galewski who, as we saw, had blandly spoken of a hoax, and had to be pressed to give his order of entry. No doubt he felt that if this affair stank the more it was stirred, it behoved him the more not to give the impression, to outsiders, that he had not even gone to the nunnery when the horrible beans were spilled. (Even so, he had to be *sent for* by the examining magistrate.) Besides, the rabble of Krakow, who had now been alerted, were out for blood, the blood of torturing monks and abbesses. And, then, what about newspaper reporters, editors, and foreign correspondents who would soon be converging by train towards Krakow from Vienna and Berlin and Breslau? Lucky, for Galewski, that the telephone had not been invented! He was spared *that* ordeal! But the electric telegraph was very much in operation, and the submarine cables, and nothing could be kept out of those deplorable newspapers.

Barbara was brought before the bishop. She fell on her knees. Then she burst out into horrible imprecations.

Galewski: "My poor woman, I am here to help you. I am a bishop."

At this juncture, the reluctant Prioress, Maria Wenzyk, decided to put in an appearance; but this stern-faced, pious old harridan was observed most carefully to avoid the "impure nun's den, which sank offensively. A bigger cell, at the other end of the long corridor, was opened for the ascetic and most delicate nose of Mother Maria. Several elderly nuns spoke up and told the bishop, in exculpation of their unspeakable barbarities: "She, the nun, is mad. She tore her clothes to pieces. Her language is filthy."

The Bishop: "Be silent, you wretches! You are the shame of religion. You are furies, not women (*Furien nicht Weiber*). Go out of my sight! Two hours of such imprisonment would drive *me* mad, let alone twenty years!"

Mother Maria showed herself extremely unwilling to obey the bishop's orders. Her attitude was: "I have spared the nunnery a scandal—done a service to God by keeping this nun walled up for twenty years." And the confessor, Father Kiewicz, actually told the bishop—perhaps not altogether without foundation—that: "You, and the ecclesiastic authorities have, for years past, known all about this affair of the nun, Barbara Ubrik."

The Bishop: "That is an utter falsehood! I suspend both you and the Prioress from all further duties." (Another account of a clerical newspaper, in Vienna, affirmed that neither the Prioress nor the father confessor was so suspended.)

Meantime, outside this nunnery, four thousand indignant citizens of Krakow were demonstrating. Stones were hurled at the windows, and attempts made to get inside the convent and lynch the Prioress, the elderly nuns, and the father confessor. (And, surely, ropes have been put to much worse use!) Troops were sent for from the barracks. They had to open fire to keep the mob outside, and forty-one people were arrested. As it was, they got inside the nunnery and would have thrown out the nuns, neck and crop, had not soldiers arrived in the nick of time. Men rushed round to the premises of the Jesuits, about whom similar stories of "brutish savagery" were circulating, smashed every window they could reach, and insulted the rector. They also attacked the Franciscan convent in Krakow. For three days, Krakow was in an uproar, and unless the Prioress of the Carmelite nunnery had been placed under the guard of soldiers, she would have been torn limb from limb. Late on the Sunday following, the Prioress and the older nuns were taken away by night, under military escort and put under protective custody in an unnamed establishment. Citizens patrolled the town, shouting: "Down with the convents!" Leading Liberals in the city addressed street demonstrations, asserting:

> "The vows of poverty of these monks and nuns lead only to mendicity. The vow of perpetual chastity is against nature, and destroys the family and the basis of the state; while the vow of obedience makes machines of men. Charity has died in these institutions, and mysticism and the contemplative life is rarely there in evidence."

The commandant of the garrison did his best to pacify the people; the burgomaster, Leitel, issued a proclamation appealing for order; and the municipal council demanded the dispersal of the Jesuits and the Carmelites, denouncing them "as instruments of brutishness and depravity fit for the Middle Ages, and not the middle of the nineteenth century."

On 23 July, 1869, the Judicial Tribunal and a medical commission again visited the Carmelite nunnery, and Barbara Ubrik was brought from the hospital of Saint Lazare to the nunnery. The Prioress, Maria Wenzyk, was also summoned, and her infamous predecessor, the Abbess Kioswikiewicz. Barbara's mouth was full of curses against the Prioresses, and the almoner—and who may wonder? She was said to have told many stories of the mysteries of the nunnery in the ten years past. They spread into the town and further enraged the people of Krakow.

Said the criminal Prioress, Teresa K.: "The nunnery is being broken up. I shut her (Barbara) up on the recommendation of the doctor of the convent, in 1848. He is dead."

The Tribunal summoned the doctor of the convent, in 1869, Dr. Babeszinski. "I have held my post for seven years," he said, "but have never once seen this nun." The Tribunal ordered that Barbara be removed to a lunatic asylum. On seeing the green grass of the convent garden and the sunlight, she, who had for twenty-one years seen only a rare beam of light through a chink in her foul cell, wept and laughed for joy. One nun had humanity enough to run forward and kiss her; the rest turned their backs. On the journey to the madhouse, she fainted. The change was too much for her. Said a Vienna newspaper:

"She gradually recovered some of her strength, and the bad smells from her body had vanished in the clean apartments. The Tribunal at Krakow have decided to arraign, on indictment, for infamous conduct, grave injury to the person, and barbaric violence the present Prioress of the Carmelite nunnery, Maria Wenzyk, her predecessor, Teresa Kosiwikiewicz, (sic) or Kozderkiewicz, and the other Prioress, Ksanara Josap, all of whom are implicated in the crime, together with several senior nuns who were willing accomplices."

Another Liberal and non-clerical newspaper in Vienna, commented that Barbara Ubrik had trembled when she entered the asylum; for she was still under the control of the Brown sisterhood of the Carmelite Order. "It is an extraordinary arrangement," said the newspaper. But the Tribunal at Krakow had run against formidable and secret obstacles. The ecclesiastical wheels, geared to the Vatican, in Rome, were turning. In Krakow, the Catholic clergy were bent on hushing all up and taking no action. Every impediment was being placed in the way of the civil legal authority. The Roman Catholic authorities had even forbidden the Judicial Tribunal of Krakow to examine the defendant nuns—and this, in a horrible case of *crime*—unless the nuns were closely veiled; so that the examining magistrate could not see or recognize them! As lawyers know, it is essential for a judge to see the face and expression of a witness if he is to form any valid opinion on his or her credibility, veracity or reliability. It was also said that the Roman Catholic hierarchy in Krakow had known in 1859—ten years before the denunciation—all about the dreadful treatment and immurement of the nun, and said nothing and did nothing. They may be called accessories after the crime.

Indeed, not only the Vatican in Rome, but the *Austrian Emperor, the Hapsburg Franz-Josef* opposed *any* inquiry whatever into the scandal. As the late King Edward VII of England said, many years later, on another occasion: "Franz-Josef was not exactly a gentleman." It was apparent that, for ten years, the Concordat had stifled any inquiry into this case. Away in Rome, Father Dominicus, the general of the Carmelite Order, had, said the Krakow Carmelite convent Prioress, Teresa Kosikiewicz, or Kozderkiewicz, one of the principal criminals, arraigned by the Tribunal firmly and inexorably set his face against the removal of Barbara Ubrik to a lunatic asylum. This hard-faced, inhumane, ecclesiastic had his own politic reasons for his inaction in 1848, when this Prioress gave the order for the nun's immurement. Besides his fear of the scandal coming to the ears of the public, he, like this Prioress, was concerned with the retention of what property the nun may have had. In fact, this infamous woman, Teresa K., actually told the Krakow Tribunal that: When she (Barbara Ubrik) had "passed 50 *years*" of this death in life, in the cell, and stinking dungeon, "she would become calmer and more composed!" And the senior nuns, her accomplices, calmly told the Tribunal: "When we become nuns we banish all human emotions."

The ecclesiastical authorities even got a clerical journalist, in Vienna, to concoct an apology, or defence, which was published at Breslau, Germany, in 1869, under the title of "Die Krakauer Klostergeschichte." This man said:

> "Barbara Ubrik was brought to the Krakow convent in a state of frenzy, in which she tore to pieces all her clothes, smashed up all the cell furniture, developed *Erotomania*," (love passion of the sort which also afflicts some married women) "called for men, shouted obscenities from her cell-window; and so it had to be walled up to prevent any from hearing or seeing her. . . ."

Why, then, if this were true, had not Barbara been transferred to a lunatic asylum?

"Because, says the Prioress Teresa, who is the daughter of a very noble Polish family: this nun, whom our General in Rome would not consent should be transferred to a lunatic asylum, would have continued this conduct in a lay asylum, have told stories of our nuns and nunnery, and brought scandal and discredit on our austere order. She was sent to Krakow from Warsaw, for a change of air; but became mentally deranged, said she was the Holy Trinity, and spent whole days and nights, shrieking for a man. . . .

"We have the reputation in Krakow, for we are of the reformed order of the ecstatic and only, Santa Teresa, of the very best character. We were willing to nurse her ourselves."

Nursing! Such an idea of "nursing," held by this ruler and her accomplices in this infamous nunnery of the barefooted Carmelites, would have qualified them all for jobs in the infamous prisoner-of-war camps which the Germans established in Poland and elsewhere, nearly a century later!

The Warsaw newspaper, the *Daily Kurier*, traced the sister of Barbara Ubrik, and was told:

"Barbara Ubrik's parents were small landed proprietors, in Poland, who died young, leaving four daughters, of whom Anna was, later, renamed Barbara. She was brought up by her aunt, and, later, sent to the school of the Order of Visitation. Here, she became ill, and was taken into her house by the Countess Dziewanowski. She became ill, in this house, and when she became better, asked to be taken to the Convent of the Visitation; but they refused to admit her. She then got an introduction to the Carmelite convent at Krakow, and since then her family has heard nothing of her; except, that she had become insane and was well treated."

This story of Barbara's sister, in Warsaw, is probably less than half true. In fact, it does not square with what the Tribunal learnt of her having been transferred to Krakow from another Carmelite nunnery in Poland.

An abominably hypocritical letter had been written, on 11 August, 1851 (three years after Barbara had been walled up and eighteen years after the denunciation to the Tribunal), by the Prioress Teresa, of the Carmelite nunnery at Wesola, Krakow. This letter had been sent to Barbara's sister, Eleanour, in Warsaw:

"Your sister, Barbara, has, for three years past, been severely mentally disordered and suffering from very violent fits. If *you* lament her unfortunate position, so do we, even more. We have to pay a great deal for her medical treatment, and are in constant fear of her. It is painful for us to hear the physician say that she had evidently suffered this illness before, and that we were never told of it. For, if we had known, we would never have admitted her to our convent. . . . We do her no harm. Be quite at ease. She would be very unhappy if she went elsewhere. The convent is a great protection to her, tho' God has made her a great and heavy cross to us."

It was the *Allegemeine Zeitung* which gave the "low down" on the development of the judicial investigations at Krakow:

"The inquiry into the Barbara Ubrik affair will shortly end. The nuns defamed urge, in their defence, that they did not act on their own authority; but that the General of the Order, in Rome, Father Dominicus, refused to authorize them to transfer her to a lunatic asylum. Dominicus had even personally convinced himself, in 1858 and 1867, that she was incurable: yet he would permit no change in her situation. In order to control these allegations, the Tribunal, through the Minister of Foreign Affairs, at the Ballplatz, in Vienna, have asked that the General be questioned about them. Krakow clergy have used every effort to stifle the inquiry, and the ultra-montanist press even deny the whole story."

Father Dominicus declined all requests for him to visit Krakow, or answer any questions put to him in Rome. He clearly felt that the more the affair was stirred, the more it stank in decent folk's nostrils.

The author of this book has found it impossible to discover whether either law or justice was administered to these infamous male and female devotees. The Bishop of Krakow, Galewski, seems to have succeeded in discretely dispersing the Abbesses and their accomplice nuns to unknown destinations, after ordering the evacuation of the Wesola Carmelite (male) convent, and the adjacent Carmelite nunnery. And the process of hushing up all, and burking the investigations of the Krakovian Judicial Tribunal, was done in the thunder of the guns of the Franco-Prussian War of 1870, when the attention of Liberal Europe was distracted by carnage and the crashing of the empire of Napoleon III of

France, and the rise of the empire of Bismarck. It was also aided by the death, on 24 February, 1870, of this poor woman, Barbara Ubrik, in the hospital of the Holy Spirit, at Krakow. She was buried in secret, in the dark of night, so that no popular demonstration might be provoked in Krakow. Indeed, she never recovered her sanity, and was never able to give *her* story of the infamous and incredible goings on in the convent of the Grey Sisterhood.

One Galician newspaper said:

"Her *bourreaux* (hangmen) were the Jesuits, alleged to be the prime authors of her segregation and sequestration. And they are now rid of all by the death of the victim, which, according to some newspapers, has been ma le to seem natural."

Whether or no the Jesuits were to blame, it is a fact that one important witness *was* removed by poison, even if, as the above newspaper seems to hint, the death of Barbara Ubrik in the asylum was not exactly the *sole* work of nature. Not many years later, the German *Reichskanzler*, Prinz Karl von Hohenlohe, himself a Catholic, told Bernard von Bulow, himself, later, *Reichskanzler*, in Berlin:

"When my brother, the Cardinal, celebrated the Eucharist, in Rome, he was always careful, beforehand, to have his chaplain carefully examine the chalice, lest his enemies, the Jesuits, had slipped into the wine powdered glass, or poison."

The important witness "removed" was the boozy friar of the Carmelite monastery of Czerna, adjacent to the Wesola Carmelite nunnery; and before this witness could be interrogated by the Tribunal of Krakow, he suddenly died and was secretly buried in the convent garden cemetery. Subsequently, it was revealed that he died by poison, *not* administered by himself, but by the Prior or some monk closely connected with the witness. At all costs the hierarchy were determined to stifle any judicial investigation.

In the meantime, there was, of course, an inevitable backwash and eddies from the rising of this tide of corruption and barbarity in the closes of the monasteries and nunneries in this corner of Austrian Galicia. The eyes of Liberal and non-clerical Europe were fixed on these domains of the Hapsburg Kaiser Franz-Josef, and the newspapers of London, Berlin, Paris, Vienna, and even Warsaw ventilated other monastic scandals, real or alleged, in which it is not always easy to apportion the precise amount of veracity. For example, the *Narodni Listy* came out with a scandal alleged to have occurred at Karolinenthal, in Bohemia (today, Karlin, a suburb of Prague, in Czecho-Slovakia), in the belfry of the convent of the Sisters of Charity, where a nun had been found self-hanged.

"An infamous lie," said the Abbess; but the nuns said: "You can keep nothing out of the newspapers, in these days." A police commissary and the parish priest went to the nunnery to investigate. The commandant of the local barracks had, for some reason, ordered soldiers to watch the belfry from a vantage-point in the barracks:

> "Early in June 1869, children came home from the convent school of this Order of the Sisters of Charity, and asked their parents not to send them back; for their teacher, a nun, had been shut up, and *they, too,* they feared, might be shut up! Several soldiers from the nearby barracks say they have seen a nun in the windows of the belfry opposite to them. They were sure that she had been imprisoned. Other people say they had also seen this nun up there, up to the 14 July, towards 6 p.m. More, the children of the convent school said, at this time, that the nun had hanged herself. Indeed, other witness assert that they have seen the body of a nun, distinctly, hanging up; whereas, in the previous days, they had seen her moving about the belfry alive. Two women, whom we may call W. and G., and who live in Jakobstrasse, promenading in the evenings, recently, swear that they also had seen the nun up there. We are told that the window of the belfry has been closed up and the body of the nun whisked away into Prague, dressed as a domestic servant. The nun's name is Damascena, and she was the daughter of a coal-merchant, named Badil. We call for a searching official inquiry." (*Narodni Listy*)

Another Prague newspaper gave details about an affair in the convent of the Greyfriar nuns, also at Karolinenthal, where "a nun, alleged to have violated her vows of chastity, has by the Prioress, been sentenced to imprisonment and punishments, and has hanged herself in the cell. At the autopsy, the nun was found to be four months pregnant." A "complete invention," said the Prioress; but the same newspaper returned to the charge with a story of a nun in a local Ursuline convent who was "tortured for eight days, in the winter of 1869, in a cellar of the convent. Here, seized with a frenzy, the nun wanted to kill the Abbess with an axe." (Only "wanted," one sees!) "No truth in it," said the ecclesiastical authorities. Finally, the *Wiener* (Vienna) *Blatte* published a *schauer-märe* (horror story), about a lusty and lecherous scoundrel of a Redemptorist Father, who appears to have been directly descended from the friar, in fourteenth-century England, who said "Benedicite! with a bolke" (belch) and was very partial to shriving handsome wives of Midland farmers and indulging in very intimate friendships with them, when the said farmers were away at markets in conveniently distant medieval towns. The Redemptorist Father's spiritual task was to confess sins and listen to penitent nuns; but, in July 1869, he had also ravished a twelve-year-old maiden—a novice—in the six-years-old nunnery of Maria Stiegen, in Vienna.

In this last case, a threat was uttered, but really *not* by the scandalized Abbess, Mother Maria Stiegen, but above the supporting signature of Padre Josef Kassenwalder, Prior Superior of the Redemptorist Order of Fathers. Unless the editor purlished an immediate retraction of the story, then certainly Kassenwalder, if not the Abbess, would have the Austrian press law on him:

"Our honour has been impugned in your issue. Nr. 209, of Friday, 30 July, 1869. No such nun has been ravished by any Father of the Redemptorist Congregation. I, as Provincial of this Holy Congregation, declare the whole story a lie which you have told about this Father and this maiden, whose name, you say, is Veronica. I demand, in virtue of the Austrian press laws, that you publish an apology and this statement in your next issue; otherwise, I shall be compelled to have recourse to legal measures. . . .

"*Wien* (Vienna), 31 July, 1869, (*signed*) Maria Stiegen. With all respect: Padre Josef Kassenwalder, Sup. Prov. Austr. C.SS.R."

It may seem, to the reader, a little odd that Kassenwalder, *alone*, spoke of "honour" impugned, while the Abbess Maria Stiegen did no more than merely put her signature first, and leave the Redemptorist gentleman to make the denial and the threat. Why this odd silence of Mother Maria —not one word from *her* about the honour of Veronica, of Maria Stiegen, or her nunnery? The impression one has is that if there was no fire, there was some queer smoke.

Chapter 5

THE MONSTER OF BRUGES

OUR twentieth century—the age of two devastating world wars; of relativity; the coming of interplanetary travel, still, however, a long way off in the future; the diabolical hydrogen bomb and the fearful weapons of inter-continental ballistic missiles; and of the years ahead of which no man cares to take a long view—has certainly seen no lack of mysteries as baffling as any that were in the centuries before.

Some years before the Second World War, I was in that city of slow time and the sound of dreamy carillons, where, if there are not now "grass-grown streets trodden by noiseless feet," there is certainly a strange labyrinth of twisting medieval streets in which it is easy for a stranger to get lost all night. I refer to Bruges. I stayed at an ancient house not far from the Rue des Tonneliers, right in the heart of this queer timeless old city, and, there, I was told a very eerie story connected with some very strange bones now in the "dry" section of a certain Belgian Medical Museum. This ancient house had formerly belonged to the order of the Black Friars, or Dominican monks; but, about 1908, it had been acquired by a private person who let out flats in it to artists, or to foreigners desiring to make a protracted stay in this picturesque, old Flemish town. As would be expected of a former monastic institution, the house had grim and massive walls, many small rooms that had once been cells, tortuous stone stairways, and very narrow passages.

But there had been complaints about the place. People came and rented the rooms and flats, for which only a modest rental was asked; but many of them packed up and left, some even before their period of paid occupancy had ended. There had been stories of eerie footsteps of something unseen ascending the stairs, not merely in the night, but in the day. One Englishman, who was about to come out of his door on a top storey, hurriedly shut it when he saw, in the dim angle of the stone passage outside, where only a crepuscular light entered even at sunny noon, what he called some "damned inhuman," but vague and bizarre object, standing and waiting. He could not make out what it was, but it shuffled and padded off, leaving behind a horrible stench, as "if it had come out of the Devil's own latrine!" There were also eerie raps on doors, and when the doors were opened, no one was seen there.

At last, the *patron*, who saw that if these phenomena continued, he would be left with an empty house on his hands—since not even the most downright sceptic can be prevailed on to live and spend his days and nights in an old house which has "something queer about it"—got in some builder's hefty men and had them break up the heavy stone flags of a very ancient and roomy stone cellar, which was believed to be the source of the phenomena. They did not find any coffins, or skeletons under the floor, nor any fruits of the clandestine amours of medieval monks and nuns, nor any sign that someone in the fourteenth or fifteenth century had by some means "raised the Devil" and couldn't get him to lie down afterwards! But when the labourers were asked to apply their chisels, and picks and crowbars to the thick *walls* of this queer cellar, they opened up something on which no pathologist could express a decided opinion. They found, right in the middle of the thick cellar-wall, a sort of alcove in which were strange bones that did not all look human.

A surgeon, who was also a pathologist, was called in, and when he examined the bones, even he, hardened to macabre sights, shuddered. He said: "This must have been some monstrosity, walled up untold years ago, and the bones all belong to the same uncanny being. *Nom du diable* . . . I confess I am unable to express any opinion on the origin of this horrible thing; nor can anyone now say if the monks knew anything about it."

All one can say is that the monstrosity was not an infant, but adult; and whether or not it was the fault of some nasty amour of the unnatural type denounced in the books of the Pentateuch, or the remains of some horrible thing teleported to Bruges from some world in space, it is beyond the wit of man to determine. All *I* can say, besides this, is that the Flemish gentleman who told me this story, and who now owns the old house, assured me that there are now no raps on doors by an unseen thing, nor charnel-house stenches; but that all is now as holy and quiet there, as the nave of a church consecrated with holy water. I had no inclination to test his assurance; but, after cogitating "Who had done the walling-up, and when?" I made tracks for a cheery pavement café off the *Grande Place* and called for an extra large glass of strong *schnapps*. It is obvious that a number of persons unknown could have told a most hair-raising story about what went on in that ancient cellar!

Chapter 6

THE MYSTERY OF
LORD KITCHENER'S CORPSE

THE news behind the news—the news a reporter dare not, or cannot tell—would surely make the most sensational book ever written; but, often, it is the book that never will be written. Let me, as an old newspaper man, tell such a story. It is the story of a missing link in the chain of fate or destiny, and in *some parts* of it, it is probably a story which I am the only man alive who can tell. For most of those who knew certain mysteries, to be related in this chapter, have gone the way of all flesh in the intervals of two world wars, and since the second one, which even now is not ended.

The first act of this queer drama goes back to the month of January, 1885, six years before the present narrator was born. On the 25th day of that month, the Dervish, Mohammed ibn Abdallah, native of Dongola, on the Upper Nile in the Sudan, and an Arab of the Dangala tribe who came from Mecca the Holy, attacked the poorly fortified town of Khartoum, on the upper Nile above the sixth cataract. Mohammed was a Sufi Dervish of the mystic rolling drum. He claimed that he was a direct descendant of the Imaum Ali, cousin of the Prophet, the camel-driver of Mecca who founded the great creed of the blood-red rose of Islam. Inside Khartoum was another great soldier and mystic, General Charles Gordon, one time of the Royal Engineers Corps of the British Army, who had, after many months of starvation, been holding the fort against the fanatic hordes of the Dervishes of the Sudan, all lit up with the flame of the Jehad, or holy war against the infidel Frank. Gordon was the Governor-General of the Egyptian Sudan, and the garrison under his command was extremely small.

As we know, Gordon had been sent by Mr. W. E. Gladstone, the Liberal Premier of the British Government of that day, to effect a withdrawal, from the Sudan, of British and other personnel; since Gladstone and some others of his Cabinet did not want to be involved in a war with Dervishes, aflame with nationalist patriotism roused to fervent heat by the preaching of the jehad, against England and western Europe, by the Sufi Dervish, Mohammed ibn Abdallah, known as *el Mahdi,* or the long foretold Messiah of Islam. On the way up the Nile was a small British military expedition intended to relieve Khartoum and rescue General Gordon, he whom the Arabs called "Queen Victoria's husband." But the relief had been gravely delayed by the desert sands and a fierce fight with fanatic Dervishes and savage Arabs. Many of the Dervishes were coal-black Negroes and formidable warriors.

At last, when a mere score of British troops—the planning by the War Office in London was little else than a sacrifice of brave men on a hopeless quest—and men of the Clan Gordon of the Scottish Highlands, of whom General Gordon was a clansman, arrived aboard two crazy paddle-steamers off Khartoum, their commander, Colonel Wilson, was horrified to see, as he peered over an armoured turret, under very heavy fire from the Nile banks, that the black and green flag was streaming from the top of the Governor's palace, where should have been the flags of old England and Egypt. To go on was madness. Wilson had actually only twenty men, with very little ammunition. He gave the order to turn the paddle-steamers round and steam back down the Nile to the gorge, where lay the main British force. He would have to fight his way back, against fanatical and brave Dervishes, and Lord help him, or any of his men, if they fell into the hands of these black fanatics. An appalling fate would be theirs. Those that died in action would be the lucky ones!

Wilson had dreadful news to carry back. Only two days before his arrival, in these crazy paddle-steamers with their rusty boilers and faulty engines, the roaring Dervishes, yelling war cries and calling out on Allah, the Prophet, and his servant the Mahdi of the Sudan, had burst the poor defences of doomed and famished Khartoum and, in the dead of night, rushed in to loot and murder. The Dervishes' vast ivory war horn, the *Ombana*, boomed appallingly—it was made of elephant tusks—and had roused these already savage paranoiac fanatics to paroxysms of wild fury. General Gordon, roused from an uneasy sleep, grabbed a revolver and rushed from his bedroom to the top of the palace stairs. One brave man against hundreds of religious madmen and yelling fanatics, coal-black and nigger-brown, all calling for the blood of the infidel. He was beaten down, and as he fell, a giant Negro hacked off his head!

The head was taken, dripping, red as the blood-scarlet flowers of the rose of Sufi Islam, shoved into a coarse sack, and carried by this giant black, whose name was Shatta, to the embroidered, splendidly carpeted tent, where waited *el Mahdi*, prophet and leader of the Dervishes, with his inscrutable and mystic smile. At the door of his black tent, *el*

Mahdi, who had lapsed from the sincere fervour and ascetic self-discipline of his devotional days, and become obese with gluttony and idleness, and the sexual indulgence of the harem, contemplated the head of General Gordon. But, strangely enough, it is said, *that head bore a cheerful smile!* In it still lived the soul of the other great mystic and soldier.

All that day and for many days, black and bloody massacres and looting raged in Khartoum. In faraway England, the British Government, to the great indignation of many Englishmen and the rage of her whom the Arabs called "General Gordon's wife," Queen Victoria, in Windsor Castle, withdrew all British troops from the frontiers of the Sudan.

El Mahdi, who, to do him justice, had ordered that Gordon should be brought to him alive—orders, however, he failed to enforce on savage Baggara and Hadendos Arabs and African Negroes—had a singular V *cleft* in the front centre of his magnificent white teeth of the upper jaw. This queer cleft, said Mohammedian mystics, was the sign of him who should come as the Twelfth Imam and conquer the whole world of infidels for Allah.

Thirteen years passed. The Sudan had been cordoned off from Egypt, whose suzeraine was then Queen Victoria, and the financial control that of the British Government. In that time, *el Mahdi* had died and been buried where he died. A shrine, with a shining white dome and white walls, had been built over the corpse and could be seen afar, by day under the hot sun, and by night under the moon and stars, brighter than we see them in our Northern climes. There came the year 1898, and on 2 September, the war drums beat for action. *This* time, they were not merely the *ombanas* of the Dervishes. The *British* were on the march, and behind the shrilling of the trumpets, sounded an extremely sinister staccato chatter of a new weapon, one against which not even the blood-red rose of Mahdi Sufism might prevail. The British lion was out, roaring for vengeance.

On the very hill where the Mahdi had prophesied that his hosts would fight a great, last and victorious battle against the British, stood a well equipped and disciplined army. They were the flower of British regiments, with trained Egyptian auxiliaries who would *not now* run at the very sight of a Dervish's ragged and patched *jubba*, or shirt. Below, on the Nile, were the most modern gunboats, firing lyddite shells; while on the heights, the army had the latest artillery and the ingenious machine gun which a certain picturesque Levantine Jew, who, in the First World War, was known as Sir Basil Zaharoff, had sold to the British Government. The army was under the command of Sir Herbert Kitchener, the Sirdar of Egypt.

Battle started. The Dervishes, in their thousands, advanced with magnificent, but insane bravery, and flashing Christian medieval swords actually taken in battle, centuries ago, by Saladin of Islam, before the walls of Jerusalem. The Dervishes had guns and artillery, but would not, or could not use them. They were mown down by the hail of bullets from the machine guns. In fact, the Dervish hosts never reached within 100 yards of the squares and ranks of the British troops! Out on the river, the gunboats opened fire on the distant dome of the Mahdi's white tomb, and, as they fired their lyddite shells, Dervishes, up above, on the hilltops, were falling like ninepins.

When the British Army entered Khartoum they found the Mahdi's tomb smashed by shells, and its dome shattered.

After the battle, the tomb of the Mahdi was razed. Of the fate of the Mahdi's corpse there are two versions:

(1), Kitchener's own story, telegraphed to Lord Cromer (Sir Everard Baring), British Ambassador in Cairo, in February and March 1899; and (2), a version derived by Richard A. Bermann, German author and traveller, and recorded in Bermann's *Die Derwischtrommel* (Berlin, 1931). The Right Hon. Winston S. Churchill (now Sir Winston Churchill) wrote an introduction to the English translation of Bermann's work, published in London, 1931. Churchill, it will be recalled, was a lieutenent in the British Army under the command of Kitchener; was present at the battle of Omdurman, and also acted as war correspondent of the London *Morning Post*.

Says Bermann, in *Die Derwischtrommel*:

"The Mahdi's head was packed in a *kerosene tin* and sent as a trophy to Egypt. Churchill says that Lord Cromer had the head buried (re-buried) in Sudanese soil near Wadi Halfa; others say that it was preserved in some medical institution in England . . . The Mahdi's head was found to be perfectly preserved and with recognizable features, and was not destroyed with the body. *Who really knows what happened to it?* Head for Head! The Mahdi had General Gordon's head on a spear outside his tent. The Mahdi's body was first disinterred and then destroyed."

Before one records what Kitchener himself had to say about the affair of the Mahdi's desecrated corpse and tomb, one should refer to the circumstances in which Kitchener was *forced* to reveal that which neither he, nor the British Government and the Marquess of Salisbury, then Prime Minister, had any intention of making public. In the January, 1899 volume of the London *Contemporary Review*, Ernest A. Bennett, a war correspondent and a man of a class to whom Kitchener was very far from partial, especially in wartime, wrote an article castigating the conduct of Lord Kitchener and the British Army after the battle of Omdurman. This article, and comments in the British newspapers, not to speak of violent acrimonious invectives at Exeter Hall, attracted much public attention. There were prompt echoes in the House of Commons. Bennett, who had been present at the battle of Omdurman not only gave the lord of the dervishes, El Mahdi, his just due, but made no bones about citing alleged atrocities committed by the British Army and its officers in the Sudan campaign. Four or five months after Omdurman, sinister stories had reached London. At Liverpool, the city authorities pressed the Government to investigate.

In the House of Commons, on 28 February, 1899, Mr. A. J. Balfour, then First Lord of the Treasury, told Mr. MacNeill, M. P., that Lord Cromer, the British Ambassador in Cairo, had been directed by the British Government to furnish a report about the desecration of the tomb and corpse. (A Bill was then before the House to create Kitchener a peer for his services in the Sudan campaign). But it was not until 16 March, 1899, that MacNeill (M. P. for Donegal), who had protested about the delay, was told by Mr. Brodrick that Cairo had replied on 13 March, and there "had been no undue delay."

Lord Cromer had telegraphed to the Marquess of Salisbury, Kitchener's reply to the charges made in Mr. Bennett's article in the *Contemporary Review*.

Kitchener wired:

"To Lord Cromer from Major-General, Lord Kitchener, Omdurman. 1 February, 1899:

> "Mr. Bennet has alleged that Dervish wounded were massacred, after the battle of Omdurman, by my troops under my orders; that the British, Egyptian, or Soudanese troops wantonly killed and wounded unarmed Dervishes; that Omdurman was looted for three days after its occupation; that, when we were rapidly advancing upon the town, fire was opened by the gunboats on mixed masses of fugitives in the streets of Khartoum . . . I categorically deny these charges. I would add that my action regarding the tomb of Mohammed Ahmed, the so-called Mahdi,

was taken after due deliberation and prompted solely by political considerations ...
  (*Signed*): Kitchener of Khartoum."

Lord Cromer had evidently asked Kitchener for more details, for on 12 March, 1899, nearly six weeks later, Kitchener wired from Khartoum:

"After the battle of Omdurman, I thought it was politically advisable, considering the state of the country, that the Mahdi's tomb, which was the centre of pilgrimage and fanatical feeling, should be destroyed; the tomb was also in a dangerous condition owing to the damage done by shell-fire, and might have caused loss of life if left as it was. *When I left Omdurman for Fashoda I ordered its destruction. This was done in my absence,* the Mahdi's bones being thrown in the Nile. The skull only was preserved and handed over to me for disposal. No other bones were kept, and there was no coffin. I was advised, after the taking of Omdurman, by Mahommedan officers, that it would be better to have the body removed as, otherwise, many of the more ignorant people of the Kordofan would consider that the sanctity with which they surrounded the Mahdi's tomb prevented us from doing so. None of the Kadis, ulemas, or inhabitants here, consider the Mahdi to have been more than a heretic to the Moslem religion. He destroyed all the mosques in the country as well as the tomb of the descendant of the Prophet, at Khatmieh. He was denounced by the religious Sheikh Senoussi as acting against the religion. He treated all Mahommedans who did not accept his changes, as heretics to be killed. I feel sure that no Mahommedans in this country feel anything but satisfaction at the destruction of his power, together with all traces of his religion."

Cromer, who heard that the Mahdi's skull was being shown around in Cairo, ordered that the skull be buried in Wadi Halfa, in the Sudan. Mr. A. B. Theobald, author of *The Mahdya*, (London, 1951), says that the action was a stain on the name of Lord Kitchener, who had ordered that the Mahdi's tomb "be destroyed by explosive," and the "body—not the skull—thrown into the Nile." The skull was said to have been buried in the Moslem cemetery at Wadi Halfa. Indeed, no one really *knows* today what eventually happened to the Mahdi's skull! It is also to be noted that Kitchener had ordered all correspondents to quit Khartoum for Cairo *before* he left to meet the French under Marchand, at Fashoda. *Kitchener,* as he himself admits, was not in Khartoum when the desecration occurred, and, so, was not an eye-witness of the *manner* in which the *trunk of the Mahdi was destroyed.* Bermann's reference to the skull of the Mahdi being sent to Cairo in a *kerosene* tin, is highly suggestive of what may have been the *real* manner of the destruction of the Mahdi's trunk.

Horatio Herbert, Lord Kitchener of Khartoum, later Earl of Khartoum and of Broome, Kent, K. G., G. C. B., G. C. M. G., was born on 14 June, 1850, at Gunsborough Villa, near Ballylongford, Co. Kerry, Eire. He was the second son of Lieut.-Colonel Henry Horatio Kitchener, his mother being the daughter of a clergyman, the Rev. John Chevalier. Before his entry into the Royal Military Academy, Woolwich, he studied at a seminary at Grand Clos, Villeneuve, Switzerland, which probably gave him his early partiality for French Army chiefs, and also saved him from the insularity his social upbringing might have ensured for him.

In March 1911, he was aboard the German Kaiser's yacht *Hohenzollern,* in the Adriatic, and had tea with the Kaiser, who talked amiably with him. It was the last time he would meet this imperial gentleman, who, seven years later, was to be in exile at Doorn, in Holland, when the late David Lloyd George, not then an Earl, was stumping the country on a so-called "crusade" "To Hang the Kaiser!" and at a time when the abdicated emperor's subjects were calling him *Wilhelm, der Fahnenfluchtige* (William the Deserter). Kitchener was popular with the British troops in the South African War, of 1899—1902, who looked on him as a stern, but fair man, but he was by no means popular with the society women who had some influence in Whitehall.

His reputation, which grew among the public in Great Britain, in the first decade of the twentieth century, as a strong, silent man, not very approachable, wove such a nimbus of shining military glory round his head, that, on the very day of the outbreak of the First World War, in August 1914, when he was on the point of sailing for Cairo, the Liberal Prime Minister, Mr. Asquith, invited him to enter the War Cabinet, as Secretary of State for War. This action was vociferously acclaimed by the public and the troops who had served under his command in the Sudan and South Africa; but the degree of acclamation from the Army Council and high officials in the War Office was distincly more tepid.

Prior to that, as Commander-in-Chief of the old Anglo-Indian Army, he had fallen foul of another autocrat, Lord Curzon of Kedleston, he who was given to pro-consular prancings, and who never seemed to sleep very much—so that a King's Messenger, with dispatches from the Foreign Office, who deemed that his errand would suffer no harm were he to leave their delivery over till the morning of a nice summer day, was greeted with the grand manner and a sarcastic comment from Curzon: "They call you silver greyhound, do they? *H-m*," with a haughty glance at the person of the messenger and his silver badge: "*I should call you a fat bulldog!*" But in Egypt, where he (Kitchener) was Sirdar and a high administrator, he showed that he had, at times, a peculiarly effective sense of humour. Informed by a British high official that a number of other British officials were so scared of the reputation that had preceded him from India, that they were, all in a body, getting ready to hand in their resignations, Kitchener replied with a grim smile: "Tell 'em that I have a cigar-box full of letters of resignation. All they need are just the signatures!" No more was heard of any resignation.

In private life, his tastes were not literary, but towards the collection of fine china, ceramics, arms and armour. In India, at the Commander-in-Chief's house at Simla, the rooms and saloons were full of fine ceramics, porcelain, china, (Sèvres, Dresden, Ming, Wedgwood, Chelsea and Bristol), pictures, etchings, Persian and Indian miniatures and paintings, the walls hung with banners taken in the Sudan wars, in bright green and yellow, and inscribed with quotations from the Koran, in gold. He was known to have a more than passing acquaintance with Arabic, Islam and the Koran. He had also a gold service for twenty-five people, and delicate glasses with gold rims, emblazoned with a gold coronet, and the monogram "K." But the military side of him came out in the arrangement of the chairs set out in stiff rows, although their patterns did not match. There was then a rumour that he was to become engaged to a lady well known in Anglo-Indian society, but only a rumour. He does not ever seem to have been a man with a woman in his life. Nor was he fond of debunkers who said that General Gordon studied the Bible, held in one hand, and a glass of brandy and soda in the other. "A damned lie!" he said, when someone mentioned the story.

Probably his greatest work in the First World War was the raising of Kitchener's Army of volunteers, some, not too "willing" volunteers, in 1915. There must be many people alive who remember the startling posters of the year 1915, with the picture of a stern, silent generalissimo with a big handle-bar moustache, a hypnotic eye fixed full on the faces of the passers-by and an arm with finger extended that seemed to bore right down into the shrinking souls of men who were wondering why the war had not been over at Christmas, as some gentlemen in the Liberal Cabinet and the War Office were known to have promised. In a silence that spoke louder than many words blared from a loud-speaker, there was over his head: "Your King and Country Need Y O U!" Other exalted bunglers, especially after he was dead, were prompt to load onto *his* shoulders, the burden of their own appalling inefficiency and calamitous mistakes, on the old and tried principle that *les absents ont tourjours tort!* They omitted to remember his rare flash of prevision when he told the optimistic War Cabinet: "This war will last four years, maybe more. It won't be over by Christmas as some of you suppose."

Kitchener's blind spot was one he shared with Sir Douglas Haig, later Earl Haig, and the supplanter of his own chief, Field-Marshal Lord French of Ypres. It was a contempt for mechanism in what was essentially a war of machines, and not only men. In 1916, Sir Arthur Sloggett, Director of Army Medical Supplies, urged on Kitchener that the troops at the front, who were suffering terrible head wounds, from exploding shrapnel, urgently needed steel helmets. For 40 minutes, Sloggett arged the matter with Lord Kitchener, who never batted an eyelid. The forty minutes up, Kitchener took out his watch, looked at it, and said: "Sloggett, for forty minutes you have been talking bloody rubbish!"

And that was that! Sloggett had to slog it off; and there were to be no steel helmets—until thousands more men had been killed unnecessarily. Of course, others had the same blind spot, symbolized by staff officers spurred in motor-cars at the front, as if a cavalry mount were in the boot. Haig, despite the initial success of the tank, on the Somme, said: "Its success can never be repeated." And this was the man who was chief of the British staff!

Blindness of this kind was not confined to the British. Field Marshal Hindenburg, when President of the so-called Republic of the German Reich, had similar traits. Told that a certain German statesman had been advocating an understanding with the Russian Soviet, "old Squarehead" summoned him to Neudeck Palace, sacked him there and then, and said: "Best thing you can do is to push off to Moscow, now!"

The last thing one would have associated with Kitchener was any form of emotion. Yet there were three occasions when he could not restrain his tears: when he was Sirdar in Egypt and a gunboat sank; on the death of the first Lady

Cromer; and when Lord Cromer (one of the Barings of Baring Brothers, the famous banking firm, and the cold and formal diplomat, in Cairo, whom General Charles Gordon so amusingly "guyed" at the end of the telegraph line in Khartoum), questioned the Sudan Government accounts. *Vide*: *Memoirs of Boyle* (British administrator in Cairo, *temp*. Lord Cromer and Sir Eldon Gorst).

In Asquith's War Cabinet, Lord Kitchener showed himself an individualist. He did not mix well with his colleagues. At this time, there was a Field Marshal, Sir Henry Wilson, later Chief of the Imperial General Staff, and who was, in 1919, shot by Sinn Feiners at the door of his house in the West End of London, who habitually referred to them as "the Frocks." Kitchener, indeed, had a poor opinion of the men in the War Cabinet, and had little to say to them. He made one exception only: the Prime Minister, Asquith, later Lord Oxford.

Arnold Bennett, the novelist, who kept a diary, and had connexions with the Government Press Bureau, wrote, on 6 March, 1916:

"Masterman," (he was a former ministerial colleague of Mr. David Lloyd George, when the latter was Liberal—Radical Chancellor of the Exchequer), "told me, at lunch, that Kitchener was no great shakes. Obstinate, not open to new ideas; no great brain power. But he had the quality of acknowledging that he was wrong, after an interval."

There were other voices, some in high diplomatic quarters, speaking, "on the quiet," things not exactly in praise of Kitchener, or qualifying any credit they gave him, with comments that discounted it. There was, for example, Lord Bertie of Thame, British Ambassador in Paris "*Is* K. a great man? A good organizer, but small-minded. He has now the Garter, but the Dukedom he wanted is postponed." Sir, later Lord, John French, the generalissimo at the front, the very cream of whose regular soldiers had been lost on the terrible retreat from Mons—owing, largely, to the blunders of French brass hats who did not know their business as modern professional soldiers—had no high opinion of the French Army chiefs; whereas Kitchener held a contrary view. Kitchener reinstated in high positions "dud" generals whom French had sent back from the front for gross inefficiency.

"K. of K.," said French, privately, "does not understand

the conditions of modern warfare. His strategy is bad, and he vacillates and sticks in the mud of old ideas."

Kitchener's relations with the British Admiralty were strained. He fell out with Mr. Winston Churchill, who had asserted that the Turkish "Narrows" of the Dardanelles, and their powerful land-forts, could be forced by battleships alone, with their 15-inch guns. "I am delighted to hear it!" said Kitchener; but his expression was ironical. Privately, Kitchener complained: "We, of the British Army, have not been consulted over these Dardanelles operations. It is a *land-operation* to smash forts."

As it happened, by the blow of fate, and, as some said, by treachery in high quarters, and espionage, Lord Kitchener was to lose his life when the same Admiralty confided him to the care of the Grand Fleet of the Royal Navy, on the fateful and abortive mission to Tsarist Russia. Whether or no it was wishful thinking, military and probably high British diplomatic quarters, in London, but *not* in Petrograd or Moscow, paid no heed to authoritative warnings about writing very visibly on the wall in Russia, early in 1916.

A Labour leader, Ben Tillett—who, some time later, was to earn the sobriquet of "Ben Tolettwicenightly," when he, at high fees, engaged in war propaganda, in hired theatres, with another "revolutionary hot air" gentleman, "Bob" Williams—called, one day, on Lord Kitchener at the War Office. It was a wintry day, and, as the shades of night closed in, Lord Kitchener and Ben gazed out of the War Office windows at the dim blackout lights of the street lamps.

"Tillett," said Lord Kitchener, suddenly, "I should not wonder if you, or, certainly, myself, before this war ends, will *be hanging on those lamp-posts!*"

Kitchener's "friends" were ganging up against him, privately, or not so privately. He was furious at being side-tracked by Lloyd George, who was backed by the Carmelite House newspaper peer, Lord Northcliffe, from any control, over munitions. Indeed, Lloyd George's star was rising, and, in July, 1915, he was said to be planning to oust Kitchener from the War Cabinet. By the end of 1915, Sir William Robertson, who became Chief of the General Staff, had partly superseded him, and Kitchener was being more and more limited in his functions. Inside the War Office, something like a camarilla was working against him. Besides Prime Minister Asquith, he had, later on, one friend, in the War Cabinet, It was F. E. Smith, later, the first Lord Birkenhead, whom Kitchener had not censured when Smith, as chief of the Press Bureau, issued certain passages about the well known "back to the wall" Mons message, for which *The Times* wanted Smith's head.

"He (Smith), was a tower of strength to me, in the War Cabinet, today," said Kitchener.

Meanwhile, behind the steel ring of the German-Austrian empires, conspirators—including an early Christian, antinomian he-goat, with hypnotic eyes and a sadistic, erotic power over certain pretty and foolish women, the monk, Grigor Rasputin, an old Russian character—were already spinning the web which the three, terrible old ladies, whom the Latins called the *Parcae* were, in due time, to slit. The Tsarina, under Rasputin's control, was already selling the Allied pass to the Germans. Certain French war historians tell a story about an alleged chief of "the Secret Service branch of the English Foreign Office," who, one day in 1916, slit open a package which had arrived from a "certain Henry Woodridge," said to be "a British strategic and diplomatic agent." (*If* so, he was a curious sort of hybrid bird for a diplomatic aviary!) This package contained a report, alleged to have been "revealed," after its discovery, in the early 1920s, "in the secret archives of a certain Allied Power." Woodridge, "Stationed abroad"—whether this meant Berlin, Vienna, or Paris is not stated—revealed startling details of treachery in Tsarist Russia. It was added, by this French historian, that "A liaison officer on Lord Kitchener's staff chanced to have seen this secret report, in Downing street, and, on his own responsibility, disclosed its contents to Lord Kitchener, who was so stupefied by these Russian Tsarist Court plots that, on the morning of 2 June, 1916, *at* 2 a.m. (!) he went to Buckingham Palace and asked for King George V to be awakened; so that he, Kitchener, might warn His Majesty. The King was awakened, and, in the audience, ordered Kitchener to sail *next day* (sic) for St. Petersburg, on a special and very secret mission."

Unfortunately, this picturesque story is *not* borne out by British official history, which is that arrangements for Lord Kitchener's mission to Russia were made about the end of May 1916, when the names of the mission and the date of their proposed arrival, in a British warship, at Archangel, were cabled to the British Mission in St. Petersburg. It is known that Kitchener himself telegraphed to Sir John Hanbury-Williams, chief of the British Mission in Russia, and used in the wire the rather curious words following:

"If there is any desire that I should not come . . . in which case, I should not think of doing so."

Hanbury-Williams sought an audience with the Tsar, who, man of weakness and duplicity that he was, less stable than the waters of the Neva, twice repeated: "I wish him to come." Kitchener's plan—it makes one smile wryly, in view of the conditions in rotten Tsarist Russia, at that time!—was to spend *only a week* in Russia, and then return.

As a curious fact, Mr. Lloyd George, was, by the interposition of fate, saved from Kitchener's fate; for, as Minister of Munitions, Lloyd George planned to accompany Kitchener to Russia. It, however, chanced that Prime Minister Asquith wanted Lloyd George to help him resolve the Irish problem after the Dublin Rebellion, in Easter week 1916. Lloyd George was forced to alter his plans.

There was a curious streak of mysticism and Eastern fatalism in Kitchener, who, as we know, had spent many years in the East. It held a spell over him. He had himself once told a friend: "I dislike the sound of breakers crashing on a shore." It may be—who knows?—that his *alter ego*, deep down in his sub-conscious, gave him a premonitory vision of a grey, cold, inexorable sea, lashed by hurricane winds, that would sing his requiem over his grave in Northern waters. "I *hate* its angry roll!" he said, on another occasion. There is a story that, in India, in 1894, when he was Commander-in-Chief he consulted a Hindu *faquir*, or a fortune-teller, who looked at his hand, and told him: "You will die on the water, or you will be captured by an enemy, and will never return." In the week-end, before he left London for Thurso, he was down at his country house at Broome, Kent. He then, it was reported, said to a friend: "I have been told I have *got* to be drowned!" On another occasion, he was walking on the sea shore with Aristide Briand, *President du Conseil de France* (20 October, 1915 to 10 March, 1917), when a wave washed near his foot: "I hate the very sight of the sea!" he said to the smiling Briand. "Yes, it has a *cruel* roll!"

"*Et comment, Monsieur*, why so, since you English claim to rule it?" replied Briand.

Kitchener's face set sternly, and his eyes looked far away to the horizon. He did not speak for some time. Then he said: "You may call it *baliverne, Monsieur le President*; but, years ago, in India, and, again, in Egypt, a palmist told me that I shall die at sea by enemy action." Whether he had any premonition that his trip from Grand Fleet base to Archangel would be his last, no one can say. Often, these predictions by seers or old oracles omitted some essential circumstance by which the predicted event might be recognized beforehand. He is said to have told a well known Society *clairvoyante*, Nell St. John Montagu, whom he saw in London, in May 1916: "I shall want your advice on matters, when I return from my business trip (*sic*) abroad." But the omens were *not* good, and on other than mystic ground.

In his "Diary," Lord Bertie of Thame, wrote, on 27 March, 1915:

"There is no such thing as a secret nowadays. Only one woman I know who does not talk."

The official version of the Admiralty is that the secret of Kitchener's mission to Russia was strictly guarded, at any rate, so far as the Admiralty and Royal Navy were concerned. Only five or six naval persons knew it, and no statement was issued to the press, nor any request for secrecy. At Grand Fleet base, at Scapa Flow, in the Orkneys, only the high command knew of Lord K's mission, and the "crew of H.M.S. *Hampshire*, by which he was to sail, heard that she was ordered to Archangel only on the day of her departure, when, to their complete surprise, Lord Kitchener and his mission came aboard." (The "Official White Paper, on the Loss of H.M.S. *Hampshire*, 1926"). But there is some reason to suppose that, inside the War Office, one of Kitchener's military enemies, or, it may be, a spy planted there (just as British War Office Intelligence is said to have planted a secret agent right in the Reich's *General Stabsquartier*, or *das Kreigsministerium*, in Berlin—for do not they *all* do so?), had passed to Russia and so to Germany, highly secret information of the forthcoming trip to Archangel, and over the single line of railway to Petrograd.

Impossible, it will be said!

Well, in 1916, there was in London, Prince Kropotkin, the famous Russian philosophical anarchist, who, says Herr Heinz Ecke, author of *Vier Spione Reden* (Four Spies) published in Berlin, in 1931, was told by an unnamed French secret agent, that Lord Kitchener was going to Russia; whereon, it is alleged, Kropotkin, fearing that the war would be prolonged, asked a Russian General Staff officer, de Ghize, to prevent the journey. De Ghize, or so it is said, passed the news onto the German Navy Department at Wilhelmshaven. De Ghize left England, in 1917, reached Holland, *via* France, and became a German spy. He was said to have been in Georgia, in the Causacus, in 1920.

But one need not invoke the hypnotic monk, Rasputin; since Bruce Lockhart, who was British Consul in Moscow, in 1916 makes it very clear that Kitchener's impending visit was known in Moscow a full fortnight beforehand:

> "On 24 May, 1916, the British Ambassador told me, in strict confidence that Lord K. was coming, and in the next few days, half a dozen British journalists must have telephoned me to ask if the news were true. At my wife's weekly reception, General Wogak, a charming and cultured soldier, announced the visit, with the date and object, as if no secrecy were needed. Long before K. had sailed from Scotland, the news of his mission was common property in St. Petersburg and Moscow . . . I do not suggest that these leakages bore any relation to the fate of the ill-starred *Hampshire*." (*Memoirs of a British Agent*, 1932).

It is obvious that if all this were known by many in Moscow and Petrograd, a German secret agent knew it, and, weeks before tipped off the German General Staff, or the German Naval High Command.

On 6 June, 1916, the Tsarina, the Empress Alexandra personally wired the Tsar, Nicholas Romanoff, who was then at the front, an amazing message:

> "Our friend," (that is, the monk, Grigor Rasputin), "says it is a good thing that Lord Kitchener has perished, as later on he might have caused serious harm to Russia."

It is not necessary to cite the quite callous and indifferent answer she had from this degenerate Tsar, who himself had urged Kitchener to come to Russia. As a well known British diplomat wrote, at this time: "The Tsarina is a *Boche* (German)." She was that both by birth and by sympathies; and yet, both these Imperial wastrels and traitors expected England to offer them a shelter and a palace, after the Russian Revolution.

It must not be forgotten that Kitchener, himself, in one of his rare flashes of premonition foretold what would occur in Russia. At Chantilly, at the *château* in the department of Oise, which, throughout the First World War, was the headquarters of the French General Staff, Kitchener, in November, 1915, had a conference with General Joffre, then the French generalissimo. Joffre, like *un bon bourgeois*, ate heartily and well fortified himself with the cup that inebriates, after which, in the height of the war when things were going badly for the Allies, he regularly retired to bed, at 10 p.m., each night, and not the crash of a thousand empires would fetch him out of bed until 8 a.m. It did not matter that urgent dispatches and decisions were arriving before and after midnight, Joffre was in bed, snoring *comme d'un cochon des Pyrénées Orientales* (like an eastern Pyrenean pig), and no one was to awaken him. This was the Army Chief who assured Kitchener that Tsarist Russia would stand by *la belle France* until the last *Boche* (German) had been killed.

Said Kitchener to this military-politico: "So you think that Russia will be with us to the end? I calculate on her being out within a year!"

History proves that *Kitchener was right almost to a day!*

Despite all the criticisms, many of them justifiable, that were leveled at him behind his back, in his lifetime, and after his death, Kitchener was *not* the *dumb* soldier that he had been represented to be. Sir John Fortescue, the military historian, denied, in 1931, that Kitchener was anything like a great organizer. "It was only in 1916 that he became less Olympian and more open to counsel. . . . It had apparently begun to dawn on him that other people besides himself possessed knowledge and brains, equal if not superior to his own." The truth was that Kitchener *had* genius; albeit of a limited sort.

Sir George Arthur, who was Kitchener's personal private secretary, when K. was War Minister—and became Kitchener's official biographer—tells a story told him by Queen Alexandra, to the effect that, on the day before Kitchener's departure for Grand Fleet base, she hurried to Buckingham Palace to see King George V. There she said: "I have had a sudden premonition that disaster awaits Lord Kitchener and his mission to Russia. Just as, when I was in Venice in 1910, I had the conviction that King Edward VII, my late husband, was very ill; despite the fact that the previous letter I had from England was that he was in quite good health . . . I beg that Lord Kitchener's journey may be postponed."

King George V shrugged his shoulders, and said he could not interfere with the urgent decision of his Ministers.

One of the last persons to see Kitchener before he entrained from King's Cross, was Mrs. Asquith. She wrote, later:

"Lord K. said he was delighted he was going to Russia. He had had enough of British Ministers, and only regretted that he was leaving one colleague, and that was my husband, the Prime Minister."

Walter Page, the U.S. Ambassador in London, had his

own grapevine telegraph and knew the attitude towards Lord K. in exalted official quarters. Page entered in his diary, in 1916:

> "There was a hope and feeling that he (Lord Kitchener) might not come back . . . as I make out. There was very little personal sorrow at his loss."

There were even *not* so exalted quarters, in London, in 1916, and long after, that hinted that "someone in the War Office," had ensured that Lord Kitchener would never return!" They included some newspapermen, and soldiers who had served under Kitchener, before and during the First World War. Who is to say what the truth may be?

Alas, the die was cast! Not even the gods on Olympus could alter or avert the decrees of the remote destiny far beyond the stars. Destiny waits for no man, and no man, however exalted, can avoid its decree. Kitchener, as a fatalist, would have recognized its inexorability.

Lord Kitchener lunched with the Commander-in-Chief, Lord Jellicoe, on the flagship, *Iron Duke* at 4 p.m., 5 June, and embarked in a drifter to board the cruiser, H.M.S. *Hampshire*. He said to Jellicoe: "I am working to a time-table. I feel I have not a day to lose." As he spoke, there was a rising gale, preventing mine-sweepers from clearing enemy mines from the Western approaches. A German submarine had also been sighted, steering west from Cape Wrath.

On 4 June, 1916, H.M.S. *Hampshire* had secret orders to proceed by a route east of the Orkneys, keeping a speed of eighteen knots as far as lat. 62° N., when she would detach the two escorting destroyers which would return to Grand Fleet base, at Scapa Flow. She would then reduce her speed to sixteen knots and go ahead. She was screened by the destroyers: although in such a night of Boreas and raging icy seas, old Father Neptune did all the screening necessary. She slipped away from her buoy at 4.45 p.m.; since, driven on by the inevitable fates, Kitchener, in face of rising wind and raging sea, would listen to no suggestions that he defer the trip until the storm blew itself out, next morning. He hastened onto his doom, instead of waiting till the channels might be swept by mine-sweepers ahead of *Hampshire*.

Later, Lord Jellicoe said, in his "Grand Fleet," "I would not have hesitated to take the Grand Fleet to sea on the same night and by the same route as that traversed by H.M.S. *Hampshire*!" (Well for him that he did *not!*)

What the British Naval High Command had left out of

their calculations was a completely new type of German mine-laying submarine that, in the spring of that year, 1916, had actually penetrated, without detection by British patrols, and laid mines right within striking distance of British Grand Fleet base, at Scapa Flow! Was it one of these mines that sank H.M.S. *Hampshire?* The answer is that no one will ever know! What *is* known, or was revealed, is that H.M.S. *Hampshire*, bucking and rolling and pitching against head winds, sent back the destroyers, which could not keep pace with her, cut down her speed to fifteen knots, and, at 7.40 p.m. on that howling night, off the cliffs of Birsay, a British gunner of the Garrison Artillery, saw a flash jet from the side of a four-funnelled grey-hulled warship, a cloud of smoke rise over her hull and decks, her lights go out, and, at 8 p.m., saw her settle down by the head, her propellers out in the air. She sank before his eyes. The local post-mistress also saw this tragedy, and yet, so near to Grand Fleet base, there was no telephone from her post office at Birsay to the base! Naval High Command did not come very well out of this lack of essential signals!

When the explosion occurred, near or under *Hampshire's* keel, stokers on the port side were badly burned, and fumes of high explosive spread below to the engine-room. True to the splendid traditions of the Royal Navy, there was no panic on board. The men were piped to stations and efforts were made to launch boats—*by hand!* H.M.S. *Hampshire* was an old ship, and, even in the height of the war, had no better means of launching boats in an emergency. Her Captain, Saville, was seen standing by his own cutter, slung from her davits. He called: "Will Lord Kitchener come forward and get into the boat?" The night was dark, the grey seas icy, the storm at the height of its fury.

Kitchener was conducted to the quarter-deck, the men making way for him and his four officers. It is not clear what then happened. If the cutter were lowered, she did not reach the water on an even keel. No one knows whether Kitchener was in the cutter. Indeed, some survivors who managed to swim away say that not one boat got away from *Hampshire* on that dreadful night. In the black night, poor flimsy things called Carley floats—of copper, with wooden gratings and nettings—were thrown into the raging waves, and all were overcrowded. Badly burned stokers and other men died like flies, on these contraptions. In so appalling a night, there was no safety for men standing up to their chests in icy water, benumbed and shivering, with the added certainty, that, *if* they reached in shore, they would be battered to death against the iron rocks of the Orkneys. Any man who lost his footing on the pitching float and fell from the wooden grating into the netting was doomed. In any case these contraptions could make no headway against wind and tide. As it happened, only one warrant officer and eleven men reached shore on a raft. Boats could *not* be launched from *Hampshire*'s decks. Men got into them, as the boats lay in the cradles, hoping that, when the cruiser went down from under them, they would be floated off; but, alas, in the vortex created by her final plunge, she took down all the boats with her!

Flotillas of destroyers were rushed to the scene, revealed the towering cliffs and shores in their powerful searchlights. Trawlers and yachts were ordered out. Even so, *two hours were lost* by the time they arrived on the scene, after the doomed *Hampshire* had gone down. The Admiralty's official statement that "more than half an hour was lost by delays" is—*misleading*. The relatives of the lost officers and men can have found little consolation in the official assurance that, in that bitter cold and darkness of violent seas, little or nothing could have been done to save life. It evades the point of the two hours' delay, and the fact, that, while there is life, there may be hope. That statement was not made until the Admiralty's hands were forced, *ten years later.*

Five years after the sinking of H.M.S. *Hampshire,* a journalist, Mr. Frank Power, provoked in a London newspaper, a controversy that roused the House of Commons. The Admiralty and its strange policy of secrecy about the events of that tragic night in June 1916, stood on trial. Power alleged that *Hampshire* was a "coffin ship," and when, "during repairs at Belfast, it became known that Lord Kitchener was to sail in her, stokers mutinied, and an ugly rumour about her seaworthiness spread." He added that "a deck hand applied for leave, and an officer already on long leave applied for sick leave, and did not sail in her." In 1926, the Admiralty said that the cruiser was "only eleven years old" and had reached a speed of twenty-one knots in the Battle of Jutland.

A well-known London newspaper published from real, or alleged survivors, a story that when H.M.S. *Hampshire* was struck, they heard three terrific explosions at intervals of a few minutes, and that her captain tried to beach the ship, but was too far from shore. "She heeled over to starboard and sank in about twenty minutes."

Another unnamed survivor told Mr. Power, it is alleged, a remarkable story:

"After many hours of aimless drifting, one of the boats from *Hampshire* was driven on the rock-bound shore, and from it only one man was able to make his way to land. It was Lord Kitchener. All the other occupants had succumbed to exposure, or been dashed into the sea. At the end of a terrific struggle with the waves, Kitchener was tossed ashore on a low-lying rock utterly exhausted, unable to make any other effort to help himself, but still alive. Meanwhile, the boat drifted away, and was eventually found run aground at another point of the shore, and was salved."

Kitchener, it may be noted, was then aged 66.

Two men it is further said, reached the shore not far from where Lord Kitchener had landed. They had neither food nor warmth, but they did their best to aid him. He lay, for two nights, prostrate on the sands, with two men, one of whom was a private soldier who left the *Hampshire* on a raft. One of the men crawled along the shore to look for a rescue ship, which never hove in sight. He crawled back, and found the hat of a Field Marshal on the edge of the rock, while, some distance away, he saw two dark objects tossed about in the waves, one of which, to his failing sight, seemed to be clinging to a large piece of driftwood.

Of course, this queer story does not explain what happened to Lord Kitchener after the man, who crawled to look for a rescue ship, had left the rock! It does not say who was clinging to the driftwood, or why so desperate a getaway had been adopted, or if the Field-Marshal's hat was left where it was! The body of Kitchener was also alleged to have been washed ashore, nine days afterwards, on the coast of Norway, having "been drifted there on a strong tide with hundreds of other corpses."

It is curious, by the way, that the Official Narrative of the Loss of H.M.S. *Hampshire* nowhere makes any reference to the complement of officers and crew that were in that cruiser when she sank. All we are told is the number of the survivors. The same singular omission is also to be noted on the monument in one of the Orkeny Islands where the officers and crew lie buried. Why was this omission continued until 1926? One can find no newspaper, either, in which these casualties by drowning off Birsay are given. The omission is so odd that one is forced to conclude that the Admiralty had some reason for the omission. If so, what was it?

Finally, the newspaper stated that Norwegian fishermen,

in a motor-boat, and a guide-interpreter made a search for the express purpose of discovering Lord Kitchener's body, and that the corpse of a tall, heavily built man, in green khaki, with a line of ribbons on his chest, was buried under a cairn. The Admiralty asserts that the officers and men buried on the Norwegian coast were those killed in the Battle of Jutland, on 31 May, 1916. "There are good reasons for regarding it as most improbable that the sea would have carried them (the *Hampshire's* dead) there."

To that, one may point out that the distance from the Orkneys to the coast of Norway, as the crow flies, is some 320 miles, compared with the distance of some 260 miles from Jutland's coast. Sixty miles or so would not make all that difference to the "probabilities" of the tide, or currents drifting the *Hampshire's* dead to the coast of Norway. Again, we ask: Why this strange secrecy about the numbers of officers and men *lost in H.M.S. Hampshire?*

The same newspaper said that there was, in the Admiralty's confidential files, a secret report to the effect that some of the "two hundred men said to be buried in cemeteries (*sic*) on the rocky shores of the Orkneys, actually survived, and, as late as 1926, were still in the land of the living. The alleged testimony of an engineer in H.M.S. *Hampshire*, who, according to the Admiralty was dead, but who was somewhere very much alive in 1926" was that the "first of the explosions occurred at 8 p.m., on the port side of the foremost boiler room:

"The Kingston valve could not be opened to flood and trim the sinking warship, then going down by the head, since the propellers were out of the water. Two other explosions occurred on the starboard side of the same foremost boiler room, and soon afterwards the ship went down. The officers on deck were quite clear that the explosions were caused by mines. Many days afterwards, a boat belonging to *Hampshire* was picked up miles away, with the hardly recognizable body of Colonel Fitzgerald, Lord K.'s aide-de-camp, aboard, jammed under the thwarts."

One may intermit, here, to point out that the official Admiralty statement is that the body of Col. Fitzgerald was found floating at sea, and not in the skiff-dinghy of the warship, by the tug *Flying Kestrel*. The body was identified by the M.O. of the hospital ship *Soudan*, on 6 June, who said he had been drowned. (It is an odd coincidence, by the way, that Kitchener's aide-de-camp's body should have been placed in a ship called *Soudan!*)

A "thirteenth survivor"—one more than is admitted by the Admiralty—said:

"Lord Kitchener was knifed in a struggle with one of the men thrown with him into the sea and onto the shores of the Orkneys."

There came forward a Mrs. Linton Orman who said that, in 1923, she was "dining with friends in London and met a man just home from Africa, who said he was a survivor from H.M.S. *Hampshire*; but, on being questioned, he said: 'I am under oath to say nothing about what happened, that night, when *Hampshire* sank!'"

The same newspaper went on to say that the twelve officially admitted survivors from H.M.S. *Hampshire* were sworn to secrecy after the official inquiry, and dispersed to all points of the world. (This may be true, when we record, later, what Lord Long, then First Lord of the Admiralty, said, in 1920 to Sir George Arthur, who was the friend of Lord Kitchener). It was also added, by the newspaper, that the "thirteenth survivor," mentioned earlier, alleged to have been with Lord Kitchener, on the rocky islet for a day and two nights, "was pensioned for life, on condition of holding his tongue." Of two other survivors—deck and engineroom ratings—"one was in South Africa, in 1926," says the same newspaper, which goes on to tell how:

"A witness at the Naval Inquiry into the loss of the *Hampshire*, held in 1916, said he saw a man tampering with the ammunition and twice reported the matter. Then a mate said to the witness: 'Shut up, you bloody fool! Can't you see "they" do not want to hear this?' This tamperer was a German spy in the *Hampshire* with forged papers. He pushed sailors into the water when the warship was going down, and, when he was found dead, German money and documents were taken from his pockets."

The "Official Narrative of Events" does not refer to this story of the "spy who pushed sailors into the water," except to say, generally: "There is not the slightest ground to attribute to H.M.S. *Hampshire* . . . a 'bad record' in the matter of spies. . . ."

Naturally, a tremendous furore in press and Parliament followed these "sensational exposures." Some Fleet Street newspapers clamoured for bureaucratic blood, and demanded that the Admiralty—whose foolish policy of secrecy was admirably calculated to draw down these very strictures! —wash the dirty linen in public. Of course, the Admiralty had *nothing* to say about what the American Ambassador, in London, said of "the hope and feeling that Lord K. might not come back." Mr. Walter Page, the U.S. Ambassador, was in touch with very high quarters, and we may have little difficulty in guessing to what exalted quarters the Ambassador was alluding. At this moment, on 10 February, 1926, Sir George Arthur, Lord Kitchener's official biographer, wrote a remarkable letter to *The Times*. He said that Lord Long, then First Lord of the Admiralty, had invited him to read the "secret and unpublished report on the sinking of H.M.S. *Hampshire*":

> "On the understanding that I would not divulge a word of it to anybody. I declined to read the document on those conditions. I told the First Lord that neglect, or, at any rate, carelessness, must be charged against the officer commanding the Grand Fleet, or the Admiralty, in the arrangements made for Lord Kitchener's voyage. The reply of Lord Long was: 'I do not think you could say otherwise!'"

It is clear that this letter, written six months before the sensation began to approach its climax, and the "story to break," was hardly calculated to allay public suspicion that here was something that had, for years, been concealed, and on which the Admiralty's high officials were determined to "keep the wraps." Finally, the Department was forced to issue a belated White Paper on the "Loss of H.M.S. *Hampshire* on 5 June, 1916, Official Narrative." In a footnote, it categorically dismissed stories of "hidden survivors." "The testimony of survivors was unanimous that no boats with occupants got away°. . . .Observers ashore who saw several rafts or boats—one man said 'four'—were probably deceived by the wild sea and atmosphere conditions. . . .

°The Secretary of the Admiralty said, on 6 June, 1916, at 1.40 p.m. time of issue, that "four boats were seen by observers on shore to leave the ship." He repeated it on 10 June, 1916, at 4.55 p.m. time of issue, by which date he *must* have received confirmation of the fact. *Ten years later,* this very categorical statement is—*officially denied.* Why? Maybe, denied by the same unnamed naval authorities who put the cliffs out of bounds to Orkneymen, who wanted to save the poor devils.

"Mention . . . of imaginary survivors . . . the Press referred to an officer alleged (by persons unnamed) 'to be in South Africa, who owned to being a survivor from H.M.S. Hampshire, under an oath of secrecy'; a 'man named Green, a servant of an officer aboard'; a 'a man named Gulliver . . . at Banbury, or living hear it, who died recently;' a 'big artificer alleged to be a German spy.' Not one of these stories has any foundation in fact . . . . No spy or ill-affected person was ever on board H.M.S. Hampshire. . . ."

Among the evidence that H.M.S. *Hampshire* struck moored German mines, is the report of Admiral Scheer, Commander-in Chief of the German High Seas Fleet, that, about mid-May 1916, he sent Kapitän-Leutenant Kurt Beizen, in minelaying submarine U-75, with other submarines, to mine positions off the British naval main bases, as far north as Scapa Flow, British Grand Fleet base. In bad weather, Beizen laid "the mines to which this ship," that is, *Hampshire*, "was to fall a victim." It is one of the ironies of war that U-75 laid them, outside one of the main exits from Grand Fleet base, at Scapa Flow, but one a route close to the western shores of the Orkneys—whether Pomona, or Hoy is not clear—this route being used, not by warships, but auxiliary patrol vessels! U-75's commander had the impression that she had dropped twenty-two mines in detached groups, several mètres under water, and (wrongly) on a regular warship route, without being seen by British patrols, in an enemy operation lasting for 2 hours and 35 minutes from 6 a.m., to 8.35 a.m. (*Vide* "Der Kreig zur See," (Band V., PP. 201-2).

The hour of Lord Kitchener's destiny had struck. The Naval Intelligence and the Fleet Intelligence did not know that any German mines had been laid farther north than the Firth of Forth, which, as the crow flies, is about 130 miles south-east of the Orkneys. It did not know, either, that a completely new type of German mine-laying submarine had, in spring 1916, actually penetrated and laid mines within striking distance of British Grand Fleet base at Scapa Flow. It is a mordant piece of irony, too, to reflect that, but for the heavy pitching of H.M.S. *Hampshire*, when she was beaten back by hurricane-force headwinds, she might easily have passed, *unscathed*, right over this German minefield, which lay seven to ten mètres (7.6 to 10.9 yards) under the waves! Of course, it is a trite commonplace to say that life is full of these "ifs" and "buts," which are the very mechanism of inexorable Fate.

Ten years afterwards, the Admiralty denied that any survivor had seen Lord Kitchener in a boat, after *Hampshire* went down. The Department also made short work of the story that Lord Kitchener's military secretary, Colonel Fitzgerald, was found with his body jammed under the thwarts of a boat. . . . "There is," asserts the Official Narrative, "no record or ground for asserting that any human body, or papers, or articles from the *Hampshire* were discovered in any boat."

It may be noted, however, that the London newspaper, in giving the story that Lord Kitchener's body was found, drifted onto the coast of Norway, and buried under a cairn, did *not* say that English civilian or naval hands had raised that cairn, but that *Norwegian* sailors, or fishermen raised the cairn and placed the corpse below it. On the other hand, the Official Admiralty narrative, in aligning these bodies with the corpses of officers and men drowned in the Battle of Jutland, leaves it to be inferred that these latter were buried by the *British* authorities, on the Norwegian coast. The Narrative adds: "None of the *Hampshire's* dead have ever been identified and buried on the Norwegian shores."

This may very well be; but the Admiralty's *disavowal by no means disposes of the allegation that Norwegian fishermen may have buried such bodies,* and identified them by means of the official tabs, or numbered metal discs, that every man carried in wartime; nor even that Lord Kitchener's body may have been buried under a cairn by these Norse fishermen. Nowhere in the Admiralty's Official Narrative can one find any indication of what the British naval authorities may even have theorized as to what happened to Lord Kitchener's body on that appalling night.

A pitiful story about the fate of one soldier who left the *Hampshire,* when she was going down is told by Shipwright Charles Phillips, in his book *The Loss of H.M.S. Hampshire,* (London, March 1932). Phillips was one of the eleven survivors from H.M.S. *Hampshire,* and in the announcement issued by the Secretary of the Admiralty, on 8 June, 1916, he is named as "Phillips, William Charles, Shipwright, 1st Cl. 343500 (Po)". Mr. Phillips's story may be prefaced by the Admiralty Official Narrative that, "this private soldier left the ship on one of the rafts, and it is not known what became of him." (He was one of the servants attached to the Kitchener Mission). "He left the ship in a float which came in at Nebbi Geo, but lost his life in its terrible passage to the Orkney shores. There is reason to think that another of the servants left the ship in the small floats and was washed away on one of the occasions when it capsized."

(*Official Narrative*).
Says Charles Phillips:

"We stood in some four feet of icy cold water, (on the Carley float), with waves engulfing us every instant. . . . Standing next to me on the raft was a soldier—he was servant to one of the officers on Lord Kitchener's staff—and he asked me in a very pitiful way if I thought we should ever reach the cliffs. I told him I thought we really should do so. He replied: 'I do not think so, mate,' and almost immediately he died, staring straight at me, and eventually slipped to the bottom of the raft. . . . Some of the poor fellows clinging to the raft, lost their reason . . . while night was drawing on and men dying very swiftly. We had *two hours* of this . . . when the float was flung onto the rocks, and a rescue party hauled the six survivors to safety."

It may also be added the the skiff-dinghy of H.M.S. *Hampshire*, in which Lord Kitchener was said, by some survivor, to have left the doomed warship never seems to have been found; or, if it *were* found, no one knows what became of it. It is true that this dinghy was believed to have been on show at Terrace Gardens, Kensington, as late as February, 1926; but when Sir Robert Hamilton, M.P., asked Lord Bridgman, the Parliamentary Secretary to the Admiralty, if this dinghy might be bought for the public by the Admiralty, Hamilton was told, in the House of Commons, that this dinghy was not in the *Hampshire*, when she went down; for it was intended to replace it with another, and on the request of Captain Herbert J. Saville, R.N., of H.M.S. *Hampshire*.

By now, in 1926, it began to look as if, in the words of an old British soldier, who served under Sir Garnet Wolseley, "now, all was serene and Sir Garnet." The Admiralty had, as it appeared, disposed of a host of "fantastic stories." Nevertheless, the "All Quiet on the Western Front" legend of the war had not predisposed a large section of the British public to swallow official denials and apologies, no matter how cogent they appeared. The Kitchener mystery, far from having been relegated to the dusty oblivion of a House of Commons State paper, was travelling towards a startling *dénouement*.

A well known London newspaper stated that Mr. Frank Power, the journalist mentioned earlier, had let it be known that, in summer 1926, he had made arrangements to get divers to examine the sunken hulk of H.M.S. *Hampshire* lying under water—in how many fathoms it was not stated—and, of course, as all salvors know, such a wreck would not be in "public domain," free for any to explore or salve, but the property of the Royal Navy and British Admiralty, whom underwriters or salvors would first need to consult. The hulk lay off Marwick Head. Mr. Power said he had indignantly refused the offer of a destroyer, tendered to him by the British Admiralty, to bring back the "body of Lord Kitchener, after exhuming him from under the cairn on the Norwegian coast." He had chartered a yacht, privately, to bring the remains back "from the cairn on the Norwegian island, where local fishermen had laid them to rest."

With the eyes on the people of England, her wartime allies, and the British Commonwealth fixed on him, Mr. Power, it was stated, had placed the corpse in this yacht which was sailing from Norway and would land the coffin at Southampton Dock.

In due time, what transpired was disclosed in all the London newspapers:

"A coffin, believed by Mr. Frank Power to contain the body of the late Lord Kitchener, has been moved by Scotland Yard officers from the private chapel of an undertaker's premises in Waterloo Road, London, S.E.1" (very near to the Southern Region railway terminal of Waterloo Station), "to Lambeth Mortuary, The coffin, which Mr. Power states, has come from Norway, was deposited at the premises of Mr. Thomas Hurry, undertaker, by Mr. Power, in the name of Fraser, late on Saturday night. Chief Constable Wensley, and other Scotland Yard officials, visited the place and ordered the coffin's removal to the mortuary. There it will remain intact, until today, when the matter will be reported to the coroner, Mr. Ingleby Oddie. Mr. Power yesterday denied that he had any knowledge of the removal of the coffin.

"He said: 'I am now waiting to hear from the authorities, and, until I do, I shall take no further steps in the matter. I spoke to the undertaker, last night, and he then said he would do nothing further until he heard from me.'

"The coffin arrived at Waterloo Station, London, S.E.1, by mail train from Southampton Docks, on Friday night, the name of the sender and consignee being Fraser. Mr. Power has sent a letter to Mr. Baldwin." (Later Lord Baldwin, and then Prime Minister of the British Government). "It was stated at the Home Office, last night, that a question had been referred to them by the coroner, and that Sir Bernard Spilsbury was to be present at the opening of the coffin at Lambeth mortuary, today."

Sir Bernard Spilsbury, at that time, was the famous forensic medical expert of the British Home Office—but he was *not* destined to carry out *this* examination, or autopsy, as will be seen, and for the amazing reasons stated below! It was not to be Sir Bernard, but "all serene and Sir Garnet!" who would have the final "say," or silence in this most strange affair.

Next day, the British and the overseas public, whose attention was riveted on this mystery, rubbed its many thousand or million eyes. The friends of authority through thick and thin were not slow to come out with the ready and triumphant: "Did I not say that this is how it would turn out to be?"

The Times, and the friends of propriety and officialdom were gratified and edified by this *very proper* announcement, in the true style of British official rectitude:

AN EMPTY COFFIN OPENED!

"The Home Office states that the packing-case, alleged to contain the coffin and human remains, which, on Saturday night was removed by the police from an undertaker's premises in the Waterloo Road, to the Lambeth coroner's court, was yesterday opened in the presence of Mr. Ingleby Oddie, the coroner, and Sir Bernard Spilsbury, the official Home Office surgeon and analyst. The packing-case was found to contain an empty coffin. The coffin was apparently new and obviously had not contained human remains.

"The official statement refers to a packing-case, which a Mr. Frank Power alleged contained the body of Lord Kitchener, which, he asserted, he had brought from Norway. Nobody in this country for a moment imagined that Mr. Power's claim would be substantiated, in view of the clear and definite statement made by the Admiralty, last week-end, that no bodies of any of those who had lost their lives in the sinking of H.M.S. *Hampshire* had been picked up on the coast of Norway. When the packing-case arrived in London, the authorities seized it and conveyed it to Lambeth Mortuary, in order to clear up any mystery that might be attached to it.

"In addition to Mr. Ingleby Oddie, and Sir Bernard Spilsbury, Chief Constable Wensley, and Dectective-Superintendent Brown of New Scotland Yard, and other officers were present, when the packing-case was opened; and when it was found that there were no human remains of any kind in the coffin, the coroner and the other officials dispersed. A large crowd had collected outside the mortuary, and shortly after the coroner had left, the packing-case and the empty coffin were removed in a motor van to New Scotland Yard. The police are now considering, what further steps, if any, shall be taken."

"Further steps?"
If any were taken, which is gravely open to doubt, the public never heard of them! And, if a very remarkable story which ran the rounds of experienced and senior newspaper men, in Fleet Street, were true, about hidden events, on that afternoon of 17 August, 1926, a few hours after the "empty coffin" had been opened, it is probably also true, that, on the well-tried principle, well-known and acted on in official quarters, "the more an unpleasant and mysterious affair is turned, the more it stinks," it was wisely and discreetly decided to let the whole mystery drop again into oblivion. One may add that no crime reporter, and no retired detective, writing his memoirs, or having them "ghosted" for him, has ever said that this empty coffin and packing-case were ever placed, or ever will be placed, in the well known "Black Museum," in New Scotland Yard!

What was that amazing story?
I, myself, then working in Fleet Street as a "daily paper" reporter, was assured—and the story was never officially denied, but discreetly ignored—that British Secret Service officers, or certain high legal officers whose identity will never be known, had secretly visited the undertaker's morgue and abstracted both coffin and mysterious corpse! Thereon, a substitution had been effected, but *not* of the mysterious corpse. *That was cremated*, and where, by whom, and when, will remain unknown.

This story was whispered in editorial sanctums and in places where newspaper men foregather in their off-hours. The newspaper man, who assured me it was true, was a responsible journalist on the staff of a national Fleet Street daily, and *not* given to lying. I, myself, offer only the comment that it is totally inconceivable that any man in his senses, knowing that the eyes of all England, the British Empire and allies beyond the seas were waiting the outcome of these exposures, would have been so incredibly foolish as to try to hoax the public and the authorities with an empty coffin-shell. He would know that his damnation would be sure and prompt if he tried to fob off an empty coffin-shell on the principal officers of the Criminal Investigation Department. And, unless he were uncommonly naïve, he would have foreseen that the Home Office, in a case where a State secret was involved, would be likely to order the sequestration of the exhibits, in the matter of the "Kitchener's Body Myth." True, at that time, the reputation of the Yard for acumen and up-to-date methods of criminological science was not of quite the high order it subsequently attained; but even so, I must again repeat that I am, myself, totally unable to suggest when, or where, or by whom, or in what circumstances this alleged substitution and alleged cremation were effected. All are dead who knew.

But, *assuming* it were true, the Dervishes' curse had worked to its fulfilment. The man who, twenty-eight years before, had ordered the burning with petroleum of the corpse of the Mahdi, he who was a sacred Mohammedam Imam and Sufi, and the removal of the head which was sent down the River Nile to Cairo, or was buried secretly in some unknown cache on the Upper Nile, had himself, in the revolution of time and war, been drowned at sea by enemy action, as he had been told he would be; and, if the amazing story be true, his body had emerged from the "salt, unchanging sea"—to be burned by flames, whether electrically generated or not.

There have been, as might be expected, numbers of sensational stories, in the American and German press, and in German war books, about alleged events on H.M.S. *Hampshire*. For example—and I disregard stories by U.S. salvors, which arouse justified derision by reputable and experienced ship salvage men—in June, 1934, there appeared a story by a Captain Borskowski, of the Polski liner, *Kosciusko*. He said, at Halifax, Nova Scotia:

"A few years after the First World War, I met a former German submarine commander who told me that two German Secret Service agents, speaking fluent English, volunteered to destroy H.M.S. *Hampshire*. With stolen passports, from Kiel, they reached Scotland, met with and murdered two of the *Hampshire's* seamen, and went aboard in their stead. They managed to reach and blow up the warship's magazine. I am sure no floating mine struck her."

Apart from the small, or *no* evidential value of this yarn, it was not explained how these spies could possibly have passed without detection by the men on board the *Hamp-*

shire. How often, too, do such speakers of "fluent English" have no accent?"

In February, 1935, the German Nazi authorities suddenly suppressed a book, whose author was said to be Ernst Carl, a former German spy, and titled: "Ein Mann gegen England" (One man against England). He said that he and an Irishman brought about Kitchener's death. The "master spy," said this book, was caught and sent to the Tower of London, where he was tried and sentenced to be hanged; but, in some mysterious way was set free to continue his work for Germany. (It may be commented that the late Sir Basil Thomson, who was then in charge of the Special Branch and contra-espionage, makes no mention of such a "master," or double spy). This story was worked up to a climax with the sinking of H.M.S. *Hampshire*. A review in the *Deutsche Allgemeine Zeitung* enlarged on Lord Kitchener and H.M.S. *Hampshire*'s sinking, but only a few copies of the book had been sold when the Nazis clamped down on it. Why, was not made known. The review described the book as "no romance, but a description of bare facts which reveal many completely new matters, and, with its drama, places many romances in the shade." (Possibly, it did not keep in the shade some information about the Abwehr, or Secret Service branch of the German "General Staff," then run by the famous Admiral Canaris, whom the thugs of Müller's Gestapo "liquidated" in 1945.)

The full truth about the Kitchener mystery is never likely to be known. Nor the truth about some after-events concerned with the sinking of H.M.S. *Hampshire*, which must be in the Admiralty's confidential files. For example, in 1938, I knew a naval man whose cousin was surgeon on the ill-fated warship. Quite a long time after the disaster, the surgeon's next-of-kin received his pocketbook and wallet; but the Admiralty firmly *declined to say where the surgeon had been buried.*

Why? What was being concealed? His next-of-kin and my informant could never find out.

One more singular matter may be noted. I was in Pomona, in the Orkneys, in 1952, and I found, that, among the fishermen and farmers in the Orkneys, strange things are told even today, thirty-six years after the *Hampshire* went down in the waters off Marwick Head. I give an account made to me by a fisherman there:

"On the night the *Hampshire* went down, our Orkneymen rushed to the cliffs where we knew that survivors would try to come ashore. There are paths up and down these three-hundred-foot-high cliffs, which are known only to the local folk who live off Marwick Head. . . . Now, I want to know—and I did, thirty-six years ago—and so did every man here, who was out on the cliffs that night, when the warship went down and poor devils were freezing in the icy waters and raging winds trying to reach the shore, we were everyone turned back by sentries when we tried to go to the aid of the poor men, with ropes. . . . Have you seen, sir, the tombstone, in the Navy graveyard in the Orkneys? It has a simple granite stone, engraved with the words:

" 'To the memory of the Officers and Men of H.M.S. *Hampshire,* who were drowned at sea on 5 June, 1916, and here lie buried.' Our own Orkneymen were among them.

"I do a bit of reading, in my shore time, and I remember a poet whose name, it was said, was 'writ in water!' "

This fisherman was a very sober-minded and serious type of man, and he told me this story in a very serious manner.

It is true that the Admiralty officials who prepared the "Official Narrative of the Loss of H.M.S. *Hampshire*", ten years after the tragic event, said that this story of the impedance of the Orkneymen is as "untrue as contemptible;" but they were *not on the spot,* on that night of 5 June, 1916, and no official *démenti* will persuade the Orkneymen, even today, so many years later, that something did not occur which, they swear with passion and anger, *did occur!* The full facts in *this,* too, will never now be made known.

All one may say is, in the words of an old Caribbean mariner who had a talent for verse:

> *"For the dead man's eyes, they tell no lies,*
> *Of a secret they do know*
> *With a hee, and a ha, and a ho."*

Author's Note: In June 1942, Mr. C. J. Selway, C.V.O., C.B.E. former traffic manager of the London and North-Eastern Railway told some hitherto unpublished facts about the last journey of Lord Kitchener. He said that the special conveying Kitchener to a northern Scottish port had left King's Cross Station, *in secret* at 5.40 p.m., when there arrived breathlessly at the stationmaster's office, Mr. Hugh Beirne, a Foreign Office official. Beirne was very agitated. He said: "It is absolutely essential . . . I *must* overtake that train; for I have highly secret and important despatches that the Head of the Mission *must* have."

"I am sorry, sir," said the stationmaster, "but she cannot be stopped. We have stringent orders that there must be no delay whatever."

Beirne took out his cheque-book. "If you can't stop the special, then it is essential that I overtake her. Look here, you must run another special in chase of her. I take the responsibility in the name of the Secretary of State for Foreign Affairs."

"Well, sir," said the stationmaster, "since you insist, we will see what can be done; but I must warn you, it will cost you £200."

"Good!" said Beirne. "Here is my cheque." He took out a blank cheque and handed it over. "The stationmaster rang up the locomotive engine-shed and ordered an express passenger locomotive to be attached to a carriage brake-van, and, in about thirty minutes, the new special left a side bay of King's Cross and was on her way north. Beirne asked the engine-driver to get the utmost speed out of his engine, and this was done. All records were broken as far as Grantham; but the special ahead had not been overtaken, nor was any telegraphic order given to any signalman to set the signals against her. It was not until York was reached, that Lord Kitchener's secret train was halted, and even then only to take in water from a tank. As the fireman was throwing the streaming hose out of the engine's tank on to the line and hitching it up to the pillars, with a roar of steam blowing off, the pursuing express locomotive, behind, ran in on to another platform. Beirne jumped out of the coach and rushed across to the first special, which was on the point of being flagged out by the guard, when Beirne clutched at the handle of a compartment and got in as she was on the move.

Next night, Beirne, who might have reflected that the King of Terrors had stood behind the driver in the cab of the chasing express locomotive, was lying drowned with the rest of the party at the bottom of the hurricane-whipped sea!

It is curious that no contemporary account, newspaper or other, named Beirne as among the lost and missing; but the cheque drawn by him for the public service on his private account, was, in 1942, in the possession of Mr. Selway, who, at the time, was Superintendent of the old Great Northern Railroad. The cheque was, in fact, never presented. Selway emphasized that it was a *secret special*, and that no one outside the ranks of high railway officials knew that Lord Kitchener was aboard.

Envoi: "The Mahdi's formerly blown-up house, re-built, is one no Sudanese, *today*, will stay in. It is haunted by *afreets*, and a British Commissioner went mad in it." (*Khartoum correspondent to the author.*)

Chapter 7

MISSING PERSONS MYSTERIES

Is THERE something about Mount Parnassus, Greece, which puts a spell on it; or is there, at times, over it, an ecstasy induced by the ancient gods who once dwelt there, so that men who go wandering alone on the mountain never return, or abandon their normal life to live that of the Delphic shepherds?

This question was asked quite seriously by one don in a common room of an Oxford University College, in the summer of 1931. David Cochrane, nephew of a former Cabinet Minister, Mr. H. A. L. Fisher, had vanished while walking over this former mountain-seat of the oracle of Apollo. It is rugged country with crumbling limestone and is very solitary and wild. Search was made by the Greek authorities; but no trace of Mr. Cochrane was found, and his uncle, Sir George Young, who took part in the search, returned to London, believing that his nephew had been murdered by bandits. The then Foreign Secretary, the late Lord Simon, even got the Vice-Chancellor of Oxford University to issue a warning to visitors that they should not go on tours of this mountain without a guide. All hope had been given up, after military aeroplanes had been used, that the mystery would ever be solved, when, a year later, the skeleton of this unfortunate young man, was found in a glen on the mountain.

But the mystery of the disappearance of John Andruss, who claimed that he had found a method of making petrol from water, has never been solved. It is stated that both the British and the U.S. Governments had been sufficiently impressed by his claims and had set up a joint panel of experts to study his specifications. Finally, the stage was reached when a tank of a motor-boat was filled with water, and Andruss poured into it a glass of his secret composition. Picked men were in the boat, and it is stated that it roared out over the waters of a lake near New York. A final test was to be made on the speedway at Indianapolis; but, on the morning of the (successful) test, Andruss did not turn up. From that day in 1925, until this, not a trace of him has even been found. He had no financial worries. Some folk held the theory that big American oil interests had hired thugs to kidnap and murder him; but, if so, no clues were ever found.

In September 1915, Dr. Thornton R. Sampson, a college friend of President Woodrow Wilson, started out on a fishing trip into the Colorado gorges, and days passed without his return. Federal agents were ordered to search for him, and one of the greatest man-hunts in history was staged. It went on for many days, and the search was given up only when the thunder of guns heralded America's entry into the First World War. He had been totally forgotten, when, one July day, in 1932, a ranger in the National Park of the Rocky Mountains came on a skeleton to whose ribs fragments of clothing were still attached. Close by was a diary. The location was in a very lonely part of Estes Park, Colorado, and the remains lay at the foot of a cliff above the shores of Odessa Lake. One leg was fractured, and it was theorized that Sampson, whose diary it was, had fallen from a high ledge, lain unconscious for hours, and died of exposure. But one may ask: what was a *fisherman* doing on a high ledge in a *cañon?*

Iceland, the Ultima Thule of Uncle Sam's northern air bases, is a land of weird mysteries and wild and eerie folklore. It is more often on and off the east and north-eastern shores and inland that one will hear of these, in this very rugged island of wild Boreas and his winds, and of the volcanic fires of Erebus. In actual fact, these wild fells, in the north-eastern part of Iceland, are very little known to natives, and less so to foreigners.

I have two mysteries in mind. The first lies on the face of a towering weather-worn and wind-beaten craggy cliff called the Hof, and located on the south-eastern shores. High up from the wild fjörd, cut deeply in the face of the rock, are a number of very ancient unknown glyphs, or mysterious signs. Whoever cut them it was certainly *not* the old Norse, or the Vikings. But it may be said that the exact counterpart of two of these strange glyphs has been found out on the walls of a dead city, deep in the still unknown *sertão*, or hinterland of the state of Bahia, Brazil. The signs may be a memorial of the old land of Chronos, or the lost continent of Iere-Atlantis, which, in a very far day, once stretched from Iceland to what is now Trinidad, British West Indies. Long ago this lost continent sank under a rain of fire from the skies, roaring volcanoes rising from a much smaller Atlantic than we know now, and an appalling deluge. But there are traditions of its existence surviving today, among the yellow Caribs and black aboriginals in some of the Carribbean islands. They speak of great cities, pyramids, and methods of locomotion unknown in our day.

However, what one is more concerned with, in this chapter, is a strange and uncanny story told of a wild and lonely region in north-eastern Iceland, known as the "Odádharhraun." This fey region is as solitary, today, as it was when the early Norse and the Vikings pushed the noses of their war-galleys up the fiords of the Northland some 1,500 years ago. The Odádharhraun is located in a quadrilateral, bounded on two sides by Longititude 16° E., and Latitude 66° N. This mysterious region is about 100 km. (162.1 miles) long, and about 40 km. (24.8 miles) wide, at its broadest part, and lies west of Mount Askja (1.2 miles high). The landscape of the Odádharhraun is like that of the ashy moon: vast expanse of riven rock, dead fields of lava, craters, sand and waste, and unearthly in its atmosphere.

A very ancient hunting song of the old Norse says of it:

"Uncanny are the things that are out in the wild lands, when the westering sun is near the horizon. They haunt the desert hills."

The region has long had a fascination for Germans, who visited it years before the First World War. Gustav Buchheim who, in collaboration with Herr Helmuth, doctor of philosophy, wrote: "In Thule, the Land of Fire and Ice" (Berlin, 1930), says:

"I had a guide and the purpose to push on towards the ill-omened and notorious Lava-field of the Odádharhraun. This territory is an endless waste, and in early times criminals were exiled there, and died in it. I was drawn to stop there and become acquainted with the long since past ancient time and the whole horror of it."

(But it is *not* Buchheim who tells the strange story below, which is akin to similar mysterious stories told of ill-omened lakes in the northern mountains of Tibet.)

Mount Askja, referred to above, is a great volcano with a crater *actually thirteen miles across*, and the scene of many frightful eruptions, which have spread far-ranging lava-fields over the Odádharhraun, that fey land. The greatest lava-field is known as the "Lava-Land of evil deeds." Icelandic farmers, who live on the edge of the region, rarely venture into it. They say it is "haunted by evil spirits who want none there."

In 1905, three young Germans of Berlin University, who were keen students of seismology, geology and petrography, left Husavik, a solitary little township of fishermen and farmers on the north-east coast of Iceland, and, on horseback—they are stunted horses, like those of the Shetlands—rode south, to explore this wild region under the Icelandic northern moon. It was high northern summer, and they were gay and lighthearted and laughed at the wild and romantic stories of the native farmers. They halted at a little village of lonely farmsteads, from which they planned to make for a "hot lake" in the Odádharhraun, which has a sandy beach, offering a good site for pitching a tent.

A farmer, whose ancestors came to this region three centuries ago, warned the young Germans that this lake had an evil reputation. "The place is uncanny," he said, "and, in twenty years, I have known only three people who ventured in there, and they would not stop there even one night. They returned here, saying that they did not like the atmosphere on the shores of the lake where you plan to camp."

"Why," said the leader of the three Germans, smiling at his friends, "what is there about the lake?"

The farmer noted the glance between the Germans and showed that he was annoyed.

"All I say is that the place is uncanny. I and my forebears have lived here for more than 300 years, and, I tell you, young gentlemen, that I, myself, would not spend a night there for 10,000 gulden!"

The German laughed. "We are students of science, not connoisseurs of old wives' tales. If you mean spooks are there, such things have no place in *our* philosophy. It sounds interesting. So, a good day to you, *mein Herr!*"

The three Germans spurred their horses and rode off, laughing, with their guide. The latter knew the region, but did not seem to share the light-heartedness of the young fellows. In due time, they reached the shores of the hot lake from which steam rose, pitched their tent, and sent away the guide with the horses. For no grass or fodder can be had in that region.

"Come back in a week's time," said the leader. "We have food enough to last till then."

The guide, casting a gloomy eye on the young Germans, tied the reins of the Germans' horses to the crupper of his own, and galloped off as if he had a desire to put as much distance as possible between him and the lake, before sundown.

Two of the Germans went out on the lake in a collapsible dinghy. They wished to gather data on temperatures and depths. The leader, the third man, who was a geologist and petrographer, rambled along the shore, examining the rocks, and became completely absorbed in his task. About half an hour later, he turned round to look across the lake for his friends. To his amazement, there were no signs of them, or of the dinghy! And the whole lake was visible from shore to shore. Nor could they have landed on the farther bank and wandered inland; for he would have seen them and the dinghy, which they would have left on the opposite shore. He shouted repeatedly, but all the answer he had was the echo of his own voice returned to him from the rocks. Where were the two men? What had become of them? He roamed the sandy beach for an hour, and then, as night fell, he went into the tent. He had no ability as a tracker, and no map of the region; and he feared that if he tried to follow the track taken by the guide, he would become hopelessly lost in that fey wilderness, many miles from the nearest habitation of men.

It may be surmised that he spent a very bad night, oppressed by the uncanny atmosphere of the place. Presently, despite himself, he began to fancy that he could see, out of the corner of his eye, shapeless things watching him, and waiting. Fear in its most elemental shape seized him. Against it none of his science and rationality could prevail. He had a rifle and some ammunition, and, towards midnight, he began to fire at shadows in the blackness. But there was no response, save the reverberations of the explosions. . . . He peered out over the dark and stealthy waters of the lake. . . .

All that is definitely known, is that the guide, when he returned with the horses, a week later, found a demented man, and had to gallop back for help. A search party was organized, and, in a boat they dragged the lake; but not a trace of the missing men, or the dinghy, was ever found. It is said that, in 1921, another German student, who derided the warnings about this lake, tried to camp there, and had to return, telling the farmers in the nearest inhabited place, that the hot lake was more than he could stand. Its eerie atmosphere was too much for his nerves. It is evidently a region, this eerie Odádharhraun, like those uncanny mountains in North Mexico, in Masefield's "Sard Harker"; "a place which its gods or demons wish not to be known!"

Any curious inquirer who may spend some time roaming the interior of Iceland, would not find it difficult to collect queer and eerie stories of vanished men. For example, 60 miles northwestwards of the Odádharhraun, is Hjeradhsvoton river, which flows into the wild Skaga fjörd. One of the lonely villages on its bank is separated from the church by the waters of this foaming river. The natives tell a story about an old farmer named Oddur Gillasory who, one Sunday, years ago, went across the river to the church. He vanished while he was crossing! And he was never seen again, nor his body found. No doubt, he fell in and was drowned? Or, maybe, he wished to commit suicide?

"Oh no," say the farmers of the village, "he just vanished from the sight of those who saw him cross! The river was dragged up and down, and he was never seen again." There are no railways in Iceland, and the "Norraena" language, spoken there, is about as intelligible to the modern Englishman as would be Anglo-Saxon of the tenth or eleventh century, which it closely resembles.

In 1926, there was solved, in a very strange way, the mystery of the disappearance of an old Portuguese explorer who had been missing for 424 years—since A.D. 1502. It came about when Professor Delabarre, of Brown University, Rhode Island, cleared up the mystery of eight truncated words cut on a weathered rock above the Taunton river in Massachusetts; and abbreviated in the manner of ancient Roman inscriptions in England. In 1502, two Portuguese explorers landed on the then lonely coast of Massachusetts, marked on old maps as "Norimbega." They vanished into the woods where only cat-footed Indians ever penetrated, and where the only sounds, save for a call of a wild beast, was the whispering of the wind, or the splashing of a waterfall. Only very old Indian trails ran through the vast forests. The story may be summarized from what Delabarre told an academic audience:

"I studied more than 600 old books and MSS., many of them in Portuguese, and I expanded the abbreviated Latin on the Taunton river stone, which read as follows:

" 'MIGUEL CORTEREAL 1511 V DEI HIC
DUX IND'

"The date 1511 gave me a clue, and I found in an old record in the archives, in Lisbon, that a captain, Miguel Cortereal, had sailed from Lisbon, in 1502, to find what had befallen his brother, Gaspar, who had vanished into the forests of Labrador and Newfoundland, as Miguel himself was to do in North America. I read the abbreviated inscription, as follows:

' "I, Miguel Cortereal, 1511. In this place, by the will of God, I became a chief of the Indians.' "

In 1929, the British Embassy, in Washington, the Federal U.S. authorities, and the French *Deuxième Bureau* were asking themselves a strange question: "What sort of criminal is he who first riddles his victim with small shot, then carefully extracts the bullets, after which he severs the head with a sharp instrument, and mutilates it?"

Behind the question lay a strange affair going as far back as 1865. But long after that, in or about 1925, people in the picturesque township of Fernandez de Taos, on the Rio Grande, in New Mexico, were shocked and puzzled by a strange murder connected with what is locally known as the "Mystic Gold Mine." Three men seeking to win gold, in this lonely region, have mysteriously vanished in the last fifty years. In two cases, bodies have been found—*decapitated!* The story would make a lurid thriller. My own inquiries of American police departments and crime laboratories showed, in 1937, that little or nothing has been recorded about this macabre mystery of the *missing heads*. In 1863 a man, named Stone, found in Colfax county a mine which he called the "Mystic Mine." Two years later, he met a man, named Ferguson, with whom he went into partnership, in order to win the gold, a certain amount of which they took out, until, in 1879, another richer mine was staked, about five miles away. It became known to gold-seekers as the "Aztec mine," and is said to share with another mine in the state of Sonora, Mexico, the reputation of being one of the two richest gold-mines in the world, or, at least, in Central and Western America.

At this stage, Stone wandered into the wilds and was never heard of again. Later, in 1882, there were rumours that he had been murdered, but no body could be found, nor any proof of the allegations. In 1895, one Manby, entered on this eerie stage and became known as a promoter of gold hunts all over New Mexico, California, and Arizona. He joined a syndicate composed of Ferguson and a man named Wilkinson, and the combine prospered. But again, sinister rumours circulated. It was said that the combine had tapped the Aztec mine by a secret tunnel and that, in 1915, Wilkinson disappeared, as had the others. However, nobody could pin anything on to a suspect. Ferguson, who died in a lunatic asylum, told an attendant, on his death-bed: "I have had a horrible dream! I saw a body with a head floating above it!" He died, and his daughter, Teresa, or Teresita, inherited her father's share in the "Mystic Mine."

The spotlight in this drama, with its Grand Guignolesque features, now became centred on A. R. Manby, who was an Englishman who had gone to New Mexico in the 1880s, where he had met with Wilkinson, whose beautiful daughter became Manby's private secretary. At this time, Wilkinson, who had disappeared, reappeared as suddenly and mysteriously as he had vanished. He had been presumed dead. But, yet again, Wilkinson vanished. Seven years went by, and then, on 3 July, 1929, the *decapitated corpse* of an old man was found in the library of a big house, alone. It was clad only in a nightgown, and when a search was made the missing head was found in a room next to the library, and concealed behind a big cabin trunk. The head was that of A. R. Manby, aged 72. Manby had had the reputation of being an eccentric recluse, and he had built this splendid house, with its library, in the manner of a hidalgo of old Castile. It was lavishly furnished with art treasures and carpeted with many valuable Persian rugs with rich Oriental coverings and tapestry. The old man had four ferocious Alsatian police dogs which followed him around the house, like his own shadow, and slept by his bedside at night.

It looked as if Manby has gone in fear of something and had taken no chance. People in Fernandez de Taos said they had last seen Manby alive on 30 June, three days before the discovery of his headless body. The last entry in his diary was dated 1 July, 1929. The local people were scared by the sinister atmosphere of this big house and the strange stories attached to it, and the mines, and they had called in the police. The first policeman to pass in through the door of the house, stopped short in his tracks when he found himself face to face with a savage dog, who snarled and bared his teeth menacingly. The policeman did not try to pacify the mastiff. He whipped out his revolver and shot him dead. Then, as stated, he found in the library the headless body.

A coroner's jury was empanelled and returned a verdict —in face of all the evidence to the contrary—that Manby had died by natural causes, and that one of the savage dogs must have mauled his body and carried it into the library, leaving the head in another room. The folk of Fernandez de Taos rightly scoffed at this absurd verdict; for they had not forgotten the previous cases of headless victims at times when no dogs were around. They might, too, have drawn the inference which the coroner had not, that whoever had committed this macabre crime, in that lonely house, was almost certainly a person whom these savage guardian dogs knew! Now, as stated, Manby was an Englishman, and his relations in England pulled the official wires so well, that, at Washington, D.C., the British Embassy brought pressure on the Federal State Department to open investigations into this very strange crime. For some reason, a French detective, from Paris, then on holiday in Washington, was ordered by the Prefecture of Police, in Paris, to go to New Mexico and look into the case. Why, one does not know; since there were plenty of agents available from the Federal Bureau of Investigation, not to speak of the New Mexico state police; and, besides, Manby was not a Frenchman. Was some unknown official averse from an investigation? If so, why?

Monsieur Henri Martin, the Paris detective, had the corpse exhumed, and found that death was caused by pellets from a sawn-off shotgun. How the coroner and his jury of what the Americans called "hicks" had been blind to these—and other—facts, might be explainable in several ways, the most reputable of which is that coroner and jury were a collection of half-wits. Martin delved into other strange riddles about the case, and particularly a forty-year-old unsolved mystery: why had the partner Wilkinson mysteriously vanished in 1915, re-appeared in 1921, and for a third time vanished? Martin met a woman who assured him that Wilkinson had been murdered by his associates in the prosperous gold mines. She said that, after his murder, Wilkinson's body had been placed in her room without awakening her; for she was Wilkinson's cook and housekeeper.

"I woke, next morning," she said, "and found Mr. W.'s body riddled with shots through his chest, and lacking his head!" (If this crime took place in Wilkinson's house, why had she not been awakened by such a fusillade, and how, too, had the entry of strangers into her bedroom failed to rouse her?) She indicated to the detective where the body had been buried in the lonely mountains, and he went there and dug up a skeleton and skull. Certainly, the whole circumstances were very peculiar, and the inference is that the woman stood in mortal fear of some very sinister assassins, and assassins with old Aztecan traits of paranoia about them!

The death of Ferguson was then investigated. It was said that he had become a drug addict before he died in the lunatic asylum, and someone inferred that Ferguson was in such deadly fear of someone else, that he deliberately took a more subtle road to death. If, indeed, he did, or did not die with his boots on, he certainly and very literally lost his head!

No doubt, robbery was one of the motives actuating the sinister assassin, or assassins of A. R. Manby; for, between the time when he was buried and the French detective's investigations started, his lavishly furnished, hidalgo-style house had been denuded of its rich art and Oriental treasures, and, too, $40,000 worth of gold-dust, known to be in the house, had vanished without trace.

At this point, we may inquire into *one* of the very Grand Guignolesque features of this mystery: what sort of criminal is he who beheads his victim *after* shooting him dead? It is to be again noted, in eight years, two of the partners in this "Mystic Gold Mine" had been found dead and decapitated. Was this very singular crime, or these crimes, the work of one man, who would present a study for a criminological psychiatrist; or was there behind it all some queer secret society dominated by a man with a warped mind? Or a man of ancient Nahuan, or Aztec descent? Students of criminology and police science knew that certain "techniques" stamp the handiwork of certain types of criminals. For example, a criminal in North America's underworld, who leaves traces of naked feet on the scene of a murder is one who has migrated to U.S.A. from one of the countries of south-eastern Europe, or from Sicily. But, in this case, the author of this book would venture a suggestion of his own: if there were not a warped type of Oriental at work, which does not seem probable, was he, say, a half-breed Mexican, who may have been of *peón* ancestry, with hereditary knowledge of the methods of the old Aztec priests of and before the days of Don Hernando Cortes, who sacrificed victims in a barbaric fashion by tearing out their hearts with obsidian, or volcanic glass, knives; or even *beheading* them? And then sticking up the skulls, in Nahua temples, to dry? These rich gold mines must have been known to south-western Indian tribes, like the Apaches, and the Mexicans in the days when either old Spain, or Mexican revolutionary governments extended their sway over what is, today, the American states of New Mexico, Arizona and California. Moreover, it is known, that, even today, Apache Indians, with lively ancestral memories of the ways of whites and sallows, forty-niner Americans, and old Castilian adventurers, keep watch over "lost" gold mines, and, from ambushes in the mountains, there are dead-centre rifle-marksmen who shoot and leave carcasses to be picked clean by the coyotes and buzzards. Nor can any sheriff, or marshal bring the Indian assassins in for trial. In fact, in at least one of these states, the sheriffs show little inclination to try to trail the Apaches. On one mountain-top, is a stone monument warning adventurers of the many deaths in fifty years that have overtaken those who tried to trail these "mystic mines."

But the strange affair did not end with Martin's investigations; for my own files show that, in April 1930, a cable from Albuquerque, N.M., to London, England, stated that an American private detective, Miles Plowman, of Bentonville, Arkansas, had alleged that "A. R. Manby, the Englishman, is alive and well *in England!*" I knew a London newspaper reporter whose editor assigned him to get on the trail of what this cable alleged. Here is what I was told:

"As representing the London 'Sunday Comet'—*N.B.* I passed my word not to name this Sunday newspaper. *Author*—'I visited the house of Major Manby, A. R. Manby's brother, which is in a spa in the eastern counties. The major emphatically denied this story from U.S.A. Some one said it was merely a red herring to divert attention from the strange lack of any real effort over there to get to the bottom of the mystery. The major said: 'I am certain that my brother was murdered, and that this story had been spread around by those behind the case who may have motives of their own for insinuating such a lie. So far as I know, my brother died intestate. *If* he were still alive, I should have been told so by my two other brothers who live in one of the western states and have been trying to investigate the murder. I am sure that the great Alsatian hound, who guarded my brother in that big house, must have known whoever it was entered the house and did that horrible murder. I saw my brother, Arthur Roche Manby, in 1914, in New Mexico, and I knew that the dog would not allow anyone to go near my brother unless it knew him as an old friend, or unless the dog had been introduced to him, or to a stranger who entered the house. I am not well informed on the subject of my brother's recent affairs. When the murder was discovered, the great dog was standing guard over the body, and the body was carefully covered with a quilt."

For some reason best known to himself, the then Governor of New Mexico opposed the re-opening of an inquiry into the mystery, and his opposition had to be overborne by the Federal authorities, in Washington, who had been subjected to diplomatic pressure from the Foreign Office, in Downing Street, and H. M. ambassador in Washington, D.C.

What is most peculiar about this strange affair is that Martin, the French detective, found that A. R. Manby's corpse had *been riddled with small shot, which had afterwards been carefully extracted, after which the head had been severed by some sharp instrument and mutilated.* Whoever killed Manby was not content with murdering and robbing him. He acted under some strange or necromantic ritual, involving decapitation and mutilation after death! And, the inference is irresistible, that more than one man, besides the master-criminal, was involved. Who was that man? Someone high up in New Mexico probably knew or suspected his identity.

From my own files I extract some more queer details:

"It seems that police investigations—maybe, those of the F.B.I.'s agents—have disclosed documents to the effect that, in 1926, three years or so before A. R. Manby's murder by people unknown, he and Miss Teresita Ferguson had, it is alleged, become members of some mysterious 'United States secret service society.' It is said that these documents were found in Manby's old hidalgo house, near Fernandez de Taos, where he was found headless. Manby is said to have entered in a diary that 'Miss Ferguson, a Spanish type of beauty, is the princess of all my dreams.' It is also said that she was to receive vast and fantastic areas of land, worth some £20,000,000, held under old Spanish grants of the late eighteenth century. Manby held a half-share in the 'Mystic' Mine, while Miss Ferguson held the other half, bequeathed to her by her father who died in the lunatic asylum. As these murders had been perpetrated in wild and lonely western mountains, sparsely populated by wandering Indians and Mexicans and roaming gold prospectors, clues were almost impossible to obtain. But Major Manby, in England, says he is positive that the so-called 'U.S. Secret Service Society,' of which there has been so much talk in U.S.A., 'was formed merely for my brother's protection, and not for his destruction.'"

British M.P.s have been the central figures in unsolved mysteries, one of the most mystifying of which happened on 10 December, 1881 when Walter Powell, M.P. for Malmesbury, Wilts, went to Bath, Somerset, with two aeronautical friends and ascended in the British Government balloon, "Saladin." Some hours later, the balloon came down near Bridport, Dorset, on the beach not far from the Chesil Bank. The two friends got out; but while Powell was in the act of following them the balloon gave a violent jerk and suddenly ascended into the clouds. Powell went up with it, and was never seen or heard of again.

The incident raised several riddles: (1) Did the balloon come down in the waters of the English Channel? No one knew; but had it done so, it seemed likely that the hydrogen gas in the envelope would have kept it afloat in the sea until a rescuing ship came on the scene. For three days, until 3 December, 1881, a steamer quartered the English Channel searching for Powell or signs of wreckage of the balloon; trawlers and fishing boats took part in the hunt; and a sweeping search of the waters was organized. Coastguards ashore were doubled, and night and day they combed southern English beaches on the hunt for wreckage, and from the tops of cliffs closely scanned the sea through telescopes. All that was found was a thermometer in a leather case.

(2) What about the mystifying reports that came from various parts of England, Scotland, western France, and north Spain? They merely deepened the mystery of the fate of Powell, lost in this wandering balloon. On the evening of the 13th, two days after the disappearance, a strange luminous object was seen quartering the sky, back and forth over Cherbourg, and three nights later, on 16 December, three Spanish *guardas de costas* (coastguards) reported that they saw "something like a balloon in the sky." They climbed to the top of a mountain near Laredo, a Spanish fishing port near Santander, on the Spanish Biscay coast, in north Spain, to get a better view of the object, and, as they watched, it shot out sparks and vanished. (It could hardly have been a balloon!) Next day the same object, or something like it, was seen over Bilbao, about 75 miles east. It was luminous and emitted a strange glow. On 15 December, at 5 a.m., a Captain McBain, of s.s. *Countess of Aberdeen*, saw, in the sky, over the sea, 25 miles off Montrose, east Scotland, a luminous object which he took to be the "gondola of a balloon, which seemed alternately to increase and diminish in size." But, when he trained binoculars on it, it appeared as a large bright object *moving against the wind*, and visible for half an hour, after which it vanished. Again, two days before, on 11 December, when the balloon had disappeared, people at Dartmouth Harbour, in South Devon, saw "two strange bright lights in the sky."

Powell was never found.

Another queer affair was the vanishing of a British Labour

M.P., Victor Grayson, the last of whose known movements was when he boarded a night train from Liverpool to Hull, where he was booked to make a speech, in June, 1920. He was member for Colne Valley, and had had a picturesque career as an adventurer, stowaway, engineer, preacher, journalist and politician. He was a graduate of Queen's College, Oxford, and an accomplished speaker on political platforms. The train arrived at Hull but Grayson never alighted from it. His health was good and he was said to have had no domestic or financial worries. Scotland Yard took up the case; but the mystery still remains on their files. Detectives three times investigated this mystery. A curious report came from Melbourne, Victoria, Australia, in September, 1942, when Mr. T. J. Smith, former secretary of the Australian Clerks Union, who had met Grayson in London, alleged that he found a man living in pitiful circumstances in a hovel at Carlton, a suburb of Melbourne, in 1922. This man soon after died and, before his death, complained to Mr. Smith who said he was the missing Victor Grayson, M.P., that the House of Commons would not listen to his pleas for the poor and down-and-out.

It *appeared* that the mystery had been solved when about this very time, Grayson's sister, living in Canada, wrote to Scotland Yard and gave them fresh clues. Again detectives took up the case and again nothing was found. In the summer of 1957 a fresh story came from Australia that Grayson was alive in Sydney, New South Wales; but the story was never confirmed. It seems curious that Mr. Smith seems to have waited for twenty years before making his story public. In any case, the mystery remains unsolved; and the story, said to have been told by the man at Carlton, Victoria, can hardly be said to convince.

In 1940, during the so-called "phoney" period of the Second World War, Lieut.-Colonel Sir Arthur Talbot Wilson, K.C.I.E., C.S.I., C.M.G., D.S.O., Conservative M.P. for Hitchin, author of many travel books and diaries relating to the East, liked in all quarters and very sympathetic to the social aspirations of the English working classes, set off in an aeroplane piloted by a flight-lieutenant of the Royal Air Force, bound for the front, then in Belgium. No one knew what happened to him, and in the House of Commons the Air Minister stated that Sir Arthur Talbot Wilson's fate was unknown. The mystery looked like being insoluble when, at the end of the war, it was discovered that he and the pilot and plane had been shot down by the Germans somewhere near the Rhine. As often happens in war, when one hears the "beating of the wings of the angel of Death," the solution of the riddle of the disappearance of a man on active service may be delayed for years, or never found at all. However, in the case of this well-known British M.P., it has never been revealed what his mission was, or how his plane came to be so far away from the British lines.

Again, did Colonel James Baldwin-Webb, Tory M.P. for the Wrekin Division of Shropshire, go down with the liner *City of Benares?* She was torpedoed by a Nazi submarine on 17 September, 1940, when she was carrying evacuees to the U.S.A.

It was believed that he had been lost, along with a former B.B.C. overseas service announcer, Mr. Lazlo Raskay; when two strange cables were received by the Colonel's sister, Miss Annie Webb. The first cable was from Baron Raskay, father of the lost announcer. It asked: "Have you any news of your brother, Colonel Baldwin-Webb?" It was followed by a second cable from Hungary, sent by Margarette Raskay, daughter of the Baron:

"Unofficial news going round here in America that our brother are safed. Please try to surch them. Let us work together."

Miss Baldwin-Webb was mystified; for not only was the cable ambiguous in meaning, but she thought that, if her brother had been rescued at sea, or had landed in the U.S.A., she would have heard officially. The mystery was never solved and the heart-breaking messages merely deepened the survivor's grief.

PART THREE

WAR AND POST-WAR MYSTERIES

Chapter 8

THE VANISHING AEROPLANES

OLD Davy Jones, with his locker, runs a neck and neck race with Daedalus and his flying coffin in the Great Mystery Stakes, and one in which the "unplumbed, salt, estranging sea" and the recesses of lonely mountains offer no prizes; for there are no "winners" in *this* race! A skeleton whose bones lie across the blade of a propeller, or whose skull peers out from the instrument panel in the cockpit of a shattered plane in a wood, or high up on the rugged flanks of a towering mountain, or in the col of a corridor walled in by frowning precipices, or on the edge of a green glacier, may be the only clue to some years-old mystery, forgotten by all save the relatives or wives of lost men.

In the summer of 1928 an American airman, Paul Redfern, kissed his pretty wife good-bye, taxied down the sands of Brunswick, Georgia, and took off into the skies on an exceedingly foolish stunt trip to Brazil. His plane had only one engine, a death trap if anything untimely befell him, and he was alone on a journey of 4,700 miles. The months passed into years and his wife gave him up for dead; for the last news she had was the report of a Hollander skipper of an oil tanker who had seen a plane streaking across the skies off the coast of Dutch Guiana. In that year air lines were in their infancy, and planes in those waters were not the commonplace they have since become. Rio de Janeiro cabled that no one in Brazil had seen or heard of Redfern, or his plane.

Then, in 1933, an engineer and explorer, Charles Hasler, came in from the green hell of the Amazonas *sertâo*, or wilderness, to Manaos, where he told a very odd story:

"Far up in the jungles of Amazonas, somewhere near the Rio Putumayo, a savage tribe of head-hunting Indians have a new chief who has become a god. It seems that he has a white skin, and one day there flew into the open space of the *aldeia*, with its cannibal cooking-pots, of burnt-clay, a 'great bird,' which roared over the tree tops and landed in a clearing. The 'bird' came from northeast. At once the head-hunters deposed their chief and elected what they took to be a mightier man. The new arrival was a modest man, and tried to decline the honour; but the head-hunters would not take no for answer. The witch-doctor gave a sly smile and the pupils of his black wizened eyes contracted. He indicated the cooking-pots. The great bird-man could choose: either godship or *that!* Anyway, if they could not have a live god, they would elect to have a trophy—the white birdman's head—to hang under the black beams of the tribal lodge! The new arrival chose, reluctantly, to become the Indians' god. But, while they fed him on the fat of the Indian land, they saw to it that he had no chance to walk out on them and ramble into the great forest."

Home at far-away Brunswick, Georgia, pretty Mrs. Redfern was overjoyed, and she passed the glad news to Paul Redfern's father, while Mrs. Redfern, the mother, said she had always had a feeling that Paul was alive, and would one day return. An expedition was organized; but alas, they could not find the "white god," or Redfern! It may be said that these stories of white men held prisoners and well treated by the Indians, short of letting them go, are not uncommon in the Matto Grosso, or up the little-known Rio Branco.

In the case of missing planes equipped with rafts or lifebelts, it has been found that devilish man-eating sharks will follow survivors for days, trying persistently to get their horny backs under the rafts or appliances, and lever or tip the castaways off into the sea! It was in July 1937 that gallant Amelia Earhart flew from Lae, New Guinea, bound for the lonely mid-Pacific Howland Island, on the equator. She never arrived, and sea and air searches found no trace of her, her navigator, nor any wreckage. A similar baffling mystery surrounds the fate of William Brophy, an Englishman, who in 1932 attempted a foolish solo flight from Manila, in the Philippines, to Shanghai, not then barred off by Chinese Communists. His route was over the South China Sea, not well-charted, even today, and thronged with little, unknown islands and sown with *vigias*, or rock pinnacles of coral.

There is some reason to suppose that Brophy was, later, sighted and left to his fate. Follows a letter sent to me by a correspondent in Manila:

"Brophy took a mascot with him for luck: a puppy. It did not help him any! A story has been cabled here from Yokohama about a Jap skipper of a lugger who, in August 1933, about seventeen months after Brophy took off for China, was passing by the rocky coast of the wild and solitary island of Yami, a practically inaccessible island, some way out beyond the northern end of Luzon. In the dusk, he saw a white man, with a dog, wandering on the beach of Yami. Only untamed savages live there. The man was looking out to sea and waving a piece of cloth in the direction of the lugger. The Jap focused his telescope on to the beach and made out the figure of a man, in rags and tatters, signalling for help. The Jap swore that the coral reefs made an attempt at landing too dangerous. So he steamed on and left the poor guy to his fate. Yami is mountainous, and the savages have a bad reputation. I know nobody who has ever landed there, and little or nothing is known of the place which is about 150 miles from Aparri, in Luzon. I guess the poor devil will stay there, unless some of Uncle Sam's airmen can reach him."

Quiet rural places, "deep in the shires"—not to be found as easily today as in the 1920s!—may also have mysteries as impenetrable as those of the big cities; even though they may have subpostmistresses of village stores who know a surprising lot about the private correspondence of "furriners and outsiders" who come to live in the place, pathetically supposing that, here, nobody will know a thing about them. They will find that the maxim is: "Do not advertise; tell a gossip." The late W. H. Hudson's charming book about his walks afoot in off-the-track England, tells how he got into a long disused and old grass-grown lane leading to nowhere. At a turn of the way he saw, below the boughs of an umbrageous oak, a deserted farmhouse standing with a thick grove of elms blacking out the skyline behind it. He was in South Devon. He wrote, in sensitive prose:

"There were a group of old farm buildings in a hollow in the woods . . . the place must have been deserted for many a year . . . the roofs had fallen in. . . . As I stood watching the vacant windows, it was as though something intelligent looked out of them and said: 'We have been waiting these many years for someone to come and listen to our story, and now you have come at last. . . .' But I was oppressed by the loneliness and went on my way, pushing through the tangled bushes, down this lonely road towards the coast."

The author of this book felt like that when, in February 1929, he was assigned by the editor of a newspaper to take the longish journey from Paddington Station, London, to the very isolated manor, or farmstead, of Allercott, near Timberscombe, which is some miles from Minehead on the Bristol Channel, the old Somerset haunt of late eighteenth-century pirates, wreckers and smugglers. For fourteen years this old place of Allercott had lain derelict and empty. All over its ruined brick walls and lichened grey-tiled roof was an aura of mystery. I have looked up what I wrote in my diary about this eerie farmhouse:

"A spell like that of the Sleeping Beauty's palace is on this old farmhouse: but, unlike the stories of long deserted houses in Chelsea, there is here no legend of a cob-webbed bridal room and table festooned with years-old layers of dust; or of a ghost, at midnight, gliding along dark corridors, and, in the angles where the moon shines moaning and gibbering and wringing skeleton hands. All round this Allercott farmhouse stretch waterlogged pastures, over which unbroken horses and wild cattle gallop and lumber madly away at the sight of a stranger. Tons of rubbish lie in the yard and the barns and ricks have thatches of green grass growing at their tops and ridges. As I touched the handrail of a ladder leading to the upper loft of a barn, it broke away under my fingers, owing to dry rot. I peered through broken windowpanes, and saw tattered curtains and rotten casements, also mouldered chairs and a mildewed sofa. I even startled a colony of rabbits who had made a warren among what must once have been choice furniture of period style. At the front door, whose timber has been blistered and weathered by years of sun and wind and rain, I attempted to force a way into a hall. All I managed to do was to tear my hands and trousers on the fierce thorns of rambler-roses which have long ago shut in the entrance to the partly collapsed doorway. It had made a quite impenetrable hedge I went round to the door at the back and, entering the kitchen, through a window long since denuded of its glass panes, saw cups and saucers and plates, covered by a layer of dust and birds' droppings. Many years ago a meal must have been laid hereon. . . . But where was the rich old lady who had once lived in this house? . . . 'We can't tell ee that,' said a rosy-cheeked young woman I saw, standing outside a cottage in a village, a mile away from the old farm. 'My husband, who is away hedging and ditching could ha' told ee how the old lady never let strangers come into Allercott farmhouse. If they come to pay her rent, or money for fruit or corn, which was when the place was cultivated, and not in the rack and ruin it has been for years now, she allus made 'em drop the money into a bowl of water that she had on the hall table for the purpose. She was mortal finicky, she was! No, what became of her we never knew; nor has any friend or relative of hers come there since.' "

Was it a case of murder? If so, the Somerset County Police do not appear to have found any evidence of it. So far as one could find, the old lady just folded up her tent, one morning, or night, and quite unlike any desert Arab, stole silently away in what was the second year of the First World War. But, if so, how account for the obvious preparations for a meal which was left uneaten? There may be a simple explanation of the mystery; but it is to be noted that it is by no means a "simple" matter to find such an explanation!

In all my varied experience as a newspaper man investigating mysteries, I have never, except in the case of the enigma of Bruges (described in this book), come across a weirder story than that of the "Skeleton in the Cylinder." This Grand Guignolesque thriller opened on a summer day in the last year of the Second World War, 1945, when some U.S. soldiers were running a bulldozer over a bombed site, behind a Methodist chapel in Liverpool. They had returned to quarters for the night when a man strolled on to the site and casually poked about among the debris. His attention was attracted by a peculiar cylinder which he could not force open. He told the police, who got a mechanic to prise off some iron bolts and rivets. They made a macabre discovery. Inside the cylinder was the partly decomposed corpse of a man, lying on dirty sacking. He had evidently lain there a long time, for part of the cranium was missing, although hair still adhered to the skull. A closer examination disclosed what appeared to be diaries, and one of the entries read:

"June 1885 . . . meeting . . . 1 p.m., F. C. Gr——dy . . . at Cons."

There were other papers, including five account sheets, all badly decayed. On one sheet there could be made out the name of a firm: "T. C. Williams and Co., Leeds Street, Liverpool" and a truncated date: "18 . . ." The police who, it must be said, did not appear to make a very good job of the investigations, recorded for the coroner at the inquest that:

"A postcard was found on the body, bearing the name of T. C. Williams, and written by a man named A. E. Harris on 3 July, 1885. The postmark was blurred and cannot be deciphered. There was a handkerchief, not marked with initials or laundry signs. Also a worn signet ring, hall-marked 'London 1859'. No money was in the corpse's pockets, and no other valuables. A brooch was also found in the cylinder."

The coroner's inquest returned an open verdict and the coroner said it was impossible to ascertain the cause of death, which might have happened sixty years ago. "I do not doubt," he sapiently said, "that the man had crawled into the cylinder. He wore clothing of good mid-Victorian quality."

"Crawled into the cylinder?" Why? On the face of it, this affair has the air of being a perfect murder veiled by the passage of many years. Why, too, did not the Liverpool C.I.D. examine the Liverpool newspaper and directories of the year 1885 and 1886, to be found in one national library and accessible, if not at the British Museum Newspaper Library, certainly at Liverpool newspaper offices, to which common law gives right of access to police or public. It is likely, too, that if a man had been reported missing in Liverpool in 1885 or 1886, the police would have had a record of him, and he may have been the man with the name of "A. E. Harris." Was any relative or descendant of T. C. Williams of this concern still alive in 1945? If so, it does not appear that the Liverpool police exerted themselves to find out; nor did the coroner make any obvious comments. Suppose, too, that "A. E. Harris" did *not* crawl into the cylinder, as this coroner suggested, but was *pushed into it*—which is consonant with the obvious deduction that "A. E. Harris," or the man who became a corpse could hardly have bolted himself into the cylinder? Here are all the elements of a mystery that would have delighted Sherlock Holmes, and have rightly called down from him some sardonic comments on both police and coroner. Admittedly, it is unlikely that a suspect or suspects might still be alive.

This was not the only mystery of a missing man in the last year of the Second World War. Two youths were exploring a pothole—a deep inlet to subterranean caves, or streams in the Peak district of Derbyshire, or the Pennines, in Yorkshire. They were in a Yorkshire ravine called Trow Ghyll. Heaving up stones which barred the entrance, they crawled into a cave and were startled to find a pair of shoes and, close to them, a man's skeleton. They had the impression that someone had barred the entrance to this cave with stones. Near the pelvis of the remains was a phial whose contents, when analysed later, proved to be sodium cyanide. A toxicologist and a forensic expert said they had never seen a phial so queerly shaped. Probably it had been used by a naturalist who was an entomologist. The police searched this cave and found in it a compass, shaving tackle, latchkey, two pairs of shoes, and a fountain-pen. If this were a case of suicide, or accident, *who had barred the entrance with stones?*

A week later, speleologists were exploring a cave a few miles from this first cave of Trow Ghyll, called Gap Ghyll, being a 360-foot-deep pothole. Here *another skeleton* was found! In order to reach it police had to descend a deep chasm in a bosun's chair. A police surgeon said that this skeleton, as the other in Trow Ghyll, showed no sign of bones or skulls and, in both cases, it could not be established how long these men had been dead. One theory was that the skeletons may have been those of two German Nazi spies dropped when the men were alive, over this wild region by parachutes from a German plane on a secret mission. But again, the question arises: who blocked the entrance to the Trow Ghyll cave with stones? How, too, came it that these two skeletons were found in caves some miles apart? One cave was accessible, the other could be only by a bosun's chair. If, too, these two mystery men had committed suicide, why had they chosen so wild a region of moors and fells miles from any haunt of men? Why, too, had the man in the Gap Ghyll cave gone to so much trouble to scramble down a chasm 360 feet below the surface when he could have jumped off a rock? If, on the other hand, he was lowered there by someone else, had it been done after his possible murder? Or *was* he murdered in the cave?

In August, 1954, the U.S. Navy and the U.S. Air Force were confronted with an enigma to which no answer has been given:

(1): A well-found B25 bomber took off at 9 p.m., on 25 August 1954, from Mather Air Force base, with pilot and crew of eight, on a routine navigation flight. The base is near Sacramento, in central California. It had fuel enough to keep it airborne until 3.30 a.m. on 26 August. The pilot, Peter D. McArthur, was experienced and the crew comprised an instructor-pilot, three aviation cadets, and a student officer. Its last radio message said that it was heading north, in slight rain, about ten miles south of Modesto at an altitude of 2,500 feet. The bomber became overdue and all available U.S.A.F. planes were ordered into the skies to search for it. At 5 p.m. a search plane from Travis Air Force base spotted wreckage in rugged mountain terrain, and which was strewn over an area 500 to 1,000 feet from a mountaintop, five miles south-east of Monticello, near the Napa-Yoko border, fifty miles west of Sacramento. It looked as if the wrecked plane had ploughed right into the rocks. All aboard were dead.

(2): Right on the heels of this disaster another tragic discovery was made. Two U.S. Navy propeller-driven planes AD-6 Sky Raiders, attack planes, took off from Moffett Field on a routine flight of two hours to Fallon, Nevada. They never arrived, and their disappearance was called "baffling" by a Navy spokesman. He said: "It is very strange that both these planes have disappeared without a word from either to base." Thirteen aircraft searched all over the route they had taken—in vain! The mystery remains unsolved.

What is the hoodoo that haunts the air in this region of California? There are people who say that a sinister type of unidentified flying object, like a flying saucer, attacked them from a hiding-place in a cloud! May be or may be not. Who can say? Dead men tell no tales.

The scene now shifts from the sierras and lonely ranges, and Joshua tree and cocti-strewn deserts of California to the plains and farms of North Dakota, where another insoluble mystery occurred in the last week of October, 1956. A pretty four-year old boy, named La Vern Enget, walked out of his father's farmyard near Powers Lake, N. Dakota, on a Sunday afternoon, to help him bring in the cows from pasture. The farmer never saw the little boy in the field and, indeed, never saw him again. The mystery started a week-long search of the prairie by 3,000 North Dakotans. Hand in hand, they formed a human chain that combed every inch of the stubble and undulated land. Sloughs, thickets, potholes, and hollows were all probed and five dogs, one of them sent by the Royal Canadian Mounted Police, picked up the little boy's trail; but each time the scent faded out or led back to the farmhouse. Two helicopters and 42 light planes circled over an area of 135 square miles, and the National Guard were called out. In vain! The little boy has never been found. He was wearing only a light shirt and overalls, and at night the temperature in N. Dakota drops below zero.

Is this one more case of the mysterious phenomenon called teleportation? Who will ever know?

There is the strange case of the New Zealand schoolmaster, Mr. H. F. North, of Broadwood District High School, North Island, New Zealand, who, on a morning in September, 1953, kissed his wife good-bye and walked from home to his school. All that happened after that is a blank in his mind. Two weeks later he found himself *walking in a street in London, England,* with not the faintest idea of how he got there! Worried and puzzled, he made tracks for a police station, spoke to a desk sergeant, and, naturally, had grave difficulty in getting the police to take him seriously. If he were not mad, then was he trying to perpetrate a hoax, of which a dim view is taken by the Metropolitan Police?

"Better turn out your pockets," advised the sergeant. "Show us what identity papers you have."

Mr. North took out a passport which proved that he had left Wellington, N.Z., on 25 August, 1953, and arrived in London on 29 August. He said he had never in his life suffered from amnesia; but he had not the faintest recollection of where he had stayed in London. The police communicated with New Zealand House and found that Mr. North had been reported missing, but they could not trace any of his movements in London. Passage was booked for him on the liner *Rangitiki*, and he sailed home on 3 October, 1953. His last words were:

"I just don't know where I have been, nor what has happened. The last thing I recall is going to school in New Zealand. Neurologists say I have been suffering from amnesia and wanted to get as far away as I could from my everyday movements. But why should I? I don't remember."

One question, however, suggests itself: who paid the not inconsiderable airliner passage fare to London from New Zealand; since it seems very unlikely that a schoolmaster, on the way to school in New Zealand, with no thought of going beyond his school, would have been carrying in his pocket wallet the fairly large sum for a trip he had not planned to take?

The year 1954, in England, was remarkable for the mystery of the bus driver who unaccountably vanished from the pretty village of Canon Pyon, in Herefordshire. On a night of full moon early in December, Derek Saville, aged twenty-five, by calling a bus driver, kissed his sweetheart at the garden gate of her cottage, said he would meet her again next day, and then set off to walk down between the bare hedges of a quiet country lane, in the darkness, on his way to his garage, where he got on his bicycle and rode to his lodgings. That was the last ever seen of him. The mystery was further deepened when his bicycle was found, propped against the bole of an elm on the road he was riding over. All round is typical English countryside of apple and pear orchards, a few hop-fields, farms and isolated thatched cottages. A search by police in cars started and, for twenty-five miles round the village, woods were explored, ditches forked over, haystacks probed, barns searched, brooks and wells dragged and sounded, public house and tavern keepers questioned, railway stations and bus depots visited; but all to no avail. Detectives acted on the theory that, somewhere on the mile-long stretch of road between his garage and his lodgings, he may have been waylaid and murdered. But no clue was ever found, nor any notion formed whether he had for some reason dismounted from his machine and left it lying against a tree, or whether someone else had done so.

His sweetheart, Ivy Wood, whispered about some unknown and mysterious man who used to whistle in the darkness in the lane outside the cottage—some would-be rival swain?—and about how Derek Saville told her never to walk alone in the darkness. But if the vigorous young bus driver had been attacked in the lane, it seems strange that no sound of a violent disturbance carried in the darkness of a calm night, in a countryside where noises can be heard a long way off. The tyre of his bicycle was found to be punctured, which suggests that he had alighted from it and leant it against the tree. The road surface was also carefully examined for signs of footprints, or a struggle. Tracker dogs were used, but with no results. Any ground that showed signs of having been recently disturbed was dug up. Five hundred people were questioned by the police. His mother, who lives near Mitcheldean in Gloucestershire, said: "I know he is dead—but I should like to know just what happened." How far is intuition, in such cases, fallible?

The vanished bus driver had no money worries; for there were about £30 in wages and savings at his lodgings. One may ask: did the missing bus driver find himself walking some road, or lost in some wild place thousands of miles from Canon Pyon, and not have a ghost of an idea how he got there? Was it a case of "psychorrhagic diathesis", or predisposition in the direction of the phenomenon of teleportation? If so, recovery from the concurrent amnesia may take years. On the other hand, if he were murdered, is thwarted love in a village quite a valid enough motive to inspire an assassin to put his neck in the hangman's noose? Again, have the police been told *everything* by those concerned? As detectives know, vital clues may be unwittingly withheld from the police sleuths by those unaware of their importance.

A mystery of a very different character now flashes on our screen, which shifts its focus from law-abiding England to the uncanny lake called Rupkund, located north of Nainital, on the foothills of the Himalayas in Uttar Pradesh (former United Provinces of Agra and Oudh, in what used to be British India). Villagers in the hills roundabout shun this lake, which they say is "haunted." Here is a report from an Indian official journal:

> "An Indian officer of the Forestry Department, named H. K. Madhwal, had reported that while he was searching for rare plants on the slopes of Mount Trisul (23,500 feet), he and a party of natives reached an overhanging cleft in a rock and saw, with astonishment, a strange spectacle on the shores of a lake fed with snow-water. About 250 bodies, in tattered clothing, and with sightless eyes stared up at him. He said: 'There was no smell of putrefaction, the air being cold, clean and crystalline. Their flesh was blown up like an inflated rubber bag, and I should say they have been lying there *many years!* Who are they? The villagers, some miles away, say that their forefathers knew them and that these corpses must date back to the year 1250, and are men who lived in the eighteenth century. Anyway, the corpses have been on the shores of that lake for *many years*. Some have supposed, however, that they are the corpses of men, soldiers of the army of General Zorovar Singh who invaded Tibet in 1841.'"

This report was made in 1944 and the Indian Government could do nothing to investigate the mystery at that time. It is not known whether the present Indian Government sent an expedition of inquiry to the shores of Lake Rupkund in the summer of 1955.

A curious problem, associated with *some* cases of missing men and women, confronted Dr. J. W. Fleming of Tenby, West Wales, in July, 1955, and he drew attention to it in the pages of the *British Medical Journal*. He said that, in that month, he had to treat three holidaymakers:

> "(1): A professional man of fifty-five; (2): a twenty-year-old student; (3): a housewife of thirty-five. None of them have had any mental illness, or been in the sea or water for long. The student went into the sea at 5 p.m., but remembered no more until he woke up in bed, next morning. The professional man and the housewife had amnesia about what took place before they went swimming."

Dr. Fleming said that he had read in a newspaper a story about a bank clerk and cashier, Mr. John Wonnacott, of Yeovil, Somerset, aged thirty-seven. Wonnacott vanished for sixty-three days at Weymouth, and found himself in Bristol, sixty miles away as the crow flies, and with no idea how he got there. Wonnacott said: "I last recall undressing in my car and going for a swim in the sea. I remember no more." Dr. Fleming wanted to know if other medical men had had cases in which the sea, or sea-bathing had apparently induced amnesia. Of course, it by no means necessarily follows that the sea or sea-bathing is more than a concomitant, or had anything causal in relation to this phenomenon, which Myers, many years ago, called "psychorrhagic diathesis."

The case following is probably on a different footing; for there may be some other reason why the youth below reached no other port than the bourne of missing men and women. It is a case in which the slow passage of time and chance—the latter one of the greatest, if most unpredictable of detectives—revealed the fate of a missing person, but at the same time cast a deeper shadow over a mystery. We may summarize the case:

21 January, 1956: In a lonely part of North Tyne Forest, Northumberland, a man, wandering by the side of a ditch saw, under a layer of pine cones and dead leaves, a skeleton. He might not have noticed it but for the accident of the sinking sun falling on the spot through a gap in the pine trees. The police were informed and, on searching around, found a pair of brown shoes and part of some trousers. The police records show that *six years ago*, in May, 1950, a young fellow named James Beattie, told his father, a farmer, that he was going for a cycle ride from the farm at Binks, Teviothead. That was the last seen or heard of him. A bicycle was later found after he was reported missing. It was found near where the skeleton was discovered in 1956.

Questions arise: how did the skeleton of James Beattie come to be in that ditch in this lonely forest? Like the missing bus driver of Canon Pyon, Herefordshire, he had apparently left his cycle but, unlike him, wandered into the wood. Why did he not return? Was it a case of murder by someone who did not ride away on his bicycle, lest it be identified? If it was a murder, what was the motive? Again, if there is a forester attached to this wood, why was the skeleton or the corpse not sighted long before? We may, or may not have, here, a case of a "perfect murder." Who can answer these questions after the passage of six long years which has annihilated every clue?

Some years ago, in a book of mine, I drew attention to the "jinx," or hoodoo which, in 1946, seemed to hang over the waters of the Bahamas, where British airliners, and U.S. military planes and all their pilots, passengers and crew vanished without trace.

Consider the following:

20 *March*, 1956: Five people—two men, two women and the pilot—flew from the Bahamas, bound for Miami, Florida. They never arrived. The wreckage of their plane was found ten miles west of Rock Sound, Eleuthera (Bahamas), scattered over an area of 100 feet and in ten feet of water. Their bodies have not been recovered.

Why was no radio signal sent out from this plane?
The same question may be asked in the case below:

6 *April*, 1956: Search planes have hunted over three states for a clue to the mystery of the secret Lockheed jet plane on an experimental flight over Nevada. They were on a high altitude test flight concerned with weather reconnaissance. No signal was received, and neither plane, nor pilot and crew can be found.

Some "screwball" people in U.S.A. suggested that the plane had been struck down by "something" aloft. May be, or not, but, in so rugged and mountainous a region as Nevada, gorge and *cañons* may hold secrets not revealed for years, or never! But the mounting toll of jet planes and airliner and military planes in these western and other regions of the U.S.A. is known to have caused grave concern in official quarters in the years 1954–7.

As we have seen above, caves and "subterraneans" may all lead to the port of missing men; and so may military forts and old colliery workings. In 1928 there was a report about the total cessation of work for one week at Bedlington Colliery, Northumberland, while all underground workers tried to solve the riddle of a very strange occurrence. A miner had left the base of the shaft to walk about half a mile along a road that led to the part of the coal face where he was to relieve a mate at hewing. He never arrived and what happened to him, somewhere along that half-mile, is an insoluble mystery. Each side of the road was boarded by stout timber palisades, interrupted at intervals with heavy timber doors, all padlocked. On the other side lay abandoned galleries, old mine workings and deep pits full of water. Not one of these doors had been opened, nor could any sign be found indicating that the miner had tried to scale the tall fence—for which, indeed, he could have no conceivable motive. After a week of intensive search of the long-abandoned workings, in which every hole was plumbed, not a clue to the fate of the missing miner was ever discovered.

In the well-known Cheddar Caves, in a gorge of the Mendips, in Somerset, there is what is called the "Spinning Hole." A young fellow, in June, 1929, entered there without guide or equipment and never returned to the light of day. For twelve days the search continued and, on the thirteenth, his dead body was found in a labyrinth. None of these witless and adventurous fellows ever think to take with them a ball of twine, or reel of strong thread; nor does it seem to occur to them that where such labyrinths are unexplored, even men not alone must expect to meet chasms in floors and rushing torrents, or deep subterranean lakes. And there are also the phenomena of strange noises and eerie acoustics which are calculated to shock the nerves of a man who has ventured in alone.

For example, as in the Wookey Caves, in the same region, no one has ever explained the eerie noises like horses galloping, groans and bubbling noises like sounds emitted by drowning or dying men, and crashing and reverberating roars which rise to a crescendo and as suddenly cease. To attribute them to air-locks is very unconvincing. Wookey, indeed, as a *carved* stalagmite shows—it is like a bearded man, or bearded female witch, and those who have closely examined it may conclude, as did the author of this book, in 1946, that it is *more* than the work of nature and water—was, in a very far day, used in necromantic rites involving human sacrifices. Human skulls have been dug up on the floor of the subterranean River Axe, in this Wookey cavern, below where the bearded stalagmite looms like some ancient god of fertility, or like the Palaeolithic magician with the hypnotic eyes, who is found in a nearly inaccessible reach of the wonderful painted caverns of Ariège. Has "something" left its abiding traces in this (Wookey's) gloomy underworld?

Few people will suppose that an old fort can lead to the port of missing men. Look at the following summary:

24 *April*, 1956: At Tavannes, not far from the Argonne, famous for the twenty-day-long battle between the Germans and the French and American armies in 1918, there is a tremendous tunnel dominated by the fort which defended the place de Verdun, in the First World War. Tavannes is an old, long disused subterranean fort, built by French military engineers about 1690. Galleries branch off in all directions, some of them dating from 1746.

On 21 April, 1956, Private First Class Gerrard Donnington, of the U.S. Army, who had come to Tavannes with his wife and two children, set off alone to explore these underground galleries. Possibly, he had the idea of finding some souvenirs of past wars. Night came and he had not returned. His alarmed wife went to the police of Verdun, who informed the U.S. Army authorities. Five hundred men started rescue operations. A broken plant was found at the top of one of the ventilation shafts, but no one can say if it were an indication that Connington had slipped, caught at the plant to save himself, and had tumbled down the shaft. Anyway, nothing was found at the bottom of this shaft. Power and light were laid on, a camp with kitchens set up, and French gendarmes were called in to keep back sightseers. All day and night digging went on. Rubble was cleared away from shafts. There came up a Monsieur Victor Pont, of Verdun who, during the Second World War, hid from Germans and the Gestapo and S.S., in these underground galleries. He said there was an underground railway that ran to the foot of the main shaft. But rescuers found that the railway tunnel was choked with fallen debris. Clearly, Donnington could not have entered *that* tunnel. All the galleries were explored, but Donnington was found nowhere in the labyrinth. Where had he gone? Echo answered with sullen roar of "Where?" He was never found. (*Summarized from French police reports*).

Even the hydrogen bomb has been indirectly responsible for a mystery of a lost air pilot:

15 *May*, 1956: Capt. J. E. Hall and an observer, Capt. Paul Crumley, took off in a small bomber on a mission to watch a test explosion of a thermo-nuclear bomb at Eniwetok Island, S. Pacific. At a height of 24,000 feet the plane went out of control and the pilot ordered Crumley to quit, and he himself used the ejector seat. Hall was later picked up by a destroyer who found him on a one-man raft; but of Crumley there has never been

found a trace, by warships and planes which searched for him.

On 6 June, 1956, there occurred another of the mysterious incidents which seem to involve teleportation. A strange man was found by the police wandering in the streets of New York City. He was not an American, and he had no papers. He appeared in a daze, and when, at the police station he recovered from his amnesia, he said: "How do I come to be here in New York? I am Thomas R. Kessell, and I work at a brewery in Johannesburg, South Africa. I have never in my life been abroad, nor have I ever had a passport. The last thing I can remember was taking a drink in a pub at Johannesburg, in April." The police could not find that any plane or ship had landed him in U.S.A. The South African consul in New York had him shipped back by liner to Cape Town.

There occurred on 26 June, 1956, another of those mysterious aeroplane disasters which, as one has said above, have given the U.S. Navy and the U.S. Air Force officially undisclosed apprehensions of what may be aloft, unseen and unsuspected, whenever these incidents happen:

26 *June*, 1956: A jet fighter plane, (9F 6F Conger), piloted by Lieut. Gordon Bennett, took off at 12.30 p.m. from Alameda Naval Air Station. North of the San-Francisco—Oakland Bridge the pilot *flew into a bank of cloud* about 1,800 feet up. He and the plane *were never seen again*. The Navy and Coast Guard searched and in the darkness of night found an oil wake near the Berkeley Pier. Whether it had any connexion with the missing plane, no one knows. A sample of the wake was taken for analysis, in order to determine the possible petrol content. But, of course, the wake may arise from some submarine oil field. The salvage department sent down divers to the bottom of the San Francisco Bay; but they found no plane wreckage.

"Flew into a cloud?" How often has that occurred in 1954–6, and the plane, or even planes concerned have never more been found? It is not enough to talk of "ascending currents" or cloud vortices. Why, in such cases, is no signal ever received from the cloud or the plane? *What lies hidden in such clouds?* Why, too, is no wreckage ever found? To where has such a plane, with pilot and crew gone? In this case, the phrase "port of missing men" may have a Wellsian connotation, and serve to point the warning given in New York, in 1956, by the famous General Douglas MacArthur, of "something sinister from out of space." Who yet knows? Indeed, shall we ever know the solution of this mystery? No wonder the Air Forces in Britain and U.S.A. keep secret all files referring to such events, and not even a really pertinacious British M.P. can extract from an Air Minister or Parliamentary Secretary more than an evasive and misleading reply. Do the high officers lead the Minister by the nose; or is he a willing accomplice in hiding the facts from the public?

I have dealt more at large with these recent baffling mysteries of military and civilian air transport, in the chapter following; since it seems that they may recur in the years to come, and we may arrive at only a very partial solution of the mystery by comparing and collating the circumstances of similar events and phenomena. The age of space voyaging, although far from "round the corner," is about to dawn; so that the subject is topical.

Let us, in this age of "sputniks" and projects of landing on the "dead," or not so "dead" moon, look at some mysteries of the skies and the air. Who, even today, forty-one years afterwards, knows what happened to Zeppelin airship L.50, one of eleven which raided England 19—20 October, 1917?

Says Freiherr Treasch von Buttlar Brandenfels, in *Die Zeppelin-flugschiffe über England*:

"L. 50, the fifth and last Zeppelin which we lost in that raid, made a forced landing in the south of France, but four men of the crew were unable to leave her in time. After a difficult landing the airship rose again, drifted across the Alps, and vanished for ever. She was thought to have come down in the Mediterranean."

"Thought?" But who *knows* what befell her?

A mysterious affair of a Zeppelin raid of November, 1916, is the fate of Private John Thomas Hollinrake, of the Yorkshire and Lancashire regiment who was in camp at Cockenhall, Durham, on that night when a raiding Zeppelin was brought down in flames. One man was missing but no trace of him could be found. Six months later a skeleton in a tattered khaki overcoat was found in a ditch at Swalwell, near Newcastle-on-Tyne. There was nothing to identify the remains, and it looks as if one has, here, *two* mysteries unconnected with each other, and equally as baffling to explain as having any connexion whatever with the Zeppelin raider. Swalwell is a good many miles from the location of the military camp, so that death by bombing from the air seems ruled out, nor is desertion a probable theory. The skeleton was buried in Swalwell cemetery, and a headstone was placed over the grave:

"A soldier of the Great War, 7 May, 1917. Known unto God."

Women of the British Legion asked the War Graves Commission to investigate the mystery. Hollinrake's widow claimed a pension but her claim was not recognized until 1932, when the court presumed that the unknown man in Swalwell cemetery was her husband. May be: but since all soldiers at that time carried identity discs, and the man buried at Swalwell had not been in action at the front, why was not a disc found near the body?

In the 1920s, flights across the Atlantic, the ocean of all others with most mysteries of missing ships and men, were far from the commonplace events they now are in these days of turbo-jet airliners, sub-stratosphere passenger planes with pressurized cabins, and Comet jet lines; and when adventurous pilots took off to fly from Paris or London to New York, insurance companies did not regard them as "good risks." Two French airmen, "one-eyed" Coli, and Nungesser flew, on 8 May, 1927, from Paris out over the Atlantic westwards. They never arrived on the other side, and their very memory had been forgotten, except by the bereaved, when, suddenly, in March, 1933, two fishermen from the French islands of Miquelon and St. Pierre, off the southern shores of Newfoundland, arrived in Paris. They said:

"We have seen skeletons in the snow near a burnt-out wreck of a plane which we think is the 'White Bird' in which *Messieurs* Nungesser and Coli vanished."

The French Colonial Ministry ordered the governors of St. Pierre and Miquelon to make inquiries, although the officials in Newfoundland denied that any bodies had been found. The mystery remained unsolved. Then, in late October, 1935, two trappers in a little-frequented part of Northern New Brunswick reported that, in virgin forest, they had found wreckage covered with moss and lichen, and they believed it was part of the lost plane, "White Bird." The Royal Canadian Mounted Police were sent out to investigate; but once more the curtain shut down on this mystery.

Few today, except students of aeronautics, remember the once-famous Amy Johnson—she was Swedish by birth—who, on a tour of Australia, in the 1930s, was said, by satirical newspapermen there, to have collected all that was going in the way of rewards and honoraria. In January, 1941, during the Second World War, Amy took off at 10.45 a.m. on a Sunday, to fly on a mission for the Air Transport Auxiliary Service. She had enough petrol to last four and three-quarter hours. She said she would fly above the clouds, since the weather was inclement. Noon came and there was no news of her. Three hundred airfields were signalled, but none reported that she had landed. At 3.30 p.m., H. M. trawler, *Haslemere*, escorting a convoy off the Thames Estuary, saw a parachute descend through the low clouds, followed by a plane which was losing height and circling around. Finally the plane was seen to land in the sea close to the parachute. *Haslemere* and the ships of the convoy stood over towards the plane, and while a boat was being launched a "youngish woman was seen in the sea." The boat was about 120 yards away, and a seaman said he heard the woman call: "Hurry! Please help!" The seaman climbed on to the bulwarks and tried to reach her with lines, but the strong tide carried her away and she vanished. The gallant commander of the trawler, Lieut. Fletcher, R.N., saw another survivor near her in the sea. It seemed to be a man. Fletcher dived in and reached him, and held him up, but the tide swirled him round and he had to let him go. No trace was ever found of this mysterious man and Fletcher, after being rescued by the boat, died in a coma.

Was this "youngish woman" Amy Johnson? No one really knows; and the mystery was deepened since, while the rescuers positively affirmed they saw a man in the sea, and told the coroner so, at the inquest at Chatham, the Ministry of Aircraft Production denied that any man, or any passenger, had accompanied Amy in her plane. The identity of both has never been cleared up.

On 14 November, 1944, Sir Trafford Leigh-Mallory, Air Chief Marshal of the Royal Air Force, flew from Britain, with his wife, to take up a new post as Air Commander-in-Chief of the Southeast Asia Command. He was bound for Singapore or Hong Kong. Up to 17 October, 1944, he had been Commander-in-Chief of the Allied Expeditionary Air Force for the invasion of Europe. He never arrived, and was never heard of again. In June, 1945, a wrecked aircraft was found high in the Cottian Alps, east of Dauphiné, with eight bodies near it. One of them was alleged to be the skeleton, or corpse, of Leigh-Mallory, but no word came to confirm it. His fate and that of his wife remain a mystery.

There are occasions when the sudden emergency into the light of day of a missing person may, *if* it be confirmed, lead to the conclusion that an innocent man has paid the last penalty of the law. Such an incident happened in August, 1948. Sixteen years before—March 1932—the famous American airman, Colonel Lindbergh, had the misfortune to discover that his baby boy had vanished from a cot in a garden of a house at Hopewell, New Jersey. Kidnappers left behind a note demanding $50,000 ransom. The police made a search lasting two years and finally arrested Bernard Hauptmannn, a former German soldier of the First World War, after a body presumed to be that of the missing baby was found in a wood some miles from Hopewell. Hauptmann was sent to the electric chair. Sixteen years passed, and then, from a small village named Hoejby, sixty miles from Kjobnhavn, Denmark, a farmhand, aged eighteen, named Erik Nielsen, said he had reason to suppose that he was the missing son of Colonel Lindbergh. As so often happens in the mysteries, no more was ever heard of Erik Nielsen and his claim.

There are seas, such as in the neighbourhood of the Bahamas and Bermuda, and in the North Pacific, off Japan, over which seems to loom a sinister "hoodoo." For example, just over three years after the close of the Second World War, two British airliners, *Star Tiger* and *Star Ariel*, vanished over that sea of weed called Sargasso, which lies in the North Atlantic, north of the Bahamas, and covers an area as large as Spain. *Star Ariel* vanished on 17 January, 1949, and *Star Tiger* thirteen days later. No distress signals came from either airliner. The Brabazon committee investigated the mystery, and even took to pieces and examined in detail a sister airliner, but they could arrive at no solution. Theories that there may have been a discharge of methol bromide, carried in the airliners' extincteurs and accidentally circulated in the pressurization system remained theories, since not a trace of any wreckage was ever found. Numbers of people, even pilots, were inclined to believe that the missing airliners encountered extraneous events unconnected with themselves. In the month of December, 1949, nine planes vanished without trace off the coast of Florida, and, again, not a bit of wreckage, or any trace of the 108 people aboard was ever found. A few days before *Star Ariel* vanished, a charter plane radioed that it was fifty miles from Miama, Florida, and that "all was well." But it vanished without trace, and all its thirty-three people. So many were the missing American and British planes in this region that there was talk of a "hoodoo" in the Caribbean and off Bermuda.

In the case of *Star Ariel,* a further mystifying sighting was reported. Two aircraft, a British BOAC plane, and a U.S. bomber saw a strange light on the sea before dawn, about three hundred miles south of Bermuda, and a floating object which reflected the moonlight. Somewhere in that area, *Star Ariel* had vanished without trace. Even when destroyers searched, in company with seven U.S. Coastguard and naval planes, flying wing tip to wing tip, criss-crossing the area of the ocean, nothing was found.

Another mystery, recalling the circumstances of the vanished British Lancastrian airliner *Star Dust,*[*] occurred in the last week of January, 1951, this time somewhere between Accra, on the African Gold Coast and Roberts Field airport, in Liberia, Western Africa. The Pan American airliner, Constellation, bound from Johannesburg to New York, radioed from somewhere in the Gulf of Guinea, at 3 a.m., that she would land on the Liberian airfield at 3.15 a.m. She, too, vanished in that fifteen minutes! There were forty people aboard her. Twelve French planes took off from Dakar, and were joined by British planes; but after an exhaustive quartering of the Gulf and the North Atlantic, nothing was found.

This mystery is as insoluble and disquieting as the strange loss of a four-engined Globemaster, which, in 1956, found two of her engines unaccountably stop at a certain latitude and longitude in the Atlantic, south of Iceland. She had grave difficulty in limping to her airport in Iceland. A few days later, when on the return trip, *via* Goose Bay, Labrador, to her base in Florida, the same Globemaster found *all* four engines suddenly go out of action *at the same latitude and longitude!* All that was found of her was a solitary broken raft after a prolonged search of the region by many planes and warships. The overworked theory of coincidence hardly seems to explain this riddle. Nor did the Globemaster run "out of petrol." Did something aloft, perhaps unseen in

---

[*]*Star Dust* vanished mysteriously in *three minutes,* after radioing, on 12 August, 1947, that she was coming in to land at the Chilian airport of Santiago. Her last message was followed by a mysterious word "Stendec," thrice rapidly repeated, which has never been deciphered. Reports that wreckage of her was found on the Andes in December, 1955, proved untrue. Not a strut, not a bone of her passengers and crew was ever found.

the sky, or/and something equally unseen below water, put on her what, in the First World War, was called a "death ray," that immobilized *all four engines?*

Who can say? On the old principle that if one has a mystery that in one time and one place appears without solution, one should wait until something similar happens elsewhere, one may draw attention to the widely reported—in the U.S. press—incident of a Negro motor-lorry driver who, on 3 November, 1957, saw a mysterious thing he called "a big light, 200 feet long, and shaped like an egg," parked in a lonely road four miles from Levelland, Texas. He told the police that when he drove near it his engines suddenly stopped, and his lights went out, but when the mysterious thing rose into the air his engine and lights came on again! No doubt the police would have concluded that the poor black, who fainted from fright, had had "one over the eight;" but another man reported the same phenomenon in the same region that night, and three patrol police saw the object. Possibly when, or if, some "sputnik" *does* reach and land on the moon, it may, if it ever returns to earth, report similar startling phenomena. In the new age of interplanetary travel we *may* become accustomed to almost any-

One may compare with this riddle of the Arctic Seas—but such riddles are *not* cnofined to those bleak and stormy northern waters!—the strange incident, below, which was "featured" in the whole American press:

22 *August,* 1956: A medium U.S. bomber being ferried from Iceland to France to be handed over to the French Air Force, took off from Keflavik Air Base, after dawn, in perfect weather. Twenty minutes later another U.S. plane took off from the same base for France. The later plane got a message from the base control at Keflavik; "Get contact with the first plane. We can get no reply from her." The second plane repeatedly signalled the first, but had no reply. "This was strange," said her pilot, "for on a previous trip from the U.S.A. we were in constant radio contact with her, I cannot understand it!" An air-sea rescue found not a trace of the missing plane or of her crew of two.

Equally as enigmatic is the mystery of the lost pilot of a British Navy plane which "force-landed" on the sea off Korea in 1954, in sight of a carrier which sent a helicopter to take off the senior lieutenant who was acting as observer. The helicopter landed the lieutenant on the carrier and, in *three minutes,* returned to take off the pilot—*but where was he?* Not a sign of him was to be seen. There was the plane still afloat on the sea, and her young and husky pilot had vanished in *three minutes!* A naval court of inquiry was held—no report of the affair ever reached the press—but neither submarines nor sharks could be adduced to explain the mystery. The missing pilot was a strong swimmer. One might ask: what put the plane out of action, in the first place? No one knew.

In March, 1957, a double-decker U.S. military Stratocruiser, C.1927, vanished inexplicably when *two hours away from Tokyo*, to which she had been flying from Travis, an air force base in North California. For nine days eleven American planes searched some thousand square miles of the Pacific, south-east of Japan, and, at one time, seventy aircraft took part in the search. They found nothing of this giant plane, nor her sixty-seven occupants. What, then, befell giant C.1927?

We may answer with another question: what is "wrong" with an area called the "Devil's Sea," *south of Tokyo* and east of the Iwo Jima and Bonin islands? Eight ships have uncannily vanished in this vast ocean area between 1950 and 1954, with the loss of two hundred persons. The mystified Japanese maritime authorities have declared it a special danger zone. Wreckage of only two craft has been washed up, and not one corpse, or any clue to the mystery; albeit, an extensive air-sea search has been mounted. There was one interrupted radio flash which had the air of panic in the sender: "Sinking . . ." Then silence. Many of the ships had good engines and carried crews of about thirty each. One ship, the *Kaiyo Maru*, making scientific observations off the Myojin reef, was blown up by an underwater explosion, synchronizing with the rise of part of the reef as a steaming volcano; but submarine vulcanism cannot be adduced in the other eight cases. Japanese fishermen shun the region. In January, 1955, an organized sea-search was made of the "Devil's Sea," about seventy miles off the coast of Japan, when a tenth ship—surveying on scientific work—mysteriously vanished with fourteen persons.

One theory is that there may be *vortices* underwater, or "anti-gravity warps," such as exist at Gold Hill, Oregon, and near Santa Cruz in California, and also at one spot in Ayrshire, Scotland. These are localized areas where normal pull of gravity and magnetic attractions are distorted, so that strange optical effects are seen, and, in the Oregonian phenomenon, men of *equal* height, only a short distance apart, seem one taller, or one shorter, than the other. (The author of this book has some remarkable photographs of these

Oregon phenomena.) Recently, the newer physics has discovered evidence of the existence, not merely in theory, of anti-gravitational or contra-terrene particles of matter, of a nature completely contrary to those known on this planet, and also of appallingly explosive character when such *contra-terrene* matter comes into proximity with matter, as *we* know it, subject to the normal thrust or impulsion of gravity. It has been suggested that, perhaps—who can say?—fragments of very high density matter are embedded in *localized* areas of the earth. (They may or may not have arrived from outer space.) Is there such matter embedded in the crust under this "Devil's Sea" off Japan? Obviously, the question cannot be resolved without extensive geodetic research.

Again, are there "blind spots" in the ocean where fog signals cannot be heard, or where radar does not function? It may be recalled that, in a recent case of a collision between an Italian and a Swedish liner, off New York, one of the ship's captains alleged that his radarscope did not record signals of the presence of a near-by ship in fog. He said he had *not* seen the blips of the other ship before the collision. As long ago as July, 1929, the Canadian Pacific liner *Prince George* came into collision with the U.S. cutter, *Agassiz*, in a dense fog sixty miles east of Cape Ann off the New England coast, where such a "blind spot" rendered sound waves inaudible.

No one knows if this theory can be adduced in the case of an American naval patrol bomber plane which vanished in the Bermuda area of the Atlantic on 9 November, 1956. No radio signals were received. Six military American planes vanished in one month in 1956, one Marine Skyraider diving into the sea twelve miles off Kanahoe on 6 November, 1956, for no ascertainable reason. In ten years, admitted American Brigadier General Caldera, director of flight safety research, at Washington, D.C., 1,225 U.S. Air Force pilots have been killed and 1,600 planes destroyed, often in mysterious accidents, as when nine jet planes crashed to earth, without warning, in one morning in a Middle Western area. Sabotage did not explain *this* mystery.

Chapter 9

HOW DID THEY GET THERE?

THERE are mysteries of the fates of those who vanished in wars which the members of War Graves Commissions can never solve. It would be some slight consolation to relatives if they knew at least what had befallen their kith and kin. Rarely is the riddle resolved as it was in October, 1927, when a man was found lying comatose late at night in a street at Brighton, Sussex. The policeman who shone his torch on the man must have started back in wonder and even in horror; for the man had his right leg off at the knee, his left leg at the thigh, his left arm a stump, his right arm partly paralysed, his spine shattered, and part of his jaw replaced with a silver plate! This is what the poor fellow told the local magistrates:

> "I was in the battle of Jutland." (When, on 31 May, 1916, owing in part to the superior armour-piercing shells of the German fleet, and the inferior qualities of British armour-plate, at the time, a rumour, aided by a strange cable-silence, got around that Britain had been defeated, and so aided plotters in New York and London to rake in millions by currency-market rigging, *à la* Rothschild, at the battle of Waterloo. *Author.*) "My name is Patrick O'Malley. I was, at the battle, a first-class petty officer and gun-layer on the battleship, *Queen Mary,* and we were sunk by German shells. I got on to a floating mess-door, and stayed there, helpless with my wounds, until the Germans picked me up. They took me to Wilhelmshaven, where I spent ten years in an asylum for the insane. . . . Three weeks ago I was put on a steamer for Tilbury as I had regained my sanity. I want to go to London to see the Admiralty."

How he reached Brighton when London was nearer Tilbury was not stated. The magistrates gave him money from the poorbox to pay his fare to London.

In the same year another mystery was solved after the passing of ten years. It began when a motor truck, with many Italian soldiers, was rushed to the front lines in 1917, intended to stem the Austrian Army push in the Tyrolean Alps. In a night of pitch darkness, the truck lost its way and vanished utterly from sight and mind in the vast cavern of San Giacomo di Lusiana, on the Sette Camini plateau in the Tyrolese Alps. This vast cave is said to be 1,800 feet deep. Three years after the war some mountaineers entered the cavern and, in its recesses, found four corpses of soldiers resting on a ledge some 240 feet below the top floor; but when they sought to descend farther an uprush of foul air and gas warned them to desist. The mystery was left until ten years later, when, in 1931, the members on the

Italian Alpine Club came from Verona with ropes and gas-masks; but, again, no one ever heard that they reached the floor of these halls of Eblis, nearly 1,600 feet below where the corpses were found, and where may be the remains of the lorry and the men.

Across our screen of the macabre and mysterious now flashes a strange spectacle of hidden vaults near Laon, seventy-five miles north of Paris. These were taken by the German Army of von Kluck and remained in German hands, very little damaged, until October, 1918, at the end of the First World War. In the vaults were found, in April, 1928 the bodies of fifty German soldiers seated at tables in lifelike and singularly realistic and natural attitudes, as though they were as dead as slaughtered cows! Poison gas had seeped in and suddenly struck them dead as they were sitting fifteen years before.

Another macabre discovery was made in 1930 by men digging earth for a new drain in a field at Saulzy-sur-Moselle. It was the complete skeleton of a German soldier, still astride his horse, both dead for at least fifteen years! Fragments of harness and uniform indicated that he was a German, native of Ulm, in Württemberg. Near the skeleton was found a purse with a twenty-mark golden piece. A shell had fallen on him and his horse and buried them in a crater, and there he had remained all those years.

In October, 1929, at Warsaw, Poland, men digging canals in the suburbs lit on three skeletons, two men, the other a woman, and surgeons say the remains had lain there for fifteen years. But who were they in life? Varsovian memories stirred and tongues began to wag. A barber went to the police and said:

"One night in December, 1914, in the First World War, I met a large body of gendarmerie standing near several motor-cars whose lights had been extinguished. Some of the gendarmes were digging a hole where you have found these skeletons."

Someone else came forward and said that, about that time in 1914, three British Secret Service agents, operating in Warsaw, had discovered secrets gravely compromising the honour of the wife of a Tsarist Russian Minister. The agents were staying at the Hotel Bristol, when it was surmised they had been trapped and murdered by the enemy spy whom they had unearthed at some dirty work in Russia. It was in that month of 1914, that two British men and one woman left the hotel in a car and were never more heard of again. The British Ambassador in Petrograd made inquiries of the Russian Foreign Office and was told that an "accident" had befallen the three British: but this story was vehemently denied by a well-known agent, Captain Reilly, of the British Intelligence Service. Reilly, one of the mystery men of the First World War, was, it is believed, shot by the Russian Bolsheviks for alleged espionage, in June, 1926. Incidentally, this mystery uncovered another: the remarkable career of Reilly, which is never likely to be told.

There is the grim story of the mysterious disappearance of fifteen officers and men of the 5th Norfolk Regiment, including a company of gardeners from the Sandringham Estate, Norfolk, of the late King George V. In the terrible days of the Gallipoli heights campaign, in August, 1915, these men, led by Colonel Sir Horace Beauchamp, were ordered to go into dense bush to clear out Turkish snipers. They were held up by fierce machine-gun fire and were never heard of again. Four years after the end of the war, a private of a British regiment was buying supplies from a Turkish farm, which lay far over in what had been enemy terrain. He picked up a Norfolk badge from a field, and showed it to the farmer, who told a strange story:

> "When I came back to this farm, after the British had been forced to evacuate the Dardanelles, I found the whole place covered with the decomposing bodies of British soldiers. I had to throw them into the ravine, yonder, as the air was foul with gases."

An official of the War Graves Commission came along, with the unpleasant duty of dragging up these remains from the bottom of the ravine. There were 122 men. He could identify only two Norfolk privates.

What is the solution of the riddle following, which was reported in a newspaper at Baghdad, Iraq, in December, 1932?

> "Men of a caravan bringing carpets from Isfahan, Persia, say that when they were in the Luristan mountains, in Western Persia, they came on 200 skeletons in a ravine. Persian troops, chasing brigands who infest this region, also came on these bones; but as armies have marched and countermarched through these wild heights since the days of Iskander Beg (Alexander the Great), in the absence of relics of metal objects, there is no clue to the identity, or their age."

A riddle like this reminds one of the insoluble mystery of certain discoveries that were *not* made when the old *Great Eastern* transatlantic steamer was being broken up at Rock Ferry, about the 1880s. This old liner had an outer and an inner hull, and during construction the shipyard workers were numbered, each day, as they entered and left the space between the two hulls. One day it was found that a taciturn man and boy were missing, while the old liner was still on the stocks. No clue to the mystery was ever found, and when, some years later, the *Great Eastern* was being broken up, men, who supposed that the unlucky career of this steamer might, on lines of old maritime lore, be explained by the fact that she had a "Jonah" aboard her, remembered the mystery of the disappearance of this man and boy, and carefully examined the space between the two hulls. They found . . . *nothing*, nor any human remains among the ship's debris! Here was certainly a case, as in the Luristan ravine, where dead men, present and not present, tell no tales.

To this day, eighteen years later, no one has ever been able to say what exactly was the genesis of a queer story told in the height of the Second World War, in 1940. A woman, travelling in a train from Marylebone Station to a place in the Vale of Aylesbury, saw, when the train was passing Rickmansworth, one of two nuns drop a book she was reading. As the nun stooped to pick the book up, the woman saw emerge from the sleeve of the nun's black *soutane* what she said was a hairy sinewy hand of, not a woman, but a *man!* Pretending not to have noticed the odd incident, the woman called the guard when the train stopped at Wendover, and he asked the stationmaster to telephone the Buckinghamshire police that two suspected spies, disguised as nuns, were in his train. Quite a wartime thriller! But, as one heard the same story told of a man who alleged he saw one of these "two nuns," in a train from Plymouth to Paddington, dropping a handkerchief and showing a man's tattooed arm, and had the train held up at a junction in order to have the "nuns" arrested, one wonders if this were just a war myth. Who, however, started it?

On Sunday, 27 October, 1940, a mystery of another type was reported when a shepherd, looking after sheep on the Sussex Downs, near Firle, not far from Lewes, said he was startled, when he happened to look up at the sky, to see how the weather was framing, a white line spread across the blue and from it a figure of Christ on the Cross formed slowly and clearly. He was reported to have said—to a reporter—that "angels with harps accompanied the figure." Later, when he was questioned by a man from another London newspaper, the shepherd seemed rather to back away from the story. "I never saw such a line in my life," said he, "but them villagers, below, in Firle, they say *they* saw it!" It seemed that the villagers, or some of them, affirmed that they *had* seen the phenomenon, and some person at Croydon, Surrey, also affirmed that he, or she, had seen an angel with a harp in the sky. Of course, the London newspaper columnists, in true "feature" style, professed themselves unable to solve the mystery; but, while that may very well be so, the author of this book may, first, point out that this phenomenon has *not* a religious basis confined to Christianity of an unorthodox or superstitious type. In 1937, Nazis, at one North German town, claimed to have seen the swastika emblazoned supernormally in the sky; while, in 1939, Finnish troops, holding the Mannerheim Line against Russian Soviet troops, declared that *they* had seen angels in the sky. Far from this phenomenon being new, it is very ancient.

It was witnessed by monks and townsmen at Dunstable, in 1138, and, again, in A.D. 1164. Indeed, there are numerous records of this phenomenon recorded in the monastic chronicles all through the Middle Ages. A woman wrote me that at Bath, Somerset, about 1905, after a very violent electrical storm, she saw frightened people on their knees in the streets, gazing up at a cross, or crucifix which they said they saw in the sky. The author of this book fears that this woman was far from pleased when he pointed out to her that it is *not*, as she urged, in her letter, "a wonderful manifestation of the truth of mystical Christianity."

What then is the explanation of this strange thing?

It is one of the numerous proofs that there is nothing stranger than the latent powers of the human mind. The phenomenon is psycho-neural and may occur in times of emotion, fear, and stress; so that visual images appear to be photographed on a background of clouds. It is *subjective* and not objective in character, and may even border on the psychotic, which means that some see such images or phantasmal appearances, and others, on the same spot at the same time, do *not*. Thus, in 1594, near Harmstedt, in Transylvania, people swore they saw, in the sky, the letters and date following: "INRI MDLVII ARE INENDEDISES REICHS." At Freiburg, also in 1594, people said they saw the form of Jesus Christ sitting on a rainbow, "as if to announce the Last Judgment." In September, 1556, people at the Hungarian town, then called "Babatcha," saw, after sunrise, two naked boys fighting with short swords in the sky, and with shields on their arms. Other visual images seen in the sky were a dead man on a bier, in 1594, with many figures in black carrying trumpets (over Saxony); men in the sky over old Rome in 213 B.C.; giant men in sky over Wittenberg, Prussia, in 1553; a flaming cross with a man in the clouds over Italy in 1118. There are many such records in old annals, incunabula, and chronicles, which it is unnecessary to cite here. Again, one may comment that there is nothing stranger than the human mind, especially in times of war and tumult.

At the time of the invasion of North Africa by the British and Americans in the Second World War, a chief petty officer, Dick Foxall, looked up, as he said, "for ten days from the deck of the submarine mother ship, *Maidstone*, gazing at an immense black cloud which helped to protect the armada, then assembled, from the massed attacks of Nazi bombers...."

He added:

"It was like the calm seas for days on end at Dunkirk; and, with the sea like a car park the Germans could not have missed killing hundreds of men. I was not alone in thinking that Providence set the cloud there."

Whether this is more than a pathetic fallacy, one must leave to the reader's judgment.

Ten years before on the same North African coast at Rabat, Morocco, the French authorities were puzzled by a boat, half submerged, washed up on the shore, and a corpse, near it, so badly decomposed that its nationality could not be told. On the boat was painted a number: "RTL. 164," but the riddle remained unsolved.

What, too, lay behind the mystery of the skeleton of an unknown woman found in the hollow of a wych elm in Hagley Wood, Worcestershire, in 1943? The police were baffled, with no clue. In 1944, writing appeared on a wall in Birmingham, in which the name "Bella" occurred, and for some reason that did not appear certain Midland coteries assumed the name "Bella" to be that of the skeleton in the wych elm. There was talk of witchcraft, black magic and ritual murder of the sort that marked the unsolved murder in a lonely field at the foot of Meon Hill, near the picturesque Tudor timbered village of Lower Quinton, near Stratford-upon-Avon when, two years later, the body of an old man was found horribly knifed, and with a ritual cross cut on the skin of his chest. (Although several people in Lower Quinton knew the murderer, even Scotland Yard, aided by a Royal Air Force plane and after questioning men over a radius as far as Salisbury, Wilts, never could solve that crime.) Ten years later, in October, 1953, the mysterious skeleton of Hagley Wood came again into the limelight, when a superintendent of the Worchestershire C.I.D. had a letter from a correspondent in the quite farming township of Claverley, near Wolverhampton. The writer signed herself "Anna," and according to the policeman, was a "foreigner of intelligence."

She wrote:

> "You will never solve the mystery of 'Bella,' found in the hollow tree in the woods at Hagley. The one person who could have given you an answer is now beyond your jurisdiction. The affair is one in which the murder was committed by a person who died in 1942, and the victim was Dutch, arriving in England in the war year, and illegally, 1941."

It seems that a specialist in forensic and judicial medicine, who examined the skeleton, believed that the murder had been committed a year before the skeleton was found in the hollow tree. No one named "Anna" was known at Claverley, but it *was* known that during the last war, men of the Dutch Army were stationed in a camp at Wrottesley Park, near Wolverhampton, and that many Dutch women secretly entered England when their own country was overrun by the Germans.

A mystery of a missing British secret agent that would never have been solved but for one of those million-to-one flukes of the long arm of chance, came to light after the Second World War. It is a case of almost incredible coincidence on which no novelist would build a story and few readers would accept as possible. On 23 January, 1943, the body of a man was found, by chance, at the bottom of a disused, very deep, well in a lonely place called Tanus, some thirty-five miles from Toulouse. There were three bullet wounds in the body, and a boulder had been tied to the neck. But there was no clue to his identity. Years passed, and then one summer day an Englishman chanced to be in the region when his car broke down, and he had to stay the night in the village *auberge*, or inn. Over a bottle of wine that night he was chatting with the *patron* when he chanced to hear about the mystery of the body found in the well, on the edge of the village. Certain of the details stuck in his memory and, after his return to England, he happened to meet, at dinner, and chat with the wife of a Captain Christopher James Lord who, said the lady, had been a secret service agent in the confidential file of the British Foreign Office. He had disappeared in summer of 1943, and no one had ever been able to trace him. "But," added the lady, who herself had served throughout the war with the French equivalent of the A.T.S. "what you say of this unknown body makes me believe, if my intuitions are not at fault, that the mystery man was my husband." What was also very queer was that the man whose car broke down was actually the brother-in-law of the man found in the well, and that he had not suspected the connexion when the *patron* was telling his story!

Mrs. Lord went to France, had the body exhumed, and identified it as that of her missing husband. She recognized his goldfilled tooth and a broken ankle he had suffered during a parachute jump. Also, the hair of the corpse was white, and she knew that when he had escaped from France with her, his wife, during the Nazi occupation in 1940, his hair had turned from gold to white. He had been at Antwerp when the Germans marched in, and had left his job at the bank to escape to Paris. When he was reported missing in France, in 1943, on a secret mission for the British War Office, a French newspaper said that he had been executed by the *maquis*, or underground resistance, because he had "bungled his mission and imperilled the lives of his associates" and the French newspaper alleged that this had been done "on the orders of the British War Office."

But the Foreign Office categorically denied the story. Captain Lord was not killed on any instructions, express or implied, by the War Office, which, indeed, had no knowledge of his death. Lord had never at any time been "a double agent" whom the *maquis* had had to eliminate. Neither was there any evidence that he had betrayed his mission or his associates.

Two Scotland Yard officers were delegated to inquire; but they could throw no light on the riddle. Although the file of Lord remains open today, the mystery still remains unsolved. Moreover, since the records of M.I.5, formerly a War Office intelligence section but now part of the organization of the Joint General Staffs, were destroyed by enemy action in an air raid on London, no light can, obviously, be hoped for from that quarter. No War Office of any country, least of all Great Britain, ever officially knows anything about a secret agent or his contacts, or, if it did, would ever reveal them. It is unlikely, unless chance—*if* it be chance!—moves again, that it will ever be known who killed Lord, and why! He is one of the legions that never were listed, and whose name will never appear on the roll of honour to which he is entitled.

Here follows, too, a mystery that only time may reveal, and probably will not: what happened to Private John R. Ellis, wounded in North Africa, in November, 1942, and suffering from acute neurosis, when he vanished from a field hospital on 4 December, 1942? He was reported as "missing." Six years later, a man, looking old and haggard, walked into Bootle Street police station, in Manchester, and said his memory was gone. He knew only his name, and seemed to recall a "place called Rhyl, many years ago." But he could not remember what he had done, where he had wandered, or how he had lived between December 1942 and December 1948.

In December, 1944, an American Army officer was shot in the head by Italian Army partisans, and his body thrown into Lake Orta. He was reported: "Missing. Fate unknown." Twelve years passed and, one day, a corpse was fished up from this fresh-water lake, and an autopsy revealed a most amazing feature. A New York radiologist, Dr. Walter Lentino reported:

"This body is in a most remarkable state of preservation, skin intact, size, shape and location of internal organs like those of a body freshly examined, although it has been six years (*sic*) immersed. . . . But when the tissues of the various organs are examined, it is seen that the individual cells and tissues are found to have dissolved; so that it is impossible to tell from what organ they came. We can merely tentatively say that he is the missing U.S. Army officer. But the examination may serve in saying how long an unidentified body has been submerged."

How many people who travel by diesel-electric trains know that an unsolved mystery is connected with their creator? It may be called a "First World War mystery." On the night of 29 December, 1913, eight months before the outbreak of the First World War, a great German mechanical genius sailed by the Harwich steamer from Antwerp. He was to have entrained for London, there to meet Admiralty officials and capitalists, who were keenly interested in a remarkable engine he had invented. His name was Rudolf Diesel. He never reached Harwich, and his non-arrival and what had happened to him remained a mystery. He was said to have been followed by a German secret agent and done away with, in order to prevent the British from acquiring his secrets. In 1915, a German prisoner of war was said to have revealed that, on instructions from the German Secret Service, he had pushed the traitor, Diesel, overboard. Diesel was a poor and brilliant inventor, the son of a German factory mechanic, but born in Paris, France.

The famous combine of Krupps, of Westfalen and the Ruhr, had originally backed him up; but Diesel ran against the powerful vested interests of American manufacturers' rings, and could make no headway with his engine, which, he said, was the most efficient in the world. Another version of the mystery of his fate has also been put forward: that he was a poor inventor and proud, owed £75,000, had assets of no more than £1,500, was too proud to beg from friends—as a matter of fact, few men in *his* position have that sort of friends!—and decided to put an end to his troubles by jumping off the steamer. But this story sounds very improbable when one recalls that he was on the way to London where, with an invention like his, and a world war known by the Admiralty to be imminent, he had reasonable prospects of success.

It seems rational to suppose that the mystery of his death remains unsolved. War and certain powerful financial interests know no law. He may well have been the victim of a powerful and ruthless foreign secret service, to whom the death of one man, and a brilliant inventor at that, with a creation of an engine of great war and military and naval importance, would have been a small affair, to be easily contrived by foul means that the night and the sea would cover. Why he was not escorted and guarded, while on board the cross-channel steamer, cannot be known.

The 1950s have been noteworthy for riddles, and here follows one which may be linked with the unknown fate of some soldier or sailor to which war and navy departments, or mercantile fleets, have not the shadow of a clue. It occurs in a very brief paragraph in an Amsterdam daily:

"7 *May*, 1950: On the body of a *headless* man cast by the North Sea tides on to the beach of Scheveningen, this morning, English coins have been found; but there is no clue to his identity or fate. It may be murder, or suicide, and whether the head was decapitated by contact with a ship's propeller, or eaten by big fishes, cannot be said."

Poland, which has supped on horrors, in the world and other wars, and whose sons and heroes—or some of them—for years buried themselves in the sewers of Warsaw to emerge, by night and day, to fight the Nazis and the thugs of the Gestapo and Hitler's S.S., has seldom seen a stranger spectacle than that which was witnessed in summer 1951, and is here summarized from a Warsaw newspaper:

"15 *June*, 1951: People in the suburbs of the port of Gdynia, at Babi Doly, shouted, screamed and fled in terror, today, when a strange man, six feet tall, with hair reaching his knees, beard sweeping his waist, lurched like a drunken man, rubbing his eyes, from the debris of an underground air-raid shelter. He had been hidden there for *six years*! He was followed by another man who, blinded by the light of the sun, staggered forward a few yards and dropped dead. The man's heart had stopped. When the police came up, they found that the men were the two survivors of a platoon of German Nazi soldiers, who had been trapped in an underground food and clothing stores, when the entrance was sealed and blocked by a German demolition party as the Russians were advancing, early in 1945. Two others went mad and committed suicide. Two more died of illness. The survivors buried them in flour, which, it has been found, mummified them. The other two existed for years. They had enough candles to last them for four years. For two years, they had periodically knocked on the subterranean walls, to attract attention from people above in the day; but the sounds were taken for ghostly knocks, and people shunned the place. How the two men managed at last to force a way from this bunker, none know. The solitary survivor is now in hospital, blind."

Just as railway disasters happen in a series of three, almost about the same time, so have mysteries of lost or missing men come to light. In July, 1953, a strange man was seen standing outside an empty house in Henniker Road, Ipswich. He was shabbily dressed and as he looked up to the notice, "For Sale," stuck on a window, he ran away from the house and jumped on a tram going to the Eastern Region railway station. People who saw him wondered if he were Seaman Albert Garrard (34), last reported as "missing after boat drill," off Curaçao, in the Dutch West Indies, on 20 October, 1950. He had an aged mother whose other son, in the Second World War, was reported drowned off Crete, during the evacuation by the British forces. Yet, four months later, this son walked into the house at Ipswich.

In another old city, on the opposite side of England, the "walled" city of Chester, in September, 1953, another soldier, this time reported missing in the First World War

Battle of Loos, in 1915, but who had been wandering over three years was taken ill in the street and rushed by ambulance to Chester Hospital. One day, in a ward of the hospital, this man spoke to a woman cleaner. "Where do you live?" he asked. Her answer was "Boughton." A glimmer of long-dead memory came into the man's eyes. "Ah, do you know a family named Walker, there?" The woman said she would inquire. She found the family, and two members of it came to see the man at the hospital. They did not recognize him. He was sixty-two, lined in the face, white and emaciated, and almost senile. "Don't you know me?" asked the man, plaintively. "We recognize your voice," said the visitors, "but how can you be Fred Walker? He had no white head, or moustache, as you have, and his name has been on the local war memorial for these thirty years. He died in the Battle of Loos, in 1915. This is the year 1953!" Said the man: "But I *am* Fred Walker! No matter if, as you tell me, mother had been drawing a war pension on my account, for many years."

He went on to say:

"A German shell splinter hit my head. We had no tin hats issued in 1915. I was with the Royal Welch Fusiliers. The Germans found me lying in no-man's land between the opposing trenches. They sent me to a hospital in East Prussia. I was there two years—had two silver plates inserted in my head. Then I was sent to a prison-of-war camp—what they called a 'Gefangenerläger.' There, a German 'Unteroffizer' smashed at my head, because I would not betray military secrets. They had to return me to hospital. I was not sent back to England until 1921; when the Germans did not know who I was, nor did I myself. I did not even know that the war was over. I was a man without a name, or memory, for two years, in a mental hospital at Southampton, where a brain specialist treated me . . . I have been wandering ever since all over these islands . . . slept in tramps' doss-houses, did odd jobs on farms, picked fruits and hops, in the season, slept in barns, and woods, trying to recover my lost memory. The accident of falling ill in the street, here, and talking to the cleaner put me in touch with you . . . You say you might recognize me if I shave off my these whiskers . . . Well, I will."

Next day, they came to the hospital and recognized him. In May, 1953, an Italian diver, groping on the bed of the Adriatic, close to Maggia Bay, Trieste, saw an air-tight cabin, part of the wreckage, as markings showed, of a Royal Air Force bomber. Inside were two bodies. Close to the wreckage was the hulk of an Italian liner, *Rex*, a ship of 50,000 tons, sunk by British bombs in 1944. For eight years nothing had been known of the fate of this lost British bomber, until this chance encounter revealed it.

A curious riddle of July, 1953, is what happened to the 2,000 men of the People's Liberation Army encircled by 10, 000 French legionaries and other troops, near the port of Hue, in Viet Nam, Indo-China. When the encircling movement was completed, the French found not *one* man in a big expanse of virgin jungle which they had surrounded, and over which French-flown American planes had surveyed every inch of ground. Some said that the whole two thousand had vanished into a labyrinth of subterranean tunnels and galleries, which sounds like a tale out of the Thousand and One Nights of the Arabians! The mystery is: who made these tunnels, and when? They could hardly have been bored in a single night, between dusk and dawn! All that was *known* was that the two thousand had vanished into thin air from a jungle hemmed in on all sides by an iron ring of troops, while warplanes flew overhead.

In an office near New Street, Birmingham, in June, 1954, another mystery of the eternal and secret East was being unfolded before a tribunal of three prosaic British Civil Servants of the Ministry of Pensions, who must have widely opened even their unimaginative, bureaucratic eyes at the queer story told by a woman, through a legal adviser. It had all the atmosphere of the mystic East, shot through with the aura of a Hindu cult with "a little green god," gemmed with rich jewels of fabulous value. The woman was a legally presumed widow, Mrs. Louisa Devine, a housewife and office-cleaner.

She said:

"I seek a ruling that my husband died on active service. He is still officially deemed an Army deserter. Eleven years ago (September, 1943) my husband, Private Robert Devine, of the 1st Battalion, of the North Staffordshire Regiment, was in the Burma jungle, surrounded by worse than savage Japanese troops, shrieking and yelling like demons or trapped gorillas. He was hemmed in, but he was a clever man. One night, in the leech-infested woods, he crept on hands and knees, and wormed his way through the dense bush, right under the noses of the Jap sentries, and saved the life of a comrade who was lying badly wounded, under a thick bush. Later, he and the rest of his battalion were sent to a rest-camp at Dinapore, near Patna, about 300 miles north-west of Calcutta. One evening, when he was there, he told other soldiers that he was going to the camp cinema. He was never seen alive again. Three months later some Hindus fished out of the Ganges, about 500 yards from the camp, the corpse of a man with black hair, like that of my husband; but it was so badly decomposed that the face was not recognizable. Nobody could positively identify him; but fellow-soldiers who saw the body believed it was that of my husband."

An Army Court of Inquiry was set up and it adjudged Devine to be a deserter; but, in March, 1952, Mr. Justice Collingwood, in the High Court of Probate, pronounced: "All the probabilities are against desertion of your husband. I give you leave to presume his death." It transpired that Private Devine, and other men in the battalion rest-camp, had heard a story about a Hindu temple, in Patna, where there was a jewel-encrusted idol of gold. The place is a holy city of the Hindu religious cults, taboo, and no white man was permitted to set foot in the quarter where the temple and idol are located, some fifteen miles west of Dinapore. No one knew what had happened to Devine after he was reported missing; but it was known that the bodies of two British soldiers had been found, done to death, presumably by natives who, on that same night, may have detected them prowling near the temple with the jewelled idol. The temple and its quarter, and the city, were out of bounds to the troops, since there had been stories of attempts to break in and rifle this temple. It was possible that the three men had ventured too near the temple-quarter and had been set on and killed by fanatics who had reason to resent the violation of a stringent taboo; but it could not be affirmed.

A barrister, acting for the Ministry of Pensions, said the case was very novel, since there was speculation, and death could only be presumed. If, he said, Devine *were* a victim of foul play, then he "had been the author of his own misfortunes in going out alone and exposing himself." There is, of course, no proof that Devine and the other two soldiers *were* associated in such an adventure.

The author of this book was, in September, 1957, at Berchtesgaden, an attractive South German township lying at the foot of picturesquely high wooded mountains, some with snowy peaks, where Sud-Bayern (southern Bavaria) thrusts a foot into Upper Austria, in the province of Salzburg. As most people know, on the top of one of these mountains is the famous eyrie, or wolf-lair, of Hitler, not visible from the *bahnhof* (electric railway station) and the streets of the attractive place at its foot. Today, one reaches the eyrie through tunnels bored in the granite on an electric trolley controlled by a uniformed driver. The author could get no answer from anyone in Berchtesgaden about a riddle which has puzzled him and many other people: "What became of the treasure of Hitler, who is known to have grossed more than a million marks from the sales alone of his book *Mein Kampf*, although he is not known to have indulged in the acquisition of loot, gold *objets d'art*, pictures and antiques, which his colleague, Reichsmarschall Göring stole from all over western Europe, in the Second World War?"

A shrug of the shoulders or a vacant smile from eyes in shaken heads was the only answer one got from folk in Berchtesgaden, or München (Munich). Over the border in Austria, one followed a clue one got in Salzburg, which led one to the shores of a lake—the Atter oder Kummer See— which lies ten miles, as the crow flies, west of Gmunden. Two years before, security officers of Upper Austria put a salvage steamer on the Atter Lake. They had information that a short time before Hitler committed suicide in the bunker of his redoubt in Berlin, he personally ordered a plane to fly to the "Alpine Redoubt" carrying a load of gold and documents, where he and other leading Nazis had planned to make a last stand. This plane, whether or not it had gone off course, plunged to the bottom of the Atter lake, and remained there, undisturbed, for eleven years until, in September, 1955, divers went down into its green waters, found the wrecked plain, and wrenched open a side-door in a cabin. But all that was then officially disclosed was a box of rusty hand-grenades, and no gold or documents. The wreck lies at about a depth of two hundred and fifty feet. A salvage engineer, *Herr* Anton Fohrafeliner, proposed to run steel cables under the plane and raise her about halfway from the surface of the water, and then check the contents of the cabins, or hold. But the Austrian authorities were holding their hands until the U.S. Army of Occupation, then in the region, had quitted the zone, in October, 1955. They feared that the American authorities might confiscate any treasure. All the author found was a complete veil of silence. Everybody who knew had orders from the Republican Government in Vienna to say nothing. It is difficult to believe that all this plane held was rusty explosives. Thus, it seems, the mystery of what happened to Hitler's treasure is likely to remain unsolved. Probate of his will, in 1957, showed only a small sum.

There is another mystery of a lost consignment of about three millions in gold, and more than a million in gold American dollars, which the German authorities seemed to have planned to remove to Switzerland. I tried to get on the trail of it. Some thirty miles as the crow flies, much more as one would normally travel, is another picturesque south-western Bavarian township, the locale of this very mysterious affair. One reached it by a most picturesque and panoramic electric mountain railway running through many tunnels, over breath-taking ravines with rushing, boulder-strewn torrents, under the Mieminger and Wetterstein Gebirge (Alpine ranges), to the township of Garmisch-Partenkirchen. To this quiet place, in 1945, before the Allies had finished the race to Berlin, the authorities of the Deutsche Reichsbank secretly sent German Army trucks, with an escort of soldiers, and freighted with many marked boxes full of gold ingots, gold coins and sacks of American dollars. The treasure amounted to several millions. What happened to it? One thing very definitely *is* known: the treasure was never restored to the vault sof the Western German Government at Bonn! Or to Berlin, whence it had come.

The author, with no little difficulty, discovered in 1957, when he was at Garmisch-Partenkirchen, that under the orders of a local German colonel-commandant—since vanished totally—these millions were hidden in a wood on mountains near the peak of the Krollenkopf. But when the Americans arrived they, acting on secret intelligence, found and dug up the boxes of treasure, some of which were missing; but, again, not a cent of it ever reached the overriding U.S. military authorities. I was told by a German in Garmisch—he had been an interpreter in one of the U.S. Bayern occupation bureaux, in Garmisch—that a certain American commandant, a German colonel, and two picturesque Bavarian owners of a schloss, or manor-house, in the region, spirited away a large part of this great treasure by night in a car, and in relays along second-class roads, through mountains, *via* Ehrwald, and along the Lechtal, or valley of the Lech, to the Austrian border at Buchs. It is supposed that the treasure was temporarily hidden in Swiss territory, somewhere between Buchs and Zurich. Of course, more than one motor trip was made, and the whole nefarious affair could not have been caried out except with an American *laisser-passer*, naturally used with no knowledge or consent of the American High Command.

All the rascals concerned vanished to either the Argentine, or the U.S.A., and as clandestinely as they removed the gold and dollars from Swiss territory overseas. Some say an international syndicate arranged to charter a plane to fly it to South America; others say a ship was used. One theory is that the gold was disposed of in Switzerland. All that definitely is known is that, to this day, not one of these "treasure hunters" has ever been apprehended and brought to justice!

There is also the mystery of the "100 millions" of loot, alleged to have been taken by the German generalissimo, Marshal Erwin Rommel—whether from Africa, which seems doubtful, or from western European countries—and which millions are said to have been sunk off the coast of Corsica by four of his officers, after the defeat of the Afrika Korps. In 1953, two rival expeditions were out on this war-path, and said to be "rushing from Paris and Rome" to get in first. One syndicate was led by a British officer, the other by Italians; and we may trust that none of them developed what doctors call *tachycardia*. Perhaps they were waylaid by some of the romantic bandits—not at all romantic with the use of long knives!—known still to be in this island, for no word has ever been heard about the fishing up of this fairy sea-gold.

However, in the summer of 1957 one read, in the *Corriere della Sera*, when one was staying for a day in Milan, a report of the proceedings of a Court sitting in Padova (Padua)—it then had been sitting for eleven weeks!—inquiring into the whereabouts of the "vast treasure of Dongo," Mussolini's gold and jewels; and, in the course of one of the sittings, there was a reference to a number of very "picturesque persons," said to be *"individui che si qualificano con i nemi piū diversi"* (people going under many different names), who were trying to sell a "secret map" containing alleged clues to the "great gold treasure of Rommel," hidden in a "certain *zone*," along with the proceeds of the looting of many banks, in Upper Italy, by mixed formations of German Nazis and Italian Fascisti, in April, 1945. *"Bonta loro"* (to the best of their sincere belief), said these picturesque altruists, these treasures were worth 100 milliards, and these "depositaries" of the secret required, as a guarantee of other people's good faith, a preliminary deposit of 25 million *lire*, *plus* 50 per cent of all the profits when the said treasures were "localized." The Italian police were anxious to meet and have a "friendly talk" with these romantic individuals.

This same Court at Padua, seems to have heard a good deal of mystifying evidence about this lost gold of Dongo, anent which at Köln, on the German Rhine, in autumn 1952, a German named *Herr* Gustav Nagel, aged thirty-two, an ex-Luftwaffe pilot, now working as a labourer, said:

"I was one of the guard of Benito Mussolini, he who was captured by Italian Resistance partisans, along with his beautiful mistress, Clara Petacca, shot outside the wall of a country house, not far from Lake Como, and subsequently hung up like a pig in a pork-butcher's shop. . . . I could tell the Italian Government where the Duce's gold lies at the bottom of Lake Como. It was worth millions and packed in many wooden boxes. They were thrown into the lake on the orders of the Italian Fascist dignitaries with Mussolini. I know the spot."

On 8 May, 1957, an Italian newspaper man, Signor Feruccio Lanfranchi, said when the treasure was inventoried in the town hall of Dongo a very large sum in Italian banknotes was missing, believed to have been diverted to a Communist centre in Como.

"A woman partisan, Signora Gianna, who vanished in June, 1945, when she was investigating the death of her fiancé, named Neri, told me that when the inventory was made, there were gathered in the Dongo town hall some 280 million lire: yet, in the inventory only 1,350,000 lire were recorded. She said she had a receipt for the gold and valuables sent to the Communist quarters in Como. One of Mussolini's lorries, with documents and letters between Hitler and Mussolini, was lost near Milan. More gold vanished at Como and Menaggio, and it was usual to see small boys, in the villages round Dongo, playing with gold coins. It is likely that some of the gold and jewels went across the frontiers, when some of the German lorries were let proceed, after the arrest of the Fascist leaders."

It seemed to be evident that an immense amount of treasure must, so to speak, have gone "up the spout," or been funnelled into a pipe-line and, no doubt, in the near, or not so distant, future knights of industry and romance and good will to all mankind, with bankers' balances to "invest," will be forthcoming with the "secret maps." Up to the time of writing, no one seems to have gone treasure-fishing in the lovely blue waters of Lake Como.

At Marsala, on the west coast of Sicily, there is a marsh where sportsmen lie in wait for wild ducks and other game birds. Late in October, 1957, a man was sighting his gun on a covey of birds, when his attention was drawn to a white bird, fluttering down from the sky and in distress. It fell dead on the beach, a few yards from his feet. He went across to it and noticed that it had a small green glass phial, tied to its leg with a silk thread or wire. Inside was a revmarkable note in Italian:

> "Many messengers. No answers. No hope. The man who may shoot this bird must tell the world about the vile things done by the Russians. We, here, have been slaving for thirteen years in these mines of the damned. We are in the Polar Arctic. We are Italian soldiers. White slaves in the mines. The men (guards?) have slit eyes. We die like flies. Listen, my mother, if you are still alive: it would be better if I had not been born. I have much to tell you. I cannot give our names, lest . . . I send good wishes to the *medico* at Treviso, Italia. There are 300 of us. God is our only hope. There are others from Friuli, Salara, Padova, Verona, Rovigo."

Is this a genuine call from hopeless prisoners-of-war in a mining-camp, twelve years after the Second World War; or is it a hoax of the marine bottle type? Why is no precise location mentioned, seeing that the Polar Arctic littoral covers a vast area of some 3,500 square miles?

The white bird, to whose leg this message was tied, is said to be—its species is not stated—a native of northern Siberia, which migrates, and is an autumn migrant to North Africa, flying *via* Central Asia through Turkey, Greece and Albania; but it was off course, since it does not normally visit Italy or Sicily. If there are desperate men dying in this mining camp "like flies," would not their hopelessness induce them to take the risk of naming the locality of this mine? Otherwise, how are the Italian military authorities or foreign office to be expected to undertake this hopeless task of discovering where this camp is, in so vast a region? Bureaucrats of *any* country are little likely to take the risk of being made fools of in a cast of this sort. Why, too, is the name of the Treviso doctor not mentioned in this message? It would be one way of authenticating it. The Italian Army authorities have kept this bottle and message and, as is comprehensible, refuse to express any opinion on it. The places mentioned lie in the Po Valley, north, west, and south of Venice. Surely, if any doctor from Treviso has been released from some Russian or North Siberian camp he would have made known the plight of those left behind?

Failing answers to these questions, before any assumption of the genuineness of this message can be accepted, we have no proof by whom and where this message, in the bottle, was tied to this bird's leg.

At this point the author may introduce a British military mystery which, even after thirty years, he cannot explain. In 1925 he was exploring some of the byways of the old Channel Island of pirates and privateers, Guernsey, with old haunted houses where none have lived for years; but where, on stilly summer evenings, those who peer across an overgrown lawn at some manor house, built in the eighteenth century may, so one St. Peter Port Guernsey man told me, see the sash of some cobwebbed drawing-room window go slowly up and then down, with not a soul within the mouldering room behind. But it is not of old houses haunted by invisible spooks, of which one speaks here, it is of a truly believe-it-or-not incident recorded on an obituary marble tablet in the quaint old church of St. Sampson's, in this island. Truly it is admirably calculated to bemuse either a surgeon or a soldier!

This amazing inscription reads as follows:

"*Dans cette église et dans le même tombeau reposent le corps de Daniel Falla, Ecuyer, de la Ronde Cheminée . . . et de Dame Susanne le Pelley, son épouse . . . décédés au Seigneur, le 30 Septembre, 1796. Ce monument est érige à leur memoire, et à celle de leur fils cadet, Thomas Falla, Lieutenant au 12me Régiment d'Infanterie, mort au siége de Seringapatam, le 6 April, 1790, âge de 18 ans, 6 mois, 25 jours, des suites d'une blessure d'un boulet de canon solide, pesant 26 livres, qui s'était logé entre les deux os d'une de ses cuisses, la dite blessure, s'étant enflammée considérablement, le chirurgeon du régiment, quoiqu'-ayant examiné la place, ignorait qu'un boulet y fut renfermé, et, ce ne fut qu'aprés sa mort, qui ont lieu 6 heures àpres l'événement, qu'il fut extrait, à la surprise de toute l'armée.*"

Translation: "In this church and in the same tomb, lie the bodies of Daniel Falla, Esquire of La Ronde Cheminée . . . and of Dame Susanne le Pelley, his wife . . . who died in the Lord, 30 September, 1796. This monument is erected to their memory and to that of their youngest son Thomas Falla, Lieutenant of the 12th Infantry Regiment, died at the siege of Seringapatam, 6 April, 1790, aged 18 years, 6 months, 25 days, of the consequences of a wound from a cannon-ball, solid, and weighing 27 lb. 10 ounces, which lodged between the two bones of one of his thighs; the said wound being considerably inflamed, the regimental surgeon, although he had examined the spot, was ignorant of the fact that a cannon-ball was lodged therein, and it was not until after his death, six hours after the event, that it was extracted, to the surprise of the whole army."

There is extant, in a private collection in Guernsey, the manuscript on the diary of an officer of the 2nd Infantry Regiment, warring against "Citizen Tippoo Sahib." It records that the inflammation and swelling of the wound were so great and abnormal, that the hole by which the cannon-ball had entered closed entirely around the wound. The soldiers, carrying young Falla off the field, noticed that he seemed heavier on one side than on the other; but they had no idea of the presence of so hefty an object as this cannonball. The poor officer asked for some water, and said in broken English—for it was the day when Channel Islanders spoke little more than French and when all epitaphs were in that language in Channel Island churches—"I weesh for to die like one soldier!" What of course is so extraordinary is that, according to this epitaph, young Falla had a *double femoral* bone; whereas most other human beings have merely a *single femur!* And the truly miraculous manner in which the regimental surgeon entirely failed to note that a 27 lb. cannon-ball was lodged behind the orifice of the wound is almost beyond the bounds of the credible!

A singular series of events happened at night in February, 1955, when two Englishmen, unconnected the one with the other, met the same mysterious fate when wandering in the suburbs of the ports of Boulogne and Dieppe. No. 1 was Samuel Braun who died in a boulogne hospital of an overdose of some narcotic, after being found unconscious in a lonely road by the French police; but whether self-administered or not was not known. How came his passport to be missing?

No. 2 was a young man of the Royal Air Force, Victor Hutton of Kendal, Westmorland. He had landed in Dieppe on a Saturday. On the Sunday, a farmer going into his barn, found a young man apparently hanged and dead. On his wrist was a watch still going, and by his side was a camera, cigarette-lighter, part of a packet of "Caporal" cigarettes, and haversack. He was Hutton, and his *passport was missing*. There were only 150 francs in his pocket—worth about half a crown. A French police surgeon said: "This young

Englishman died about two hours before he was found, and the police found on him a Royal Air Force card."

If he had been murdered, who took his passport and left the other personal articles?

War mysteries belong, of course, to no one age. For example, in January, 1955, an archaeologist, excavating a ditch outside an Iron Age fort, at Sutton Walls, Herefordshire, found twenty-four groups of human bones, all of tall men, with the exception of a boy about twelve who may have been a messenger; but some of the skeletons were *headless*. Radio carbon tests showed that the age of the skeletons was about 2,000 years. Their ages ranged from twenty to forty. Why were they *decapitated?* This feature is sometimes associated with ritual of the black magic type. Were they Iberians from Spain, or Gauls from Brittany? Done to death by Roman Legionaries about the year 55 B.C.? Was it a war atrocity intended to strike terror into hill fort defenders?

After studying these ancient bones for three years, Dr. Cornwell, archaeologist of the University of London, was not sure of the explanation of this mystery. In the words of the well-known hymn:

> *"Time like an ever-rolling stream,*
> *Bears all its sons away.*
> *They fly forgotten as a dream*
> *Dies at the opening day."*

But sometimes the "opening day" sees the deposition on the shore of time of debris that is more eloquent than learned and dusty tomes. We have merely echoes that return no answer to our questions about mysteries that ingenuity and science cannot solve.

PART FOUR

MYSTERIES OF SPACE-TIME

Chapter 10

TALES OF CREATURES AND PEOPLE OUT OF THIS WORLD

OUR MID-TWENTIETH century age of nuclear fission and thermo-nuclear fission, radar, television, electronics and the special and general relativity theories associated with Einstein, have brought us to the theoretical pass where an atomic particle may behave as a wave one minute, and a particle the next; so that the physicist is driven to call in the metaphysics of Kant and the "unknowable noumenon" in order to arrive at even a temporary hypothesis about the nature of man, mind, matter and the universe. The scientist is like the man who consulted the old seagod, Proteus, who was difficult of access and often refused to give an answer to a problem. He assumed different shapes if not properly secured in fetters and, in the end, vanished in a flame of fire, a whirlwind, or a rushing stream.

Nature, as Bertrand Russell has said, presents us with "the wave with nothing to wave in." It ought not, therefore, to arouse derision or undue scepticism if one adumbrates, or prophesies that, for science, a time is rapidly approaching when the scientist willy-nilly, may have to attempt a fusion of physics and meta-physics, which will bring him into contact with the uncomfortable and mysterious worlds of the fourth dimension, whose plane lies at right angles or, sometimes, seems parallel to our own everyday world of three dimensions. Our world which that other very mysterious world seems, at times, to interpenetrate.

There is, so to speak, "a hole in the wall," or, to vary the metaphor, the occurrence of a vortex in matter-energy through which certain people of all social classes and ranks, animals, and objects, involuntarily and unexpectedly may pass, and from which there may, or may *not* be a return to the world from which they were "teleported." If they do return, it will usually be found that the experience of this weird phenomenon is accompanied by amnesia, entire forgetfulness of what happened just before, during and after the phenomenon. This weird phenomenon is not an abstract affair, but is, has, and will be connected with the mysterious disappearances of people in cases where no normally physical or criminological explanation can be found. In order, however dimly and very imperfectly to conceive what happens when a man or woman, an animal, or object vanishes from the third into the fourth dimension of the continuum of space-time, we may assume the hypothesis of a two-dimensional object, with length and breadth, being lifted up into the third dimension of height, and so transcending the bounds of the circle which confined it. It would be re-deposited again in the two-dimensional plane outside the circle, and so, after it had vanished, it would reappear, mysteriously, at another point in space.

Or, again, if the object, or actor, were the norm of our own world of three-dimensions, such an object or actor, passing into the four-dimensional world might, and very often might *not,* come back from that unknown and mysterious bourne to which he or it had been teleported.

To pass through the "hole in the wall," or the warp, or crack, or vortex, or rift, in space, the sentient object, the man or woman, may require to have a functional peculiarity, or unconscious, or sub-conscious "knack," which the learned Victorian, F. W. H. Myers, called "psychorrhagic diathesis," by which, in conditions we do not yet know produces a breaking-through of the stuff of mind-energy-matter and may affect a sort of inversion of the space-time continuum. The actor falls through the warp, or vortex, in space, somewhat in the way a swimmer may be carried away by a current under ice, in a lake, or a floe, and, thereafter, he may, or may *not* rediscover the point of entry. If he does not, the world from which he mysteriously vanished will know him no more!

The phenomenon may be a two-way one. It may involve an involuntary, unexpected and certainly undesired transference or teleportation from our own three-dimensional world to the unknown one of four dimensions, or even vice-versa. One may conceive, as, indeed, the relativity theory suggests, that worlds may exist not, as we empirically suppose, in succession, but side by side, one being invisible to the other, and connected with it only through a space-vortex, or the "hole in the wall in space-time." The strange phenomena recorded in this chapter, and also, here and there, in other parts of this book, were and are not confined to the nineteenth and twentieth centuries, or to any age in the past or present, but were experienced in the early and later Middle Ages, and, naturally, mis-interpreted according to theological preconceptions. They *were,* however, recorded often by learned monastics who have been smiled and laughed at for their pains and their "superstition." And, no doubt, the phenomena occurred in the earlier ages of Egypt, Babylonia, Sumeria, India, Rome and Greece, or Carthaginia and Etruria. They belong to every age, in fact.

We may preface accounts of these weird and bizarre phenomena with a brief narrative of a strange incident that occurred no longer ago than the afternoon of 23 September, 1880. I summarize from various contemporary newspapers in the U.S.A. :

On that afternoon, a man named David Lang, who had a farm about twelve miles from the small township of Gallatin, in Sumner county, Tennessee, spoke to his wife and two children on the veranda of their farmhouse, and, in sight of them, walked across a forty-acre field* and was never seen again. As Lang was walking across this pasture-field of close-cropped grass, an attorney and Lang's brother-in-law were driving up a lane, in a buggy, towards the farmhouse. The attorney saw Lang in the middle of the field, and was about to shout to him—and there were no hedges, trees, boulders, or fences at or near the spot—when, to the attorney's amazement, Lang vanished from sight instantaneously, as if the earth had suddenly opened and swallowed him up! The alarmed wife and the two men at once went to the spot, found no crack in the turf, or soil, and nothing whatever to indicate what had happened or where Lang had gone. One moment, Lang was, the next he was *not!* Every inch of the field was searched by the police, but with no result. A surveyor and a geologist said that limestone bedrock lay a few feet under the soil, and no crack or fissure could be found in it. The search went on for a month, all in vain!

A year later—and this has reference to one's point that there may often be "no return" to our own world, for the luckless actor, or patient!—a very strange thing occurred:

On a day in early August, 1881, the missing man's boy and girl were walking over this field, when they noticed that the grass at the spot where their father had mysteriously disappeared showed a 20-feet wide circle of high and rank grass. All outside the circle had been cropped by sheep, or grazed by cattle; but no cow, or sheep, or horse would venture into the circle, not even a cricket or grasshopper. They would not approach it, but shied away in fear. . . . For some reason, the girl was impelled to shout out: "Father, are you anywhere around?" She repeated the inquiry four times, and the boy joined in. No reply came, and then they were about to walk away, thinking how silly they were, when, of a sudden, they heard a voice call for help. It seemed faint and faraway—in, but not of this world! The startled mother was told. She went to the spot in the field, and called, and her husband an-

---

*Later, in this book, I shall refer to another queer case of three missing children in a field also called the "Forty Acres," near the old Midland Railway sheds at Gloucester, and the adjacent Great Western (Western Region) lines to Paddington and South Wales. It happened in 1906, on a site today in a built-up area close to the Royal Air Force records office. (I took part in a search in this case.)

swered. They went back for several days; but each day the voice grew fainter, and at last was heard no more.

It seemed that Lang, wherever he was, or had been precipitated, could not find the point of re-entry to the world of three dimensions.

In the reign of King John Lackland, of England, about the year 1200, there lived a learned English monk and traveller who was related to the Earl of Salisbury and who spent some time at the court of the Holy Roman (German) Emperor, Otto IV, at Aachen, or Aix-la-Chapelle, where he wrote a very early Latin encyclopaedia, titled *Otia Imperialia*. His name was Gervase of Tilbury. He gave two very strange accounts of fourth dimensional phenomena, to the second of which we shall refer, later, in this chapter.

"In the county of Gloucester is a town called Bristol, of wealth and noted for prosperous citizens and merchants. From its port, men sail to Ireland. It befell on a time that a man of Bristol left his wife and children at home, and sailed for Ireland. Then, after a long voyage, as he sailed to a far-off ocean, he chanced to sit at a dinner with the seamen. It was about the hour of tierce (9 a.m.), and, after eating, he washed his knife in the salt water over the ship's side. Suddenly, the knife slipped from his hand. Now, at the same hour, at Bristol, the knife fell in through the roof-window, which men call a dormer, and in his own house stuck in the table, at which his wife was then sitting. She was dumbfounded at so strange a thing, and recognizing this well-known knife laid it aside. Long after that, she learned, on her husband's return, that the incident happened on the very day when she found the knife."

On 25 February, 1956, the author of this book had a remarkable letter from his brother, Mr. Gordon Wilkins, who lives in the city of Gloucester, in this same county. He wrote:

"One day last week, an elderly lady wrote to the office saying she was unwell, and asked me to call at her house off Calton Road, Gloucester. I found, when I called, that she wanted me to act as co-witness to her will. As I was leaving, the other witness said to the old lady: 'Amy, have you found that knife yet?' The old lady, Mrs. G., said: 'No, and I think the people who were here may have taken it.' Mrs. G. then turned to me and said: 'Mr. Wilkins, I want to tell you of a very peculiar thing. My late husband was a linesman employed by the Midland Electricity Board.

One day he was sent to erect some overhead power lines in a field near Brockworth, as you know, about four miles from here. When lunch-time came, he pulled out his bread and cheese, and found, to his annoyance, that he had forgotten to put a table-knife in his lunch-box. He bent down, and there, on the grass in the field lay a fine new table-knife which certainly had not been there when he came into the field. He took it home and we kept it until, a short time back, some years later, after my husband died, it mysteriously vanished. . . .'"

It is a very odd coincidence that this phenomenon, associated, in both cases with a knife, should have occurred in the same English county at an interval of about 750 years!

Of course, as psychical research people know, phenomena like these, above, of the fourth dimension may be associated with spooks, whose "translunary" world beyond the grave seems to have many fourth-dimensional features.

We now come to the bizarre incident of the "two Green Children," which, even today, is still spoken of by Suffolk people who live in the countryside near Bury St. Edmunds. It happened in the twelfth century, either in the reign of King Stephen of England (1135-54), or in that of Henry II. who succeeded him. In the medieval chronicles of that age it is referred to as *De Viridibus Pueris*, and was about the emergence of two strange children, a boy and girl, sister and brother, with *green skins*, at a place today called Woolpit, then called "Wulpets," in the hundred of Thedwardsty, Suffolk.

The place-name, Woolpit, is said to signify a den of wolves (*fossa luporum*). The old Jacobean encyclopaedic writer, Burton, of the "Anatomy of Melancholy," roundly expressed his opinion that these two green children "either fell from the sun, or were dropped from the moon!" It is also curious, by the way, that believers in the phenomena of the flying saucers as extra-terrestrial, reported to the police, the American Air Force and the press of at least five American mid-western towns in 1955 and 1956 that, when they were driving cars, along lonely roads at night, they were scared at encountering unpleasant manikins with green skins, and also in green dresses, who stood in the highways close to strange blazing discs parked in fields or near woods. One policeman, on night patrol in a town in Indiana, swore that he saw them—he did not say they were green—standing close to a railway viaduct!

However this may be, and whether or no someone was "hallucinated," one might theorize without over indulgence in fantasy that, in a cold planet like Mars, where the sun appears much smaller than we see it from the earth, the flora may be blue or green, as is found in Alpine heights, as in the Hindu Kush or Karakorum Mountains; that the extreme rigours of the climate may have long since forced humanoid beings to live underground, where their pallor would be tinged with green or bluish-green. It is a fact that thermo-couples have detected heat coming from the interior of Mars.

The earliest chronicler to report this queer affair of the green children was William of Newburgh, whose family name was Pettit, or Parvus (the Little), and who was born at Bridlington, Yorkshire, in December, 1135 or '36. He was a learned Augustinian monk, and rationalistic for his times. He says, in his *Historia Rerum Anglicarum*, that it is "well known that it occurred *sub rege Stephani* (in the reign of King Stephen), *in Anglia* (England):

"Although the thing is asserted by many, yet I have long been in doubt about the matter, deeming it ridiculous to credit a thing supported by no rational foundation, or at least one of a mysterious character; yet, in the end, I was so overwhelmed by the weight of so many competent witnesses that I have been compelled to believe and wonder over a matter I was unable to comprehend and unravel by the powers of my intellect...."

He adds:

"The place is called Wolpittes after the ancient cavities or pits for wolves, near it. The boy and girl were completely green in their persons, and wore garments of strange colour and unknown materials when they emerged from the pits. They wandered thro' the fields in astonishment, and were seized by the reapers who took them to the village. Here they were for some days kept without food and gaped at by persons from far and near. By degrees, after many months of food and bread, they gradually changed their colour and became like ourselves and learnt our language. The boy was the younger of the two and died first. They said they lived in a twilight land, not warmed by the beams of the sun. 'A certain luminous country is seen not far distant from ours and divided from it by a considerable river.'"

The other testimony is from Abbot Ralph of Coggeshall, who, in 1207, was abbot of the reformed Benedictine Abbey which once stood in the picturesque village of Coggeshall, in Essex. He says that the incident happened in the reign of

Henry II (1154-89), and that he was told the story by Sir Richard de Calne, in whose house at "Wykes," the two green children resided. If this were so, Abbot Ralph heard the story later than William of Newburgh—say some thirty-five to forty years after it had happened—whereas, Newburgh appears to have been a contemporary and questioned many eye-witnesses about the matter. The green girl, after she became white, lived as a domestic servant, for some years in de Calne's house and later on, seemed to have married a man at King's Lynn in Norfolk.

In his *Chronicon Anglicarum*, Coggeshall says:

"This boy and girl, brother and sister, came out of holes at St. Mary de Wulfpetes, next the edge of a pit found there. They had all the members (limbs: *forman omnium membrorun*), like those of other men; but in the colour of the skin they differed from all other mortals of our earth. For all the surface of their skin none could understand. At that time, weeping inconsolably, they were taken, out of astonishment, to the house of Richard de Calne at Wikes. Bread and other food was placed before them; but they would not eat it, and, indeed, with great hunger from fasting, they were a long time tormented, because, as the girl afterwards confessed, that all that food could not be consumed by them. However, at last, beans cut off or torn from stalks, were brought to the house and they fell on them with great avidity. So now those beans were given to them and they broke open the beanstalks, *not* the pod or shell of the beans, evidently supposing that the beans were contained in the hollows of the stalks. But not finding beans within the stalks they again began to weep, which, when the bystanders noticed, they opened the shells and showed them the beans themselves. Whereupon, with great joyfulness, they ate beans for a long time, entirely, and would touch no other food. The boy, however, grew weaker and weaker, and died in a short time. The girl, indeed, always enjoying good food and growing accustomed to whatever food one was pleased to set before her, completely lost the green colour of her skin and by degrees regained (assumed: *penitus amisit*) a normal red-blooded condition of the body (like our own). And, after being regenerated by the holy waters of baptism, for many years remained in the service of the soldier, aforesaid, as from the same soldier and his family we often heard. She showed herself very wanton and lascivious (*nimium lasciva et petulans exstitit*). Indeed asked frequently about the men of her own country, she affirmed that all who dwelt in her land, or had lived there, were coloured (dyed: *viridi fingerentur colore*) green, and no sun was perceived there, but that a brightness or shining (*claritate*) such as would happen after sunset (was seen there). Asked in what manner she had come from the land, aforesaid, with the boy, she replied that they were following sheep (or small cattle: *pecora*), and arrived at a certain cavern. On entering it they heard a certain delectable sound of bells and, in trying to reach the sweet sound, they wandered for a very long time through the cavern until they came to its end. Thence, emerging, the excessive brightness of our sun and the unwonted, warm temperature of our air astonished and terrified them. And for a long time they lay upon the edge (or mouth, or end: *super oram diu speluncae jacuerunt*) of the cave. When overcome with disquietude, they wished to flee, but they could not in the least find the entrance to the cavern, until they were seized by the people of the countryside."

Passages in this curious narrative of Abbot Ralph of Coggeshall, above, seem to imply either that the world from which they came was subterranean, and in some terrestrial "antipodes," or that their fourth dimensional world existed side by side with ours, and in some sort interpenetrated it. It may also—who can say?—imply that they had been teleported from some world in space, beyond the earth, where men live underground.

In England, in 1817, a strange girl suddenly appearing at the door of a cottage near Brislington, Bristol, spoke an unknown tongue which no linguist could identify, and even wrote unknown glyphs. There was at Nürnberg, Germany, in 1833, a boy named by Germans—not by himself—Kaspar Hauser, who gave a *Herr* von Feuerback the impression, so complete was his deficiency in terrestrial knowledge and his horror of all terrestrial customs, that "he might have been a citizen of another planet transferred by some miracle to our own." I have given an account of this, and other similar phenomena, in another chapter of this book.

Gervase of Tilbury, who may have been contemporary with Abbot Ralph of Coggeshall, says that the green children were sitting in the pits, weeping, when the beans were brought to them. This seems to imply that the two children had gone back to the pits to try to find "the hole in the wall," that is, the point of re-entry from the third to the fourth dimensional plane; so that they might be teleported back to the world from which they had so mysteriously come to the England of the twelfth century.

Gervase says that the girl, later, married a man at Lynn, "where she was said to be living, a few years since" (that is, at the end of the twelfth, or in the early years of the thirteenth century). When asked whence they had come, they replied:

> "We are folk of St. Martin's Land; for he is the chief saint among us. We know not where the land is, and remember only that one day we were feeding our father's flock in the field when we heard a great noise like bells, as when, at St. Edmunds (Bury St. Edmunds, Suffolk), they all peal together. And on a sudden we were both caught up in the spirit and found ourselves in your harvest-field. Among us no sun riseth, nor is there open sunshine, but such a twilight as here goes before the rising and setting of the sun. Yet there is a land of light to be seen not far from us, but cut off from us by a stream of great width."

Gervase's story gives the impression that the strange children's story had been "touched up" by some learned medieval cleric, who had put to them a leading question about "St. Martin's land," in order to advance a theory of his own. But, here it may be said that Martin's mass was the time of death, or slaying. St. Martin's Land, or Merlin's Land, was the land of "grammarye" or necromancy; or a twilight land, or subterranean land to which the old gods or god-men were forced to descend after a cataclysm which sank an ancient continent. Beans were deemed by the Pythagoreans to contain souls in the first stage of metempsychosis, and to be a mystic link with the dead. Again, St. Martin's Land was deemed to be at the Antipodes, the assertion of whose existence, that is, of the Antipodes, brought down on the head of the Irish saint, Fergil, the thunders of excommunication from Pope Zacharius, in A.D. 780! It was held by some curious monastic speculators of the early Middle Ages that the way to the Antipodes was through vast subterranean tunnels and caverns. Among the Amero-Indians, all the vast way from Alaska to Patagonia, there still exist myths and legends and traditions about great tunnels and a subterranean world in which civilized men were forced to dwell, ages ago, after vulcanism, floods and collision of the Pole with a tremendous aerolite had sunk a long-lost continent.

Indeed, even today, in this region of Suffolk, there are people who have never heard of these chroniclers, but who still talk of these two green children in a way suggesting memories handed down from remote East Anglian ancestors, and something more than mere fairy folk lore! Before passing on we may draw attention to Saxo-Grammaticus (*fl.* thirteenth century), an old Danish historian, who wrote, in Latin, the oral myths and traditions of Denmark. He speaks of an underworld, called "Hadding's Land," after "Hadding, son of Gram," an ancient King of Denmark, "in the days of the giants." Hadding followed a woman who carried "sweet green veronica" in the depths of winter

> "through deep, musty clouds, along a well-worn road, where they passed nobly-clad men, in rich robes, to sultry fields of purple, and thence to a bridge by the River of Blades, where two armies of ghosts of slain soldiers were seen fighting. From this underworld, mentioned in old Gundrun's lay, as the long lyng fish* or serpents, of Hadding's Land, the culture-gods stole and steal all the beasts of the underworld for the use of men on the surface."

Gervase, monk of Christ Church, Canterbury (*fl.* 1188), tells a curious story of a strange boy who, in 1138, mysteriously appeared in the wine-cellars and vaults of the "noble monastery of Prüm," in the diocese of Trier, or Trèves, in the Eifel country of Rhenish Prussia. Apparently this queer story was circulated in many abbeys in Western Europe, and probably reached Gervase from some traveller given hospitality in the guest-house of an abbey at Canterbury; or it may have come from some German monk, sent on some monastic business to Canterbury:

> A.D. 1138: "Among the things that flew around is this report of a miraculous event. In the archbishopric of Trèves, is the site of the noble monastery called Brumia." (Prumia or Prum, dedicated in honour of the holy apostles, Peter and Paul, and founded in ancient times by Pepin, king of the Franks, Pepin le Bref, father of the Emperor Charlemagne).... "One morning, the cellarer (*celarius*) and his man went into the wine-cellar, to draw wine for the altar-sacrifice. They found that one of the casks that had been left full the preceding day was emptied right down the bung-hole (*usque ad foramen obicis*), and the wine spilled all over the flagstones. In great dismay, the cellarer sharply rebuked his man, telling him that he must have fixed the spigot carelessly the evening before. He enjoined him to tell no one what had occurred, and added threats. For

---

*"Lyng fish:" a symbol, as in ancient Central American myths of Votan, heart of the world, whose emblem was the *green* emerald, for vast subterranean tunnels of the "snake-men," or men of the underworld.

he felt that if the abbot were told he, the cellarer, would lose his job.

"When evening came, the cellarer returned to the wine-vaults and, before the monks had retired to sleep, carefully secured the bung-holes of all the casks, and shut the cellar door, and went to bed. But next morning, on entering the cellar, he saw that another cask had been emptied. . . . Not knowing whom to blame, he was filled with despair and wonder, and again ordered his servant to say nothing. He went to bed after fastening all the bungs with extreme care, and carefully re-locked the door. Rising at dawn and going down to the cellar he found a third cask emptied. The bung had been extracted and wine spilled all over the flagstones. Being greatly alarmed he decided to keep silence no longer, and hastened to tell the abbot. The abbot took counsel with the senior monks, and ordered that, towards evening, the bung-holes of all full casks should be anointed with chrism *(holy oil)*. . . .

"At dawn of next day, the brother *(frater)*, going into the cellar, found a marvellously little black boy, or dwarf *(pueruium nigrum mirandae parvitatis)* clinging by the hands to one of the bungs *(in uno de pessulis manibus haerentem)*. Hastily seizing him, he took him to the abbot and said: 'My Lord, here is the urchin who has done all the damage in the cellar!' The abbot, astonished at the strange appearance of the boy, took counsel with the senior monks and ordered that the boy have a monk's dress prepared for him, and associate with the youths who were scholars of the monastery *(cum scholaribus puerulis in claustro conversari)*.

"The strange boy lived with these scholars night and day but never took a drink or food, never spoke, either in public or private, and while the others were sleeping at night or in noontide, he sat upon his bed and constantly moaned or deeply sighed. Meantime, the abbot of another monastery came to perform his devotions in the church. And the scholars frequently passing before him as he sat with the abbot and the older monks, he saw the little boy stretch his hands toward him as if to ask a favour.

"So often did the strange boy repeat this gesture that the abbot, noting his small stature, said to the monks who sat near him: 'Why do you keep so little a boy in your convent?' They replied, smiling: 'My Lord, he is not what you suppose!' They told him the story of the cellar, and the abbot groaned deeply and said: 'Expel him at once! He is clearly a devil in human form; but, by the mercy of God and the merits of the saints, whose relics you have here, he has been held from doing you more injury.' At the command of the abbot, the boy was at once brought before him, and while they were in the act of stripping off his monastic dress he vanished from their hands like smoke (*inter manus eorum ut fumus evanuit*)."

The mysterious black and dwarfish boy had "found the hole in the wall" and, as if he had been teleported to early medieval Germany from some tribe of Central African pigmies, he had as mysteriously returned to that unknown bourne whence he had come. Here, again, we have a story in part garbled by medieval monasticism.

Ralph, the Abbot of Coggeshall (Essex), mentioned above, tells another curious story which he may have heard, in the ancient guest-house of his abbey, from some traveller. Abbot Ralph is reputed to have been a careful and conscientious writer who took trouble in order to get at the truth about an event, in his late twelfth century day:

"In the time of King Richard I (1189-99), at Daghewurthe, in Suthfolke" (west Suffolk, two miles north of Stowmarket), "in the house of Lord Osberne of Bradwell, a certain fantastic spirit appeared often in the family circle of this soldier, imitating the voice of an infant, and calling himself Malkin. He asserted that his mother and brother were staying in a certain house, and spoke chidingly against them. On that account, he had separated from them and presumed to speak with men. He performed wonders, and spoke with laughter, and sometimes revealed the hidden and secret acts of others. At first the knight's wife and family were truly terrified at his conversation; but, after a time, become accustomed to his ridiculous words and actions, they gained confidence, and spoke frequently and familiarly with him, and asked him questions. He spoke English according to the idiom of that reign, also now and then Latin, and discoursed of scripture with the knight's chaplain. He could be heard and felt; but not all seen, save on one occasion when a chamberwoman (housemaid) caught sight of him in the form of a child, but only for an instant when he was clothed in a white tunic. He had beforehand begged the girl that he might make himself visible; but she would not consent until he had sworn by God that he would neither touch nor violate her."

This poltergeist, or familiar, made a confession implying that he had been *teleported*:

"He confessed that he was born at Lanaham" (Lenham, Kent, or Lalnafan, near Aberystwyth?), "and, while his mother took him (or abandoned him) into the country, or field, where she was working as a harvester, she left him alone in a certain part of the field, when by a certain other he was forcibly carried and transported to another place. And he remained seven years in that same place and, after seven years more, he was returned to his former habitation. He said to a certain chaplain, and to others with whom he was familiar, that he would again become invisible. Many times he demanded food and drink from those standing near him, and they set it on a certain chest and he was not seen any more."

Giraldus Cambrensis, or de Barri, born at the castle of Manorbier, in Pembrokeshire, in 1146 (?), and called "Sylvester" by his enemies, in allusion to Pope Sylvester who was accused of black magic and necromancy, was connected with Rhys ap Gruffydd, prince of South Wales, and made archdeacon of Brecknock. He tells a story of a case of teleportation in Denmark. He died about 1220.

"In our days in Dacia (Denmark), an unknown priest acquired the favour of an archbishop by his obsequious bearing. He had a good memory and a general knowledge of letters. One day, talking with the archbishop, about ancient history and unknown events, he alleged that Christianity had lessened the power of demons over mankind. 'Some leapt into the sea, others hid in hollows or crevices in rocks, or hollow trees, and I, myself, leapt into a well.' Here he blushed for shame and went away. The archbishop and company were astonished, and asked many questions of each other and much conjectured, while they waited the strange man's return, as they had expected. The archbishop sent a servant to call him, but in vain, for he had vanished and could nowhere be found. He never was seen again. Later, two priests, sent by the archbishop to Rome, returned, and when they heard of the affair they asked how and when it happened. 'Why,' they said, 'on that very same day, and hour, we met that man in the Alps, and he said to us: "I have been sent to the Roman court on business (*ad curiam Romam*) of my master, the archbishop of Denmark!"'"

Giraldus adds the comment, so characteristic of the middle ages that the man "must have been a demon in human form." The passage about "jumping into a well" is "explained" in another curious story, told by Giraldus, about a strange, red-haired young man who suddenly turned up in the house of Eliodorus de Stakepol, in the "province of Pembroch," Pembrokeshire, West Wales. (It may be noted that in Stackpool Church, Pembrokeshire, there can still be seen, today, the effigy of a twelfth century cross-legged knight named "Eliodore de Stakepole.")

> "This strange man said his name was Simon. He took the keys from the seneschal, and took over, also, the seneschal's job; but he was so clever and finished a manager that nothing was ever lost or wanting in the house, which ever more became prosperous. If the master or mistress thought of something they would like, and did not even speak their thought, he read their minds and, hey presto, he got it, and no orders given him! He knew where they cached their gold and jewels. He would say to them: 'Why this niggard care of your gold and silver? Is not life short? Then enjoy it, spend your gold or you will die without enjoying life, and the money you so cautiously hoard will do you no service.' He had an eye for the good opinion of menials, and rustics, and he gave them the choicest food and drink."

This quite aristocratic type of mysterious man held some very modern views. Indeed, he must have been a very early Socialist! For he said that "those who have abundance ought to give bounteously of that which by their labourers' toil they had acquired."

> "He knew all the secrets of the lord and lady of the manor-house, and what he wanted done, were it pleasing or displeasing, *was* done! This strange red-haired man set his foot in no church, used no breviary, and uttered no Catholic word or religious sentiment. He did not sleep in the manor-house; but was always on hand to serve and spring forward to give what was wanted."

But the "Stakepols" did not know when they were well off, and their progeny had more of that niggling and prying middle class morality than became members of the "country gentry." They were very curious about this strange young man, a rare-jewel of a servitor, who had suddenly appeared from nowhere, in a West Wales country house:

> "The young Stakepols took to spying on him in the grounds of the manor, and, one night, peering out from behind a holly-bush, when the strange man was, by chance, gazing

hard into the waters of a still mill-dam, they saw him moving his lips as if in converse with something unseen."

Next morning, the knight and old Pembroke "gentleman," Stakepol, summoned the young man to the private chamber and sacked him there and then. He had done them no harm, but much good, and it may be suspected that some sour-faced fanatic of a padre, or monk, had spoken to the lord of the manor of some old Christian folk lore about how "demons" could be known by their gazing into still water, or jumping into wells:

"As they took the keys from him, the lady of the manor asked him: 'Who art thou?'
"He replied: 'I am begotten of the wife of a yokel of this parish by a demon who lay upon her in the shape of her own husband.'
"He named the man who was so cuckolded, who was lately dead. The mother was still alive, and when strict inquiry was made of her, the thing was certified to be true by her public confession."

We seem to have, here, merely the early medieval interpretation of the phenomenon of teleportation, in terms of the barbarous monkish superstition of incubi and succubi, generated by the nasty minds of monastics suffering from suppressed sex. But do we, today, *know* much more of this phenomenon than they did in the days of Giraldus Cambrensis?

The answer must be: We do *not!* Nor will the derision of orthodox scientists advance the bounds beyond our nescience.

Besides phenomena which seem to relate to teleportation of human beings, the ages of faith have, in many records known only to highly specialized scholars, or to Orientalists, told of the appearance of animals or monsters, apparently unknown to zoologists or herpetologists. Often the stories are passed over with a smile or a scoff as just travellers' tales. However, in this chapter, that need not deter us from mentioning some of them. Abu Hassan al-Masudi, an Arab historian and geographer, descendant of one of the Prophet's companions and native of Baghdad, travelled in China, India, Egypt, Persia and the Caspian region, in or about the year of the Hegira 332 (A.D. 946), and tells, in his *Meadows of Gold*, about an adventure of one, er Rashid:

"One day, he was hunting in the country, near el-Mausil, when a white falcon in his hand became uneasy, and he let it go. After a long time, it came back with an insect like a serpent, or a fish, with wings like fins. . . . Some observers have told me that, in Egypt and other countries, they have seen white serpents in the air, moving from place to place as fast as lightning; that they lit sometimes on an animal and killed it; and that they are sometimes heard flying by night, when, in their locomotion in the air they are accompanied by a noise like that made when new cloth is unfolded. Persons who have no knowledge of the subject and superstitious women are heard to say that the sound proceeds from witches flying on quails' wings. But it seems to prove that animals live in the upper elements."

This oddity would have appealed to the late Sir Arthur Conan Doyle! The Chronicon of Denys de Tell-Mahre, a patriarch of the Syrian Jacobites, who was born in Mesopotamia (Iraq) about the end of the eighth century A.D. records as follows:

"A.D. 774: "Before the reign of the (Byzantine-Greek) Emperor Leo IV (that is, prior to A.D. 774), there raged a plague, followed by the appearance of frightening and terrible animals who feared nothing and no man. They fled from no man and, indeed, killed many. A very little they were like wolves, but their muzzle was small and long, and they had great ears, like those of horses. The skin on their dorsal spine resembled the bristles of pigs, and stuck straight up. These mysterious animals committed great ravages on the people in the Abdin Rock region, near Hoh. In certain villages they devoured more than 100 people, and in many others, from twenty and forty to fifty. Nothing could be done against them for they were fearless of man. If, by chance, men pursued them, in no wise did the monsters become scared or flee, but turned on the men. If men loosed their weapons on a monster, it leapt on the men and tore them in pieces. These monsters entered houses and yards, and seized and carried off children (*pueri*), and went out, no one offering resistance. They climbed in the night on to terraces, abducted children from their beds, and went off before any could oppose them. When they appeared, the dogs did not bark, so that for this reason alone the countryside suffered a more bitter experience than it had ever known before. Two or three men dared not move around together, and no more were cattle seen in the fields, for all had been devoured by these monsters. Indeed, when one of them attacked a herd of goats, or flock of sheep, it took away several at a time. . . .

These monsters passed into Arzanene," (region in southern Armenia, on the borders of Assyria) "and badly ravaged every village, as well as in the country of Maipherk and on Mt. Cahai, and they caused damage at Amida," (on the Upper Tigris). . . . *Several pages are here missing in the original MS.*

What were these strange animals and whence did they come?

The Chronicon of Frodoardus—he is named, variously, as Frodardus, Flordardus, or Flavellus, was born in A.D. 894 at Epernay, and became a regular Benedictine monk, writing his Chronicon at the mature age of seventy in A.D. 963—tells of a phenomenon several times recorded in the following six centuries, in England and France—and still as mysterious today:

A.D. 943: "Exceedingly great tempest and whirlwind completely overthrew very old and very strongly built houses of cement on the hills of the Martyrs" (Montmartre, Paris.) "where St. Denys was martyred. It was reported that things like demons or horses (*feruntur daemones tunc ibi sub equitatem specie visi*) were seen at the height of the storm, which struck a church . . . destroying the beams and removing walls, and laid waste all with the vines on the hills."

Some people in America, today, would suggest that these so-called "demon horses" may have been flying saucers!

Abbot Ralph of Coggeshall Abbey, Essex, has, in his Chronicle, a very odd story of another phenomenon in a storm, *not* of a type appealing to modern meteorologists, zoologists, or marine biologists:

24 *June*, 1205: "In the holy night of John the Baptist, all night thunder roared and lightning, terrific, incessantly flashed all over England. A certain strange monster was struck by lightning at Maidstone, in Kent, where, in the highest degree, the most horrible thunder reverberated. . . . This monster had the head of an ass, the belly of a human being, and other monstrous members and limbs (*caput asinorum ventrem humanum . . . portentosi membri*) of animals very unlike each other. Its black corpse was scorched (by the lightning) and so intolerable a stench came from it that hardly anyone was able to go near it."

As to the last feature, any modern farm-worker, hardened

to the foul smell of silo-pits, could have managed the approach to an interesting animal that may remind us that Loch Ness monsters, or what the Irish call "piastes," are not necessarily merely the products of imagination and overworked Scottish or Irish distilleries (I, myself, and another man, saw, on Tuesday, 5 July, 1949, at 11:30 a.m., an even weirder sight in the creek of East Looe, at Cornwall. A young news editor of the *Daily Mail* promised to investigate this, but did not do so.)*

Abbot Ralph records another eerie incident in a violent electric storm, on 29 July, of the same year, 1205:

"In the night of the festival of the holy martyr, Felix, horrible thunders and cracklings and incessant lightning raged over all England, all night long; so that one thought the Day of Judgment had come. Men nearly died of fear and horror. Men, women and cattle were killed, houses burnt to ashes, corn crushed flat, with great stones the size of goose eggs, with sharp stings (or pointed, *aculeati*). Trees torn up by the roots and carried to other places. Ropes appeared as if whirled round and some torn to pieces right in the middle. . . .

"Next day certain monstrous tracks (*vestigia*: hoofprints, or pointed feet) were seen in several places, and of a kind never seen before. Men said they were the prints of demons."

The Abbot seeks to explain this phenomenon as a "war in the skies" (*Ex Ethico Jerome*), in which "good angels" cut "demons to pieces and thrust them into chasms in the earth."

---

*Two remarkable saurians, 19-20 feet long, with bottle-green heads one behind the other, their middle parts under the water of the tidal creek of East Looe, Cornwall, apparently chasing a shoal of fish up the creek. What was amazing were their dorsal parts: ridged, serrated, and like the old Chinese pictures of dragons. Gulls swooped down towards the one in the rear, which had a large piece of orange peel on his dorsal parts. These monsters—and two of us saw them —resembled the plesiosaurus of Mesozoic times. In that month of 1949, the Gulf Stream showed an aberration from its normal course; so that fishermen at Mevagissey, not far away, were scared when they netted a 20-foot-long tropical turtle, never seen, normally, off Cornwall. Unfortunately I had left my camera behind. It is futile to report such phenomena to marine biological stations. *Author*.

He says: "The philosophers care to dispute this more than other high matters."

It is curious that, in August, 1956, *peónes* with farms on the flanks of the southern cordilleras of the Argentina went, badly scared, to the local *jefe de policia*, and told him that they had seen monstrous tracks in the snow of the higher Andes which were made by no beasts known to them. Whether or no the southern Andes has the counterpart of the Tibetan "abominable snowman," one cannot say.

The *Chronicon de Melrose* (Cottonian MS. Faustina, British Museum), compiled by the old monks of the Cistercian Abbey of Melrose, spoke of a queer incident at Scarborough, Yorkshire, in A.D. 1065. It is of a type usually relegated to folk lore, as merely medieval superstitions about the "Devil riding a black mare." Today, one might talk of a Loch Ness monster, or some "sea serpent" wandering inland from Scarborough in a hurricane:

> *August*, 1065: ". . . Great tempest and thunders at York, when the old enemy was also seen by many in that horrid tempest, mounted on a black horse." (In margin of MS: *diabolus visus*, the devil seen). "The monster was of very large size and preceded the storm. He was always flying towards the sea to tread it under foot, and was followed by the blast of thunder and the flash of lightning, with horrid cracklings. Indeed, the tracks of this horse, aforesaid, were seen, of enormous size, imprinted on a mountain (*sic*: *de monte*) at the city of *Scandeburch* (Scarborough), whence he leapt into the sea. Here, on the top of several ditches, men found, stamped in the earth, prints made by the monster, where he had violently stamped with his feet. . . ."

Abbot Ralph of Coggeshall, Essex, tells of another phenomenon rather like that which terrified the Argentinian *peónes*, *supra*, more than 760 years later. As before, there is little or nothing new under the sun, as the Abbot, doubtless, would agree, were he alive today:

> "In the time of King Richard I, of England" (1189-99), "there appeared in a certain grassy, flat ground human footprints of extraordinary length; and everywhere the footprints were impressed *the grass remained as if scorched by fire* (*herba velut igne ustulata remanserat*). This was in the province of York." (Oddly enough, about this time there was found on the seashore, in the county of York, the

head of a giant [*caput giganteum*], and "the finder said it would hold the highest capacity of corn." Whether this was the head of some unknown monster of the deep, one may confidently leave to the cogitations of a marine biologist, knowing well, beforehand, what he would say! *Author.*)

We may pass on to the year 1293, of which Raphael Holinshed, or Hollingshead, son of an old and decayed family of Cophurst, Cheshire, and who travelled all over England collecting curious items told, in his *Chronicle* published in 1577, at the "signe of the Starre, in Aldersgate," a very singular thriller, and horrifying story:

circa 1293: "At a solemnization of the second marriage of King Alexander of Scotland, after the 31st year of his reigne . . . as the bridegroom was leading the bride in a dance, a great number of lords and ladies following them, there appeared, closing in the rear, a creature resembling death, all naked and flesh and *lire* (?) with bare bones, right dreadful to behold, which spectacle the king and the residue of all the companie were sore astonished by, and put in such feare that they quickly made an end of their dance for that time."

Quiet folk of today, who live near public dance-halls, would like to hear that a phenomenon of this sort was around at midnight, or after!

In passing, one may note that Holinshed, like some of his twentieth-century successors, was outspoken in criticism of the Queen Elizabeth of his day, and did not exactly mince his words in his accounts of Elizabeth Tudor's tortuous, feminine policy, ever vacillating in accord with the old French poet's criticism of fair or unfair women:

> "*Souven femme varie,*
> *Bien fol qui s'y fie.*"
> (*Fickle woman changed her mind.*
> *Big Fool believed her, went and whined.*)

In Holinshed's case, the reverend greybeards of Elizabeth's beruffed Privy Council removed, not him, indeed, but parts of his *Chronicle!*

In another little known—this time, *French*—chronicle, appeared a curious item which again seems to imply that it is not only men, women or children who may pass involuntarily through the "hole in the wall" of the space-time continuum, but fauna or arachnidae. For example, *scorpions* are, outside, the zoological gardens, as rarely seen in Paris, France, as are "Portuguese men o' war" at Hastings, Sussex. Yet, says the author of *Le Journal d'un Bourgeois de Paris*—he may have been, in his fifteenth-century day, a cleric in the Université de Paris:

> A.D. 1421: "The English army occupied Paris and, in this year, there were found, at Paris, *escorpions* that one had never been accustomed to see at this time."

Joseph Ritson, an antiquarian who died in 1803, in a lunatic asylum, found, about the year 1785, in some old library in a manor house in the shires of northern England—which he did not locate, as he should have done—a very curious ballad which, from the evidence of its style and vocabulary, must have been written by someone who was a contemporary of William Shakespeare of Stratford-upon-Avon. The ballad is certainly older than the year 1636. He titled it: "Bateman's Tragedy;" whereas, really, he ought to have called it "The Mystery of the fate of old Jerman's pretty young wife." Ritson inserted this ballad in his "Ancient Songs and Ballads from the reign of Henry II to the Revolution" (of Oliver Cromwell). Among them is a fine old Christmas carol of the thirteenth century, which Ritson must have found in the Sloane MSS. in the British Museum.

"Bateman's Tragedy" was intended, as a "Godly Warning to all Maidens, by the example of God's Judgment shewed upon one, Jerman's wife of Clifton, in the county of Nottingham who, lying in childbed, was borne away and never heard of after."

Ritson was almost as curious an old fellow as this singular ballad. He was born, in 1752, of a family of yeomen of Stockton-on-Tees; but, apparently, when he saw the light, the family, like Thomas Hardy's "Durbeyvilles," must have run through their property. Ritson had some odd vicissitudes; at one time he was a servant employed by a tobacconist, then by a merchant of Stockton-on-Tees, but his admirable urge for betterment took him to London, where, from serving as an attorney's clerk, he was called to the bar at Gray's Inn. For some unearthly reason, Ritson took to a permanent diet of milk and vegetables which he kept up till death, and it "made him a very morose man." In Ritson's old age, this dreary diet may have contributed to his going insane when he was living in rooms in Gray's Inn. One day he set fire to a very valuable collection of old MSS. and ballads, and such volumes of smoke poured out of his chambers that the Treasurer of the Inn, fearing that the whole stuffy Inn, with its musty landings and winding wooden stairs, would be set on fire, broke down old Ritson's doors. Whether it was true that Ritson offered the Treasurer a glass of milk and two cold potatoes, after sternly rebuking him for the invasion of a legal gentleman's rooms, is hard to say, but it is, unfortunately, too true that the Treasurer, who was a fine-old-port-vintage-bottle man, had to arrange, some days later, for poor Ritson's removal to an asylum, where Ritson died of a "brain-tumour."

"Bateman's Tragedy" is the story of "a fair and comely damsel" of Clifton, a village in Notts. Her "cheeks were like the crimson rose," and her shapely legs and arms as white "as swan's down." But, alas, along with a fair face, the lady had a "false heart!" "Many sought in marriage-bed to embrace her body," but she would have none of them at Clifton until there came along "a proper, handsome youth named Bateman." He plighted her his troth, split a gold coin in two—no matter what our Sovereign Lord, the King, might say and threaten about defacing coin of the realm—and gave one half to her:

> " 'The other half, as pledge, dear heart,
>   Myself will have,' said he."

Said she:

> "If I do break my vow to thee,
>   While I remain alive,
> May never thing I take in hand,
>   Be seen at all to thrive."

Alas, not two months went by ere she jilted the Bateman, and had the wedding-bells tolled at Clifton Parish Church to celebrate her marriage to "old Jermans," weighed down with bulging money-bags, and encumbered with streets of decaying houses! True, old Jermans had slight drawbacks, such as rough and grizzled cheeks which had never known Boreham's Scented Soap and Mr. Cut-throat's Patent Razor. His legs were spindly and hairy; but he "was of greater wealth and better in degree" than the Bateman.

The Bateman vowed revenge—posthumous:

> "Thou shalt not live one quiet hour,
>   For surely I will have
> Thee, either now alive or dead,
>   When I am laid in grave."

His rhymes were a trifle "rocky"; but his intentions were pretty clear. On the day she married old Jermans, the Bateman, failing to heed the spirit of the advice of some Tudor predecessor of Sir John Suckling:

> "*Are there not others fair as she?*
> *If thou canst not make her,*
> *Why, the Devil take her!*"

hitched a cord round his neck, shoved the other end over a branch of the old medlar tree, and hanged himself. But the lady was to find that his spook would, anon, be right in the married bed-room, peering behind the "cramoisie" tester-curtains for the time when she was cradled in the senile arms of the aged Jermans. That was the signal for this unsporting poltergeist to make the hour of love hideous with groans, howls, sighs, and voices assuring her and old Jermans that: "I *will* have her, not thee, old bald pate!" As the ballad puts it, the lady, in a manner *most* unusual, as cynics say, in this peculiar case, hugged old Jermans "mortal close and tight" in the marriage-bed; *not* because she was smitten with a strange passion for this old Methuselah, but so that, if the Bateman carried out his ghostly intentions, he would have to bear away both what he sought, and, eke, what he did *not*.

In due time young Mrs. Jermans was "delivered of a child"; but whether or no old Jermans wished it, she pressed her far from eager friends to stay in the bedroom all night, and not leave her alone until broad day had come. The spirit of the friends was far from willing; and as the nightly racket had unexpectedly ceased their drowsy heads nodded in the haybags with which old Jermans had been compelled to cushion the hard, angular Tudor chairs. The flesh proved decidedly weak:

> "*So being all full fast asleep,*
> *To them unknown which way,*
> *The child-bed woman that woeful night*
> *From them was borne away.*
> *And to what place no creature knew,*
> *Nor to this day can tell.*
> *As strange a thing as ever yet*
> *In any age befell.*"

It is curious that, while the eighteenth-century compilers of protracted country histories often bore us to distraction with their uninteresting accounts of the fee simples and Latinized tombstones of dull medieval knights and Tudor lords of the manor, or of guttling and guzzling sporting eighteenth-century parsons, remembered in after times only by grave women of the parishes who deplored the number of base-born brats laid at the said parsons' doors by deceived and abandoned wenches in the villages, yet not one antiquarian who speaks of Clifton, in Nottinghamshire, has seen fit to spare one word, or tear, or even to mention the Bateman, old Jermans, or the lady, whose name no one knows.

From the pathetic vim of quaint Joe Ritson, one might infer that *he* had been jilted by some saucy country maiden, and that was why he took to a permanent and unrelieved diet of milk and cold vegetables.

We now come to the most mysterious affair of the "black dog of Bungay," in the county of Suffolk. The overture to this mystery of the days of Queen Elizabeth Tudor, which mystery old Abraham Fleming, in his black-letter brochure (imprinted at London, by Frauncis Godly, dwelling at the west end of Paules"), called "a horrible shaped *Thing* sensibly perceaved by the people (there assembled)," opened at Blibery, (Blythburgh, near Halesworth, Suffolk), "on Sundaie, 4 August, 1577, between the hours of 9 and 10 o'clocke, in the forenoon":

"Whilst the minister was reading of the second lesson in the parish church of Bliborough, a towne in Suffolke, a strange and terrible tempest of Lightning and Thunder strake through the wall of the churche into the grounde about a yarde deepe, drave downe all the people on that side, above 20 persons, then renting (rending) the wall up to the revestre (vestry), cleft the doore, and, returning to the steeple, rent the timber, brake the chimes, and fled towardes Bongie (Bungay), a town aboute five miles off. The people were striken downe and were found grovelling more than half an houre after; whereof one man, more than fortie yeares, and a boy of fifteene yeares old, were found starke dead. The others were scorched. The same, or the like flash of Lightning and crack of Thunder rent the parish church of Bongie, 9 miles from Norwich, wrong in sunder the wiers (wires) and wheeles of the clocke, slue two men which sat in the belfreie, when the other were at the procession, or suffrages, and scorched another who hardlie escaped."

Abraham Fleming, in his black letter, with quaint woodcut of the "Thing of horrible shape," tells what happened at Bungay, the same Sunday morning, 4 August, 1577:

"The parish Church at Bongie (Bungay) did quake and stagger under the violence of a storm, such as never before hath been seen. There were terrible cracks of thunder and flashes of lightning. It struck into the harts of those that were present such a sore and sodain feare, that they were in a manner robbed of their right wits. Immediately thereupon, there appeared in a most horrible shape and similitude to the congregation . . . a *Thing like a black dog*, at the sight whereof, together with the fearfulle flashes of fire, which then were seen, aroused such admiration (wonder and fear) in the mindes of the assemblie, that they thoughte doom's day was already come. This black dog, or the divil in such a likenesse, running all along down the body of the Church with greate swiftnesse . . . among the people, in a visible form and shape, passed between two persons as they were kneeling . . . and occupied in prayer, as it seems, wrung the neckes of them both at one instant, clene backwards, insomuch that, even at a moment where they kneeled, they strangely dyed! . . .

"There was at the same time another wonder wrought; for the same black dog, still continuing in one and the self-same shape, passing by another of the congregation, gave him such a blow in the back, that therewithall he was presently drawen togither and shrunk up, as it were a peece of leather touched with a hot fire, or, as the mouthe of a purse or bag drawen togither with a string. This man, albeit he was in so strange a taking, dyed not; but it is thoughte, is yet alive. . . .

"Moreover, before this, the Clark of the said Church, being occupied in clearing the gutters of the Church, with a violent clap of thunder was smitten down, and beside his fall had no further harm, unto whom, being all amazed, this strange shape . . . appeared. Howbeit, he escaped without daunger, which might peradventure seem to sound against trueth and to be a thing incredible. . . . At the tyme, the Rector, or Curate of the Church, being partakers of the people's perplexity, comforted the people and exhorted them to prayer. . . .

"And now, as testimonies to the force which rested in this strange shaped thing, there are remaining in the stones of the Church, and likewise in the Churche dore, which are marvelously renten and torne, ye marke, as it were, of his clawes or talons. Beside that, all the wires, the wheeles and other things belonging to the Clocke, were wrung in sunder. . . . At the time the tempest lasted . . . the whole Church was so darkened . . . yea, so palpable was the darkness, that one person could not perceave the other . . . but only in the great flashing, when the fire and lightning appeared."

Fleming adds what Raphael Holinshed cautiously omits, in our citation above: that the Thing also raised hell in the parish church at "Blibery" (Blythburgh), "not above 7 miles from Bungaie:"

> "The like Thing, in the same shape, entered the Church at Blibery, where, placing himself upon a main balke or beam, whereon sometyme ye Rood did stand, sodainly he gave a swinge down through ye Church, and there, also, as before, slew two men and a lad, and burned the hand of another person . . . among the rest of the company, of whom divers were blasted. This mischief thus wrought, he flew with wonderful force to no little feare of the assembly, out of the Church, in a hideous and hellish liking. . . . These things are reported to be true, yea, by mouthes of eye-witnesses of ye same."

Fleming, of course, had little doubt of whom or what this "Thing" was: the Devil and all! But, in our more (?) rational age, we may ask *was* this a thunderbolt! If so, it was a very strange one, whose behaviour no meteorologist or physicist would care to certify, or corroborate.

Nor was this the first time on record when a phenomenon of this type was reported. For example, Bertin, a French historian who lived in 1160, and wrote or compiled the *Annales Francorum Regum*, and seems to have had some connexion with the monastery of Sithieu, founded by St. Bertin in A.D. 707, at St. Omer (Pas de Calais), says:

> "A.D. 856: In August, Teotogaudus, bishop of Trier (Rhenish Prussia), with clerics and people was celebrating the office, when a very dreadful cloud, with thunderstorms, and lightning, terrified the whole congregation in the church, and deadened the sound of the bells ringing in the tower. The whole building was filled with such dense darkness that one and another could hardly see or recognize his or her neighbour. On a sudden, there was seen a dog of immense size (*canis nimiae enormitatis*) in a sudden opening of the floor or earth (*subito terrae hiatu*), and it ran to and fro around the altar."

The *Chronicon Saxonicus* also reports that, in A.D. 867, a thing like a great dog was seen at Trier, in the pontifical chair of the great church.

It was a "thing like a *pig*" that was "teleported" in the case of a church at Andover, Hants, in 1171:

"A.D. 1171: On the night of the birthday of the Lord, there were thunderings and lightnings, of which the like had not been heard before. And at Andover, a certain priest, at midnight, in the presence of the whole congregation, was cast down by lightning, with no other injuries . . . but what *looked like a pig (porcorum sicut)* was seen to run to and fro between his feet, not haphazardly (*scientibus*)." (*Story told by an unknown monk of Malmesbury Abbey who wrote the "Eulogium Historiarum."*)

According to Holinshed, the electric storm at Andover happened in A.D. 1172, on Christmas Eve, lasted all Christmas Day and terrified people all over England and Ireland. The priest was struck and killed at the altar, at 9 a.m., Christmas morning, and his brother, running to his aid, was consumed in the fire. Again, Holinshed cautiously omits any reference to the "thing like a pig." Holinshed would have qualified as a leader-writer of the London *Daily Telegraph*, which has never forgotten the alleged Roman inscription found carved on a post on the Southern African veldt, in the early years of the twentieth century, which it incautiously certified as authentic; until some scoffer analysed the inscription as being: "This yer post is fer catel to scratch thur baks on!"

But it is another Tudor historian who tells a queer story of a Bungay-like phenomenon happening in the church of St. Michael's, Cornhill, London, in or about 1538. He is John Stowe, or Stow, born in the parish of St. Mary's, Cornhill, old London, in 1525 (?), and who died in 1605:

"In the reign of King John thunder and lightning killed many men and women, and children, burnt cornfields, and fishes of strange shape, armed with the helmets and shields, like armed men were caught, only they were much bigger. . . ."

He adds the story of the mysterious monster found blasted by lightning near London—he meant Maidstone, Kent—and relates a story told him by his father:

"My father told me that, at St. Michael's church, in the Cornhill ward, London, on the night of St. James, certain men were ringing the bells of St. Michael's, in the loft, when there arose a tempest of thunder and lightning, and a thing of an ugly shape and sight was seen to come in at the south window, and it lighted on the north. For fear whereof, all the ringers fell down and lay as dead for a time, leaving the bells to ring and cease of their own accord.° When the ringers came to themselves, they found certain stones of the north window to be rased and scrat as if they had been so much butter, printed with a lion's claw; the same stones were fastened there again, when it was repaired, and remains so to this day. I have seen them oft, and have put a feather or small stick into the hole where the claw had entered, three or four inches deep. At the same time, certain maine Timber posts at Queen Hith were scrat and cleft from top to bottom, and the Pulpit Cross in Paul's churchyard was likewise scrat, cleft and overturned. One of the ringers lived in my youth, whom I have oft heard to verifye the same to be true, and I have oft heard my Father to report it."

What sort of monster was this who left claw-prints *four inches deep in stone?* One might as well ask whence the *Thing* came! Hardly a fire-ball, meteorite, or thunderbolt?

Another case of real or apparent teleportation of a human being, in an electric storm, is cited by the Jesuit de Lozeran du Fech, professor royal of mathematics of the University of Perpignan, who published at Bordeaux, in 1762, a "Dissertation on Thunderstorms:"

"Wolfgang tells of a thunderstorm that lifted up a man and transported him to a place so far away that he never reappeared any more. This happened on a high road, where there were many witnesses, during a storm. And, so, the thunder (*sic*) served very well to veil an assassination."

Obviously Wolfgang, and, it seems Lozeran du Fech, must have believed that some mysterious and unknown entities had operated behind the cover of an electric storm, even if "they" had not actually created the tempest! Who really *knows,* even today, on the threshold of the age of interplanetary travel?

°In Tibet, wild "hielanmen" scare off devils by blowing on trumpets made of human thigh-bones. Even so, the original use of church bells, so delightful a sound on summer mornings and evenings in the English countryside, was really to scare off demons and devils whose portraits may be found in the medieval church gargoyles.

We come to non-living objects that appear to have come from nowhere, or to have been teleported.

St. Gregory of Florence, or Florentin, Archbishop of Tours, who wrote the *Historia Francorum*, has a story of a phenomenon happening in A.D. 588:

> "In several houses one found, in A.D. 588, earthenware vases engraved with different signs, whose meaning I know not. These unknown characters it was impossible to remove or delete. This phenomenon was particularly seen in a town in the territory of Chartres, or Chartrain (*Carnotenae*), and coming to Orleans and Bordeaux reached its terminus without omitting any intermediate town." (*Also recorded in the "Annales Rerum Francicarum," written in the monastery of St. Arnulfus of Matensis Metz, of which St. Armoul was bishop, prior to his death at Remiremont on 16 August, 640.*)

St. Gregory Florentin also records as happening in 588:

> "Luminous rays or serpents appearing in the sky in the North and some people saw serpents fall from the clouds, and others say that a whole village of houses and people perished and suddenly disappeared."

The latter phenomenon, as he does not say, happened in Germany, and has a very odd sound today, when mysterious disappearances of jet aircraft and their skilled pilots occur at a time when the hostile type of flying saucers, called "serpents" by Gregory of Florentin, have been registered on radarscopes. Again, there is little or nothing new under the sun, in our mysterious planet!

Roger of Wendover, Bucks—he was a monk of St. Alban's Abbey, and a chronicler, who was born at Wendover, and died in 1236—records, in his *Chronica sive Flores Historiarum*, a case of teleportation by some mysterious and unknown agency, in the sky. It is an early example of a phenomenon recorded, many times, as happening in western Europe in the nineteenth century:

> "Clodesindus, of Metz, was flying from her husband when an angel conveyed to God the covering of her head . . . whereat, she committed herself to God."

Marcus Frytschius, who lived in 1563, mentions in his *Catalogus prodigiorum atque ostentorum*—he was a native of Laubanum (Lauban), in Schliessen, Prussia—a queer case of the teleportation of earth:

> A.D. 822: "This year a prodigious portent occurred in Thuringia: a foot and a half of turf was seen suddenly to be lifted into the air from over a total area of twenty-five feet. It also happened on the borders of Saxony and Misnia," (Meissen, near Dresden, ancient capital of Misnia) "that the earth swelled up and erected itself in a heap near Lake Aonseum, creating a mound nearly 3,000 paces long."

Again, what mysterious and unseen agent, aloft, was operating on turf, far below?

The *Chronicon Ecclesiae Sancti Bertini,* compiled at St. Bertin's Abbey of St. Sithieu, in what is now the Pas-de-Calais, says that, at the time St. Lothair's coronation, in 840:

> "In Thuringia, a clod of earth over fifty feet long, fourteen feet broad, and six feet thick, no hand touching it (*sine manibus a terra pracisus*) was cut off, and raised into the air. In Saxony the earth was puffed up like a mound of one *leucae*" (a league).

It is impossible to say whether this phenomenon happened twice in the same place or whether the compiler-monk made an error in the dates, giving a discrepancy of eighteen years.

One may compare this ninth-century mystery with what Stowe, the Tudor annalist, says happened "In the Hermitage, in Dorset," on 3 January, 1582:

> "On that Sunday, 3 January, 1582, in the valley of the Cerf Blanc, in Dorset, a piece of earth suddenly quitted its place of former time, and was transferred and transported forty yards to another paddock, in which were alders and willows. It stopped the high road leading to the little town of Cerne. Yet the same hedges which surrounded it still enclose it today, and trees that were there are still standing. The place this bit of land occupied is now a great Hole."

Chapter 11

THE SHEPTON MALLET MYSTERY

UNDER THE SHADOW of the beautiful Mendip Hills, over which, on summer days, the deep white cumulus clouds like wind-blown galleons glide, lies the small town of Shepton Mallet, in the county of Somerset. It has a colliery which once belonged to the very old Anglo-Saxon patrician family of the Earls of Waldegrave, who were thanes in old England long before the arrival of Bastard William the Norman and his bandit knights. It has, also, a military "glass-house" which the British Army authorities do *not* advertise; and, too, a fine old market cross with a 52-foot-spire, an unusual hexagonal "shelter," and a brass plate, dated 1500, which the townsfolk very proudly show to the visitor. Despite the holocausts of two world wars, this quaint old township, going far back to old Saxon sheep-trading days, is still, today, a "bride of quietness and slow time"; the drowsy chimes from the fine old church tower distil an opiate oblivion of the busy world outside.

None of the expresses from the North and the Midlands to Bournemouth and the New Forest stop here to set down passengers; so that very few people know that Shepton Mallet is the home of one of the world's unsolved mysteries. Nor do the local guide books advertise this mystery which goes back to the year 1768, the month of June, when "Farmer" George, the third, had been on the British throne for eight years. On that balmy summer evening, Owen Parfitt, aged about seventy, living in a cottage on the turnpike road to Wells, at Wester Shepton, Board's Cross, was the involuntary actor in a riddle which, today, 190 years later, remains as totally without solution as it was then.

He was a tailor; but for years had been bedridden, crippled and could not stir an inch without assistance. A sister, older than himself, looked after him in this humble cottage before the door of which many people, on foot and in wagons and carts, passed up and down, all day long, on the busy turnpike road. The evening was warm and sultry when Owen Parfitt was lifted from his bed by his sister and another woman, and carried downstairs, to be set in a chair, at the door, which opened directly on the highway. He was left there, alone, with his great-coat across his chest, and clad in his sleeping-dress. His sister then went upstairs to clean his bedroom and make his bed, and the other woman went home. About a quarter of an hour later the sister, then upstairs, heard, according to one witness's story, "a noise," and running hastily downstairs found, to her consternation, that her brother Owen had vanished! She at once gave the alarm which spread all over Shepton Mallet and, at once, parties of men started to search the roads and fields for many miles around, even as far as Wells.

They sounded wells, dragged brooks and streams, explored woods and copses; but all in vain. No one had seen or heard Owen Parfitt; and if he *had* gone along the road—and he was bedridden and a total cripple—people, who, all round were haymaking, must have seen him. The township's population was about 3,000, and everybody knew old Parfitt; for many of whom he had made their clothes before he became totally crippled. It may be inferred that he was paralysed. He was never again heard of; nor was any trace of him found.

Forty-six years passed and then, in 1814, when there were still alive in Shepton Mallet people, not *all* in extreme old age, who were either eye-witnesses or participants in the hunt for him, and remembered the circumstances of the baffling mystery, a local attorney, William Maskell, and two or three well-to-do residents, started to examine these witnesses. One witness said that Owen Parfitt had been a soldier in the British Army, and had seen service in "Africa." He had been discharged and worked at his trade as a country tailor. But another witness, a woman distantly related to him, said that Parfitt had never been a soldier. He had no pension for service. Indeed, he had been in his youth a "wild boy," and went away to America and Africa. It may be inferred that he had a very hectic career of unusual adventure; but not a word of it has come down to our own day. More's the pity; because it is evident that we should have had a very interesting story of a wild Somerset man's adventures in strange places in strange times. He was far from an ordinary homekeeping rustic.

In 1877, Maskell's son, a writer of miscellaneous books and pamphlets, now very rare, wrote a brochure about the mystery, in which he points out what is true: that it is very unusual to have, in this type of mystery, so much valid and contemporary evidence of what occurred nearly half a century before the day of William Maskell, his attorney-father.

Let us see what these witnesses said:

Susannah Snook, aged 71, in 1814: "I was the woman who helped his sister carry Owen Parfitt down and set him in his chair before the door of his cottage, I was then twenty-five. It was 1768. I knew him very well. He had been in the British Army and served in Africa. He was a complete cripple; but although his sister was of very advanced age and feeble, she looked after him. I used to help her set Owen into his chair, whilst the bed was being made. This chair was usually placed either in the passage or just outside the door, to give him air. On the day he disappeared, I helped her put him into the chair outside the door, and he was in his sleeping-dress, with an old great-coat thrown over his shoulders. The bed was made and, leaving the sister upstairs, I left the house. In fifteen minutes an alarm was given that Owen Parfitt had disappeared. I came back to the cottage and found his sister, Susannah, much agitated. She was crying bitterly, and could not tell what had become of him. She said to me: 'I went upstairs and, on coming down again, and not hearing him, I called: "Owen, where are you?" There was no answer. I found only the chair, with the old great-coat lying in it!' The alarm spread in Shepton Mallet, and people searched for miles around. It was in vain. No trace of him was ever found or heard of. On the day, the weather was warm; but it turned sultry after the alarm and thunder and lightning came on. His sister did not live for long, in the same house afterwards; but left and was boarded in another house. I often talked with Owen Parfitt and thought he was a fair character." (That is, his character was fairly good.) "He was of middle stature and rather stout."

Samuel Bartlett, who said he was about twenty, in 1768, gave a similar account of Parfitt's character—"quiet and sober . . . I, with others, searched ponds and wells for him. All in vain."

A third witness, Jehosaphat Stone, added evidence of what is an accompaniment of some cases of the phenomenon of teleportation. He said that Owen Parfitt's sister, upstairs making the bed, *heard a noise and found that her brother was gone, and the chair moved*:

"I knew Owen Parfitt well. He was a tailor. Many folk round here at the time believed that Owen Parfitt had been spirited off by supernatural means."

Joseph George: "I lived at Wester Shepton, Board Cross, at the same time as did Owen Parfitt. He made my clothes. I was then a young man. After he had gone I searched a well near the house. But in vain. He was not a very good or a very bad man. Sometimes he was violent."

The evidence of these contemporary witnesses was sent to Dr. Butler, headmaster of Shrewsbury, and, later, Bishop of Lichfield. Butler seems to have had some sort of local contact with Shepton Mallet. For some reason not stated, Butler was struck with the testimony about the noise, and questioned Susannah Snook about it. Snook said that Owen Parfitt's sister told her she heard no noise at the time Owen Parfitt vanished. The chair, she said, was not displaced. Of course, one is not in a position to say whether Butler or the attorney, Maskell, put some leading questions to her on this point; for witness Stone was very positive about it. "There *was* a noise," he said. Moreover, on Susannah Snook's own showing the sister had been too much agitated at the time to be questioned by Snook, and it seems improbable that, *when the mystery occurred*, Stone, who was quite uneducated, would have invented the question about the "noise." Possibly, Parfitt's sister recollected it later, when she was calmer:

Snook: "The storm came on an hour after Owen Parfitt had disappeared. The search lasted all day and night, and went on next day. Owen Parfitt could not move at all without aid of someone else, and, when he vanished, had been a cripple for many years. William Millard, aged 70: "He vanished between 6 and 7 p.m. The alarm was given about that time. . . ."
Joanna Mills, aged 70 or 80: "I was a distant relation of Owen Parfitt. He was neither in the King's service, nor had he any pension. He was wild, and went away in his youth to Africa and America."

It was said that, at Board Cross, a lane from a place called Catsash debouched into the Wells turnpike road; but if so, no one saw Owen Parfitt staggering up that lane. In fact, such a feat in his condition would have been as unlikely as the story that the late President Franklin D. Roosevelt, who was also lame, "hoopled and leapt" on the strand of the pirate and treasure island of Cocos, off Costa Rica, when landing there from a U.S. warship in the 1930's!

Now, as happened in the case of the mystery of the disappearance of the British diplomat, Benjamin Bathurst, forty-one years later at Perleberg, in Prussia, another mystery was unearthed, very near to Owen Parfitt's cottage at Board Cross, much about the time when Maskell was questioning these witnesses. And the second mystery, as in the Bathurst case, *seemed* to hold the clue to the first mystery. In 1813, one,

Henry Strode, was digging in a corner of his garden at Board Cross, the garden being about 150 yards from the site where, in 1768, Owen Parfitt's cottage had stood. A small field separated his garden, and the width of the turnpike road, from Owen Parfitt's old cottage.

Strode told lawyer Maskell:

"Two feet under the surface of the soil, I dug up a piece of a very old wall and found, at the end of it, a skeleton lying face downwards. It seemed as if the person had been thrown in hastily, after death; for the skeleton lay all in a heap. I picked up a skull."

It was found that when Parfitt had disappeared, the house with the garden, in 1813 occupied by Strode was, in 1768, tenanted by a woman named Lockyer, distantly related to Parfitt; but it also appeared that, at the time, no suspicion attached to her. Dr. Butler heard of the discovery and asked that the skull be sent to him, along with the skeleton. It was packed in a box and sent to Shrewsbury. At first Butler was confident that, at long last, the mystery had been solved: this was the skull of Parfitt! *But*, when a surgeon and anatomist was shown the remains, he said they were those of a *young woman*. It is, by the way, odd that we hear of no coroner's inquest on this skull and skeleton, and no attempt made to try to find who the young woman was; although, *prima facie*, a murder seemed to have been committed. We know neither the approximate date when the body had been buried under the wall, nor where the wall had been; so we cannot say whether or no the woman Lockyer had had a hectic past in Shepton Mallet. This second mystery, also, was never cleared up. All the circumstances point to a murder and a hasty and clandestine concealment of a crime. As Sherlock Holmes once pointed out to the "dumb" Watson, his foil, rural places and small towns may be the scene of horrible and sadistic crimes, and are by no means always as Arcadian and innocent as they may appear to outsiders.

Lawyer Maskell's son, William, the pamphleteer and miscellaneous book-writer, appeared, in 1867, to have been inclined to agree with the opinion of the folk of Shepton Mallet in 1768, and later that "the devil had spirited away Owen Parfitt, in the body;" for he refers to Glanvil's "History of Witchcraft," and recalled the saying of the mystified folk of this old Saxon sheep-trading township, in the shadow of the Mendips, that "Owen Parfitt had said that in Africa he, Parfitt, had associated with necromancers and magicians." Maskell also recalls that Glanvil said that witches and wizards, in the seventeenth century, were common in Shepton Mallet and the surrounding countryside.

Again, as one has stated, Somerset county lore has missed a good thing in not having any record of Owen Parfitt's hectic and colourful past. One would give a train-load of theological junk and antiquarian "tombstone" volumes, by Dr. the Rev. Theophilus Dry-as-Dust, for just one small Newgate ballad book on: "My life among the rapscallions and bloody pyrats, in the New England and Massachusett's Bay plantations and the necromancers of Africka, by Owen Parfitt, tailor of Shepton Mallet, in ye yeres 1720 to 1735. All other stories are false, this being certified as the onlie true accompt by ye chaplaine of Newgate Jail."

Lawyer Maskell appears to have fallen down on *this* part of his job, in *not* rescuing from the jaws of old Time and the bony King of Terrors what some of the old timers, still alive in 1814, in Shepton Mallet and Board Cross, could probably have told him of Owen Parfitt's interesting past. This tailor of old Shepton Mallet had a story to tell; for there are dim hints in the evidence of Joanna Mills, aged seventy or eighty, and also in what Owen Parfitt probably told Joseph George, what time he was running the tape measure round George's breeches and waistband. "He was sometimes *violent*," said Joseph George. Yes, the sort of violence characteristic of a man who had lived rough, seen horrors and missed being swung off, in the manner of life of Mister Billy Bones, mate of Flint's old and bloody ship "down to Savana," and who had small patience with hairy hay-seed men and bacon-chawing Shepton Malleteers, in the 1750's.

The question is bound to arise: did Owen Parfitt hide some shameful secret under that old wall in a neighbour's garden? Who knows? All one can say is that, in our own modern phrase: "One would not have put it past him."

It might even have befallen Owen Parfitt, walking in the streets of godlie Boston, Mass., "in ye yere 1720," that he suddenly woke up to find himself tramping on the beach off Table Bay, or the ungodlie strand of Caffraria, with not the ghost of an idea of how he came to be meeting up with very unrespectable and wild Hottentots when, a minute before, he had been dodging the catchpoll of the vestrymen of Boston, Mass., with an order to lay him by the heels and have him soundly flogged for being seen to kiss a saucy young woman under the shadow of a baulk down in Boston Harbor at midnight.

Collinson, the Somerset historian, theorized that perhaps Owen Parfitt had been suddenly seized with frenzy, as he sat in the chair at his door on that warm evening in June,

1768, and had wandered away along the turnpike road. But, unless Collinson supposed that Parfitt had re-enacted the part of the gentleman in the Scriptures, who took up his bed and walked after being cured of paralysis, it is difficult to believe that Parfitt, in his paralysed condition, could have performed that feat. And, even if he had, how he could have avoided being seen by the people of Shepton Mallet and the region around who, at that very time, were all haymaking in fields bordering each side of the turnpike road. Also, a turnpike toll-collector would have seen him.

Collinson adds a few details about the personality of Parfitt that others do not give. He also says the mystery happened in 1763, five years earlier than other contemporaries say:

> "Owen Parfitt had been a soldier in America in his younger years. . . . He became bedridden after a long illness and had a melancholy turn of mind. He had become almost as emaciated as a skeleton. He depended on his neighbours for support, and was taken care of by an aged sister. By his own desire he had several times been brought downstairs in an elbow-chair and placed in the passage of the house for benefit of air. In this situation he was left one evening for a few minutes; but, on his attendant's return, strange to tell, this helpless man was missing, and no where could be found; nor has he ever been heard of since. A man of his description was observed, the same evening, in the west woodlands of Frome; but his person could not be identified. . . .
>
> "*History and Antiquities of the County of Somerset,*" *by the Rev. John Collinson (pubd. in* 1791).

Frome is ten miles north-east of Shepton Mallet, as the crow flies; but even had this been Owen Parfitt, in the wood, the difficulty still remains that he was a paralysed and bedridden man, hardly likely to have been seen *walking* in a wood.

In 1933 a Benedictine prior, at a meeting of the Somerset Archaeological Society, put forward a theory that Owen Parfitt had drowned himself in a well and his body had been carried up into an adit. Apart from the fact that no well with such an adit is, or was, known, the same objections apply to *this* theory.

This mystery has been marked not only by Victorians in old England, but by very modern journals in the U.S.A., and, alike in both cases, has been barefacedly garbled. Dr. Butler, then Bishop of Lichfield, Staffs., must have often told the story of Parfitt's disappearance at garden parties, on summer lawns; for, in 1859, an anonymous contributor foisted off on Charles Dickens, then editor of "Household Words," a yarn in which Parfitt is transferred—but not by name—to a "cottage in a scattered village outside the gates of a gentleman's park in Shropshire," seated in a chair to bask in the sunshine while the whole family went off to the fields to make hay. When they returned, he was gone. The faker artfully drew in sentimental references to a lady who told him, or her, the story, "with all the quietness that always marked her simple narrations . . . she was a cousin of the Sneyds, related to Baron Giles Fosdyk of Merrydown Park, and her most respectable father a patron of the beautiful Miss Linley." To make more weight, the names of various nobilities in Debrett's Peerage were also foisted into the story and sold to Charles Dickens, who, having his own secret sentimental past, did not care to investigate the past of the quiet and simple lady of the faker's acquaintance.

In summer 1956, a Middle Western American Journal, catering for the "strange and the unknown, all true stories," proved it by publishing a yarn, under the authorship of a native Middle Westerner, to the effect that Owen Parfitt vanished from his chair in a Somerset village, *in the year* 1937; that his sister "rang up" the Shepton Mallet police station; and that the "full story may be found in the archives of the local police!" Again, in October, 1957, a well known American cartoonist said that, "Believe it or not" Owen Parfitt vanished from his chair, in a cottage garden at Shepton Mallet, in 1763. Well, he was only five years "previous!"

All *we* can say, 190 years later, is that bedridden Owen Parfitt never found "the hole in the wall" from the fourth back to the third dimension of our everyday world; that he had no money to make it worth while for anyone to kidnap him; and that, finally, he never returned to the world of men, like Rip van Winkle, to find that all who knew him were long dead and gone. Or, all, save Joanna Mills, aged seventy or eighty, or Joseph George, how old he could not really say, with memories that, while they certainly would *not* have solved the mystery, would probably have delighted grave women of the parish of Shepton Mallet, who would have been very agreeably shocked by revelations of Owen Parfitt's hectic past, and especially about the young and mysterious woman's skeleton found under the old wall!

PART FIVE

THE QUEER AND THE BIZARRE IN THE TWENTIETH CENTURY

Chapter 12

WHAT KILLED HARRY DEAN?

The 1930s and the 1950s, leaving apart the terrible interregnum of the Second World War, were, in England and America, remarkable for numbers of mysteries, connected with the enigmatic "port of missing men," which are included in the two per cent of cases which Captain John Ayres, formerly of the New York Police Bureau of Missing Persons, admitted remain insoluble. It was estimated, prior to 1939, that, in America alone, 3,000,000 people had, in one decade only, vanished without trace. Nor had any of them been identified when corpses were laid out on the slabs in morgues. Each year, New York police, alone, were called on to investigate reports about 10,000 missing persons, in regions ranging from Birmingham (England) to Bombay (India); Tientsin (China) to Vienna (Austria); and Montreal (Canada) to San Diego (Calif.). Captain Ayres urged that everybody ought to have his or her fingerprints taken and filed for identification.

But the *insoluble* cases did not include vanished persons subsequently traced to wards in lunatic asylums, prison cells, hospitals, marines, foreign legions, and the ends of the earth. It is odd that, for every two women and girls who disappear, there are three men; but these were often cases of deliberate or planned disappearances, where false clues were laid. In England, in the 1930s, there was one case of a man suspected to have decoyed into an old car a homeless tramp whom he hit over the head with a spanner and killed. He then soaked the car with petrol, set it on fire, and vanished, leaving the victim to be incinerated. He had arranged with a confederate to collect the insurance money on the car, but he left what the French police call *traces révélatrices* on the site of the crime and the police collected him instead!

A well-known American detective, Wm. J. Burns, told of a case of this sort in Iowa:

"On a lonely road a corpse was found at the wheel of a burnt-out automobile. It was handed to relatives, who buried it as their relative. Later, someone proved that that corpse had been embalmed, and, later, stolen from a cemetery. It looked like an attempted swindle on an insurance company. Then a fellow pumped his own car full of bullets and left the car on a road. But he was found, later, in the Marines, having baulked the matrimonial halter on the wedding morning. Again, a toy-maker, in New York State vanished when on the way to his works. He was carrying $10,000, the wages of his workers. He left a note in the back of his car: 'Has been bumped off. Look for body in the river.' But the river was ice-bound! Eight years passed, and then he was accidentally seen and recognized in a park, 1,500 miles from New York. All he had was a desire to sow and reap some wild oats, so darned wild, that, to harvest 'em, you'd need to steal up on 'em in the dark! He sure had had a fine run with his workers' wages, and had given the slip to a battle-axe of a wife. . . . What causes us endless and needless trouble is the deliberate failure of 'sorrowing' relatives of some missing guy to show us vital clues. For example, a buyer of a large store, near Detroit, did a fade-away from his hotel with $50,000 of his employers. In his New York hotel, out of which he vanished, the fellow had even left his shaving-brush with the cream still wet on it. We broadcast photos of him, and, a year later, a cop at Saskatoon—a smart guy—walked up to a gentleman in a park and showed him this photo—*his own!* We were sure riled to find that his family had not shown to us his annotated note-book, on the margin of which he had noted the name of a character in a popular novel. It was the name he was sailing under when the cop spotted him."

Many years ago, a clerk at the old Bank of England was found guilty of forgery, and was hanged. His unfortunate sister lost her memory, and, year after year, harrowed the officials by calling every morning at the bank to ask for her brother. Among the files of the New York Police's missing-men bureau is a parallel case, to which Captain Ayres refers:

"One morning a delivery boy, employed by a maker of faked jewellery, vanished. He was fourteen years old. Maybe someone had stuffed him with a yarn that the jewellery was the real thing. Or, maybe, some crook, who thought so, slugged him in a quiet lot. Anyway, his poor old mother comes every week to the station where she can see, on the wall, a graph showing the number of missing people, about 130,000 in ten years. We show her that only two per cent of our cases remained unsolved. So she is hopeful, alas!"

Old England had some queer cases of missing people in the years preceding the Second World War. In a few of them something more, or other, than a criminological element seemed to have been involved.

The author of this book himself took part in a search by scores of people, in the summer of 1906, of some lonely fields; and, again, in another case, in 1940 and 1950, quartered a well-known outlier of the Cotswolds, Bredon Hill, three miles from the Bredon Bells, made famous by A. E. Housman who listened to the bells, ringing from all the shires around, on a summer Sunday morning, with the larks high in the sky, and wrote a poignant poem on a murder. In the *first* case, which happened on a June day, in a big pasture, locally known as the "Forty Acres," close to a locomotive engine-shed of the old Midland Railway, and marshalling yards of the Great Western line, then a mile outside the city of Gloucester, three children, a boy aged about ten, and his two sisters, aged three and five, went into this field and never returned. For three days and nights, scores of people, including the cleaners from the locomotive shed, searched every inch of the "Forty Acres." (Today, the site of the field has almost been lost, for on it stands a big records department of the R.A.F., small factories, and some new streets and many houses). We paid particular attention to the north-east corner of the field, where the pasture was bordered by tall, old elms, a thick hedge of thorn and bramble, and a deep ditch, separating it from a corn-field. Every inch was probed with sticks, and not a stone left unturned in the ditch. Had a dead dog been dumped there, he would certainly have been found. Not a trace of the missing children was found.

The affair was headlined by all the newspapers, and quite large sums for the aid of the family were collected from the readers of Sunday newspapers. The father was a rather uncouth railway goods guard, or brakeman, named Vaughan, who, said his neighbours, was soon "rolling in money" sent him every post by sympathizers. Indeed, a special staff had to be put on at the local post office, in order to deal with the numerous postal orders he received. The vicar of his parish called on him, only to be told, by Vaughan, that he "wanted no b—— parsons a rappin' at his door," nor any sympathy from them.

The mystery had been given up by both local police and public as beyond solution, when, just after 6 a.m. on the fourth day (they started early in those times) a ploughman went to work in a nearby cornfield, and, looking over the hedge, saw, in the bottom of the ditch, the three missing children, asleep! He informed the police and claimed a share of the reward which had been collected by the *News of the World* for anyone who could throw a light on the mystery. He was clearly entitled to it. But a local bigwig, who was then superintendent of the Gloucester City Police refused to hand over to the ploughman any share of the money; and, indeed, insinuated that, in his official view, the man had probably kidnapped the three children and held them in order to claim the newspaper reward.

The poor ploughman lived in a cottage, one of about a dozen others, in a hamlet called Coney Hill, and it was really quite impossible for him to have done what the Gloucester police superintendent had alleged, or insinuated, without his neighbours, all of the provincial sort who know all and more about their next door neighbours' private affairs, being at once aware of the presence, in the man's cottage, of three hidden children about whom a national hue and cry had started. Moreover, there was the trifling circumstance that the farmer, by whom he was employed, would certainly have become aware that his field-worker had absented himself from work in order to remove the children; for the farmer closely supervised the work in the field, harvest-time being near. The ploughman never received a penny of the reward, and became slandered into the bargain, with the local police by no means playing the slander down. Nehemiah Philpott, the police superintendent, thus had the last word in the affair. He died years ago.

One of the missing children is still alive. (They may all be; for the longevity of folk in Gloucestershire is well known to statisticians). He is now a man in the late sixties, and, at the end of the Second World War, someone, who remembered this case of 1906, questioned him, and Vaughan replied that he had not the slightest recollection, nor ever had had, of what happened between the time when he and his sisters were missing in the Forty Acre field, and when he and they were found, asleep in the ditch. If this be so, here, again, is the characteristic of the amnesia which marks these phenomena. It may be added that there was no financial incentive for anyone to kidnap these three children, and, moreover, the reward offered by the newspaper had been offered only after they were missing. No one, indeed, spoke of kidnapping until the local police superintendent put it forward as a too obvious solution. The affair remained a mystery; for who, in a country town like Gloucester, in 1906, had ever heard of the phenomenon of "teleportation," or would have had the ghost of an idea of what the "outlandish" word meant?

The other affair is even more mysterious, and has some very singular aspects not marking other cases cited in this book.

At 5:30 p.m., on 9 May, 1939, Harry Francis Dean, aged 49, a solicitor's clerk (former newspaper reporter), and an accountant employed in the department of the Town Clerk of the old Tudor timbered town of Tewkesbury, Gloucestershire, with its fine Norman abbey and battle-field made famous in the Wars of the Roses, left his office, and, instead of going home, boarded a service bus which put him down at the lonely hamlet of Westmancote, whence, through quiet lanes, close to the Vale of Evesham, he took a cart-track which led him to the summit of Bredon Hill, about 1,000 feet high. Dean seems to have been fascinated by this queer hill and its aura of ancient mysteries; although, whether he knew or sensed much about those mysteries, cannot be said. All that we know is that he was never seen alive again.

He and his wife had planned to put up a tent, somewhere on this lonely hill and spend a summer holiday there. It is easily accessible only on the side he took, being covered with loose screes and of very rugged and difficult terrain on other sides facing his own township. Indeed, to ascend it at all, requires sound wind and an able body. On its summit stands an ancient camp of the Iron Age, to the stockaded protection of which, thousands of years ago, the prehistoric people, in the vale below, drove their flocks and herds, when threatened by savage invaders from what is now Belgium or North France. In one corner of this prehistoric camp, with grassy mounds rising above it, stands a queer fissured stone called the "Bambury" stone. The word "Bambury" is from the words, "Ambroisie petrie" which are of Saxon origin and mean "anointed stone." It was anointed with something more sinister than oil!

Midnight came, and Dean had not returned home. His alarmed wife notified the police and an organized search by police and civilians started. It went on all night till dawn. It takes an able-bodied man hours to walk round the perimeter of Bredon Hill. Also, even on a summer day, one may wander over the hill for hours, and never meet a soul. At dawn, on 10 May, 1939, the police found the dead body of Dean lying at the foot of a curious boulder in an eerie, abandoned quarry, which has been called "Death Quarry." I believe that it has been the scene of more than one fatal accident in modern times. He lay huddled up and it *looked* as if he had fallen *strangled*. Yet the boulder, which I visited and climbed in

1940 and 1949, is not more than three feet high. Had he, in fact, *fallen off that boulder?*

Dean was no weakling. He was an athletic man and played county cricket, hockey, and strenuous Rugby football. He was in good health, had no financial or other worries, no known enemies, and, indeed, his wife and widow, told the police and South Worcestershire coroner, that her husband certainly did not intend to commit suicide. He had often walked over the hill and was deeply interested in its surroundings. It was true that, when playing rugby he had had a minor accident which slightly weakened the cartilage of one of his legs; but it did not give him much trouble. A woman doctor, who examined the body informed the coroner, who agreed with her findings—very odd findings they were, too!—that, in her opinion, Dean had climbed the boulder in order to look around him in the quarry, he had slipped off it, and, in falling, only three feet, had been choked by constriction between his collar and tie and neck. What an expert detective, or criminologist or police scientists would have said of this most improbable theory one need not waste time in suggesting.

Now, this queer quarry, which has been abandoned for years, is bounded on all sides by cliffs of rock which vary from thirty to eighty feet high. At the end of it where stands this boulder, the cliff is edged with a copse of pines, beyond which is a broken-down, dry-stone wall over which a child can climb with ease. By standing on top of this boulder, neither Dean nor anyone else could or can see any more than he, or they would, when standing on the dead-flat floor of the quarry.

At the inquest, the coroner said:

> "I am convinced that Mr. Dean did not fall more than three feet, and that he slipped, and displaced the cartilage of his leg. In great pain, he fainted, and was choked, owing to the unfortunate position in which he fell. It is a case of accidental death." (*Press report*).

But it was also said, at the inquest, that the coroner's own officer, a hefty policeman, had also visited the same quarry *in that week of May* (there is a significance in this mention of the month of May, as will presently be seen), and had a nasty fall and ricked his ankle rather badly.

Knowing this hill very well, I made some investigations in May 1940, at the time when bomb-craters, near the hill-top, had been left by Nazi planes coming from an attack on Birmingham. The entrance to this "Death Quarry" is also the exit. On every side, it is bounded by high rocks looking down on a dead flat floor, which looks as if it had been, and probably was levelled by ancient man, and at a time long before the Iron Age, which archaeologists guess was about 750 B.C. On this flat floor grow medicinal herbs and wild flowers, and, at about the four cardinal compass points, stand four curious and weathered boulders, three of them badly fragmented. It was at the base of the one at the south side that Dean's body was found. This boulder looks as if it had been rudely sculpted, and it appears as flat as the cap-stone of a trilithon of some megalithic monument. None of these boulders seem ever to have been shifted by those who quarried there, years ago.

Outside the entrance to this quarry is an ancient, grass-embanked causeway, on the sides or top of which are numbers of still unopened barrows of the Stone Age and the turf is deep and immemorial in age. Not many yards away, close to a copse of tall trees, stand two ancient obelisks called the "King and the Queen stone." These stones are masses of whitish oölitic rock through which were passed, up to about 1870, old men or women from villages and hamlets, in the Vale of Bredon, who were suffering from rheumatoid or arthritic complaints. It was a magical ceremony, for which these two stones were whitewashed, and must date very far back into Neolithic times; for here, as in Wilts., there remain ancestral memories possibly handed down to these people by ancestors contemporary with these two magical stones and their ancient magic ritual. Anyway, the ritual was deemed to ease their aches and pains, nor did they care a bean what the pa'son said about it.

Indeed, in this Vale of Bredon, as late as 1880, "corn-dollies" were carried on the harvest wains, which was, beyond doubt, a sublimation of the rites of human sacrifice and fertility carried out on the hill top, about 600 feet above, at the weird "Bambury," or "anointed stone." Above the copse and these two magic obelisks is a very ancient ditch, or prehistoric trackway.

One passes from this grass-grown causeway, leading from these King and Queen stones and the "Death Quarry" entrance, along an ancient path leading up through rough fields of bent and thistles, through a wood and pasture to the summit of Bredon Hill, where stands what is said to be an early Iron Age camp—actually it is *far* older than that!—with *valli*, now grass ramparts, where once stood stockades. It is evident that a very bloody battle was waged here, for, inside an old fort there have been found the remains of fifty young men fallen in a struggle with savage Iron Age invaders from what is now Belgium, or northern France. Their bodies were barbarously mutilated, heads, hands, feet, legs and arms being hacked off and cast down anyhow. Into this old "fort," the peaceful prehistoric farmers from the vale below drove their small sheep and cattle, and dug primitive fodder-pits.

But what attracted my own attention was the weird, badly fissured and weathered "Bambury" stone, shaped like a squatting elephant, standing at the foot of a towering grass-bank in one corner of this ancient grass-grown camp, or fort. It clearly is older than the fort or camp for it occupies no central position and must have been an object or focus of awe and veneration to the people of the Early Bronze and later Iron Age. Today, people smash beer bottles against it, and children pop-bottles! But on this stone was laid, ages ago the bodies of a chosen youth and maiden, whose throats were cut and the blood sprinkled on the stone by grim, skin-clad priests of a barbarous cult of fertility, which had its exact counterpart in the Aztec, or Nahua blood-cults, which Don Hernando Cortes and his Castilian soldiers extirpated, in old Mexico, in A.D. 1520. This weird "Bambury" stone was also a focus for black magic and witchcraft ceremonies, in the later Middle Ages and in the sixteenth and seventeenth centuries.

Rising steeply above this stone, threading through deep turf, run ancient paths, very clearly marked by immemorial use. It may be deduced that the "Death Quarry," about a mile below, was the open air temple where were celebrated the primitive rites preliminary to the human sacrifices on this "Bambury" stone. What it was "anointed" with, was, of course, as one has said, human blood! It is a macabre spot and it would seem that the evil aura is by no means extinct, especially in the *month of May*, when the rites were celebrated.

I had a rather eerie experience when in summer 1940, I sat on the middle of this "Bambury" stone and got my brother to photograph me. It was a clear windless day, not a soul was around and only a predatory black crow cawed overhead. On a sudden we both heard a thud in the grass above. We at once cast around, but could find no stone that had been displaced, thrown or fallen. "Something" eerie and sinister had demonstrated its presence, and its objection to the photographing of this weird stone, and our rational contempt for what it anciently stood for!

Now we may theorize what had possibly happened to Dean on that night *in May*, the anniversary of the grim and macabre rites on this eerie hill of Bredon. *He never climbed the boulder*, in the "Death Quarry," at whose base he was found strangled. He had no reason to do so, as one had already pointed out. In the dusk of that May night, in 1939, he may have approached the ring of pines on the edge of the northern rock wall of this quarry, and, there, in the May darkness, something, some unpleasant entity, quite invisible, clutched his throat as he peered over the edge, and hurled him violently on to the floor of the quarry, some fifty or sixty feet below. Or, it may be that he entered the quarry, this ancient open air temple of paranoiac fertility rites, and was strangled by this unseen entity as he stood, in the dim light, at the base of that boulder. He had no known enemies, and had any strange man committed this murder, it is most unlikely that such a man would not have been seen by some in the villages at the foot of the hill; for countrymen are quick to note the appearance of a stranger. Moreover, on the night of his death, when police and civilians were quartering this hill, and the hue and cry were on, it is improbable that such a stranger would have been undetected by someone. What proof is there for this theory?

None, certainly, that any legalistic mind, or a coroner of the average type, would accept. He would regard such a hypothesis as fantastic and the imagination of a crackpot. But, to assert as did the woman doctor, at the inquest, and the coroner, that an athletic man, as was Dean, climbed a boulder, in the dusk, just to look round him—at what?—and slipped and fell only three feet and was choked by the constriction on his neck of his collar and tie is even more absurd and improbable. This vast and lonely hill is not a good place to roam on in *May darkness*. Even in broad summer, I have gone miles up and down it, and on several sides including, the trackway past the "King and Queen stones," and have not met a soul, or anything but cawing crows on lonely and long derelict barns.

I have, myself, as in September, 1956, proved that strange phenomena can, at broad and blazing noontide under a southern Italian sky, intrude on the stylobate of a roofless Ionian Greek temple, erected to Poseidon, *circa* 600 B.C., and leave their strange record on the film of a perfectly efficient camera.

Just a final word about this strange Hill of Bredon: it forms one side of a rough quadrilateral, and due east, thirteen miles away, is another hill with a sinister repute. It is known as Long Compton Hill, and has on its top a strange circle of megalithons known as the Great Rollright Stones. Round these Rollright megalithons, in the sixteenth and seventeenth centuries, local witches of whom there were many in nearby Long Compton Village, danced in a circle round a mysterious Man in Black, who was taking the part of the very old horned god, Pan, or a nature deity whose rites go back to the time of the Palaeolithic cavern of Ariège, as, in its innermost recesses, a remarkable portrait of an old Stone Age magician, with hypnotic eyes, shows. Pan is still worshipped today by cattle-drovers and their women at Killorglin, in Co. Kerry, where they dance round a white goat on a platform.

In another angle of this same quadrilateral is a sinister hill called Meon Hill, where, on St. Valentine's night, in 1945, a seventy-five-year-old man, a hedger and ditcher, was found in the corner of a field, murdered and horribly mutilated, and with a ritual cross cut on his chest. He had lived in the Tudor-timbered village of Lower Quinton, not far from Stratford-upon-Avon, and was the son of a woman at Lower Compton, reputed by the villagers to be a "black" witch. Someone—maybe, several people—in the village of Lower Quinton, today, in 1958, knows, or know the identity of the murderer of this old man, but no one will speak, for the old man was credited with using the "evil eye" to "kill cattle." Scotland Yard's detective force, even with aid of the Royal Air Force planes, and the British Army, were beaten entirely after three weeks of intense investigation.

In the New England state of Vermont, there is a mountain, height about 3,800 feet, named Clastenbury. Between the years 1945 and 1950, it has been the focus, or vanishing point of the mysterious disappearance of six people, only one of whom was subsequently found, and, even so, in a condition which threw no light on the mystery. The singular circumstances are set out, below, in chronological order:

(1): Early in November, 1945, a professional guide, named Rivers (aged 75), conducted a party of hunters—four men—into the forest, on the slopes of this mountain. They set up a base camp, and then, Rivers, after helping them pitch a temporary camp, in what is called "Hell Hollow," departed, apparently to return to the base for some equipment; but was never seen again. Although an old man, he was sturdy, cheerful, and had no suicidal tendencies. Police and state troopers searched for six weeks, but found no trace of Rivers, nor any clue to his disappearance.

(2): In the first week of December, 1946, a pretty, blonde girl, Paula Welden, aged 18, an art student at a Vermont college, started from the nearby township of Bennington, on a ramble over this mountain. With the self-confidence of young girls of our day, she did not elect to have any escort, or girl friend with her. Someone gave her a lift in his car, and set her down near the slopes of Clastenbury Mountain. She was never seen again, alive or dead. Nor has a reward of $5,000 for her alive, or $3,000 for her dead body brought a clue, or in any way aided the police.

(3): On 2 December, 1949, a man named Tatford, or Titford, got on a 'bus for a veterans' home at Bennington. No one saw him alight, and someone, if not the conductor, made the extraordinary statement that Tatford must have vanished into thin air while he was still aboard the bus! No one had heard him say that he intended to hike into the forest, or on the Clastenbury Mountain, but popular rumour in Bennington was not backwards in linking the affair, however apparently slight the connexion, with Clastenbury Mountain. No trace of the man was ever found.

(4): 15 October, 1950: A man, named Jepson, drove his motor truck into a glade of Clastenbury Forest, left his eight-year-old son in it, and went off to gather wild fruit. On his return, he found the boy missing, without trace. The police took tracker-dogs to the place; but, it is said that the dogs lost the boy's scent about the spot where the girl, Paula Welden, was last seen.

(5): Another case of a missing person also took place in this year 1950, when, on 28 October, a woman, Mrs. Langer (aged 50), went for a ramble in Clastenbury Forest along with her cousin, a man. She tried to ford a shallow brook, slipped off a stone and was wetted to her underclothing. Scrambling out, she told the man she was going back home to dry out. For some reason, the man did not follow her, but remained roaming in the woods. Mrs. Langer was said to have been handy with a sporting gun, to know the forest well, and to have knowledge of woodcraft. She was never seen again. The cousin and another man searched the forest and mountain, and the police also hunted around. There was a sequel in May 1951, when the woman's corpse, badly decomposed, was found in a glade of the forest already searched. There was no sign of interference or violence, but the remains were too far gone to permit a thorough examination. *If* this were a case of teleportation with accompanying amnesia, the victim, or patient, may have subsequently found the "hole in the wall of the fourth dimension," and have been too dazed, with snow thickly covering the ground, so that she perished of cold exposure. But, of this theory, there is obviously no proof.

The year 1950, ended with a *third* case for that year alone!

(6): On 6 December, 1950, in falling snow, Miss Frances Chrisman started out from her home to visit a friend in a cottage near Clastenbury Forest. She had merely to traverse a stretch of about half a mile of road. She, too, never arrived. Spring came, but nobody was found under the thawed snow. No clue to the mystery has ever been found, since.

Some light *might*, possibly be cast on these riddles, if one knew more of the psychological pattern of these missing persons. One might inquire if they had ever shown any predisposition, or diathesis in the direction of previously vanishing and re-appearing, with symptoms of amnesia. Were this so, then it *may* be merely a singular coincidence that they vanished in the regions of this Clastenbury Mountain. But, were this so, the problem would not be one merely for a police detective or criminologist, but would form a suitable incident for the case-book of an expert on para-normal psychology. The strange phenomena do not necessarily reside in any given lake, mountain, road, or township, but may be immanent in the peculiar psychological make-up of the man or woman concerned. Yet, all said, there is something "fey" about Clastenbury Mountain and wood.

But not only men, women and children may vanish as individuals: whole races may do so! This has been the case in the secret heart of South America and in Central Asia. When the British Government were delimiting the boundaries between Guiana and Venezuela, in the late 1890s, many old Spanish documents from the archives of the *Casa de Contratación* (the Spanish Council of the Indies) and Simanacas were examined. I here translate and summarize one of them, which attested, as did many other old Spanish documents and viceregal reports, the existence of an *El Dorado* which was not totally a glittering legend woven out of the crazed imaginations of gold-bitten Castilian adventurers:

In 1537, Juan Martinez, gunner of the expedition led by Don Diego de Ordaz, far up the Rio Orinoco, had the bad luck to explode a flask of gunpowder which blew up the ammunition of the expedition. The Don marooned the gunner in a canoe and set him adrift. Four years later, a man, naked, blackened to the colour of coal under a hot sun, emaciated, and sick almost unto death, staggered out of the jungle onto the beach of the north-east coast of Venezuela. He signalled to the captain of a Spanish trading ship, who took him off the beach and landed him in Puerto Rico. Here, dying in a convent of the Dominicans,

Martinez told the prior a strange story. It was about a great and wide city of gold inhabited by clothed Indians, near-white, far south-west of the Guianas. It lay behind a screen of high mountains and vast stretches of bush and jungle, and it took a day to walk across it! There "were splendid palaces and mansions of lords." The roofs glittered in the sun, being tiled with a metal that shone like gold. The king freed him but forbade him to quit the country. Later on, the king let him go, but on condition that he did not reveal where the strange country lay. In the middle of the land, was a great lake on which the city stood, and its sands were full of *chispas* of pure gold. Centuries of Spanish, English and Dutch expeditions sought this land of gold, but in vain. Most of them left their bones on the trail, to be gnawed by jaguars. . . ."

All one may point out is that a good Spanish Catholic of the day of Martinez did not tell lies on his death-bed, when being shriven by friars. He feared the fires of hell!

In Central Asia, once lived the "Tocharians," but all that is known of them is that they were a race of advanced culture who disappeared about the year A.D. 1000

In 1931, Russian and German scientists and explorers tried to solve the riddle of a lost people of the Pamirs, on the roof of the world. They were said to inhabit a lonely mountain region back of the Hindu Kush range. A theory was that here lay the original home-land of the white Aryan peoples. Another theory was that this lost race of highlanders were remnants of an ancient civilization allied to that which left buried cities in the sands of the Gobi Desert. A third theory was that they were descendants of the Greek and Macedonian soldiers of Iskander Beg, Alexander the Great, who invaded old Hindostan from Afghanistan (Ariana or Bactriana, the "Oriens" of classic Roman maps). Present-day nomads told a fantastic story of a strange people in these mountains who possessed supernormal powers. Yet expeditions in the eighteenth and nineteenth centuries failed to find them, or even penetrate the land of the Pamirs. The Russian and German caravan started from Turkestan, and, at the approaches to the Pamirs, enlisted the services of a tribe of nomads, who led them over the mountains, and into the icy world on the roof of the globe, where people must live in the lowest valleys, because of a strange disease, brought on by rarefied air, which takes a heavy toll on lives.

Here, the Russians and Germans travelled through great fields of "ice ferns," scaled a 21,000-foot-high mountain, and sought for the lost people. Led on by rumours, the expedition crossed and criss-crossed unknown territory, but even in the most remote mountainous recesses, apparently, uninhabited, they could not find the lost race. Yet, the scientists were sure that there was a real foundation for the stories. It was planned to equip another expedition to search more thoroughly, but the clouds of world war "stymied" the plans.

Chapter 13

THE STRANGE PILTDOWN MAN PUZZLE

ON A SUMMER DAY in the year 1908, a country solicitor, who had a taste for natural science and palaeontology, was walking up a lane with high hedges and field-banks, leading to the Sussex South Downs, when his eye was caught by a strange, round, brown object lying in a ditch. He bent down and picked it up, and peered closely at it. It looked as if it had been broken by contact with a metal tool. Workers near by were opening up some new gravel pits, and one of them caught sight of "a gen'l'm'n a-peerin' at summat he 'eld in 'is 'and." The gentleman saw him and beckoned him to approach. A short examination followed.

Solicitor: "What is this object, my good man?"
Labourer: "Well, zur, I think it be a coker-nut."
Solicitor: "Coco-nut? But what is a coco-nut doing in this ditch? There have been no fairs in these parts for a long time."
Labourer: "Well, zur, all I can tell 'ee is that I found 'im in the gravel pit. I smashed 'im with me pick as I 'owked 'im out."

The country solicitor bent down and picked up a splinter from the side of the ditch. It looked like brown bone. "Thank you, my man," he said to the labourer, pressing into brown palm what the labourer, later on, in the Old Brown Cow at Piltdown, that evening, called "a 'arf dollar." "This you call a 'Coco-nut' is a petrified human skull turned brown by ferric oxide. I am taking it away with me." So saying, the solicitor walked home to Uckfield leaving the bemused labourer with an awed look in his eyes, and a dawning theory which he also unfolded that evening in the four-ale bar at Piltdown, about "summun as must ha' bin 'it over the yed, years agone and chucked into that thur gravel pit."

The country solicitor's name was Charles Dawson, and he had started a train of very singular events which were to end up in the House of Commons when six M.P.s moved a vote of censure on the Trustees of the British (Natural History) Museum, and many very distinguished savants were astonished and annoyed for several reasons, and more especially because they had given learned lectures before learned societies. What was much worse was that one cannot easily eat one's words when one has put them into print! They had called him the "Piltdown Man;" the "oldest man in the world."

Now, home in his big house at Uckfield, Sussex, Charles Dawson had a small chemical laboratory. He was a versatile man, by no means limiting himself to the study of conveyancing and mortgage deeds, and documents of powers of attorney, or the suitable investments of clients' moneys. He treated the skull with bichromate of potassium, in order to harden it, and placed the skull in his little collection of artifacts and palaeontological specimens. For a long time he tried to find from what geological stratum the skull had come. Three years later (1911), he said he found further fragments of the skull-vaulting in heaps of rubbish near the same gravel pits of Piltdown. Again, in 1915, he, or someone else, found parts of the cranium of another "dawn man" in a field two miles from Piltdown. But three years before that (1912) Charles Dawson went to see Arthur Smith-Woodward, keeper of the Department of Geology at the British (Natural History) Museum, South Kensington. In past two years Dawson had sent many fossils to the British Museum, and had become known as a distinguished amateur in the field.

Smith-Woodward gave his professional opinion to the excited Dawson. It was that the layer, from which the labourer at Piltdown had exhumed the skull, was Tertiary, and that fossils of mastodons and the Stegodon, in the line of the ancestors of the elephant, had been found there. It looked as if Charles Dawson had found part of the skull of a dawn man who lived in the last age of the Tertiary, the Pliocene. Then came on the scene Père Teilhard de Chardin, a famous palaeontologist and specialist on pre-history. He went with Dawson to Piltdown. It appeared that, some time before that, about 1912, Smith-Woodward had himself found at Piltdown a fragment of skull that fitted the fragment picked up in the ditch, there, by Dawson in 1908. Also, Charles Dawson, in the presence of Smith-Woodward, dug up at the same spot a simian underjaw with a few teeth. It was also odd, or fortuitous (?), however, that, the jaw was discoloured with bichromate of potash, which chemical, of course, would *not* be found free and in a state of nature in a gravel pit. But nobody, at this stage, commented on this odd chemical "coincidence," or whispered that, perhaps Charlie Dawson had been doing a bit of palaeontological "salting," in the earnest desire to "advance the progress of science."

No; everybody said that Charles Dawson, while he might be a solicitor, or attorney, was yet a very upright man of strict probity, and would not deceive a baby, let alone world-reknowned palaeontologists. There was old Gaffer Giles who, part time, scythed up the grass between the tombstones in Piltdown village churchyard, and who stated, in the bar of the Old Brown Cow, that "Mr. Dawson was a real 'genilman' allus good for a bob, or 'arf a dollar, when I brought up a fosseel as I found at the bottom of the new graves I dug."

More finds were made at Piltdown. They were primitively worked flints which looked like the eoliths or primitive tools of the dawn men. Père Teilhard de Chardin found in the Piltdown gravel pits what looked like a semi-human, or semi-simian—have it which way you like!—canine (tooth), which he believed might have belonged to early man's cousin, the most ancient type of chimpanzee. It also seemed that, later on, Père de Chardin felt it might be something else: a tooth fallen out of Charlie Dawson's half-simian underjaw! And he was the more confirmed in his later view when Charlie Dawson or someone else—it is not clear precisely whom—howked up from the Piltdown workings a remarkable object that looked like a petrified club, possibly used by a half-simian gentleman to brain a pal with; or, as might have been, a recalcitrant female, whom some gentleman of a very ancient species had regrettably found it necessary to "treat rough." Some time, subsequently, another peering and prying investigator was moved enviously to state that it was no petrified club of dawn man, but proof that Charlie Dawson had been "getting his hand in at stone-chipping."

The interesting stage now arrived when Smith-Woodward of the British Museum (Natural History), and a lot of other savants, had a rare old time trying to fit all these skull fragments together. Although the pieces did not make a fit anywhere as "true" as an anatomical suture; yet it seemed as if the Piltdown man had the skull-vaulting of homo-sapiens, along with the lower jaw of a big ape. Smith-Woodward felt called on to do the right and gentlemanly thing by Charlie Dawson, and try to save all useless argument and silence the rival sceptics who demanded to be told what in Heaven, or the other place, this Piltdown "guy" was doing with a man's skull fitted to an ape's jaw. (Well, of course, none of them had ever seen Battling Bill, heavyweight world champion, in action.) So, to put it once and for all on a proper scientific footing, or, as it might be, heading, Smith-Woodward of the British Museum called the thing "Eoanthropus Dawsoni."

That put the thing in its evolutionary place, and gave the credit of the discovery of the exhibit to the proper gentleman. It was the missing link from the forbidding Tertiary Age.

However, it may be noted that, in the camps of both archaeologist and anthropologist, the word *Tertiary* is not merely of explosive significance; it is also a "darned nuisance." Since, in the quite recent past, unwelcome finds have been made in mines, on the shores of lakes and other places that have proved nothing but a "darned nuisance," the Doctor Dingbat who, were he forced to admit their authenticity, would be called on to revise some nicely classified and catalogued theory of hypothesis by which he has made his name.

But these palaeontologists are not easily won over to acceptance of another rival gentleman's views, and the less so if he happens to be an amateur, even a *gifted* amateur. Sure enough, one learned gentleman arose with a snort and said to another savant: "How came this 'dawn man' to have the muzzle of a beast with the head and cubic brain capacity of a primitive Neanderthal man who lived, according to the best and most honourable computation, 800,000 years later than dawn man's day?"

It seemed a fair and reasonable question. Much very acrid argument followed and, after a considerable time, it was decided, if not exactly to bury the hatchet for all time, at least to dismiss this Piltdown Man as a fellow who had a past, but no future. He was merely a misfit, a sport of nature who had half-finished a job, got tired of it, and tossed it on to the scrap heap of *no*-evolution. In 1916 Dawson died, and was given the honour of a plaque, on a glass box enclosing the skull of Piltdown Man in the Palaeontological Department of the British Museum. He was also given the even greater honour—it all depends on the point of view—of a sign-board on an inn, at the foot of Piltdown.

About thirty-six years passed by before Professor Dingbat, the debunker, got on the trail of Charlie Dawson, deceased. If Professor Dingbat hails from Bloomsbury, he may be relied on to do his fell work by casting out not only the dirty bathwater, but the baby with it. It had been felt in more than one exalted palaeontological quarter that this fitting of anatomical fragments together, and making 'em join like a piece in a jigsaw puzzle was rather reminiscent of the ways of a classical gentleman named Procrustes, who, if the body of a gentleman-boarder—nothing is said about ladies—did not happen to fit a bed, lopped off part of a leg, or arm, to make the rascal fit the bed, anyway! True, the late Sir Arthur Keith, director of the "dry" department of the Royal College of Surgeon's Museum, in Lincoln's Inn Fields, always to the day of his death believed the Piltdown Man to be genuine. Sir Arthur was always a very courteous gentleman of the older Scottish school. It was soon seen there were others who had other views.

In 1935, a dentist and palaeontologist who had personally known Charlie Dawson, found, in another gravel pit at Swanscombe, Kent, a skull of a man estimated to have lived some 400,000 years ago, along with no fewer than 600 fine stone tools of the Acheulian Age, and a hand-axe in the same layer as the skull. But what was to be said of the gentleman, called the "Piltdown Man," who had lived even 200,000 years earlier?

The dentist and palaeontologist was the man to say it! As a professional, he turned his attention to the teeth of the Piltdown Man. These teeth, he roundly said, mincing no words about them, were those of a *true ape*, or prehistoric chimpanzee of the Tertiary Age; but the skull was that of a man who had lived in the later Ice Age. The dentist, whose name was Alvin Theophilus Marston, had no luck in the promulgation of his theory. Some folk there were who demanded to know why the underjaw of a human skull had not been found on the site at Piltdown, and not that of a prehistoric chimpanzee who, they asserted, had never been known to have lived in what was then prehistoric Britain?

A few more years passed and then the skeleton in the Piltdown cupboard was rudely taken out of its bag and given a shaking. Biological chemists were now on the warpath. Two of them, Oakley and Hoskins, of the British Museum, had discovered a fluorine test whereby the age of fossils and bones, could, to some extent, be determined by the fluorine content, which increases in proportion to the time the fossils and bones lie in the ground. Like the celebrated and later carbon 14 radio test, it is not 100 *per cent* reliable; since chemical conditions in soil vary greatly in time and place. Marston wrote to Oakley and asked him if he would test the Swanscombe remains and those of Piltdown Man. It was found that the Swanscombe Man, by this fluorine test, was probably of early Neanderthal and Ice Age in time, while the Piltdown Man was only 100,000, or, it might be, 50,000 years old and of the later Ice Age—far from as old as Tertiary. Marston wondered if the deceased Charlie Dawson had done something more than merely find a jaw on the same site as parts of a skull. Had he, in fact, *put it there to be found?*

The result of fluorine, carbon 14 radio, nitrogen and iron tests, in various laboratories, seemed to show that the underjaw bone of Charlie Dawson was actually a most skilful piece of fakery. The jaw was that of a quite modern chimpanzee, or orangoutang, polished and treated with chemicals to make it resemble ancient skull fragments. It was now decided that the jawbone had been coloured, as had the skull, by impregnating them with bichromate of potassium.

But something even more remarkable and mysterious came to light in these micro-chemical-biological investigations! The canine tooth found by Père Teilhard de Chardin on the site at Piltdown was, said the scientists, that of a young anthropoid ape, and highly skilled and most delicate precision work had been done on it to file it away and make it look like a prehistoric human tooth. The ducts of the canine tooth were found to contain tiny grains of fossilized ironstone, apparently introduced from outside by a master hand, or dentist of supreme or almost superhuman skill. The Piltdown splinters were, beyond doubt, genuine, being impregnated with iron, as fossilized bones, human and other, always are; but the jaw had been artificially treated—its interior was *modern!*—with a coating to make it look like skull fragments.

Nice questions here arose.

Who had filed the tooth and applied this coating? Whence had the faker obtained the jaw of an ape corresponding to the very ancient skull? It would have been almost impossible in the short time that the Piltdown finds had been made. Had Dawson, or someone else, dug up the simian jaw a long time before the skull fragments were found at Piltdown?

And, again, what was the motive? Certainly not money, which Charlie Dawson had *not* made out of his discoveries. It would appear that the core of the mystery was put by the dentist and palaeontologist, Marston, at the meeting of the London Geological Society in the first week of December, 1953.

He asked:

"How could Dawson, or anyone else, in 1912, have been able to operate on a tooth duct of a young ape, as was contended by the British Museum and other experts, so as to leave inside the ducts tiny grains of fossilized ironstone, and compel the deduction that, here was a canine tooth some thirty-five million years old? Who had had the skill—very high and of amazing precision—so as, in 1912, to be able to file away the coating of the tooth of a modern young ape and make it look exactly like a prehistoric human canine tooth?"

Oakley showed, or contended, that the fluorine and nitrogen content of the Piltdown jaw establishes the fact that the ape, to whom it belonged, died not much earlier than A.D. 1900.

Nothing on this planet of many mysteries is more strange than man himself! Dawson was a capable amateur palaeontologist, and he was also a lawyer by profession; and it would appear extremely unlikely that he could have possessed, or acquired this remarkable technical skill, which would have been beyond the powers of even the most skilled masterdentist in 1912. But had he had behind him some *very* skilled and unknown technician? A technician who had astoundingly introduced into the duct of an ape's tooth almost microscopic particles of ironstone? It would appear that Marston, as a skilled dentist, believed that it was at least highly improbable that this most delicate operation had occurred in fact. Marston, as a palaeontologist, believed that the *jaw*, found at Piltdown, was *really* that of a prehistoric ape or chimpanzee, "Proconsul," who lived in the middle Tertiary, an epoch dating back some twenty million years ago. "Proconsul's" skull has, in fact, been found in Africa.

But this, of course, leaves open the authentification of the ancient *skull* fragments round the parts of the petrified human skull thrown into the ditch by the labourer, who prised it up on the end of his pick, in the gravel pit at Piltdown. It has *not* been decided that it is not genuinely prehistoric. In fact, it was *not* a fake, and was not "planted" there by Charlie Dawson. What may remain still doubtful is the exact age of these Piltdown skull fragments; since none of these chemico-radiological or biological tests are, or can be 100 per cent accurate.

Dawson has now been dead for forty-two years, and the mystery remains. One is forced to agree with Marston that it seems almost impossible that Dawson could have introduced microscopic particles into the very fine duct of a tooth and have accomplished the delicate precision work involved in the alleged filing of the canine tooth. It seems also extremely improbable that Dawson could have found a masterly technician to do this for him who would remain unknown and silent all these many years.

The final chapter in the Piltdown affair was written by fate on 25 November, 1953, when six M.P.s, in the House of Commons, presented a motion which the Speaker, amid the laughter of the House, refused to accept. This motion was one of "no confidence in the Trustees of the British Museum (Natural History), for their delay in discovering that the skull of the Piltdown Man is partly a forgery."

PART SIX

RIDDLES OF THE SEA

Chapter 14

THE FATE OF THE *GROSVENOR*

WHEN THE HOARY, squinting, grinning, tarry-faced, evil-eyed familiar of Poseidon of the thunder-brows, Davy Jones, sits on the lid of his famous locker emblazoned with the skull and cross-bones, and takes up a stolen, piratical, gold-handled quill which once belonged to the general of an ancient fleet of Spanish galleons, he outdoes the most skilful forger who ever spent a long "stretch" in an English or American convict prison or penitentiary for faking drafts on the Bank of Wickedness Unlimited.

For your land-lubber forger usually limits his mischief to his own day and generation; whereas, old Duffy Jonah, of the mahogany countenance, forges a document which becomes a continual draft on a credulous posterity which knew not the forger of the original document. And that old mystery sprite of the deep sea is the more dangerous to his land-lubber victims in that he knows so well how to play on that very human failing which fills all our jails. He is the diabolical fiddler in the Sea-Devil's own orchestra, where he wails out that ancient Tzigane fantasia: "Something for Nothing, or the Crooked Shepherd's Air of the Purse-string."

In the case-book of old "Duffy Jonah"—he, by the way, is really a Caribbean Negro sea-devil, whose name has been anglicized by old "shellbacks" and ancient mariners as "Davy Jones with his Locker"—there is a mystery nearly a century older than that of the derelict *Mary Celeste*, which mystery is of special interest to the people of the South African Union. It is also of special danger, not only to South Africans, but people in England and America. Danger, because an anonymous forger of documents has in the last eighty years and more, caused the robbery of the gullible "investing" public, and the simple, avaricious folk of small means and great faith in dividends of 300 to 1,200 per cent.

The affair dates back to the month of August, 1782, when a famous East Indian ship, the *Grosvenor*, west ashore on a spot, still not certainly known, on the shores of South-east Africa, and in circumstances which cannot be deemed creditable to the ship's navigator, and her captain's efficiency as a seaman. More than a century and a half has passed, and it is high time that the truth be told about this famous old English wreck, and, *perchance,* ingenuous and naïve people saved from parting with that money which becomes the patrimony of knaves and swindlers.

The *Grosvenor* was a ship of 741 tons, with three decks with a "between-height" of 5 feet 10 inches, a keel about 112 feet long, a hold 14 feet 3 inches deep, a bottom 4 inches thick, and an armament of twenty-six guns. No one knows of what timber she was built, or whether she was sheathed when one, Wells, launched her on the River Thames, in old England, in the year 1770. She had already made three voyages to India, when in March 1782, she lay tied up to the bollards on the wharf of the old East India Company factory of Fort St. George, in the Presidency of Madras. Lord Macartney was then President.

England was then at war with the Dutch and the French, and the French fleet suddenly appeared off the Coromandel coast just at the time when the *Grosvenor* was about to cast off for England. That blockader's *contretemps* delayed her voyage and forecast her doom. Lord Macartney sent by another ship a message warning the "Honble. the Court of Directors for the Affairs of the Honble. and United Company of Merchants of England, trading to the East Indies" that the French fleet's appearance had delayed the sailing of the *Grosvenor,* till the offing was clear of the scented Mounseers. Then his Lordship added a paragraph which should be pondered by would-be "investors" in modern syndicates to salve the alleged millions of treasure in this wrecked ship:

"She is now dispatched to you with a full lading of Coast Goods. . . . The supply of cash received in consequence of advts published for granting bills of exchange on Yr. honours . . . fell far short of our expectations or our wants. We have therefore extended the term of receiving money into the Treasury on the same conditions the 1st May next, and the *draft on you by this ship** amounts to Star Pagodas 82, 811 . . . 8 . . . 26 . . . *Para.* 16. The invoice by the *Grosvenor* amounts to Star Pagodas 162, 378 . . . 22 . . . 69 and the Register of Diamonds to S.P. 24,444. . . . 31 . . . 69." (*Extract from the E.I. Court Minutes, vol. DG. of June* 1782).

It will be noted that no word in this official contemporary

---

*My italics. *Author.*

document supports the legend that the *Grosvenor* was carrying boxes of gold bullion and silver ingots, and cases of rubies and gems and jewels. Indeed, their place, except as to diamonds, was taken by bills of exchange, a lading of coast goods, and East Indian produce. In faraway London, at the very time the *Grosvenor* was sailing the Indian Ocean, the managers and charterers of East India Company's ships were complaining to the Court of Directors that it was onerous and unfair for them—the cargo owners and charterers—to have to accept the responsibility for bullion and diamonds shipped to London from the East, when they received no freight on their delivery in England.

"No matter," declares the autocratic and conservative Joint E.I. Committee of Correspondence and Shipping, "we decline to depart from long-established customs. The matter is your responsibility."

The captain and officers of the ship were allowed to carry private ventures in East Indian goods provided they declared them to the factors before sailing. Accordingly, before the *Grosvenor* sailed for England, in 1782, her captain, Coxon, writes Charles Freeman, Esq., secretary at Fort St. George (23 March, 1782), asking that goods on his (Coxon's) account in the ship appear in the manifest as instructed by the East India directors in London. He did not want to forfeit them. "My goods," he says, "are marked *I.C.* 34 bales of piece goods, and *IH^c* 11 casks, 10 cases indigo."

These details do not make thrilling reading, but they are of public interest to "investors" in this "treasure" wreck.

On 13 July, 1782 (ominous number!) the *Grosvenor* shook out the reefs in her topsails and stood out of the harbour of Trincomali, Ceylon, bound on the long voyage round the Cape of Good Hope, for the Thames, London. Now, as events were to show, Captain Coxon was not one of the type of English seamen gifted with qualities of ready resource or improvisation in emergency. He had, too, the misfortune to be served by an incompetent mate who would have been probably better employed in a wherry on the Thames—and, even then, *not* in a storm—rather than in an East India Company's deep-water ship, sailing on dangerous seas between India and Africa, in that year 1782!

The navigator was probably working by charts which were of French, and Dutch origin—either the "East India Pilot" or the French "Neptune Oriental," or the Oriental Navigator of the East Indies, by Monsieur d'Après de Mannevillette (from his journals, and the observations of the Honble. East India Company). In any event, their charting of the southeast African coast, from the Great Fish River to Delagoa

Bay, was derived from no later information than Manoel de Mesquita Perestrello's "Descripcao da Costa de Africa Meridional," which that Portuguese navigator made for King Sebastiano of Portugal, in *November* 1575. That mariner who had already been shipwrecked, or run aground in the Rio de Infante (Bashee river [?], S.A.), aboard the *San Benedict* in 1554, with Fernan Alvares Cabral, commodore of his fleet, surveyed the eastern coast of modern Cape Colony up to Cape Correntes, from the deck of a ship. Perestrello's object was to find harbours in which ships might shelter from heavy gales blowing from the westward and raising high seas. His topographical and nautical information was copied into the Dutch map of Arnoldus F. à Langren,* published in Holland in 1596; and, beyond the limit of the Dutch Farms, on the Great Fish River (Cape Colony) in the year 1782, no later survey of the coast had been made. Perestrello's charting was as accurate as the instruments of the day allowed. Indeed, had late eighteenth- and early nineteenth-century cartographers paid a little more heed to Perestrello's description of the South-east African coast, up to Delagoa Bay, they would possibly not have made the grotesque mistakes which the "Englishman," De Riou, made when he tried to chart the course of the 1790-91 expedition of Jacob von Reenen, in search of the wreck of the *Grosvenor*.

In any case, names of creeks and rivers on that coast changed in three centuries, and it is not easy to identify Perestrello's catholic nomenclature with those, later on, derived by the Dutch from the Kaffirs and the Zulus.

The *Grosvenor*, with 142 people aboard, sighted no land after leaving Ceylon, and had an uneventful passage across the South India Ocean. At 3:30 a.m. on 4 August, 1782, John Hynes, a seaman, was aloft on the fore to 'gallant yard, straining his eyes ahead. His seaman's instinct told him that grave danger was at hand. Suddenly, in the dim crepuscular

---

*The "Neptune Oriental, ou Routier Général des Côtes des Indes Orientales, et de la Chine" was published in 1745. Monsieur Jean Baptiste Nicolas Denis d'Après de Mannevillette issued his chart "Carte réduite de l'Océan Oriental, qui continent la Côte d'Afrique, depuis le 9° de la lat. S. à 30°" (reduced scale chart of the Eastern Ocean, with the coast of Africa, from Lat. 9° to 30° S.), about 1760. The "East India Pilot, or Oriental Navigator" saw the light, in London, in 1780. Arnoldus F. à Langren's "Delineatio Orarum maritimarum Terrae vulgo indigetate Terra de Natal . . . (Aft-bleedinge der custen des Landes genaempt Terra do Natal)" appeared in 1596, at the Hague.

light, he thought he saw a line of white breaking against a dark grey shadowy outline ahead.

He called down to the mate on the deck below:

"Land ahead, sir! Breakers on a reef!"

The mate looked up and ordered him below.

"Shut thy stinking gob," said he, "and take the sand out of thy bloody peepers! Dost thee think theest know more than the cap'n and officers of this 'ere ship? Man, we are *hundreds* of miles from land!"

At 4 a.m. the watch was relieved, but Hynes* did not turn in as others in his watch did. He had a foreboding of disaster. He was still on deck, half an hour later, uneasily straining his eyes ahead into the growing lightness of the sky and sea. The white ribbon ahead took form. It could be no less than breakers on a lee shore. He felt implied again to warn the mate who had snubbed and jeered at him.

"Blast!" said that lunatic, to the anxious mariner. "It's the reflection of the sea in the sky. I shall not put the ship's head to the sea. Get thee down below, and let me see no more of thy poke-nosing face, or I'll ha' thee lashed at the foot of the mainmast!"

But standing by was the quartermaster, William Nixon, who distrusted the mate. He overheard the colloquy and at once went into the Captain's cabin. Coxon immediately came on deck and ordered the mate: "Wear ship! We are on a lee shore!"

The order no sooner left his lips than there was terrible grinding and jolting of timbers and the *Grosvenor* jarred from stem to stern.

"All hands on deck!" roared Coxon.

The *Grosvenor*, heeling over, was beating out her bottom on the reefs of Africa. Now, the wind gave a sudden shift, and blew offshore. Men hoisted the fore-tops'l to back her off the rocks, but she was hard on. The force of the wind twisted the ship's head offshore, while her poop and stern lay on the reef. She now began to fill with sea-water, and part of her hull drifted ashore where the waiting Kaffirs,

---

*An earlier unfortunate predecessor of Hynes, who was on board H.M.S. *Anson* warned the captain that *she* was perilously near the coast of Cornwall, England. His reward was, by order of the martinet, Admiral Sir Cloudesley Shovell, to be hanged at the yard-arm for daring to contradict his superior officer. While the poor devil's body was still dangling in the ropes, *Anson* struck the iron reefs off the Lizard, and she went to a watery grave, taking with her idiot Shovell, and all the rest.

who had been watching the ship from the edge of the reefs, clambered aboard to get copper and iron which they valued far above gold. She parted her chains at 1 a.m.—which implies that she must have been stranded on the reef for about thirteen hours—and, says Hynes, "we got the ladies out by the starboard-quarter-galley. . . ."

"She remained with her head on shore, till she went to pieces and when she parted the (each) side sunk down into the sea, and with them all upon it, floated into shallow water, when the sailors helped the ladies and children on shoar, in the sandy bite."

By another account:

"There was a creek into which many of the things drove, particularly a cask of wine, and one of our sows, which was killed against the rocks, but the creek was full of rocks which we passed over at low water. Plenty of timber from the wreck and the booms of sails were cast ashore, sufficient to have built and fitted several vessels, nor were tools, as adzes, etc., wanting—plenty of beef and pork ashore, and all in pieces."

The latter passage was the "Authentic Account" of the surviving seamen, Price, Lewis, Warmington, and one landsman, Barney Larey, as published in most English newspapers, in July, 1783.

Hynes, the seaman whose repeated warnings were fatally disregarded by the egregious mate of the *Grosvenor*, told his story to the English historical portrait painter, George Carter, whom he met aboard ship on a voyage to India in 1789 or 1790. He then gave a fuller story:

"The *Grosvenor's* stern lay high on the rock after she struck, and the wind blew off-shore ten minutes after she struck the reef. She was within a cable's length, or three hundred yards of shore. She broke in two before the mainmast, and the bows veered round towards the stern. The wind then shifted towards the land and people had got out on the poop as that was nearest shore. The wind, in conjunction with the surges, lifted us in, and that part of the wreck, on which the people were, in an instant rent asunder, fore and aft; (so) that the deck, splitting in two, in this distressful moment, they crowded on the starboard-quarter, which soon floated into shoal water, the other parts continuing to break off those heavy seas that would otherwise have ingulfed or dashed them to pieces. . . . No water was found in the hold when she struck, the stern lying high on the rocks and the forepart being considerably lower, the water had all run forward. . . . A raft was made, and launched overboard from the wreck and veered away towards the stern of the *Grosvenor;* so that women and children might the more readily embark upon it from the quarter-gallery."

When the ship struck, or some time after, five persons were drowned. In the forepart of the wreck was Captain Talbot, R.N., and he and some others came ashore on that part of the wreck.*

Hynes supposed the ship was wrecked somewhere between 27° and 32° south latitude on the coast of Kaffraria. Now that is a stretch of territory about 250 miles, as the crow flies, from Cape St. Lucia, in Zululand, to Umtata in Pondoland. Alexander Dalrymple, employed by the Honble. East India Company's "secret committee," London, in autumn 1782, to buy maps and charts reported (August, 1783) to Sir Henry Fletcher, Bart., chairman of the Court of Directors of the E.I. Company:

"I have examined the several persons saved (who) are now in England (Robt. Price, Capt. Coxon's servant), Warmington, bosun's second mate; Thomas Lewis, seaman; and Barney Larey, Landsman; and, from the description they give of the coast . . . compared with that given by the Portuguese pilot (it) must have happened under the Lat. 31° S., as they represent. . . . It is obvious the ship was lost in the Coffrey country, which terminates on the south by the Gt. Fish River, in about the Lat. of 30°, which they passed on their journey towards the south, and after they were shipwrecked they travelled three months before they came to the Dutch Farms at Swartkops river, in about 31° S. lat."

Daniel Corneille, writing home, in 1783, from the Cape to London, England, says the seaman brought to the Cape varying accounts of where the ship struck, between lat. of 27° and 32° S.:

"The Dutch cannot exactly ascertain the spot; some saying it was on a point called in Dafris' chart Pointe des

---

*Vide: *Sussex Weekly*, 7 July, 1782, and Correspondence from the Cape, Home Miscell. Ser. vol., 1783.

Fumies, others on Pointe des Fontes . . . among the passengers were Messrs. Taylor and Williams, from Bengal."

It may be observed that, in Arnoldus F. à Langren's chart of A.D. 1596 the Pointes des Fontes is the Peneada de fontes, located south of the Rio do Infante of Perestrello's chart. The "Pointe des Fumies" is probably the Terra dos fumos, in Langren's chart, located about the lat. 27°, which gives a stretch of about 500 miles, with the wreck lying anywhere between the "pointes."

Captain Coxon's lack of *savoir faire* in the matter of navigation off a dangerous lee shore, in unknown African territory, is matched by his and the castaways' lack of common sense *on*-shore. They had a carpenter with them, tools and plenty of timber to hand, and they might have waited for better weather and constructed a ship out of the debris, which might, or would have carried them till they crossed from Kaffraria, into the region occupied by the Dutch. One hundred years earlier, in 1683, an English ship, the *Johanna*, was wrecked about the region of Delagoa, and the castaways were aided by blacks who furnished them with guides who led them southwards to a river, where another set of guides escorted them to the Cape. The shipwrecked mariners covered more than one thousand miles in forty days. Unlucky Captain Coxon, however, came ashore in a part of Southeast Africa where the Kaffirs happened, at the time, to be at war with or certainly unfriendly to the whites.

Once on shore Captain Coxon called the survivors together and said he hoped to reach the Dutch settlements—at Zwartskop—in fifteen, or sixteen, or seventeen days. Now, assuming that he supposed his party could march about twenty-five miles a day, this suggests that the Captain of the *Grosvenor* believed the ship had gone ashore about four hundred miles from the nearest Dutch Farms, on the Great Dutch Fish River. If he estimated aright, the location of the wreck would be on the northern border of Natal, or the coast of Zululand. The party would travel across unknown territory and keep, as much as possible, to the seashore. . . . "And," says Hynes, "in this the Captain was not much mistaken, the shipwreck happening somewhere about the 29th degree* of Southern Latitude, and the most northern of the Dutch colonies extending beyond the 31st degree:

---

*This position would locate the wreck on the coast of modern Zululand, which squares with the story of Levaillant, the French traveller, cited later in this chapter.

"this might have been done, had not the intervention of the rivers, which lie between, too much retarded them."

Then began the tragic trek towards the outposts of civilization. In the column led by Captain Coxon were Colonel and Mrs. James, Mrs. Hosea, Mrs. Logie, Mrs. Dennis, Miss Wilmot, Miss Hosea, Master Saunders and Master Chambers. Two sailors were left behind at the wreck: John Bryan, lamed and unable to walk, and a mental defective, or "fool," Joshua Glover. On the march the castaways were molested by Kaffirs hovering in their rear; then there came up a light-coloured man with straight hair, whom the sailors called a "Malay." Actually, he was a renegade Englishman (?) named Trout who had fled from the Cape after committing a murder, and dared not return from the Kaffir wilderness.

"*Engles, Engles?*" said he, clapping his hands—which suggests that either Mr. Trout had forgotten his native tongue, or was posing as a man of another race.

Then, speaking in Dutch, he said: "The Cape is a great way off . . . no, no, I cannot guide you there, no matter what reward you offer me."

(We shall hear of Trout again, ten years later.)

The castaways saw Trout a second time, when he had returned from the wreck with copper. About a week after they had left the *Grosvenor*, the sailors carried the lady passengers over a small river, in water breast-high, which was tidal. Ten days after leaving the wreck, the party split in two, and the sailors pushed on ahead, leaving the "disheartened captain with the ladies." He still, however, had provisions for them. None of this rear party was ever heard of, except in a cloud of unverifiable rumours. Their fate remains a mystery.

One hundred and sixteen days later three surviving sailors staggered into a Dutch farm at the Zwartkops. Here, one cannot help saying, that, if the location of the wreck *were* off the coast of modern Pondoland, then the mystery of sailors wandering over a stretch of about 250 miles in 116 days, and mostly keeping to the sea-shore, partakes of the same unfathomableness as the children of Israel wandering for forty years in the little peninsula of Sinai!

Here they were succoured by Daniel König, a Hanoverian and member of a German settlement which still remains on this part of the coast of Cape Colony. *Herr* König promptly sent out Hottentots to escort the distressed mariners towards the Cape. And, when the news reached the Dutch Governor, although his country was at war with Britain, he humanely sent out an expedition of a hundred Europeans and three hundred Hottentots to search for other survivors. The wagons of this expedition met the three survivors at the Sondags river. König joined this expedition and took brass, beads and copper to induce the Kaffirs to surrender their luckless white captives. Two other survivors, De Larso and Evans, who had reached Zwartkops, joined this expedition of about forty wagons—a commando led by Captain Muller—and went back towards the wreck. They were five days' journey from it, when their horses foundered and the "Mambookers" (Tembu) barred the road.

"They left the wagons at the River Nye (Kei?), which is a very large river full of stones and has a rapid stream. It is near Bamboe Berg, and is fresh water, and in their journey from the wreck, they were obliged to go up it three days before they could cross, on account of the great stones. The country is inhabited on both sides. The wagons were absent a month."

This expedition reached within a day's journey of where the Kaffirs had robbed the *Grosvenor's* survivors, but came short of the wreck. In the hut of a Kaffir, the whites saw a great-coat, which *might* have belonged to Captain Coxon, but they found no signs of the ladies or of the Captain himself. The Dutch Governor's expedition rounded up, it is said, three white men, seven Lascars and two coloured women; but it is *very* doubtful if these unfortunates were from the *Grosvenor*.

One of the passengers of the *Grosvenor* was a Mr. Williams of Bengal. His fate was a tragic one. He gave a gold watch-chain to renegade Trout, and other passengers gave the man rupees. Trout promised to bring them food; for they were starving. But he went away and never came back. Poor Williams, crossing a large river, was caught by Kaffirs on the bank, and thrown into the water, where they stoned him to death. It is a curious fact, that, in 1927, there was living at Clarence Square, Cheltenham, England, a gentleman who is a descendant of Williams. He, if still alive, is Mr. A. W. Gordon Graham and he wrote to the India Office:

"The part-owner of the *Grosvenor*, I understand, was my great-grandfather, a Mr. Williams. I have always understood . . . he had with him a very large amount of bullion, gold, silver and precious stones, his own personal property."*

---

*The charter-party, mentioned, in a letter to Lord Macartney, at Fort St. George, Madras (on 2 February, 1782) from Captain Coxon, as part-owners only David Mitchell and Thomas Walley Partington.

The India Office, in London, replied that the Directors:

"corresponded only with a Part-owner, David Mitchell . . . he acted on behalf of other owners here, but their names have not been traced in the records here. No complete list of the ship's complement of passengers is included in the records. Nothing further concerning Mr. Williams is known here."

Our narrative, which we have interspersed with new, albeit dry documentary details—for a very definite purpose of public interest, as will be seen—must now flash back, in the manner of a movie film, to old London, in the year 1783. The relatives of the missing officers, crew and passengers in the *Grosvenor* had become anxious about the lack of news. They were pressing the Honble. the East India Company's directors.

Says the London *Daily Advertiser,* on 9 April, 1783:

"The Court of Directors met at East India House, in Leadenhall Street, on 8 April, 1873, and read advices that the *Grosvenor*, a missing ship, was not arrived at St. Helena."

The first news of the ship reached Lloyd's who, no doubt, had insured her cargo and, perhaps, bottom. It came on 22 April, 1783, and it was bad news. Here, it may be said that Lloyd's records perished in a disastrous fire at the Royal Exchange, London, in 1828, and no log or manifest of the *Grosvenor* is to be found there—as syndicators are apt to state:

"April 22-23, 1783, *Daily Advertiser*: Advices are said to be received at Lloyd's, stating that the *Grosvenor*, East Indiaman, on her Passage for Europe, was lost on 12 October (*sic*) to the Northward of Lagoa, about 180 Leagues from the Cape of Good Hope. The crew was saved. The above intelligence was brought by a Gentleman who left the Cape, 17 December, 1782, in a vessel bound to L'Orient, which vessel was taken and carried into St. Lucia, from which place he came home passenger in the Sandwich Packet, and says that four of the crew of the *Grosvenor* are arrived at the Cape."

More bad news came when a Captain Dumeney of the Dutch East India Company was taken in his passage from the Cape of Good Hope. A British frigate took him prisoner; for the Dutch were then at war with England. Said he:

"The ship was driven on shore near the River St. Christopher, on the African coast, about forty leagues to the eastward of the Cape of Good Hope, on or about 10 October, 1782, and on 11 December last, four of the crew arrived at Moselle Bay and gave an account of the loss of the ship to the Dutch East India Company. The Dutch governor at the Cape was very friendly to the unhappy sufferers and sent a party of soldiers to protect them from insults that may be offered by the natives. I had written an account of all the particulars; but, when I was taken, it was thrown overboard with the rest of my dispatches."

By now, the people of London and Britain were much agitated about the fate of the ship. It will be noted that not one contemporary reference is made to any bullion, or specie, she was carrying. All the *Gentleman's Magazine* of London said was:

"She was carrying cargo from Bengal valued at £300,000."

No; the furore was all concerned with a matter of very human interest. For, unlike the late G. Bernard Shaw, the people of England in that day, did not believe in miscegenation as a cure for the ills of some of the poor white race. The story of the lost "*Grosvenor's* Lady Passengers" had become real live news in the London journals.

Says the *Morning Chronicle* of 25 April, 1783:

"The situation of the female passengers who were on board the *Grosvenor* Indiaman must have been the most dreadful that imagination can form, or humanity feel for. This ship was lost upon the coast of the Kaffrees, a country inhabited by the most barbarous and monstrous of the human species. By these Hottentots, they were dragged up into the interior parts of the country for the purposes of the vilest, brutish prostitution . . . and had the misfortune to see the friends who were their fellow-passengers sacrificed in their defence."

This theory of the fate of the women—and some of the men—from the *Grosvenor* seems like an intelligent anticipation of what the blacks told Captain Stout, thirteen years later.

Women in London were keenly interested in the fate of their sex, and here, again, no girl, old or young, said a word about any treasure in the *Grosvenor*—not even about the ineffable, gorgeous, scintillating Golden Peacock Throne. No, it is to be seen that these "females," as a London newspaper called them, were wallowing in delightful vicarious delights and shuddery images of "brutish," grinning African blackamoors kissing, or, more likely, they thought, fiercely embracing and raping, in cave-man style, helpless white females who screamed and fought against fellows bearded worse than any pard, and bristling with assegais and wooden clubs. It was almost as good as one of Mr. Richardson's *rather* suggestive novels for the refined wives and daughters of London City tradesmen and merchants.

For example, there was the *Morning Chronicle*, again. What said the editor, on 28 April, 1783? This:

> "A female correspondent, not being able to support the idea of the fate which, it is said, befell the unhappy ladies, passengers in the *Grosvenor East Indiaman*, would esteem it benevolent, if any one in possession of *authentic* information on the subject, would give it to the world, through the channel of the *Morning Chronicle*. Everybody who has a heart must feel it interested in this unhappy catastrophe. . . . Who were the ladies? Were they married or single? Were they mothers or daughters? These are the questions asked by everyone still hoping that the information is not in all points true, and that the inhuman Kaffrees dragged them dead, not living, to their diabolical haunts. Some of the male passengers, it seemed, remained alive. How can this be possible? Could an Englishman, *whilst he lived*, suffer such a fate to befall his country-women?"

Things went with a far slower tempo in those happy, nonmechanistic days, and the next news of the *Grosvenor* did not reach old London till 22 July, 1783, when the East India Company, sitting at East India House, ordered the "sailors of the *Grosvenor*, just arrived at Portsmouth, in a Danish ship from the Cape, to appear before the Committee of Correspondence."

Some time passed, ere the East India Company, in London, learnt from Daniel Corneille, their correspondent at the Cape of Good Hope that the first Dutch expedition had reported to the Governor at the fort at the Cape:

> "We reached the spot of the wreck, and found all her cargo on shore, totally rotted."

This I repeat, was the cargo of which the *Gentleman's Magazine*, of London (1783) said:

"The ship was returning from a Bengal voyage, and the cargo was valued at £300,000."

Even then, a year afterwards, we find not a word about the "Ten boxes of gems, valued at £517,000, and 720 gold bars, and the 1,450 silver ingots in the lazarette, not counting the passengers' valuables and the crews' savings"—*nor* the Mogul's Golden Peacock throne.

The tragic fate of the women passengers held the imagination of the English at home and abroad, and of the French and Dutch. It remained the one subject on which all interest and discussion was focused for more than a hundred years afterwards.

Of course, the East India Company tried to solve the mystery. Captain d'Auvergne made inquiries at the Cape, in October, 1783, and sent his report home to England. I have not been able to find that report in the India Office records. The British Admiralty ordered Lieutenant James Loveday to search for any survivors of the *Grosvenor*. He was to have gone out in the brig, *Swift*, to the "Kaffre" coast in 1783, or in January, 1784; but his ship was paid off at Deptford, in March, 1784. I have seen the *Swift's* logs in the Public Record Office, London,, but neither in 1783 nor 1784 is any mention made of this expedition to Africa and India.

Then there was the question of a court-martial on the Captain of the ship. The East India Company (committee of shipping) met, on 21 January, 1784, and decided it:

"felt incompetent, for want of proper information to determine whether the loss of the *Grosvenor* was unavoidable."

Monsieur Levaillant, the French traveller, journeying through Kaffraria, about the year 1788 met some Kaffres, north of Pondoland (?), and questioned them about what they knew of the fate of the missing captain, officers, and passengers of the ship. The Kaffres (or Kaffirs), had seen part of the goods taken from the wreck, which had been exchanged for cattle:

"Even the Kaffres, now at my camp, possessed some trifling part of the goods. One showed me a silver coin, which he wore at his neck; another had a small steel key . . . They had divided a watch among them. They said the most valuable of the effects had been taken by their countrymen of the sea coast, who were in possession of a great quantity of pieces similar to that they had shown me. As for the people who had escaped the wreck, they had been told some were found dead upon the sand, but that others, more fortunate, had reached some country inhabited by white people."

Here is about the only contemporary, non-official reference to the fact of *any* treasure being on board the *Grosvenor*: the existence of "great quanities of silver pieces" (?) looted by the Kaffir wreckers from the hulk of the *Grosvenor*.

In 1790-91, the Dutch made a third attempt to solve two mysteries: the real location of the wreck, and the unknown fate of the Captain, officers and women passengers. Jacob von Reenen set out on his expedition, and after a journey of 226 hours, covering a league an hour, he and his comrades reached a village in the country of the yellow-skinned, frizzy-haired "Hambonas," where, on 4 November, 1790, they were greeted with joyful shouts of: "Our fathers are come! Our fathers are come!" It is not stated what views *Mijnheer* van Reenen may have had on the subject of miscegenation: but we hear that these joyful roarings came from some "bastard Christians," or mulattoes, who were descended from Englishmen or Englishwomen shipwrecked on the coast and carried up-country to Kaffir kraals. There were three old white women (sisters) who said to the Dutchmen:

"We were children when our ship was wrecked on this coast. We don't know how old we are, or what nation. We were too young to know."

Then, on the banks of the Umzimvubu,* which the Kaffirs had corrupted to "Sinwoewoe," a fellow stood and bawled across the river. What he roared was not the apostolic: "Come over and help us!" but something else. The Dutchmen, indeed, had the impression that the stranger—very coy and wary—felt that it might be a case of "God help *him*, if he came any nearer!"

He said:

"There is nothing to be seen of the *Grosvenor*, but cannon, iron ballast and lead. The crew are dead, some killed by natives, others by hunger."

Unfortunately, his news was confirmed by some of van Reenen's party who had just returned from the wreck which,

---
*The St. John's river, in modern Pondoland. *In Zulu, Umzimvubu means "abode of the sea-cow."*

they said, lay about two days' journey from the River Bogassie. The wreck lay four hours from a certain spot, and there were seven rivers to pass, "for which we had no name:"

> "On this day, with some others of the party, I rode to the spot of the wreck, but saw nothing but five cannon and a great quantity of iron ballast. It was plainly perceived on a spot of ground between two woods that the poeple had made fires and sheltered themselves. Likewise, in the rising ground between two woods was a pit where things had been buried and dug out again, thus confirming to us what the runaway slave (Trout) had told us, that everything had been dug up and dispersed very far into the country. We also understood from the natives that the greater part of the goods had been conveyed to the Rio de la Goa, there to be sold, which place, as we could learn, was from this spot a journey of four days." (*Van Reenen's Report*).

Levaillant, already mentioned, was travelling in this region about six years after the foundering of the *Grosvenor*, when he met some Kaffirs on the march. He questioned them about the location of the wreck: They said:

> "This wreck had, indeed, foundered above the coasts of Kaffraria. According to these indications, I judged that this unhappy event had happened beyond (above) the country of the Tamboukis, as far up as Madagascar, towards the Mozambique channel; they added that, without knowing the difficulties one would encounter after passing their frontiers (*limites*), it would be necessary to cross, among other rivers, one much too wide to swim, or, instead, to go back much to the north in order to find a ford; that, in the meantime, they had seen several whites in the Tamboukis' country; and that they (the Kaffirs) had, on their behalf, exchanged some merchandise with the same Tamboukis, and especially, many nails proceeded from the debris and breaking apart of the wreck . . ."

Thus, if Levaillant's information were even approximately correct, the *Grosvenor* had gone ashore north of Cape Corrientes, in the present Portuguese territory of Mozambique and the river, too wide to swim, *might* be the Limpopoo.

Here we come against the riddle of the location of the wreck. De Riou, who made the chart to accompany the

Journal of van Reenen's expedition—a chart based on another map whose provenance he makes a mystery about—apparently committed a serious error. He spread these seven nameless rivers over a tract of about five hundred miles reaching up to modern Delagoa Bay. On the other hand it seems that van Reenen, on horseback, went no more than about seventy miles up the coast from the southern border of Natal. A glance at a modern chart of this coast shows seven such rivers located in a short stretch of territory north of the river St. John's, or Umzimvubu.

If, however, it be correct that van Reenen's party travelled "226 Leagues from the Great Fish River," then the location of the wreck would be, as de Riou says, somewhere north of Point St. Lucia, in modern Zululand. Was van Reenen misled into identifying the Portuguese Delagoa with some other *lagoa*, named by the old Portuguese navigators, and known under that name to the natives but actually located much nearer modern Durban?

In 1829 John Cane, who came in the embassy of the Zulu king Chaka to Cape Town, said the wreck lay forty miles east of the Umzimvubu, that is, in Pondoland. He said:

"I have frequently heard of some survivors of the wreck, and I recognized Kaffir corruptions of names such as Jeffrey, Thomas, Michael and Fortuin. I understand the armourer died about 1825."

Then the Gweak, or Greak Faku, King of the Pondos, once questioned about the *Grosvenor,* is said to have answered:

"I was only a little boy when I saw the ship broken on the rock. A little time later, it vanished altogether."

George MacTheal, the well known and erudite South African historian, thinks the wreck lies a few kilomètres north of the Umzimvubu river.

A well known English salvor, Mr. J. B. Polland, who has advised previous *Grosvenor* expeditions, and who has held wrecking concession from the Government of the Union of South Africa, holds that the real location of the *Grosvenor* wreck must be south of Durban (and north of Port Grosvenor); but against his theory—which has much to be said for it—are the stories of Levaillant, van Reenen, and the odd fact—already commented on in this chapter—that the surviving sailors took 116 days to travel the distance of 300-380 miles from Pondoland to the Dutch Farms, on the Great Fish River. Only the positive finding and identification of the wreck can solve this riddle of the location.*

People, therefore, who are asked to invest money in *Grosvenor* Treasure wrecking companies must stop and ask themselves one question: "Has the wreck been found?"

The answer is "NO!"

Harking back again to the mystery of the fate of the women and Captain Coxon, one finds that a dim light was shed in what the Kaffirs told Captain Benjamin Stout, of the U.S. ship *Hercules,* lost at the mouth of the Beka river, on the coast of Kaffraria, on 16 July, 1796. The *Hercules* was caught in one of those appalling hurricanes on this coast, which have doomed far bigger ships since her day—the *Waratah* liner, for example. The ship was wrecked off the mouth of the Rio de Infante (24 miles or more south of the Rio São Cristovana or Kei river). Stout questioned the natives about the *Grosvenor*. They (Hottentots) went on a sand-hill, and, pointing towards the place where they said the wreck was lost, asserted that:

"Captain (Coxon) he was slain. A chief wanted to take two of the white women to his kraal, and Captain, he say 'No!' Sailors say 'No!' They try to fight, but no arms, no guns, no spears, Chief tell his men killum at once. They die."

---

*Arguing for his theory, Mr. Polland reports to me that he, about thirty years ago, once spent all night wandering on a beach, near Durban, trying to find a path through the bush fringing the cliffs to a road where he had left his motor-car. The bush is thronged with poisonous snakes. No steamer can take in ballast there without finding her holds, later on, tenanted by snakes. Mr. Polland had, on the previous afternoon, descended the bush path in company with a Durban newspaper reporter who was afflicted with a cork leg, and who, in the night, would have perished with cold had it not been for the efforts of his companions. Their quest was the hut of a diver who was watching some treasure chests, sunken in a cleft of a reef, off-shore. Not before dawn did any help come, in the forms of Hindus hunting bait, along the foreshore, with twinkling lights, which Mr. Polland saw from a distance. The Hindus told Mr. Polland that he had passed the track, in the darkness, half an hour previously.

One of the Hottentots told Stout that one of the ladies of the *Grosvenor* died a short time after reaching the kraal. "The Hottentot showed real concern," says Stout. The other lady, the black said, was still living, and had several children by the chief . . . "but where she is now, they knew not."

The historian MacTheal notes that two white men, for some years lived near the wreck, but adds that it is not certain who they were. One of them lived with a Kaffir woman and had a son by her. This man had a son who, in 1824, was a servant to Mr. F. G. Farwell, in Natal. He told Mr. Farwell that two women also, for a time, lived near the wreck; but that when a tribe invaded the country from the west, the women hid in a forest and there starved to death:

"It can hardly have been women wrecked in the *Grosvenor*. The women were with their husbands and protectors, when last seen. No trace of them has ever been found." (*Hist. and Ethnog. of South Africa, vol.* 3.)

As late as the year 1885, *Chamber's Journal* of Edinburgh published a pathetic piece of fiction about the three young daughters of General Campbell who had been forced to enter the harem of a Kaffir—presumably a Pondoland chief—and that the Gweak, or Greak Faku was the grandson of one of the Misses Campbell. All that can be said is that there are no Misses Campbell mentioned in the list of the *Grosvenor*'s passengers. Nevertheless, while the India Office in London admits that no complete list of the ship's complement and passengers is in the archives, fond believers in the romantic story of miscegenatory harems may still cling to their firm faith in the legend.

It was about a century after the wreck of the *Grosvenor* that the interest shifted its focus from the fate of the women passengers to the jewelled legends of lost treasures lying on a reef off Pondoland. Some syndicate operating in South Africa, in the nineteenth century, acquired a document purporting that the British Admiralty sought to salve the wreck in or about 1788; but the only official reference about that date that one has been able to find, concerns the dispatch of the brig H.M.S. *Swift*, and there is, as shown above, nothing to support this story of an early salvage attempt. Then (stated this syndicate) a Captain H. Bowden, called a "port captain"—his name is *not* in the Navy List of 1842— is alleged to have made thirteen trips to the wreck, at the order of the Admiralty, and to have reported, in July, 1842, that he had fished up no treasure; that the hulk was settling down, and that he had taken cross-bearings of the timbers,° which he had entered in a log for their lordships' perusal. It seems odd, by the way, that no report of Bowden's attempted salvage appears in *The Times* in 1842. That newspaper had, at that date, a keen eye for such matters. It is curious, too, that a prolonged search of the British Admiralty records for 1842, made by the writer of this book, has not disclosed the original of this letter by Bowden. It *ought* to be in the In-Letters of the Secretary, but is not, and there is no reference to it in the Index of letters for that year. No one knows of what South African port(?) Bowden was a captain, nor the particular port from which he wrote to the Admiralty in London. It is also very doubtful if the Admiralty would have displayed this interest in a faraway wreck after the lapse of sixty years from her foundering.

In 1855, Captain Turner, skipper of the trading steamer *Lady Wood*, of Durban, said the debris of the *Grosvenor's* hulk were among rocks in surf:

"which makes diving difficult. Dynamite has been used in the rocks, and then the sands scraped with buckets. A great number of small coins were found in a cannon, which I burnt (*sic*). The natives' chief at that point will not allow the guns to be touched."

He, or someone else, at this time, heard of a legend handed down among the inhabitants of the district—presumably of the Pondoland coast—to the effect that a sailor took a box ashore and buried it, and that treasure is hidden somewhere.

Another story has it that, in 1892 (?) Turner found hundreds of coins and golden star pagodas on the same coast; though it does not necessarily follow that these came from the *Grosvenor* wreck; since many wrecks are found off these shores.°

°Mr. J. B. Polland, the well known British and South African salvor, points out to me that this story of cross-bearings—a thing quite unnecessary to do, in the circumstances—makes a *professional* and experienced salvor suspicious of the authenticity of the whole yarn.

°This Pondo chief, Umquikela, did not see eye to eye with Captain Turner in the matter of granting trading conditions with a new port, now called Port Grosvenor.

Then, in the "A. and S. Regimental News of the 91st Highlanders," quoted by the *Times of Natal*, in 7 May, 1885, we hear of coins alleged to come from the *Grosvenor* wreck:

> "They have been handed to the *Mollah* (a mullah, Moslem priest) at Durban, and he says they are of the time of the Emperors of Delhi, the oldest being those of Shah Alim: 'A. 11, A.D. 1107-12'. The *Mollah* could not give an account of the two small coins that have a three-quarter figure impressed on them, the stamping having slightly split the edges. A few Venetian sequins have also been obtained. One of these coins is now in the possession of Lieutenant Colonel Robley. The figure of St. Mark is on one side in an oval of sixteen stars; on the other he is blessing a diminutive Doge whose name, abbreviated, is that of the Doge *Al Mocenigo*-1763-76. The gold is of a bright colour, and in good preservation. Captain Turner, of the trading steamer, *Lady Wood,* of Durban, says that the debris of the *Grosvenor* wreck are amongst rocks and in the surf, which makes diving difficult. Dynamite has been used on the rocks."

The romantic story of the sailor who cached a box on the strand inspired some person unknown to invoke the aid of Davy Jones, marine forger. The treasure legend now began with the statement that:

> "the majority of the passengers aboard carried large quantities of valuables with them, as they were homeward-bound from the Indies, and had spent many years in the East. Everyone got ashore but the cook's mate, and no portion of the cargo was saved. There were 150 people aboard."

We have seen what happened to the cargo. The "circumstantial account of four surviving sailors," London, 1763, says there were 142 people aboard; but not one of the contemporary accounts mentions any cook's mate. However, the ball had been started rolling, and the legend, as is the way in such matters, began to pile up as each land-romancer and sea-rover kittled up his five wits in the bar of old Tom Tiddler's bodega, or by the light of the binnacle lamp when anchor-watch yarns were spun in the doldrums.

In 1896, Alexander Lindsay is said to have picked up "hundreds of coins" and more golden star pagodas, on the Pondoland coast.

He sifted the sands in the pools, among the rocks, and

found more copper and gold coins, a cannon-ball, and a deep sea lead.

It was in the 1900s that a picturesque seafaring adventurer who had evidently been reading that Sherlock Holmes detective story, in which figures of dancing match-sticks provide a crook's simple code, called on the late (Sir Arthur) Conan Doyle and told a fresh version of the mystic Kaffir yarn about the sailor caching a chest on the Pondoland strand. He had picturesquely added to it and provided a chart, which I give below:

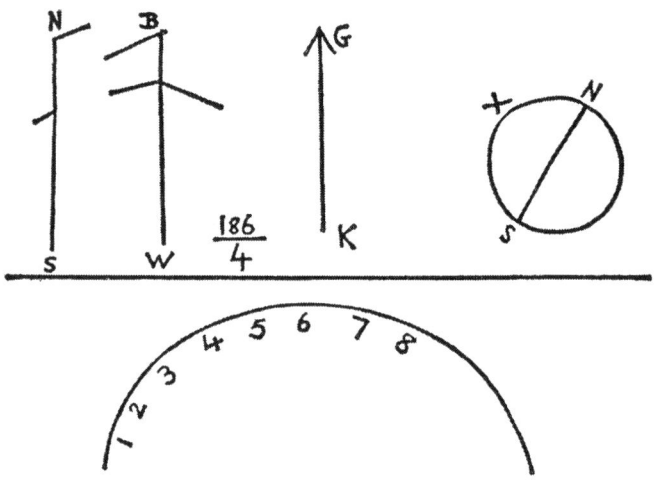

Said Conan Doyle:

"I believe the old crown regalia of Delhi was in the ship. It is surmised that the sailors buried this near the spot, and that this chart is a note of the spot. Each man, in those days, had his own semaphore code, and it is conjectured that the three marks on the left are signals from a three-armed semaphore. Some record of their meaning might be found even now among the old papers of the India Office. The circle on the right gives compass bearings. The larger circle may be the curved edge of a reef or rock. The figures above are indications of how to reach the X, which marks the treasure. Possibly they may give the bearings as 186 feet from the 4 on the same semi-circle.

Memories and Adventures.

Alas, semaphores were *not* in public use, *on land*, until 1796 in Paris, and 1816 in England. They were certainly *not* in use in any ship—East India Company's or British Navy—in 1782.

In 1906-7, H. S. Lyons of the Grosvenor Treasure Recovery Syndicate hired a dredger, the *Duiker*, from Table Bay, but nearly lost his diver when the main airpipe was cut on a sharp reef. *From the beach,* Lyons salved more gold star pagodas, Venetian gold sequins, bronze money, pieces of silver, old spectacle rims and a silver decanter. He made two attempts on the wreck—or *some* wreck—and "went bust" when appealing for £2,500 more capital for a third attempt— "to recover the treasure, *if it exists*" significantly said the shareholders' resolution. (*Vide Natal Mercury,* 6 June, 1907). Lyons had put in nearly a year, and he said the wreck was "difficult to locate, as it lay in a rock-crevice between banks of sand and shells . . . On the beach we picked up a silver brooch, shoe buckle, strings of brass pins, bits of china and glass, and a few gold coins in the shore-end of the gully."

Apparently, the guns which Turner was forbidden by the native chiefs to touch, were shifted by Lyons, and the late Cecil Rhodes took thirteen of these cannon home to the barracks of the Cape Mounted Rifles. How it was known that these guns were those of the *Grosvenor,* one is not told. It was *not* the custom of the East India Company to stamp the name of their ships on the armament they carried as defence against pirates or enemy warships.

It may have been about this period—or earlier, between the 1880s and 1890s—that another person unknown, or an unarmed naval officer was inspired to put forth the magnificent "boloney" about the Gorgeous Peacock Throne, to which Conan Doyle refers, above:

"A wonderful peacock throne from the Mogul's palace at Delhi. It is shaped like a bed on golded legs, and has a canopy supported by slender columns encrusted with seed pearls, rubies and emeralds, over the throne. Two splendid peacocks stood behind the throne, with wings outspread, made of gold with precious stones."

To give an air of verisimilitude to the story probably taken from the *Six Voyages,* some romancer cited Jean-Baptiste Tavernier, the famous French traveller and jeweller, who was in India at the Court of the Mogul Emperor in or about 1676, and saw this throne. Whoever the romancer was he did not know that Nadir Shah, the brigand-king of Persia, overran Hindostan and looted the Mogul treasures some years *before* the *Grosvenor* sailed on her last voyage. Nadir Shah was not the man to overlook so gorgeous a treasure and glorious a booty as the Peacock Throne.

In 1922 the secretary of the Grosvenor Bullion Syndicate wrote to the India Office, in London, about this Mogul throne:

"Among the documents collected by my Board are . . . two letters (one from an Army officer, a captain, and the other from a naval officer). These letters make mention of the same valuation of treasure to be found in the *Grosvenor*. Both mention precious stones, rubies and emeralds. One letter states that two golden peacocks from the famous Golden Peacock throne, in Delhi, were cemented into a strong room on board the ship. . . . My board desire to ascertain as near as possible the contents of the *Grosvenor* before reaching her, in order that the Greatest Care can be exercised in the handling of cases and boxes."

The India Office answered that "nothing is known of the two Golden Peacocks."

The writer of this letter—whether he was an Army officer or a Naval officer one does not know—cites the unknown forger's story, which the forger asserted had been copied from a manifest and (or) log. This faked document purports to detail a lot of the treasures the *Grosvenor* was carrying when she hit the reef off the African coast.

It is usually stated to be "an extract from an official report made by a survivor after the disaster that occurred in 1782," and is worded as follows:

"The precious stones, which were in 19 boxes, are stored in the strong room beneath my cabin, and could never have been got out. Their value is £517,000. The gold bars are also in their position and valued at £72,000, there being 720 bars, each £100 in value. The silver bars are 1,450 in number, and stored amidships, in the lower hold, the specie (coin) being in the bottom of the lazarette, and amounting to £717,000. Nor was any effects of the troops, or crew saved, nor their savings which, I regret to say, were under my care in the lazarette."

It may be noted that the word "lazarette," in this forged document, is spelt in its nineteenth-century form. The earliest use of the word, in the meaning attached to it in this document, occurs in *The Shipbuilder's Assistant*, by William

Sutherland, shipwright and mariner, who published his book in London in 1711. He says:

> "*Lazarette* is a place on board of a Merchant Ship, for the Conveniency of the Commander, as Store rooms are on board of Men of War, to lay up Provisions and Necessaries for the Voyage."

Dr. William Burney's edition of William Falconer's *Marine Dictionary* (London, 1830), calls it the *lazaretto*: "in some merchant ships, the *lazaretto* is the fore-part of the lower-deck, parted off for reception of provisions and stores." *But,* Falconer, who compiled this *Marine Dictionary*, at Chatham Dockyard, in 1767, does *not* give the word in his first edition, London, 1769; nor in the editions of 1771 and 1784. Again, the word appears in one of Colebrook's letters, written in 1783:

> "The Duke of Athol, Indiaman, took fire by neglect of the steward, in drawing off rum in the *lazarette*."

Lastly, I find it in the *Naval Chronicle*, of 1799, where, in a story of the fire on board the *Daedalus* transport, in December, 1792, it is said:

> "The fire must be in the *lazaretto* below."

To anyone, therefore, acquainted with the language and phraseology of the late eighteenth-century sailor, the style of this precious production shouts in his ear the words: "Liar and clumsy forger" even were the forgery not exposed by the anachronism in the spelling of the word "lazarette."

One thing the circumstantial forger forgot: to say that the value of the *crew's* savings may be estimated at another million or so! Who shall say where this faker is now, or whether he is smiling down, from the heavenly kingdom of pure whisky, on the sweating foreheads and blasphemous mouths of the divers and delvers whose borings and diggings through the sandstone strata failed to take them to this vault of a maharajah of Ind?*

Does a genuine copy of a manifest or log of the *Grosvenor* exist today?

The fire taking place at the factory and fort of St. George,

---

* The cargo of the *Grosvenor* was probably of a perishable nature, and not coin or bullion." (*India Office to Grosvenor Bullion Syndicate,* 26 April, 1922.)

Madras, some years after the loss of the ship, probably destroyed these essential documents. The India Office in London and the Office of the Imperial Records at New Delhi, as successors of the old East India Company, have no copy of them and know nothing about them. Nor has either of them the log of the ship. Lloyd's of the Royal Exchange, the probable insurers of the ship or her cargo, was burnt out in a disastrous fire, in 1828, when as we said above this and other documents and archives were utterly destroyed. Nor does the British Admiralty know anything of log or manifest.

Says the India Office, London:

"The Captain's log did not reach England, and was probably lost. The Manifest cannot now be traced. Most of the documents connected with the East India Company's shipping were destroyed many years ago." (*Letter to the Grosvenor Bullion Syndicate, of Johannesburg,* 22 September, 1921).

As to the "passengers' valuables," be it noted there was a war on with the French and their Dutch allies, and bills of exchange were the usual method of transmitting cash from India to England in those troubled and dangerous times. True, the ship carried a register of diamonds, amounting to Star Pagodas 24,444 worth £8,977 12s. (English sterling of 1782). Who, however, in his senses, would look for diamonds, which must have long since been scattered over the bed of the sea, on a coast where raging hurricanes pound and shifting currents drag the bottom?

It would be a job for Davy Jones' locker or for the fellow who went to look for a needle in a haystack, on a dark night in a raging gale, with a farthing candle stuck in a horn lantern, whose cover would not latch, and let in the wind. All the engineers of the Zuyder Zee in Holland and the Wash in old England would not be equal to such a job. And certainly, I see no Hollander—man of a cautious race proverbially averse from speculative "fliers"—busying himself and putting his money—his *own* money—in such a project! It would be instructive, indeed, to know how much money, from the *Netherlands,* has ever been invested in the *Grosvenor* treasure wrecking schemes, of the past.

It is significant that later salvors have rather boggled at the Golden Peacock throne, and, until 1952 and 1957, that gorgeous phoenix had never risen from the ashes to make its appearance, in a prospectus, renewed with youthful vigour and inspired with all the attributes of Juno whose chariot, it will be recalled, was drawn by these proud birds. Come, come, can it be that there are men who boggle at the gnat of the peacock while avidly swallowing the golden camel of the many boxes of gold ingots and gems? Or have their enraptured minds and eyes grown wise—with the wisdom for a man's self, as Francis Bacon has it—suddenly discerned that Iris of the golden rainbow who stood behind the Golden Peacock throne? Did some African Falstaff roar like a red-faced butcher or brewer's butler. "Go to, ye whoreson knaves . . . I'll have no peacock's feathers in my brewage. Nay, all shall be simple of itself—gold and gems . . . Besides, think ye Nim and Bardolph . . . will *they* stand for it . . . stand for it? Go to . . . by this round belly, lined with fat capon and soused in sack . . . NO!"

The Star Pagodas, 162,378 mentioned in the invoice from Fort St. George, Madras, represented merely the value of the cargo:

It is interesting, again to note that Captain Coxon had a living descendant, Lieut-Colonel A. W. Coxon, who lives or lived near Farnham, Surrey, England. He took shares in one wreck syndicate . . . for "sentimental reasons." Smirke's print of the wreck has high cliffs which, he rightly points out, do not fit the flatness of the spot on which so many *Grosvenor* wrecking syndicates have operated. A silver tankard in his possession is engraved "Success to the *Grosvenor*."

It must needs be said that, in 1922, the gullible investing public in South Africa and, to some extent, even in old England, were heavily "salted" over this old wreck. A syndicate had heard of the late Lord Headley's picturesque plan which he propounded in an address to the London Society of Engineers. Headley's plan never advanced beyond the stage of theory, but it was ingenious. His imagination had been stimulated by the thought of the hundreds of wrecks, from the days of the Roman Count of the Saxon shore to that Earl Godwin who gave the sands his name, on to the European war. Millions of lost treasures, he said, lie in the centuries of wrecks—a thousand years of them—on the Goodwin Sands, off Deal and Dover.

Why not sink a big concrete tower in Trinity Bay and run tunnels from this base, in any desired direction, towards the Goodwins? Borings would then reveal the presence of the sunken craft, and it would be an easy matter to bore an upward shaft to the timbers of the hulks. Lord Headley advised that first there should be an *accumulation of reliable data* on the subject of ancient wrecks. Then he would establish a line of three belts of borings, about 100 feet apart, covering the ten miles in area of the Goodwins, running north to south. Over three thousand borings would be needed in each belt, and by means of water-jet appliances, augers could be rapidly sunk to secure specimen cores of oak, elm, and teak timbers. Of course, there would be the risk of missing the mark, and a great deal of money might be vainly spent on the engineering; but the location of one valuable wreck, say, with £2,000,000 aboard her, would repay a good deal of the outlay.

He had also in mind the 3,000 sunken and torpedoed merchant ships in the First World War, whose aggregate cargo-value would be around £300,000,000. "So near and yet so far!" The problem was a knotty one, but more sound than many mining propositions he had known . . . for, at least, one knew the gold was *there*, in the sands!

The Grosvenor Bullion Syndicate started to work on this idea. They bored a "tunnel drive" (about 450 feet long) from the Pondoland shore, through the sandstone strata, towards a fissure in which it was presumed the hulk of the *Grosvenor* lay, in a bed of sands and shells, thirty-five feet below the surface of the water. Arriving at the spot, a vertical shaft would be driven upwards.

Thousands of pounds were spent on the scheme, and the South African press, especially the *Rand Daily Mail*, became critical and sceptical. A special correspondent, Mr. Cyril Campbell, administered a cold douche. Then the newspaper published a report in the form of a letter from a member of the Webster Grosvenor Bullion Syndicate. He repeated the old story of the letter from H. P. Bowden to the British Admiralty. He went further:

"The *Grosvenor* carried eight to ten tons of gold, and the manifest bears it out. The late Wm. Basley always said he saw the stumps of the mast of the *Grosvenor,* standing in the last fifty or sixty years. . . . I am certain the lower portion of the hull is intact, but buried in sand. I knew Mr. Charles Turton, aged seventy-five, who lives in Griqualand. He says his brother visited the wreck, and that a Spanish warship was wrecked on the Pondoland coast, the same time as the *Grosvenor*."

Eleven days later, on 21 August, 1921, the *Rand Daily Mail* reported:

"There are news stories from the coast, reaching Johannesburg, to the effect that the wreck of the *Grosvenor* has been found twenty-four miles from the village of Lusikisiki. It is intact from keel to deck. But The Rev. John Allson of

Durban, one of the last of the old-timer missionaries, and now an aged man, points out that the *Grosvenor* cannot now be intact; since she was smashed by a big rock which still, today, stands as sentinel, to the sea, marking the scene of the wreck, and bearing traces of it. How came cannon on top of the rock? Was it not because when seas broke up the timbers of the hulk, they left behind the heavy metal of the guns? The rock is about fifteen feet high, though, at low tide, it stood considerably higher out of the water. It appears that four cannon can still be seen on the rock."

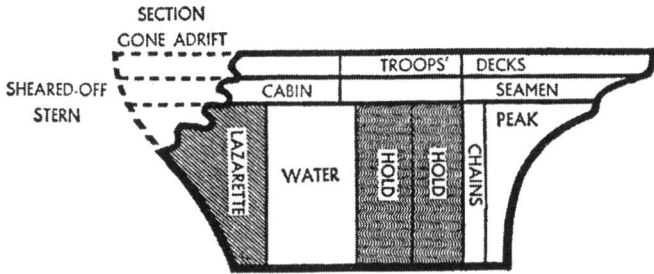

The syndicate even published a chart of the hulk of the ship. I append a sketch of it, from which the candid reader may see that it hardly fits the case of the *Grosvenor*, which broke in two by the mainmast, and then under the force of the surges on the reef, the poop, on which the people had taken refuge, sundered in two, fore and aft. A works manager of the syndicate said he was sure the wreck lay on a rock, three miles from Port Grosvenor. Only one hundred and

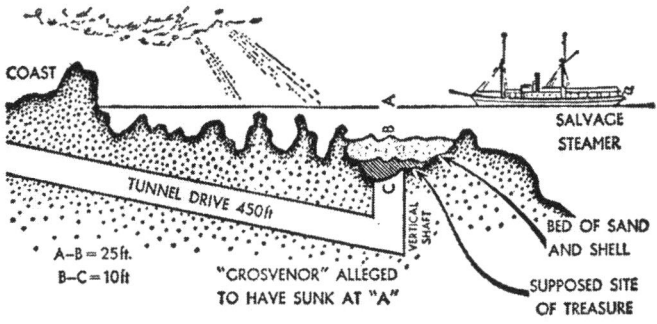

fifty feet more of the tunnel needed to be built, and by the end of September 1922:

"a most interesting position should be reached. We know the treasure is still there."

Mr. Campbell of the *Rand Daily Mail* unkindly retorted with some details about the contemporary evidence relating to the location:

"There were steep rocks southward of where the ship was cast away; but there are no steep rocks south of the Port Grosvenor location, and no mast stumps were visible above the water forty years ago. If the ship were intact, she should be in view; since she is said to be lying in eleven feet of sand, with eleven feet of water above. She must have been broken up, however; for pig-iron ballast has been found."

In 1923, South African investors had become rather perturbed, and to allay their natural anxiety, someone published the sworn report of the diver, Richard Foley. He had had Admiralty experience, and from aboard the SS. *Namaqua*, in harbour at East London, he wrote, on 6 February, 1923:

"When I got down to the ocean-bed I saw my objective in the form of a huge bed of hardened shells and sand, extending right across the gully, which was approximately 110 feet. . . .
"There was rust—probably from guns, and other material, which had mixed with the sand to form a conglomerate almost as hard as cement."

Foley had found the sea so rough and the shores so wild and dangerous that he was able to reach the sea-bed only four times in five months.

Then a member of a syndicate, formed to fish up the "*Grosvenor's* bullion," published in the South African newspapers an alleged affidavit on which it is not necessary for me to comment, in view of what happened after the old East Indiaman smashed herself on the rocks:

"There is an affidavit that the diver, in 1907, *stood on the deck* of the *Grosvenor below water*. Also there are sworn copies of the bills of lading of the *Grosvenor*, in which values are stated in terms of Star Pagodas."

The reader now knows precisely what was stated—and

what was *not*. It was also promised, that, "very soon," core, or section of the *Grosvenor's* wreck-timbers would be produced; for the divers were "very close to the wreck," the South African press were assured.

In November, 1923, the *Rand Daily Mail* commented ironically on the failure of the much-advertised core from the wreck to make its appearance. It pointed out that one man had told the shareholders that he had acquired all documents about the exact position of the wreck, in return for which he was to be given a large parcel of shares. He had besides a fair salary and travelling expenses to and from the wreck. Then this gentleman resigned his job; £12,210 had been spent by the syndicate, with nothing to show for it.

Again the legend of the jutting masts came in for ridicule:

"The masts had been cut down, both fore and main. How then could they have been seen sticking up from the seabed? Were they so seen in 1880? The answer is NO! As the ship split in four, the section containing the alleged treasure has long since been tattered to pieces and dispersed."

Rand Daily Mail, November, 1923.

How about the tunnel to the wreck?

Two watertight compartments, or air-locks were to have been built in the tunnel before the engineers broke through the silt and shells into the sea-water. From these air-locks it was proposed that the diver should work in locating and fishing out the treasure from the timbers of the ancient hulk. How the salvors planned to get rid of the rocks and sands of Sisyphus which would have inevitably rolled back into the workings as fast as they were removed, did not appear.

By October, 1923, the tunnel was fifty feet short of the site—and short too, of more capital to complete the job. In 1924, the *Rand Daily Mail* once more commented ironically on the failure of the core to appear. "Where is this much-advertised core, which three months ago was only twenty feet from the wreckers?"

Echo, with a marine lion's roar, answered down in the sea-caves: "Where? Oh, where?"

The Webster syndicate died a natural death; and then in June, 1927, Pitcairn, an American salvor, tried his hand on the scheme. He drove a tunnel towards the wreck and found sheet lead which he thought came from the hold of *Grosvenor*. After £12,000 had been spent on the job, an experienced British salvor, Commander J. B. Polland, R.N.V.R., who had tackled the difficult and dangerous job of raising the hulk of the torpedoed warship, H.M.S. *Glatton*, blocking the fairway in Dover Harbour, warned Mr. Pitcairn that if he drove the tunnel any further under the soft strata of the sea-bed, inrushing water would be almost certain to seep in through the roof and drown the divers working in the bore. The advice so impressed Mr. Pitcairn that he abandoned the quest for the alleged hulk of the *Grosvenor*.

In 1935, the Italian Sorima Company, the well-known wreckers of Genoa who fished up the treasure in the P. and O. liner *Egypt*, refused to send the steamer *Artiglio II* to operate off the coast of Pondoland, unless South African financiers guaranteed to raise the money to finance the Sorima expedition. Webster still held the lease of the wreck, but saw little hope of another attempt. Webster's son told the reporter of the newspaper *Cape Argus*:

"I was there in 1922, while my father was at work and I saw my mother pick up several golden coins on the beach. My father revisited the scene of the wreck in 1934, and is still keenly interested in the treasure. It is, of course, a very difficult proposition; for the sea may be calm at dawn and too rough for diving a couple of hours later. This means that a salvage steamer has to stand off and on, awaiting orders."

In the same newspaper, it was stated that the value of the treasure aboard the wreck is, "after careful research," estimated at £2,000,000. No doubt by 1958 it will be £22,000,000.

One must hope that the research-workers do not base their calculations on the forged document that I cited, *supra*.

One journal which gave the publicity to the legend of the millions in the *Grosvenor*, was the *Wide World Magazine*, of London (January 1939). The editor was less excusable in that, in 1921 he was in correspondence with the India Office in London about this wreck, and thereby ought to have known the facts about the alleged treasure of this hulk which he now put forth as a "well authenticated treasure." In an article (in this magazine) by one Commander J. C. Capstickdale, R.A.N.R. (retired), we find it stated:

"The *Grosvenor*, wrecked near Port Shepstone in 1780 (*sic*). The vessel had under her hatches perhaps the greatest treasure ever carried in an East Indiaman; there were nearly two million pounds worth of specie, and gems, silks, ivory, etc., to well nigh equal value."

The writer, who does not seem to have gone to much trouble in the compilation of these "facts," also mentions, as a "fact," the legend of the dispatch by the Admiralty of a salvage expedition, "seventeen years after the loss of the *Grosvenor*." (Query: Does he mean in 1797 or 1799? Anyway, it is nonsense.) This (legendary) expedition, he says, raised £1,100 of specie and other articles. Then we are told that the wreck was found broken up, the timbers being scattered over a wide area. Again, sixteen years later, the wreck was reached by tunnelling. One of these yarns cancels out the other.

Thus is a fresh heap added to the growing mountain of legend, the unearthing of *truth* thereby becoming an increasingly difficult task. There is certainly a lot of *romance* under somebody's hatches.

In 1938-39, there had been a revival of the *Grosvenor* affair. Johannesburg speculators, envisaging some "easy money," seemed very much interested in the mysterious wreck.

In 1939, the Grosvenor Engineering Company proposed to plant beacons in the sea, around the reef, "about 100 yards from the grassy slopes of the wild Pondoland shore, where the *Grosvenor* ran ashore. This reef abuts on a little cove, into which this wreck swung and sank. The sea floor, at this point, is fissured with traps out of which it is well nigh impossible for the waves to have removed such articles of high specific gravity as gold and silver. The sides of the gully will be enclosed by a breakwater, whose limits will be determined by the beacons. The wall will be double. It will be twenty-five feet at the top parapet, and up to two hundred feet at its base. Behind the outer wall will be groutings of clay and cement to halt seepage of water. When the wall has been built, the enclosed area will be pumped dry, and the sand removed from over the wreck from which teak and lead were dredged in 1921."

Once again someone had made mention of the "priceless peacock throne of the Moguls, in the hulk."

Yes, *priceless* is the word. I trust no one of the *projectors* will fall into the "traps" when groping around in the bed of the mystic dyked lagoon, or catch a crab in Davy Jones's locker. Wooden legs will be a "mighty poor" combination with wooden—or wily—heads.

In June 1952 and again in 1957, this lure for fools or optimists was once more being dangled before the noses of those who scent "easy money." South African newspapers stated that treasure hunters believed they had found "the wreck of the *Grosvenor*," with a cargo now believed to be worth £10,000,000 in her holds. Once more mention was made of "the Golden Peacock throne, of gold and silver bars, diamonds, rubies, sapphires and emeralds." Diver Tommy Devonshire had, it was true, *not* found any of these splendid treasures; but he *had* located "eight old cannon and small box-shaped objects lying on the rocky seabed."

The myth further developed when the newspapers spoke of "police mounting a watch on the wild coast of Pondoland for a 'pirate ship' seen cruising in those waters, right over the site of the fabulous treasure of the *Grosvenor*." One, Dr. Nico Baartman, whom the Cape Town newspapers said was head of the "Grosvenor Treasure Recovery Company," said the "pirate ship" had modern diving equipment and a skilled diver; but he reminded all concerned that he "held from the South African Government a licence to recover the *Grosvenor*'s bullion and jewels worth £10,000,000." He and others may hold fifty licences; but they will not enable him or anyone to recover bullion and a mystic throne that never were in this East Indiaman!

It was the advice of a famous old English cookery-book writer that you had first to catch your hare before you fricassee'd or roasted him. No doubt a wreck *does* lie in that gully off Port Grosvenor, or near to Port St. John; but that it is the hulk of the *Grosvenor East Indiaman,* one must leave to the imagination or decision of the reader of the facts set out in this chapter.

Speaking as a writer who has wasted many years of his life in getting at the incontestable facts about ancient and modern wrecks, and land treasure caches in all parts of the globe, I am willing to wager the two Golden Peacocks of the Moguls gemmed and glittering throne against any forged documents, based on a non-existent log and manifest of the year 1782, that had this or *any* gorgeous regalia, or those boxes of gold and silver ingots and cases of gems been stored or hidden aboard the East Indiaman, in that month of August, 1782, some surviving sailor would have mentioned the fact. They invariably did so in those years, when any rich East Indiaman or other good ship chanced to be wrecked in the waters of India or off the shores of Africa.

Author's Note: The Golden Peacock Throne, or the "Takhts Tavos," as Persians call it, is today in the Imperial Treasury at Teheran. Lord Curzon of Kedleston saw it in the 1900s. Since it was looted by Nadir Shah its gorgeous canopy of pearls and other jewels has vanished.

Chapter 15

NEW LIGHT ON THE *MARY CELESTE*

WHICH COUNTRY has, in its mercantile marine records, the most baffling mystery ship? Which has the marine riddle that has most severely strained the wits and inborn tendency to truthfulness of landsmen and seamen the world over?

That distinction falls to America, and her mongrel name of *Mary Celeste* has given her a false aura of respectability at variance with her hectic and highly disreputable history.

Old time salts of windjammers had two superstitions about ships: *first*, that some of them, from their building and launching to their watery ends, or breaking up in the wrecker's yards, were unlucky; *second*, that to change the name of a ship ensured certain misfortune. Or, as the splendid and genteel scoundrel, Long John Silver said: "I never knowed any luck as came of changing of a ship's name. Now what a ship was christened, so let her stay, I says." In both respects the *Mary Celeste* would have been deemed a hoodoo ship with a powerful "jinx" on her!

Built in a Nova Scotia shipyard in 1861, she was named the *Amazon*. In 1867 she was stranded off Cape Breton, Nova Scotia, was sold to another man who put in a Yankee skipper of the illiterate, coarse type of that age, who renamed her with the bastard appellation of *Mary Celeste*. Perhaps he thought the name more suitable than that of a pagan Greek! And again she is said to have gone ashore off another part of stormy Cape Breton. She was seized for debt, sold at auction, and her new owner, an illiterate skipper who had turned broker and ship's agent at New York, under the style of J. H. Winchester and Co., put in a hard-shelled, pious New Englander, Captain Benjamin Briggs as skipper. Winchester had been forced to rebuild her and give her a copper-bottom; since her timbers had suffered dry rot. He ordered her to sea with a cargo of alcohol in casks. It may be said that she was quite seaworthy and what happened to her in 1872 was a matter for the red-robed caller, in the great hall of Lloyd's Corporation, London, at that date located in the Royal Exchange, who tolls the "Dead Man's Bell," in order to announce to ship-brokers and underwriters that some ship has sunk, or become missing, how, or where, no man knows.

In this chapter of queer revelations, which sound like voices speaking from the land of dead and damned shades, one will signal to the electricians to roll up the drop curtain before the stage of this marine drama, in order to reveal some curious facts that have long been hidden. It must seem passing strange that of all the skeletons in Davy Jones's locker, this now eighty-six years' old mystery of the sea is still as fresh and green as ever. It ranks with the ever popular and enduring legend of the "Flying Dutchman;" but it has never yet seen the Wagner who will create from this riddle of the American marine a libretto for an opera, in which will be caught up the Atlantic's thunder of roaring winds and rushing waters, and cacophony of drowning human beings, sucked in and mastered by the wild waves, but leaving "no smiling eddies to dimple on the main." Yet the "electrician," who, rightly, should roll up this curtain should be Jack Ketch, with his hangman's rope in his hand. Or his American counterpart with the "hot chair" for a seat.

It was in November, 1872, that this staunch ship was found derelict in the North Atlantic. She had been so hastily abandoned, that the crew aboard her had left their tobacco pipes behind. A brigantine of 282 tons, or, according to her owner, Captain Winchester of New York, 232 tons, the *Mary Celeste* had left New York harbour on 5 November, 1872, bound for Genoa with a cargo of some 1,600 casks of alcohol, and in "fine sailing trim." There is an oil painting of her to be found in the museum of the township of Aulec, New Brunswick. Benjamin Briggs, the captain, was a strait-laced, stern-faced New Englander of old Puritan stock, aged thirty-seven, and was part-owner with Captain James H. Winchester of New York City. On board her were his wife and baby daughter, the mate Albert C. Richardson, second mate Andrew Gilling, steward Edward C. Head, and four German seamen: Walkert Lorenzen, Boy Lorenzen, Arian Hardene, and Gallhib Gondschatt. I mention these names of the crew because forgers and fakers have added to the crew ancient and disreputable mariners and crooked "shellbacks" utterly unknown in her sailing list, and have adduced pier-jumping for which there is not a tittle of evidence.

For about seventeen days she held on her course across the North Atlantic, until at 8 a.m., 25 November, 1872, someone wrote on her deck slate log, that she passed to the north of the island of Santa Maria, in the Azores, which bore away S.S.W., six miles distant. Then something strange and inexplicable happened which caused the *Mary Celeste* to be hastily abandoned by all on board. What that was is one of the most baffling riddles of the sea.

Twelve days after this last entry the British brig, *Dei Gratia*—it will be observed that there is at least an *odour* of piety about the *names* of these two ships!—of Nova Scotia,

Captain David Read Morehouse, skipper, bound from New York (which she left eight days after the *Mary Celeste*), to Gibraltar, for orders, sighted a strange ship, with jib and foremast staysail set, sailing on the starboard tack but in so strange and erratic a fashion that Morehouse decided to close in and hail her. He signalled but got no answer.

"Guess she's a derelict," he said to his mate, Oliver Deveau, and ordered the mate and two seamen to go aboard and investigate. When their boat got under the ship's counter they read her name *Mary Celeste*, and knew it very well as that of a ship that had been in harbour at the same time as themselves. They climbed aboard her, searched her thoroughly, but found not a soul aboard, not even a cat or dog. The seamen shouted but got no response to their hails. She seemed sound and seaworthy, had plenty of food and water, but no papers. Deveau examined her log book and saw the last entry: 24 November, 1872, lat. 36, 56 N., long. 27 20 W.

The startled boarding party found a strange sight in her cabin. All six windows were battened up with wood planking and canvas and resembled a *miniature fortress!* On the table was no food or drink. It looked as if the officers had abandoned her in hot haste or sudden fright. In the fo'c'sle, the seamen's chests of clothes were quite dry, and razors left behind showed no trace of rust. There did not seem to be a crack in her paint or planks; and if she had met with rough weather just before she was so mysteriously abandoned, why did a phial of sewing-machine oil stand upright by a reel of cotton and a thimble? Would not the motion of the rough seas and the wind have spilled that oil? Why too, as was the case, were spare panes of glass, stowed away in the ship unbroken, and a harmonium, music and books in the captain's cabin, dry and undamaged?

Morehouse ordered his mate Deveau and two of the crew of the *Dei Gratia* to navigate the derelict into Gibraltar, which they reached on 13 December, 1872, a day after the arrival of the *Dei Gratia*, and a remarkably quick passage. Lloyd's List thus refers to the affair:

"16 *December*, 1872: Gibraltar, 13 December, 1:45 p. m., *Mary Celeste* Australian (*sic*) brigantine, from New York to Genoa, with alcohol, has been found derelict at sea, and brought here by three men of the *Dei Gratia*, British brigantine. 17 *December*, 1872; Gibraltar, the *Mary Celeste*. British (*sic*) brigantine, is in the possession of the Admiralty Court. 21 *December*, 1872: Gibraltar. Arrived 12 December. *Dei Gratia*, Morehouse, New York."

"There were no boats found aboard the *Mary Celeste*," says U.S. Consul Horatio J. Sprague, reporting from Gibraltar to the American Assistant Secretary of State at Washington, D.C. (This of course, disposes of the fantastic legend that the boats were still slung on the davits, when the derelict was boarded on the high seas). "The vessel is said to leak some, but her new crew had no difficulty to bring her into this port. She is now in the custody of the British Vice-Admiralty Court and treated as a derelict. The Master of the *Dei Gratia* claims salvage."

Sprague was, however, mistaken in saying that the *Mary Celeste* was leaky; but he lets us on to what is the real mystery about this amazing derelict: *Why did her officers and crew leave her in such frantic and inexplicable haste?* She was perfectly seaworthy!

Now, the amazed British naval authorities at Gibraltar, and the judge of the Supreme Court there, were confronted with a marine riddle such as not even the most experienced man among them had ever heard or read of in a long life. An inquiry was at once started, and lasted for weeks. Every day the affair grew more mysterious and enigmatic. Mr. Austin, surveyor of shipping at the port, a diver Ricardo Portunato, and Vecchio, the marshal of Queen Victoria's Vice-Admiralty Court, explored every nook of the derelict. Her cargo of alcohol was all in good order and stowed well in the hold; except for one cask that had started; the exterior of the hull below the waterline showed not the least sign of damage, as by collision; the ship herself, inside and out, on deck and below, mast, yards, and superstructure, was in excellent order, and even the pitch in the waterways had not started during the voyage, suggesting that the *Mary Celeste* had not suffered from bad weather.

But the sea sleuths noted one apparently sinister feature: marks, seemingly of *blood,* stained the top-gallant rail of the derelict, and both bows had been "intentionally slashed." The ship's bills of lading and manifest were missing; and when the investigators examined and compared the logs of the *Mary Celeste* and the *Dei Gratia,* they were surprised by a very remarkable circumstance, which deserves more attention that it has yet received at the hands of those who profess, or have attempted to solve the mystery.

Between 25 November and 5 December, when the *Mary Celeste* was apparently abandoned by her crew, and when she was actually sighted by the *Dei Gratia*, the derelict ship seems to have held on her course, for ten days, with the wheel loose, and no one at the helm in all that time. Now the distance of the longitude of the place where the *Mary Celeste* was found, from that of the island of Santa Maria, the derelict's last entry in her log is, according to reckoning of the Admiralty experts at Gibraltar, 9 minutes 54 degrees (eastwards), which, at latitude 40, is equal approximately to 507 land miles. "It appears almost impossible," say these experts, "that the derelict should have compassed within the same time a distance of 9.54 eastwards, at all events on the *starboard* tack, upon which she was met by the *Dei Gratia,* when the log of the *Dei Gratia* shows that the wind was blowing from the north all that time, and the ship was on the *port* tack all that time."

Stripped of its nautical technicalities, this seems to mean that, during the ten days the position of the sails of the *Celeste must* have been altered by someone, and the "obvious inference is that the *Mary Celeste* was not abandoned till some days after the last entry made in her log." (F. Solly Flood's report to the British Board of Trade).

Here arises a startling question! *What was happening aboard the* Mary Celeste *after 24 and 25 November, which prevented the captain and officers from making any entry in deck or ship's log?* There must surely have been some remarkable occurrence to cause this breach in the normal duties of the ship's navigators, leading up to the climax when all hastily abandoned her to the mercy of wind and wave. A special correspondent of the *New York Herald,* writing from Bangor, Maine, on 21 January, 1911, says that in the cabin of the mate of the *Mary Celeste,* Albert C. Richardson, there was found a slate bearing the words: "Fanny, my dear wife," at the end of records of wind, weather and temperature.

I may say that I am the first man to have obtained from the Archives of the Vice-Admiralty Court at Gibraltar, the reports of the trial and salvage investigation into the mystery of this derelict. I have, by my side, the photostats of this evidence, which I paid for, from the Gibraltar archives in 1930—and I can find in these official reports of the Supreme Registry Court at Gibraltar, no hint of such an apparently tragic entry. It would certainly have been mentioned in the trials of the case; since the Admiralty Judge, Sir James Cochrane, was, and *rightly so,* extremely suspicious and held the strong opinion that there was a mysterious and criminal element hidden behind the enigma of the hurried abandonment of the *Mary Celeste.* Richardson was a native of Stockton, Maine and later on in this chapter I shall cite a letter about him which is like a voice from the dead. One thing no one today knows; where is the log of the *Mary Celeste?*

When the Marshal of the Vice-Admiralty Court at Gibraltar (Mr. T. Vecchio) entered the cabin of the derelict, he picked up from the floor a curious sword . . . "I have examined it," writes Consul Sprague to the Assistant Secretary of State at Washington, D.C., "and it is evidently of Italian make, and bears a Cross of Savoy on the hilt. It remains in the custody of the Court. The chronometer and ship's papers cannot be found."

Meteorologists in Great Britain note that the year of the sailing of the ship was the "most remarkable weather year of the century, rain and cold prolonged far into the summer, and succeeded by an amount of electrical disturbances of the atmosphere unparalleled within living memory. Several gales raged all over the Atlantic, in the latter part of November (1872)." (So the *Annual Register*, 1872).

Letter-writers of *The Times* in the autumn of 1872, commenting on the remarkable appearance of "shooting stars" and meteors—there were, on 29 November, 1872, alone, no fewer than two and a half columns of such letters to *The Times*—were, on 17 December, 1872, joined by one, George A. Welch, of the British Royal Navy, who was then on board the steamer *Rock City*. Welch gave an extract from the steamer's log, between 22 November and 14 December, 1872, on her voyage from Quebec to London. He says: "For brevity's sake, I will here add that, during my long experience of nearly thirty years at sea, I never witnessed such a fearful succession of heavy gales and terrific seas as we encountered crossing the Atlantic." The inevitable consequence of such Atlantic hurricanes—and the Atlantic is peculiarly notorious for mysteries of derelicts and ships that were lost without trace—was seen in the extract following, from "Lloyd's List," dated 12 December, 1872:

"The *Ebenezer* of Arendal, Birketvedt, sailed from New York on or about 22 August, 1872, with maize, bound for Queenstown, Ireland, or Falmouth for orders, and has not since been heard of."

Yet, there was no evidence of storm-damage to the Mary Celeste.

The story of the growth of legend about the mystery of the *Mary Celeste* is remarkable for the brazen lying, forgery of documents, and all kinds of romantic accounts for the mystery. None of them I humbly suggest have tried to focus attention on the evidence of a most important eye-witness—the man who was the first to board the derelict, on the high seas. Other writers did not consult, as I did, the archives of the Supreme Court Registry at Gibraltar, which I believe I was first to do, in 1930.

Oliver Deveau, the first mate of the *Dei Gratia*, offered some remarkable testimony when the inquiry into the abandonment of the *Mary Celeste* was heard before Sir James Cochrane, Knight, Judge and Commissary of the Vice-Admiralty Court of Gibraltar, on 18 December, 1872. Two remarkable facts emerged from this evidence—damaging to romantic accounts. One legend was that, when the boarders first entered the cabin of the *Mary Celeste* they were startled to find a table laid for breakfast, which had been only half-eaten. Listen to the sworn evidence of Oliver Deveau on these and other accounts:

> "I went into the cabin within a few minutes of sounding the pumps. On the table there was the log slate, but I cannot say what else might have been on the table . . . I do not know whether there were any knives. I saw no preparations made for eating in the cabin. There was plenty to eat, but all the knives and forks were in the pantry. The rack was on the table, but no eatables. There was nothing to eat or drink, in the cabin, set out on the table. But preserved meats were in the pantry. I examined the state of the ship's galley. It was in the corner of the forward house, and all the things, pots, kettles, etc., were washed up. Water in the house was a foot or so deep. I cannot say how the water got in, but the door was open and the scuttle hatch off. The windows were shut. There were no cooked provisions in the galley. I never saw the water come over the topmast of a vessel. There was a barrel of flour in the galley, one third gone. We used the provisions found on board the *Mary Celeste*. We used potatoes and meat, and she had, I should say, six months' provision on board."

The second remarkable fact—and one which may be full of significance for any attempt to solve the mystery of why this well-found and provisioned ship was abandoned—is one which is certain to be new to those who have tried to get at the facts about the mystery ship. Oliver Deveau and another sailor found, to their great surprise on their first entry into the ship, that the cabin, slightly raised above the deck, had all its six windows *battened up with canvas and boards.* The evidence in Court does *not* suggest that it was merely to keep out water coming inboard!

> "There were six windows, two in the captain's, one in the mate's, one in the W.C., one in the pantry, and one facing bow of the ship. They were all battened up with canvas

and boards. I knocked one off in the mate's room. All the others remained the same as I found them."

Deveau's story of the sighting of the *Mary Celeste*, as he told it on oath to Sir John Cochrane, is an interesting and refreshing one.

"I left New York on 15 November, bound for Gibraltar for orders, Captain Morehouse master. On 5 December, about 1.30 p.m. sea time, being my watch below, the captain called me and said there was a strange sail on the windward bow, apparently in distress, requiring help. By my reckoning, we were 38 degrees 20 N. lat., 17 degrees 15 W. long. We hauled up, hailed the vessel, but found no one aboard. I cannot say whether the master or I proposed to lower the boat, but one of us did, and I and two men went in her to board the vessel. The sea was running high, the weather having been stormy, though then the wind was moderating.

"I boarded the vessel and the first thing I did was to sound the pumps which were in good order. I found no one on board the vessel, which had three and a half feet of water in the pumps. The pump gear was good, but one of the pumps was drawn to let the sounding rod down. There was no place to let the rod down without drawing the box, as is often the case in a small vessel. . . . I only used the other pump on my way here, and the first pump I left in the same state as I found it."

"I found the fore hatch and the lazarette hatch both off. The binnacle was stove in. There was a great deal of water between the decks, the forward house was full of water up to the coaming and is on the upper deck. I found everything wet in the cabin, in which there had been a great deal of water. The clock was spoilt by the water. The skylight in the cabin was open and raised, and the compass in the binnacle was destroyed. I found all the captain's effects had been left—his clothing and furniture. The bed was just as they had left it, and that and the other clothes were wet. I judged there had been a woman on board. I found the captain's charts and books in the cabin—some were in two bags under the bed, and two or three loose charts lay over the bed. I found no charts on the table. I found the log book in the mate's cabin on his desk. The log slate I found on the captain's table. There was an entry in the log book up to 24 November, and an entry on the log slate, dated 25 November, showing that they had made the Island of St. Mary. *I did not observe the entry on the slate, the first day, and made some entries of my own on it, and so unintentionally rubbed out the entry when I came to use the slate, at least I thought so.* I did not find the ship's Register, or other papers concerning the ship, but only some letters and account books.

"I found the mate's note book in which were entered receipts for cargo . . . I found also the mate's chart in his cabin, hanging over the mate's bed, showing the track of the vessel up to the 24th. There were two charts in the mate's cabin, one under and one hanging over the bed, as I have said. I am not positive whether the chart with the ship's track marked on it was found above or below the mate's bed. There seemed to be everything left behind in the cabin as if *left in a great hurry*, but everything in its place. I noticed the impression in the captain's bed, as of a child having lain there. The hull of the vessel appeared in good condition and nearly new. There were a great many other things in the cabin, but impossible for me to mention all. The things were all wet. The sky light was not off, but open. The hatches were off, the cabin was wet but had no water in it, as the water had naturally run out of it. The masts were good, and the spars, but the rigging was in very bad order and some carried away. The foresail and upper fore topsail had apparently blown from the yards, and the lower fore-topsail was hanging by the four corners. The main staysail was hauled down and lying on the forward house as if it had been let run down. Jib and foretop staysail set. All the rest of the sails were furled."

Here the Judge interposed with a few questions, to which Deveau replied with emphasis that the *Mary Celeste* was brigantine rigged, of over 200 tons, and "I should say was seaworthy and almost a new vessel. Her anchors and chain were all right."

"There were no boats and no davits at the side. It appeared as if she carried her boat on deck; for there was a spar lashed across the stern davits; so that no boat had been there. I went back to my own vessel and reported the state of the brigantine to the captain. I proposed taking her in. He told me well to consider the matter as there was great risk and danger to our lives as well as to our own vessel. We consulted among ourselves and the crew and resolved to bring her in a distance I estimate at six to seven hundred miles. . . . The captain gave me two men, the small boat, a barometer, compass, and a watch. I took with me my own nautical instruments, and whatever food our steward had prepared. I went on board the same afternoon, and about the 5th hour afterwards, hoisted the boat on deck, pumped her out and took charge of her. Augustus Anderson and Charles Lund are the names of the two men I took with me. They are not the same men as I took with me when I first boarded the brigantine, whose names were John Wright and John Johnson. We arrived in Gibraltar on the morning of 13 December.

"When we first went on board we had a great deal to do to get the ship into order. I found a spare trysail which I used as a foresail. It took me two days to set things to rights so as to proceed on the voyage and make any headway. We had fine weather at first and until we got into the Straits when it came on a storm; so that I dare not make the Bay but lay to under Ceuta, and afterwards on the Spanish coast to the east. When I arrived at Gibraltar I found the *Dei Gratia* already there. I had seen her almost every day during the voyage and spake her three or four times. We kept company with her until the night of the storm when I lost sight of her. I saw between decks the nature of the cargo—barrels marked alcohol on the head of them—and likewise in the note of the mate of the *Celeste;* whereby it appeared he had given receipts for so many barrels of alcohol at a time. . . . I found the sounding rod on deck alongside the pump."

Solly Flood (Queen Victoria's Advocate and Admiralty Proctor): "Would you call the *Mary Celeste* a good sailer?"

Deveau: "I call both the *Dei Gratia* and the *Mary Celeste* fair sailers . . . Supposing both vessels to have been equally well found and manned and sailed, she would have been faster than our own ship."

Solly Flood: "Did you pass any other ship on your voyage before you sighted the *Mary Celeste?*"

Deveau: "We spoke one other brigantine on our voyage, bound to Boston; but we did not pass nor see any other vessel of a similar class on our outward voyage. So the first time we could have seen this ship was the day we found her as we did, deserted. I cannot say, without referring to my log where our ship was on the 24th or 25th. I do know we were to the north of the other vessel from seeing her track traced on her chart. We were between Latitudes 40 and 42. We did not sight St. Mary's Isle during any part of our voyage. I do not know the lat. and long. of St. Mary's without seeing a chart. I have made only one voyage from New York to Gibraltar before, and we did not sight St. Mary's then. I never was at St. Mary's

—never have seen it. . . . From 15 to 24 November, we had stormy weather. Most time we never took off our fore hatch since we sailed. . . . The *Mary Celeste* has only two hatches, fore and main, besides the lazarette."

The witness then described, under Solly Flood's expert cross-examination, the disabled and broken state in which he found the rigging and gear of the *Mary Celeste*. He added some queer details about the behaviour of the abandoned ship:

"Her head was westward when we first saw her. She was on the starboard tack, but the wheel was not lashed. The wheel gear was good, and with her foresails set she would not come up to the wind and fall off again. With the sails she had set when I first saw her she might come up and fall away a little, but not very much. She would always keep those sails full. The wind was blowing from the north, but not strongly then, though blowing heavily in the morning. We allow for a current running easterly, but the currents there depend very much on the winds. The first point I made when I could take my bearings was Cape St. Vincent. . . . The vessel's sheet was fast on the port side, and she was found on the starboard tack. The wind would entirely govern the tack she was on at the time. Both vessels going one way might be on the port tack, the other on the starboard tack on the same day. . . ."

The legend that the crew of the *Mary Celeste* quitted the ship in a highly mysterious way in which the ship's boat or boats had no part was not, of course, borne out by the evidence of Oliver Deveau, who made some remarkable statements about her boat accommodation and the probable methods by which her captain, officers and crew quitted her in their panic-stricken flight for no apparent reason:

"The *Celeste* had not accommodation on deck for two boats. One could see where the boat had been lashed across the main hatch, but that was not the right place for her. There were no lashings visible, therefore I cannot swear that the *Mary Celeste* had any boat at all. But there were two fenders where the boat would be lashed. Assuming there was a boat, there was nothing to show how the boat was launched. There were no signs of any tackles to launch her. We launched our boat that way from the rail of the vessel without tackle or hoisting her up, with a tow rope only to secure her."

It is clear that the legend, so well propagated, was based on the words of Deveau: "Therefore I cannot swear that the *Mary Celeste* had any boat at all."*

Deveau went on to describe his entry into the cabin— which we have already quoted: "The way down into her hold is through the hatchways, which is quite different from the Cabin. Into the Cabin, the entrance is through the companion way down the steps."

Solly Flood: "What else did you notice about the ship when you boarded her?"

Deveau: "The binnacle was injured when I went aboard. I fixed it and used it on our way here. Its glass was broken and the binnacle was washed away from its place. It is lashed on the top of the cabin above the deck, being a wooden one, the lashings had given way, and a cleet was gone. The second time I went aboard I found the cabin compass in the mate's room. There were two quadrants in the second mate's room. The cargo seemed to be in good condition, well stowed and had not shifted. As far as I could judge the cargo was not injured. I found no wine, beer, or spirits whatever in the ship."

Sir James Cochrane (the Judge): "Did you see anything to make you conclude that the *Mary Celeste* had been overset by a storm or heavy waves and had been thrown onto her beam ends?"

Deveau: "The vessel was perfectly upright while I was on board and I saw no signs whatever to suggest that she had been on her beam ends at any time. . . .

"If she had been thrown on her beam ends, her hatches would have been washed off. But if she had been thrown on her beam ends, and her hatches had been all close, she might have righted again without her cargo shifting, or without showing any indication."

Sir James Cochrane: "Can you form any idea why the officers and crew so mysteriously abandoned the *Mary Celeste*?"

Deveau: "*My idea is that the crew got alarmed, and, by the sounding rod being found lying alongside the pumps,*

---

*There was only the appearance as of one boat having been on board. I could not see any means or tackle for hoisting the boat on or off the deck, and therefore conclude the boat must have been launched. I saw no remains or pieces of a painter or boat's rope fastened to the rail." (*Evidence of Deveau*, in cross-examination by Flood, on 4 March, 1863, Vice-Admiralty Ct., Gibraltar.)

that they had sounded the pumps and found perhaps a quantity of water in the pumps at the moment, and thinking she would go down, abandoned her.

"The pumps would be sounded perhaps every two or four hours. In order to make entry in the log of 'pumps carefully attended to,' the pumps should be sounded every watch of four hours—if the vessel were leaky, more often. The fact of finding the vessel with only four feet of water when I boarded her, shows that she made little or no water, about 1 inch in 24 hours, and therefore I conclude that all the water found in her went down through her hatches and through her cabin."

The Attorney-General then read the entry on the *Mary Celeste*'s slate log, dated 26 November, 1872.

Deveau: "I never used the side of the slate upon which this entry now appears. I left the charts on board the *Mary Celeste*. I have been master of a brig myself (*this to the judge*). I have no master's but a mate's certificate."

When the inquiry into the mystery was resumed two days later, Solly Flood closely cross-examined Deveau on the state in which he found the Captain's cabin, when he first boarded the *Mary Celeste*:

Deveau: "I have said that there was the appearance on the bed in the captain's cabin as though a child had slept in it. There was room in the berth for a child and a woman, and also for the captain. I saw articles of child's wearing apparel, also child's toys. The bed was as it had been left after being slept in—not made. I saw female clothing. An old dress was hanging near the bed, also india rubber overshoes. The dress was dirty as if worn, but it was not wet. The bedding was wet. I should say that the water had got through the windows near the bed, or perhaps it got through the skylight. The windows were battened up. There had been rain and squalls the morning we found the *Mary Celeste*, but I don't think it was that which had wetted the bed. There were two boxes of clothing—in one box, male and female clothing mixed together. The box was shut, but not locked and the clothing was not wet. The other box had only remnants of cloth in it. Both boxes were open. I afterwards found some clothing in two drawers under the bed, which I afterwards took out and put into the second box, which was nearly empty.

"The clothing found under the bed place was mostly

men's clothing, and some of it was wet, especially that found in the lower drawer. The clothing was of the usual sort worn by men and women. There were also work bags with needles, threads, buttons, books and a case of instruments, a dressing case and other things in the drawers. The two boxes were in the cabin. There was also a valise which I could not, nor did open; a writing desk, and a bag of dirty clothing man's, woman's and child's, hanging up in the water closet. They were damp, but I cannot say how they got damp.

"There was a stove in the fore cabin, but I made no fire in it. Also, there were a few old coats and a pair of sea boots, but the clothes were not those of a passenger; for they were a seafaring man's clothing. The stove was not in the captain's cabin, in which there were swinging lamps on each side—one in the fore and one in the captain's cabin. They were paraffin lamps, but there were no signs of damage by fire, nor of fire or smoke in any part of the ship. The stay sail which had fallen down was on the stove pipe of the galley. There were plenty of provisions and water on board the *Mary Celeste*. A harmonium or melodium was in the cabin."

At this stage, the chart of the *Mary Celeste*, with her course marked on it, was produced in Court and shown to Deveau, who said:

"I found that chart on board the *Mary Celeste* with the ship's course marked on it. I used it afterwards for our track here. The words written '*Mary Celest*e abandoned 5 December, 1872,' are in my handwriting. I put it down merely by guess as the place where I supposed we found the vessel as nearly as I could. The arrows shown on the chart show the way the currents are supposed to run, but they often practically run just in a contrary direction. The chart was found in the mate's cabin."

Sir James Cochrane (the Judge): "How do you account for the fact that, as you say, the *Mary Celeste* ran 500 or 600 miles, with no one aboard, and the sails set as you found them?"

Deveau: "I cannot give an opinion as to whether the derelict could have run the distance where we found her, in the intervals with the sails she had set. We passed to the north of the group while the *Mary Celeste* passed to the south. Between the 24 November, and 5 December, the wind was blowing from the N. to S.W.

"She was going steadily from 1½ to 2 knots when we

saw her with the wind off her beam. She might have had more sails set at first, but she would not run steadily before the wind with her rudder unlashed. She had two head sails set, her lower foretop sail was hanging by the four corners. The wind was North her head was to the West. She was on the starboard tack, going in the opposite direction to ourselves when we met her. She probably had changed her course more than once. She was going backwards. It is impossible, therefore, to say how long or often she had changed her course. . . . There were four berths in the forecastle with bedding, in the *Celeste,* but only three sea chests. Often two sailors chum for one chest. The bedding was damp and looked to have been used. A berth in the second mate's room, or boatswain's room, had been apparently occupied, with the captain's making eight all told besides the woman and child.

"The *Mary Celeste* was sheeted on the starboard tack when we found her. The wind during the last four days before we found the vessel was northwesterly.

"The men's clothing was all left behind, even their oilskin *boots and even their pipes, as if they had left in a great hurry.* My reason for saying they left in haste is that a sailor would generally take such things with him, especially his pipe, if not in a great haste. The chronometer, the sextant, the navigation books were all absent and the ship's register and papers were not found. There was no log line ready for use. The carpenter's tools were in the mate's room. The water casks were on chocks, which had been moved as if struck by a heavy sea. Below, the provision casks were in their proper places, and not overthrown as they would have been if the ship had capsized."

The second mate of the *Dei Gratia,* by name John Wright, said he first went on board the *Mary Celeste* with the mate Oliver Deveau, and seaman John Johnson, while another seaman stopped in the boat alongside.

Solly Flood: "How long was it before you boarded the derelict, after first sighting her?"
Wright: "About two hours. When I first saw the vessel it was the state of her sails that caught my attention. She yawed some, but not much. Two hours later we lowered our boat to go aboard her.
Solly Flood: "What did you see when you went down into her cabin?"
Wright: "I went down into the cabin after assisting to sound her pumps. . . . There is a door to the companion

stairs. The door was open. The top of the cabin is above the deck, about ten inches . . . The windows were nailed up on the starboard side with plank, but not on the port side. The windows on that side were shut, but would let the light in. *I could not say whether the windows were fastened up for the voyage, or had been fastened during the voyage.* On the starboard side the planking was nailed outside the glass. On the port side the windows were shut with glass only, and were not broken. When below in the cabin there was plenty of light to see what was on the table. I did not see any of the skylight glass broken. I saw that the binnacle had been knocked off its stand and was lying on deck alongside the wheel, which was not lashed. But there was nothing the matter with the binnacle. It had not been destroyed. But the compass was destroyed, and its glass cover knocked off."

Wright: "The door was open. It was in a bad state. The stove was knocked out of place. That could have been done by a sea striking the galley and the stove through the door. . . . The main hatch was fastened and lashed with two rough spars. Why they were put there I can't say."

On the third day of the inquiry, Augustus Andersen, A. B., seaman on board the *Dei Gratia*, said there were 3½ feet of water in the *Mary Celeste*'s hold, and a good deal of water between decks. "Everything in the cabin was wet, the clothes and all."

One Cornwell, proctor for James H. Winchester, claimant of the *Mary Celeste*, asked the Judge for restitution of the ship on payment of salvage expenses, and, in open court, on Friday, 31 January, 1873, the Judge sharply commented on the conduct of the salvors:

"There are certain matters which have been brought to my notice respecting this vessel, and I have already very decidedly expressed my opinion that it is desirable and even very necessary that further investigation should take place before the release of the vessel can be sanctioned, or before she can quit this port. The conduct of the salvors in going away as they have done has, in my opinion, been most reprehensible and may probably influence the decision as to their claim or remuneration for their services; and it appears very strange why the captain of the *Dei Gratia* who knows little or nothing to help the investigation, should have remained here, while the first mate and the crew who first boarded the *Celeste* and brought her here should have been allowed to go away as they have done—the Court will take time to consider the claim for restitution."

According to a letter in the archives of the State Department, at Washington, D.C., Winchester, who was an illiterate old shellback, wrote that the Judge, Sir James Cochrane, and the Attorney General at Gibraltar, "were goein' to arest mee for hiring the crue to make way with the officers the Idear was verry rediculas but from what everybody else in Gibraltar had told me about the Attorney General I did not know but they might do itt as thay seam to doe just as they like . . . So, after tarkin' with the consul at Cadiz, I decided to come home."

Whether or no Winchester was repeating mere hearsay, it is pretty clear that Sir James Cochrane strongly suspected that there was something more than a nigger hidden in this marine woodpile! What sort of "nigger" was hidden, we shall disclose later in this chapter.

The sequel to this reprimand was that, on 14 March, 1873, the Queen's Advocate, F. Solly Flood, applied to the Judge to have the salvors charged with the cost of a chemical analysis, which, he said, had been rendered necessary by this departure of Deveau on the voyage to Genoa.

The Admiralty Marshall (Thomas J. Vecchio), at Gibraltar, was later examined by Solly Flood about the personal effects of the master, officers and crew Vecchio found aboard the derelict *Celeste*:

> "The pocket-book and letters now produced by you in this Court are some I found on board the *Mary Celeste* on my first arresting her in December—also the two yellow envelopes addressed to Captain Briggs by Captain Winchester. I found the letters in the bottom drawer in the Captain's cabin. They were wet and damp when first found, but I dried them as they now appear.
>
> "I also found a sword, now produced in Court, as well as some photographs in the captain's private chest. I found, besides, a paper in the forward cabin house, next the cook's galley, having the entrance facing the stern. This paper was in a chest in that cabin. In the envelope are eight photographs and a Post Office order for 35 dollars currency."

On the same day (3 March, 1873), David Read Morehouse, captain of the *Dei Gratia*, superior officer of Oliver Deveau, gave some rather surprising, not to say suspicious testimony respecting the boarding of the derelict *Mary Celeste*, on the high seas. As will be seen, the *Dei Gratia*'s people appear to have gone out of their way to interfere with, if not, indeed, to render invalid what French criminologists would call "les traces révélatrices" of what happened aboard the derelict before her abandonment. H. P. Pisani, for the salvors calls the master of the brigantine *Dei Gratia*, Captain David Read Morehouse, who, being duly sworn says:

"I left New York on 15 November, 1872,* at 8 o'clock civil time, in the *Dei Gratia*, bound to Gibraltar, for orders. My cargo was refined petroleum, 1,735 round barrels, and 499 cases of petroleum and one in dispute. We had heavy weather, but met with nothing extraordinary, till 5 December sea time one o'clock p.m., when I came on deck, saw a sail on the weather bow, bearing E.N.E., wind about N. We were then steering S.E.½E. by compass—38 degrees 20 N. Lat., 17 degrees 37 Long., by chronometer. It was the abandoned *Mary Celeste*.

". . . We passed alongside her, at 3 p.m. at about 400 yards distance, hailed her, got no answer and saw no one on her decks."

Mr. M. W. Stokes (for the owners of the cargo) cross-examining Morehouse: "Where were you when you fell in with the *Mary Celeste*?"

Morehouse: "More than 600 miles from Gibraltar . . . I am not aware that the *Mary Celeste* sustained any damage on the run to Gibraltar."

It should be noted that this answer has some relation to the mysterious cuts around both bows of the *Celeste*—a feature of the case which has perplexed inquirers at the time of the salvage inquiry and since, and has never been cleared up!

Morehouse added:

"My vessel is a heavy vessel to handle, so much that the Mate and his two men handled the *Mary Celeste* with as

---

*Lloyd's List, for 1872, shows that the *Dei Gratia* put to sea from New York harbour on 2 October, 1872, but her actual time of sailing was not reported. On 6 December, 1872, it reported that the *Dei Gratia* had been spoken to, on her voyage from New York to Gibraltar, at Lat. 41 N., Long. 66 W., on 19 November. This position approximates to some 552 miles eastwards from New York.

much ease as I and my four men could handle the *Dei Gratia*."

Solly Flood, the Queen's Vice-Admiralty Proctor, here interjected a question to which there is reason for suspecting that Captain David Read Morehouse returned a reply which is a deliberate lie and perjury.

Solly Flood: "When did you first go aboard the *Mary Celeste?*"
Captain Morehouse: "*I did not go on board the Mary Celeste at all until she came into the Port of Gibraltar*:
"I could see with my glass that both gangways on the top gallant rails of the *Mary Celeste* were off—were unshipped when we found the vessel. I am sure of that. I made the remark to my Mate that they had probably removed the rails to launch their boat. I also saw the marks on spauls on the bows of the *Mary Celeste*. . . . As we were steering, we should have left the *Mary Celeste* on the port tack. We were on the port tack. She was on the starboard tack. We should have passed to the southward of her. . . . It would have been possible for the vessel under the canvas she had on to have gone quite round without having had a rope touched and to have gone on the other tack. I think the jib was trimmed on the port side when we first met her, although she was on the opposite tack. I have seen vessels behave so strangely that it is impossible to say how or what they will do."

Solly Flood then produced the log and log slate of the *Mary Celeste* and read out last entry made by the ship's officers—on the log or deck slate: "Monday 25 November: 1 o'clock. 8 knots and 9 knots. Total 162."

Solly Flood: "What report did your mate, Oliver Deveau make to you about the state of things he found on the *Mary Celeste*, at his first visit?"
Morehouse: "He said nothing particular about the state of the deck, except that things were in a state of confusion—hatches off—ropes about. The flag, or what I thought was a flag from the port yard arm, we found, when we got to it, was part of the upper topsail hanging down torn. I think the sail now shown me in Court is part of the fore topsail. I think it has been cut across with a knife—although I have seen sails torn by the wind in every sort of way, across and against the grain."

A sensational turn was given to the case on 4 March, 1873, when the keen sleuth's nose of Solly Flood, Her Majesty's

Advocate and British Vice-Admiralty Proctor, had been scenting the mysterious alleged bloodstains found on the deck of the *Mary Celeste* and on a sword in the cabin of the same derelict. Oliver Deveau, the mate of the *Dei Gratia*, who had, without permission, withdrawn himself from the jurisdiction of the Court, had returned from a voyage in his ship to Genoa, and he was put through a severe cross-examination about these marks, and also about an admitted falsification of the log of the *Mary Celeste*, which he kept—or, rather, did not keep—after the 5 December, the date of boarding of the *Mary Celeste*, until her arrival at Gibraltar. The reader will now see for himself, or herself, why I have accused the captain of the *Dei Gratia*, David Read Morehouse, of deliberate perjury on an important point. Deveau had evidently destroyed some mysterious "vessels" or container—a presumably vital piece of evidence—about which the records seen by the author of this book are far from explicit. Enlightenment was also sought by the Queen's Advocate on the origin of the equally strange cuts and slashes about the hull and rails of the *Mary Celeste*:

> *Oliver Deveau*: "I saw no remains or pieces of a painter or boats rope fastened to the rail, and I noticed no mark of an axe or cut on the rail. I did not see this cut in the rail now shown me to notice it. The cut appears to have been done with a sharp axe; but I do not think it could have been done by my men while we were in possession of the vessel. I did not see any new axes on board the *Celeste*, but we found an old axe. I did not replace the rails of the ship found on the deck before I returned to the *Dei Gratia* the first time. I can form no opinion about the cause of the axe cut on the rail."
>
> *Solly Flood*: "Have you any opinion to offer the court as to the origin of the blood stains on the deck?"
>
> *Oliver Deveau*: "I noticed no marks or traces of blood on deck. I cannot say whether there were any or not. We never washed or scraped the decks of the *Mary Celeste*. We had not men enough for that. The sea washed over the decks."
>
> *Solly Flood*: "Salt water contains chloric acid which dissolves the particles of blood."
>
> *Oliver Deveau*: "If there are some parts of the deck or rail scraped, I did not notice them and they were not done while we were on board."
>
> *Solly Flood*: "Did you pick up a sword aboard the *Mary Celeste*?"
>
> *Oliver Deveau*: "I saw a sword on board the vessel. I

found that sword under the captain's berth. I took it from there, and looked at it by drawing it from its sheath. There was nothing remarkable on it, and I don't think there is anything remarkable about it now. It seems rusty. I think I put it back where I found it or somewhere near. I did not see it at the foot of the ladder. Perhaps some of my men may have put it there. I was not on board the *Celeste* when the Vice-Admiralty Marshal came on the ship to arrest her, and, therefore, I did not see him find this sword."

Solly Flood: "The sword has been cleaned with lemon, which has covered it with citrate of iron, which has destroyed the marks of the supposed blood, which therefore is not blood at all as at first supposed, *but another substance put there to disguise the original marks of the blood which were once there."*

The Court records do not state what reply, if any, was made by Oliver Deveau to these highly significant statements of the Queen's Proctor. Did Deveau clean this sword, and if so, for what reason? On the other hand, of course, it *may* be, although it seems unlikely, that the original owner, Captain Briggs, may have cleaned the sword. But, in that case, why did Sir James Cochrane, the Judge of the Vice-Admiralty Court, censure Deveau for "doing away with the vessel which had rendered necessary the analysis of the supposed bloodstain?"

Deveau's evidence, on that day, Tuesday, 4 March, 1873, concludes: "It did not occur to me that there had been any act of violence. There was nothing whatever to induce one to believe or to show that there had been any violence."

Solly Flood (Queen's Advocate): "All these questions are necessary in the ends of justice, in order to endeavour to solve the mystery of the abandonment of the ship by her Master and Crew. I alone represent the interests of the Master, Briggs, the owner of the equity of redemption of some of the shares of the *Mary Celeste.*" . . . (To Oliver Deveau, the mate of the *Dei Gratia*): "Who cut the topsail of the ship?"

Deveau: "I knew nothing about its being cut. I don't know that my men cut it to obtain a piece of old canvas, nor have I seen any pieces of canvas about the ship."

Deveau then admitted, under persistent cross-examination by the Queen's Advocate, that he (Deveau) had not only been guilty of an unpardonable dereliction of duty as navigator of the *Celeste*, in neglecting to keep a log at the proper time and place, but was actually misrepresenting the facts, in an entry concerning a visit to the derelict *Mary Celeste*, by Captain David Read Morehouse, of the *Dei Gratia*, on 6 December, 1872, on the high seas, the day after Deveau, his mate, had first boarded her. Alternatively, as lawyers would say, if Deveau had not been "inaccurate" in the matter of this particular entry, he convicted Morehouse, his own captain, of perjury in the witness-box of the Vice-Admiralty Court at Gibraltar!

Here is Deveau's sworn statement:

"I kept the log of the *Mary Celeste* after I got on board that is to say, *I wrote it by memory after we got in to Gibraltar.* I did not write it down at the time, but the Captain of the *Dei Gratia* having *come on board and said he wished I had done so,* I said I thought I still could do it from memory, with the help of my chart on wh. was the ship's course and the latitude and longitude, and from that I entered the Log up as it now appears.

"The entry made on Friday, 6 December, 1872 *is not correct. I see that it is stated that the Captain of the Dei Gratia came on board, that day, of the Mary Celeste.* That is not so. The entry 'Captain Morehouse came on board with a *letter of instructions*' is not correct. In point of fact, Captain Morehouse did not come on board. He had stated that he should come on board, but he sent the letter of instructions in a boat by two men without himself coming. I cannot explain otherwise how I made the error."

Solly Flood (the Queen's Advocate): "Has Captain Morehouse already seen this entry and previously spoken to you about it?"

Deveau: "No, he has not seen the entry or spoken to me about it; my attention is now called for the first time to the error by you. I cannot say positively whether the letter of instruction was brought to me on that day or the day before. It was on the first or on the second day."

One shuffling perjury to cover up that of another!

The evidence of the Marshal of the Vice-Admiralty Court, who was called by H. P. Pisani, for the salvors, on the same day, shows how well the people of the *Dei Gratia* had collaborated in the work of destroying the value, as evidence, of the "traces révélatrices" of the crime, or mystery of the *Mary Celeste*:

"When I first went on board the *Mary Celeste* to arrest

the vessel the things in the bottom of the Captain's trunk and of the Mate's trunk were very wet. It took me many days to dry them and some of them I have not been able to dry, which induces me to believe they were wetted by salt and not fresh water. The things belonging to the lady were only damp. They were not wet or stained as they should have been, since some of them were silk dresses

"*The things were handed to me by Captain Morehouse.* In the Captain's cabin, the things in the lower drawers were all wet and damaged, while the things in the upper drawers were quite dry. I have kept on board the *Mary Celeste*, since she has been in my arrest, no less than five men by the advice of the Port authorities, and two anchors in the water, and one ready to drop." (*Evidence of the Marshal, Thos. J. Vecchio.*)

Solly Flood: "Will you be good enough to tell the Court more of the circumstances in which you found the effects of the people of the *Mary Celeste?*"

The Marshal: "There were four drawers in the Captain's cabin. In one, the lower drawer, only, were the things wet. The things were dry in the three upper drawers. There was or had been more water on the starboard than on the port side of the cabin—owing, it is supposed to the inclination of the vessel. All the articles, or almost all had been removed from the *Mary Celeste* on board the *Dei Gratia* for security, and were afterwards brought back again from the *Dei Gratia* and given up to me, when I arrested the *Mary Celeste*.

"*The particular position, therefore, in which any article was found by me is not to be relied upon as indicating where it was found when the vessel was abandoned.*

"The skylight extends over the two cabins. The water closet opens into the Captain's cabin. The pantry opens into the other cabin. The chart found in the mate's cabin was in use and was high up over his bed and quite dry and uninjured. The harmonium was exactly under the skylight when I found it, and was quite dry and uninjured. It was of rosewood. The musical instrument and the articles of her dress and ornaments found in the cabin lead to the belief that Mrs. Briggs was a lady of refined tastes and habits. The child's things pointed to the same belief.

"With the exception of one box which contained the Captain's white summer clothing, *all the other boxes were open when I received them in charge.* I found a silver watch and some gold money. The mate explained to me the mystery of the clock face being found upside down. He had taken it down to dry and clean it and try to make it go; but, not succeeding, had put it up as we found it."

Solly Flood's report to the Board of Trade, made on 22 January, 1873—this report has since been destroyed by the officials of this Whitehall department—stated, *inter alia*:

"I proceeded on the 7th inst., to make, with the assistance of the Marshal of the Vice-Admiralty Court, a still more minute examination for marks of violence, and I had the honour of being accompanied and greatly assisted by Capt. Fitzroy, R.N., H.M.S. *Minotaur;* Capt. Adeane, R.N., H. M.S. *Agincourt;* Capt. Dowell C.B., R.N., H.M.S. *Hercules;* Capt. Vansittart R.N., H.M.S. *Sultan;* and by Col. Laffan R.E., all of whom agreed with me in the opinion that the injury to the bows had been effected by some sharp instrument. On examining the starboard topgallant rail, marks were discovered, *apparently of blood*, and a mark of a blow, apparently of a sharp axe. . . ."

The British Admiralty investigators reported that, "on being drawn out of its scabbard, the sword showed signs of having been *smeared with blood, and afterwards wiped*."[*]

Mr. James H. Winchester, the New York shipowner, arrived at Gibraltar, to claim the abandoned brig, and represent the New York underwriters. He seems to have been questioned by Consul Sprague about the reputation of the captain, officers and crew of the *Mary Celeste*. Sprague reported to Washington that the master Briggs is well known and bore the highest character for seamanship and correctness; besides, he had his wife and young child with him and was part-owner of the *Mary Celeste*.

The sword and woodwork stains on the derelict were analysed by Dr. J. Patron of Gibraltar, and, as the U.S. Consul said: "The result is considered to negative anything like blood existing thereon." But we shall have something to say about this analysis later on in this narrative. It is not quite so simple a matter as these words imply, and not by any means so easily to be brushed away.

Two curious facts emerged from the analysis of these al-

---

[*]No one *knows* how Captain Briggs came by this sword; nor why he carried it in the ship. It was never returned to his family. One would have thought they would have demanded its return. Lawyers, as one knows, are prone to retain documents and objects which are *not* their property. It seems to be a "failing," which, even today, their guardian Law Society has laid down no rules about.

leged blood stains on the *Mary Celeste*: when the salvage case was tried on 14 March, 1873, in the Vice-Admiralty Court at Gibraltar, the Judge awarded £1,700 to Morehouse and the crew of the *Dei Gratia*, but censured the "conduct of the master of the *Dei Gratia* in allowing the mate Oliver Deveau to do away with the vessel which had rendered necessary the analysis of the supposed spots or stains of blood found on the deck of the *Mary Celeste*, and on the sword." The *Dei Gratia*'s men were charged with the cost of the analysis. In the absence of a transcript of these records of evidence, still presumably in the archives of the Supreme Court at Gibraltar, but which the author of this book has not been able to trace, it is impossible to say what *was* the "vessel" done away with by Deveau, the mate of the *Dei Gratia*, at a time when he surely must have realized its importance and the nature of the act he was doing.

The other curious fact is that, three weeks after the date of the salvage award, Sir James Cochrane, the Vice-Admiralty Court Judge, and F. Solly Flood, Queen Victoria's Advocate-General at Gibraltar, not only, as the U.S. Consul Sprague reported, refused to let him have a copy of the report of the analysis of the blood stains, but also withheld that information from the British Governor of Gibraltar! "I write this confidentially," says Sprague reporting to the State Department at Washington.

It is evident that keen curiosity about the results, if not the nature of Dr. Patron's analysis of the alleged bloodstains, had been heightened by this strange and unexplained refusal of Advocate-General Solly Flood to allow even the highest authority at Gibraltar to see a copy of the report of the analysis. Not till 28 July, 1887, fourteen years afterwards, was U.S. Consul Horatio J. Sprague able to obtain from the Registry of the Supreme Court at Gibraltar a copy of the analysis, which he had been specially requested by Mr. Worthington C. Ford, of the American Department of State at Washington, to secure. During all those years, the secret report had lain in the archives of the registry, enclosed in a sealed envelope, which had not been opened since it had been deposited there either by F. Solly Flood, the Proctor and Advocate-General, or Sir James Cochrane, the Judge.

"It is rather remarkable," said Mr. Edward Baumgartner, the Registrar, when he handed the envelope's contents to Consul Sprague in July, 1887, "that the analysis, or report was so brought in under seal on 14 March, 1873, and the seal remained unbroken until I opened it for the purpose of giving you the copy."

Here is a minor aspect of the mystery which may never

be explained, since the author is long dead and gone; but let it be said at once, that, far from setting the major mystery of the fateful *Mary Celeste* at rest, this analysis merely heightens the sense of mystery and makes the whole affair a greater riddle than before Dr. Patron went to work.

Patron's report, dated 30 January, 1873, says:

"At the request of Her Majesty's Attorney General at Gibraltar I proceeded on board of the American brig, *Mary Celeste,* anchored in this Bay, for the purpose of ascertaining whether any marks or stains of blood could be discovered on or in her hulk.

"After a careful and minute inspection of the deck of the said vessel, some red brown spots about a millimetre thick and half-an-inch in diameter, with a dull aspect, were found on deck in the forepart of the vessel. These spots were separated with a chisel and carefully wrapped in paper No. 1.

"Some other similar spots were equally gathered in different parts of the deck and wrapped in papers numbered 2, 3 and 4.

"Paper No. 5 contained a powder grated from a suspicious mark seen on the top-gallant rail, part of which was obtained on board, and part from a piece of timber belonging to the said vessel, in Her Majesty's Attorney General's chambers.

"I carefully examined the cabin, both with natural and artificial light; the floor; the sides of the berth; the mattrasses; etc., were minutely searched and nothing worth calling attention was seen that could have any relation with the object of my inquiries."

Dr. Patron adds that on 31 (?) January—there must be an error here, since the report is dated 30 January—at 2 o'clock, he received from Vecchio, Marshal of the supreme court, the five papers and a sword, with its sheath, found on board the *Mary Celeste*. Here are the crude methods of analysis used by Dr. Patron in his examination of the evidences: he cut the spots in papers 1, 2 and 3 in pieces about ¼ inch long and broad, passed a white thread through them, and suspended them inside test tubes, half an inch from the bottom, containing distilled water. The contents of No. 4 he put "in a small filtering bag, their minuteness would not allow of any other process of maceration" (softening by soaking). "The like was done with No. 5," but after 2½ hours of the softening process the "water was clear and bright as at the beginning of the experiment," and, 23 hours later, the water was still as transparent, "being then heated with a spirit lamp, (and) as no precipitate or cloudy aspect appeared, I considered the experiment over and of a negative character."

Next, Patron passed his finger over the stains on the piece of timber—holy smoke, think of the profanity, or laughter such extraordinary methods would excite in any modern professor of an up-to-date laboratory of police technique, such as they have at Marseille, in Paris, Chicago, Lyons, Lausanne, or Berlin and Vienna, and how infallibly they would cause the instant dismissal of any bungling agent de police!—and, behold, his finger was neither stained or tinged! He now peered at No. 5 spot, "macerated in the bag," and placed under a microscope, when "Nothing particular was seen, but a few particles of rust (carbonate (sic) of iron)" and woody fibres.

Now came the turn of the sword, and, for the moment, it looked as if Dr. Patron might at least wear a leaf of the bays of the criminologists, Niceforo, Grosse, or the late Dr. Edmond Bayle of the Laboratory of the Judicial Police of the Parisian Prefecture of Police. On the middle and end of the blade were stains, "small and superficial," "reddish," "in some parts brilliant like albuminous coloured substance. . . ."

"My first impression," says he, "was that they really were bloodstains. Examined with an eight- or ten-diameter magnifying glass these stains presented an irregular and granulated surface, the granules becoming smaller in proportion of their distance from the central and thickest part."

Alas, again was poor Patron let down—"Out, damned spot! Out I say! One, two, three, four, five . . . !" he must have said, parodying Lady Macbeth, and no doubt like that lady, he washed his hands after instead of before the operation of passing his finger over the evidence. For were not those days when, as Sir Frederic Treves said, an old coat was the patrimony of the London hospital surgeon, and a small piece of soap to wash his hands *after*, instead of before the operation? One-and-three-quarter hours' "maceration," heat and the microscope, and a negative result as in the case of the deck!

However, Patron the Pathetic, the indomitable, carefully grated the largest of the reddish spots from the sword blade:

"and put it under a microscope of Dr. Hartnack, objective No. 7, and ocular No. 3. corresponding to a magnifying power of 330 diameter. A yellow and imperfectly crystallized substance resembling citrate of iron, presenting here and there some red granules, was seen with some fragments of vegetable ramified fibres; but no blood globules could be detected.

"Three other stains were tested with hydrochloric acid, and after a perceptible effervescence a yellow stain was produced of chloride of iron; the insufficiency of the liquid would not permit of any other experiment.

"The blade, heated under the flame of the spirit lamp, recovered a natural brilliancy after the removal by heat of the superficial crust. The sheath of the sword was clean inside and with no mark of any kind.

"From the preceding experiments, I feel myself authorized to conclude that according to our present scientific knowledge, there is no blood either in the stains observed on the deck of the *Mary Celeste,* or on those found on the blade of the sword that I have examined.

(Signed) J. Patron. M.D."

What a different result might have followed had the brilliant scientists of one of the modern European continental, up-to-date British or American police laboratories, or institutes of forensic medicine examined these long-ago-destroyed evidences from the *Mary Celeste!* Patron, of course, lived long before the days of the radiologist, using the invisible rays of the spectrum, and there was then no Wassermann or Uhlenhuth, with a chemico-biological anti-serum test to detect if the stains were human or animal blood, or of what nature they might be. Even 30 years after stains have been made on linen, these modern tests have proved whether they were animal or human in origin, or have detected their real nature. In fact, says Biffi, the criminologist, "the time may come when the reaction of blood to a serum test will show the individual who has committed the crime." It is the fact that were these evidences of the *Mary Celeste* in existence today, their age would not affect the validity of this method of the biological chemist.

What about the strange cuts and slashes on the bows of the *Mary Celeste?* The surveyor, Mr. Austin, could offer no theory to account for her abandonment. There were no wines or spirits aboard, and after the most careful and minute examination of every part of the derelict, he found no trace of explosions, fire, or of anything calculated to create such an alarm. The *Mary Celeste* was not leaking. The strange cuts on both bows, "both slashed at the same time," two to three feet below the waterline, and on seven feet of an outer plank, were "very recent, and not due to weather."

Captain R. W. Shufeldt, of the U.S. warship *Plymouth,*

chanced, at the time, to call at Gibraltar, and at the request of the American consul, went aboard the *Mary Celeste*.

"I reject the idea of a mutiny," he says. "There is no evidence of violence about the deck or in the cabins; besides, the force, aft and forward, was so equally divided that a mutiny could not have had such a result." He thought the cuts on the planks of the derelict were mere splinters forced off them by the action of the sea, and that the captain and crew had been picked up by a passing ship bound for a distant port. "But if we should never hear from them again, I shall, nevertheless, think that they were lost in the boat in which both Master and men abandoned the *Mary Celeste*, and shall remember with interest this sad and silent mystery of the sea."

The Federal authorities at Washington, D.C., energetically canvassed all quarters likely to come by information throwing light on the mystery. William A. Richardson, Secretary to the U.S. Treasury, on 24 March, 1873, sent out a circular letter to Collectors of Customs and others, which shows that the American authorities at least provisionally favoured the theory promulgated by F. Solly Flood:

"You are requested to furnish this Department with any information you may be able to obtain, affording a clue wh. may lead to the discovery of the facts concerning the desertion of a vessel, found on 13 December last, in lat. 38 degrees 20' N., long. 17 degrees 51' W., derelict at sea, and which was towed into the harbor of Gibraltar by the British vessel *Dei Gratia*, and there libelled by the salvors. From the log of the abandoned vessel, she is supposed to be the American brigantine *Mary Celeste*, bound from New York to Genoa, and it is supposed she sailed from New York, and that her master's name was Briggs. The circumstances of the case tend to arouse grave suspicions that the master, his wife and child, and perhaps the chief mate were murdered in the fury of drunkenness by the crew, who had evidently obtained access to the alcohol with which the vessel was in part laden. . . ." (The letter recapitulates Flood's report, but says that *"marks of blood were also found on the sails,"* and adds that "many other details are in the possession of the Department, and, if necessary, they will be furnished upon application."

(*Signed*) William A. Richardson, Secretary of the Treasury."

F. Solly Flood, the Advocate-General at Gibraltar, whose reports about the *Mary Celeste*, the present writer compelled the reluctant officials of the British Board of Trade, in Whitehall, London, to admit, in January, 1930, have since been entirely destroyed in consequence of a Treasury order, said:

> "My theory is that the crew of the *Mary Celeste* got at the alcohol, and in the fury of drunkenness, murdered the master Briggs, his wife and child, and the chief mate; that they then damaged the bows of the vessel to give it the appearance of having struck on rocks or suffered a collision, so as to induce the master of any vessel that might pick them up to think her not worth attempting to save, and that they did, sometime between 25 November and 5 December, 1872, escape aboard some vessel bound for some north or south American port, or the West Indies."

Consul Sprague, writing to Secretary Worthington C. Ford, of the U.S. State Department, on 26th July, 1887, justly says the case of the *Mary Celeste* "appears to be one of those mysteries which no human ingenuity can penetrate sufficiently to account for the abandonment of this vessel, and the disappearance of her Master, family and crew, about whom nothing has ever transpired."

Solly Flood's guess, however, ignores other facts of the case, and no more solves the mystery than the contention of later solutions that a sudden explosion of alcohol* frightened the crew into a panic flight at an instant's notice and that when they were in the boat, the brigantine's sails filled with wind, and she sailed so far away from them that they could never board her again. The mere starting of one keg of alcohol in her hold is certainly no adequate explanation of such a hurried evacuation of the ship.

What about the character of one of the principal agents and actors in this drama of the mysterious Atlantic?

Benjamin Briggs was, as we should say, a distinctly "stuffy" nautical gentleman. He bore a blameless reputation, but a portrait which the author possesses shows him with long hair, chin-whiskers and moustache, and a stern no-nonsense-my-man-look about his eyes. He was not the man to wale out belaying-pin soup to Cape Horn stiffs soused in kill-em-at-

---

*Had there been an explosion in the hold of the *Mary Celeste*, caused by an exact mixture of alcohol vapour with air, there would have been signs of fire in the hold. There were *no signs of fire*. The surveyor at Gibraltar, John Austin, stated that, after a minute examination of the vessel, he found no traces of fire or explosion. He also added: "I find nothing in the ship calculated to create an alarm of explosion or fire."

forty-rods rye or Bourbon; nor would he have welcomed aboard the *Mary Celeste* wharf rats shanghaied in the dead o' night, by Manhattan or Bowery crimps. He was teetotal and came of a line of limejuicer captains and pious New Englanders. Mr. Solly Flood reported that the books found on the derelict were mostly of a religious nature, and it is pretty clear that his ship would have had small attractions for the tattooed pier-jumpers, and hard-swearing whisky-swallowers who have been so liberally fathered on him by fantasts. To them, he would have been no father, but a Dutch uncle; unless those eyes of his belied him!

He and Captain David Read Morehouse, of the *Dei Gratia* are said to have been old acquaintances; and certain friends of the Briggs' family have roundly asserted that, despite Morehouse's oath to the contrary in the witness-box at Gibraltar, he, Morehouse, most certainly had gone aboard the *Mary Celeste*, if not at the same time as, assuredly not long after Deveau had gone. The reader of this chapter will have seen how closely Morehouse lay to the wind in this matter. The reader too, may ponder why Morehouse took an *alias, and clean vanished from sight of mortal and seafaring man, not long after the year* 1872.

What, then, about the character of the crew?

Numbers of ancient mariners, in the last thirty and more years, have turned up in British ports, claiming to be the sole survivors of the *Mary Celeste*, and have spun yarns of gore and piracy on the high seas. It may suffice to say, that, while the inquiry was proceeding at Gibraltar, Sprague received a letter from a German official, T. A. Nickelsen, of Nettersum, Isle of Föhr, Prussia, who wrote that the mothers and wives of two of the crew of the *Mary Celeste* were anxious to know whether the log-book had been found aboard, when the crew quitted the ship, and if there were any signs of disturbance aboard. "I know three of the sailors personally," wrote Nickelsen, "they are peaceable and first-class sailors."

In October 1929, there appeared in the *Boston* (Mass.) *Herald*, a letter from a woman, signing herself "Mrs. D. T. (*sic*) Morehouse" who said she was the wife of the Captain of the *Dei Gratia*—if so, it is to be presumed that she was near eighty years old—and in this letter she gave a testimonial to Captain D. T. Morehouse, and mate Deveau as "good honest men." It is curious that, since she wrote this letter from Buffalo, New York, the postmaster of that town wrote me that he had no record of her address, "and her name is not listed in this city directory." The methods of the American Post Office for tracing people, were, in 1929, very thorough. I had asked her if she could tell why her husband, the captain of the *Dei Gratia*, had vanished under an *alias*, and never more was heard of—by official inquirers.

When the crew and officers abandoned the *Mary Celeste*, they left behind chests of clothes of no great value, one trunk marked as belonging to "Arian Hardene," and in the captain's cabin was found the property of himself, his wife, and baby daughter, already mentioned. But there is one essential piece of evidence: the log-book of the *Mary Celeste*, which no one has been able to examine; since it has long vanished. It was known to have been sent to American Consul C. M. Spence at Genoa; but does not seem to have been handed back to Winchester, the part-owner of the derelict. Nor can it be found whether it has for many years reposed in the archives of the appropriate Department at Washington, D.C. If that Department has the methods of some of the officials in other organizations, the log has long since been deputed, by the head of a department, to a messenger to "destroy." It is just possible, although, in view of the character of ships' logs since the beginning of the age of steam, not too probable, that it may have entries throwing light on the mystery of the *Mary Celeste*'s sudden abandonment. As we have seen, a deck or temporary slate log spoke of the *Mary Celeste* sighting the island of Santa Maria, in the Azores; but no trace of the landing of the officers and crew, in that or any other island, was ever found, or reported, or even rumoured.

Little or no attention seems to have been paid by contemporary British newspapers to what was and is a first-class mystery of the sea, which, today, would cause even the most Olympian and "heavy father" of London newspapers to break into a foam of headlines with a backwash of leading articles and the sage comments of "our Shipping Correspondent." Indeed, more than thirty-five years passed, before this mystery was cast up to the stars by a nautical journal of a popular seafaring character. This journal then dropped a brick into a pool of mystification whence the concentric ripples have spread and spread and enlarged until they have broken on the legendary shores of the Never-Never-Land of British Broadcasting Corporation "radio thriller dramas." Why British newspapers even of the year 1872 should have ignored this queer story of the trial of a derelict by a British court at Gibraltar, I cannot say; unless the reason be that the ship was of American ownership. Even so, the mystery must for many years, after 1872, have remained the talk of the fo'c'sles and dog-watches in merchant marine ships and H.M.S. wardrooms in every sea of the world, until it became the stock-in-trade of authors and journalists.

On the American side, this mystery of the disappearance of a well found ship with all her officers and crew, and a woman and child on the high seas, right in the track of merchant shipping, of all nations, was recognized as an item of good news value. Says the *Boston* (Mass.) *Post*, of February, 1873:

"It is now believed that the fine brig *Mary Celeste* of about 236 tons, commanded by Captain Benjamin Briggs, of Marion, Mass., was seized by pirates in the latter part of November, 1872, and that, after murdering the captain, his wife and child and officers, the vessel was abandoned near the Western Islands, where the miscreants are supposed to have landed.

"The brig left New York, on 7 November, for Genoa, with a cargo of alcohol, and is said to have had a crew consisting mostly of foreigners. The theory is that some of the men probably obtained access to the cargo and were thus stimulated to the desperate deed."

The New York *Nautical Gazette* on 29 March, 1873, added further details, under the heading of:

A MYSTERY OF THE SEA

"We published, over a month ago, the main facts connected with the supposed loss of the crew of the *Mary Celeste*, and the account has been taken up and enlarged on by nearly all the papers of the country....

"Captain Shufeldt's conclusions are, however, in direct opposition to the opinions of the surveyors who examined the ship on her arrival at port, and though we hope he may be correct, yet we confess grave misgivings of the fate of the crew. The Secretary of the Treasury is evidently impressed with the same doubts, as the following document ... shows (*quoted elsewhere in this chapter*).

"The *Mary Celeste* sailed from New York for Genoa, as our record shows, on 7 November. The last record in her log-book was 24 November, and she was discovered by the *Dei Gratia* ten days after, that is, 4 December. It is not yet too late to hear that the wanderers were saved; but every day which elapses without tidings from them lessens the chance of their safety. We append a list of the crew, obtained from the original record:

"*List of the crew*: Albert G. Richardson, aged 28, of Maine; Edward William Head, aged 23, of New York;

Volkert Lorenzen, aged 29, of Germany; Ariam Harbens, aged 35, of Germany; Bos. Lorenzo, aged 25, of Germany; Gottlief Goodschaad, aged 23, of Germany."

We note that the captain and mate are omitted from this list. It seems curious that the *N.Y. Nautical Gazette* should not have known that Albert G. Richardson was the mate of the *Celeste*.

A document alleged to have been transmitted to the U.S. Department of State, at Washington, D.C., by U.S. Consul "Johnson" from Gibraltar, on February 1873, speaks of one "Henry Bilson," the missing mate of the *Celeste*:

"Document 139. Brig *Marie* (sic) *Celeste* cleared for Naples under command of Captain John Hutchins, sent out by the owner from New York for the purpose. Forwarded to Mrs. Bilson of New York, effects of Henry Bilson, missing mate of brig *Mary Celeste*. The brig's last voyage."

At first sight, it would seem that Consul "Johnson" confused the two ships, since Captain Hutchins took over the command of the *Dei Gratia*, while her substantive Captain, Morehouse, remained at Gibraltar to answer inquiries arising out of the arrest of the *Mary Celeste* by the Marshal of the British Vice-Admiralty Court.

Who, however, is this "Henry Bilson," missing mate of the *Mary Celeste*, whose name is so strangely omitted from the list of the crew and officers supplied by Captain J. H. Winchester, her part-owner, to the Court at Gibraltar?

The answer is that this *document 139 is a deliberate forgery*, perhaps by some sea-faring crank, suffering from *Mary Celeste* mania in an acute form. Henry Bilson was the nephew of Mrs. 'Arris, Sairey Gamp's legendary friend, and this forgery of document 139 will, here, have the nail put into its coffin and hammered well home by the letter following, dated 21 September, 1931, and transmitted to me from the Assistant Secretary of State, of the U.S. Government, at Washington, D.C. :

"You are correct in assuming that the American Consul at Gibraltar, in 1873, was Horatio I. Sprague. I am instructed to say that it does not appear from the Department's records that there was an American Consul named Johnson serving at Gibraltar, or at ports near Gibraltar, during the period 1870-73. I have pleasure in forwarding you a photostat copy of despatch No 139, dated 25 March, 1873, from Consul Sprague.

       Very respectfully yours,
       ALBERT HALSTEAD. (Signed).
      American Consul General in London."

It should be clear, from the above, that the forger had seen a *genuine* document No. 139; but one may at once say that this photostat shows not one word, in this genuine document, regarding either of the two mystery ships, *Mary Celeste* and *Dei Gratia.*

Just before the Second World War I made some further inquiries about the lost log of the *Mary Celeste*, and I was courteously informed by Captain H. C. Cocke, U.S. Navy, Superintendent of Office of Navy Records and Library of Navy Department, at Washington, D.C., that neither the American Secretary of State, nor the Secretary of the U.S. Navy, both of whom at my request, were good enough to order searches of the official archives, can find any trace of the *Celeste's* log-book. Unless a merchant ship be libelled, says Captain Cocke, her log remains the property of the captain or owner. With considerable difficulty, in 1931, I traced the still *surviving widow* of Albert G. Richardson, mate of the *Mary Celeste*, then alive in a New England port, and asked her if she knew where this important piece of evidence may be found. She could not say—but later in this chapter, I shall cite an amazing letter she wrote me, about this mystery of the lost ship's officers and crew. Finally, I discovered the address of a gentleman who is the grandson of Captain J. H. Winchester, part-owner in 1872, of the *Mary Celeste.* He wrote me from New York City:

To: Mr. Harold T. Wilkins.   17 November, 1931.
 England.
"Dear Sir.

This is the first letter I have had from you, so that your first letter of 12 May must have gone astray.

I wish I could give you the information you desire, but I fear you know much more about the *Mary Celeste* than I do. I also read that the log contained the words you quote: that is "Fanny, my dear wife" alleged to have been written by Albert Richardson at the end of the log, but I have no personal knowledge of this. This office has no original documents or records connected with this case. My grandfather, Captain J. H. Winchester, was the managing owner of the vessel, but the event took place six years before I was born. I have heard my grandfather give his opinion that gases in the hold caused spontaneous explosions which overturned the hatch cover, and the crew, knowing the nature of the vessel's cargo, immediately took to the boat expecting the vessel to burst into flames. As no such thing happened, the *Mary Celeste* sailed away from them and they were unable to overtake her, and so were left to their fate at sea in an open boat.

I wish I could give you more definite information, but really I have no personal knowledge of the matter.

Yours very truly,

WINCHESTER NOYES. President of Messrs. J. H. Winchester, Inc., Steamship Owners and Brokers, New York."

In this place, one may say something about a most ingenious and romantic yarn which not a few people, interested in the lore of the sea, believe is the solution of the mystery of the *Mary Celeste*, all others being fables, as the old Newgate pirate-book compiler and chaplain said.

In 1913, there appeared in the now unfortunately defunct *Strand Magazine*, of London, a story, titled "The *Marie* (sic) *Celeste*. The True Story of the Mystery." (It is a pity that at the start, the writer was so careless about the *real*, if mongrel name of this ship!) He was an Oxford M.A., and he introduced to the fiction-loving public—then very largely males— a most ingenious deceased faker, who, being dead, could not, therefore, be questioned. The faker's name was said to be "Abel Fosdyk," who before "he passed away to a better land," which may *not* have been the better for his passing, said to the son of his employer, who was Mr. Linforth: "Among three boxes of my papers will be found, after my death, an account of the *Marie* (sic) *Celeste!*" The faker's story was "examined" about 1912 or 1913, and purported to tell how Fosdyk shipped aboard the *Marie Celeste*, whose captain went mad on a voyage to Europe, having by some marvellous legerdemain, not to say "gift of the gab," previously persuaded the whole ship's company to stand on a crazy platform, rigged on to the ship's side or bowsprit, and watch him, Capt. Ben Briggs, while he swam round the ship in a mad race with the mate, what time a man-eater shark appeared. On a sudden, the platform collapsed, and threw the whole crew into the sea, including Mr. Abel Fosdyk, who, after hectic dreams, afloat on a raft, all about the old mystery of George Washington who simply could *not* tell a lie or fake a yarn, woke up on the strand of the Ivory Coast of

Western Africa. Woke up to find a dusky beauty pouring palm wine into his smacking lips.

"Whar yo' from white man?" said this lovely Negress. "Wha's your name?"

"My dear," said the gentleman, come so nicely ashore, "to *you*, I am Abel Fosdyk; but there are others, far away in London town, who have not been brought up so nicely as I was, who say my name is Howard Linforth, M.A. (Oxon). But to *you*, my dear, I am just Abel. Now, just you roll out another barrel of that wine, for I have been shanghaied off a Yankee teetotal ship, and if any man ever needed a good belly-cheer it's me. I guess even an earthquake won't shift me off these African shores, while you and this lovely wine are around."

Oddly enough, despite the assurances of Abel, or Howard, that the square-toed truth and nothing but that had been bequeathed to posterity in these papers, and the fact that *somebody* had been looking up annual registers, seafaring magazines and old newspapers, there were people in England, in 1913, who hinted that Howard Linforth, M.A. (Oxon), knew a lot more about the *real* identity of Abel Fosdyk than Howard was prepared to admit. Also, these people asked why a man who had been shanghaied off a ship, as alleged, was not even able to spell its name properly? Among these was the editor of the defunct London *Daily Chronicle*, who asserted that, in his opinion, the whole yarn was fiction. Mr. Howard Linforth, deprecating this scepticism, even wrote a long letter to the *Daily Chronicle*. He said, *inter alia*:

"I should like to express my regret that the *Strand Magazine* did not see its way to publish the document in full. I have reason to believe that the story will soon be published in book form, in which case, the whole document together with some other particulars, will be disclosed to the public. When, however, these papers were handed over to the *Strand Magazine*, the editor took great pains, as I did myself, to verify matters. Finding it impossible to trace more than the most meagre outline, the Admiralty were approached. At a cost of £14, a search was made at Gibraltar amongst documents which had not been disturbed for nearly 40 years, and what was the result?

"First, their accounts of the incident stated that two square cuts had been made on the bows of the *Marie* (*sic*) *Celeste*, the starboard side cut being a foot higher and a foot farther back, than the port cut. No suggestion was made as to their use. This is what would have been found if the platform had been supported by stays. . . .

"Second: a few extracts of the log were found, which I now give to you, and which you can make public—so far as I know—for the first time; for they do not appear to have been mentioned, even in 1872 and 1873, when the mystery may be described as 'at its height.'

"(a). A new topsail and foresail were bought for the voyage. (Says Fosdyk: 'Happily, we had bent our new topsail and fore sail').

"(b). A curious and inexplicable rumbling noise in the hold is three times alluded to as causing some alarm among the crew.

"Unfortunately, the *Strand* has cut out an actual account of this . . . ('And at times a deep, mysterious growl as of an imprisoned wind would come up from the hold, till baby would cling tighter to me and murmur in an awesome whisper—'I fright'—she always said 'I fright' for 'I am frightened'.)

"The log makes frequent mention of bad weather. On the whole, the log was very badly kept, and makes no mention whatever of the Ebenezer incident." (The finding of a ship turned turtle with one man decomposed and two dead, when a fourth man was taken aboard the *Marie Celeste*, who was heard gasping out the dying words 'Ebenezer, Bristol.' So Fosdyk.)

"The captain's name was Briggs, as Fosdyk gives it. In every account I can find it is given as Griggs. I am not, of course, prepared to say it does not appear correctly elsewhere . . . the Admiralty account shows the writer to have been in possession of facts which, so far as can be ascertained, were unknown to any living soul. . . . Fosdyk shows the number of the crew to have been fourteen . . . I am not at all sure that Fosdyk is not to be added to this list—of men of natural genius and philosophy, such as Aesop the slave, and Bunyan the tinker. Fosdyk had received an excellent education and wrote for his own amusement and pleasure a number of poems and stories now in my possession. He could have sold these for a high price, but he preferred to keep them secret. . . . His reasons for not disclosing his identity were all sufficient; but though I am prepared to disclose most things about him, upon this I must remain silent."

But was not Aesop, too, a teller of *fables?*
Mr. Howard Linforth died in summer 1937, and there are people who say that they would like to have been present on the other shore when Mr. Linforth performed the Janus-like feat of shaking hands with his *alter ego, Abel de Fosdyk.*

Tweedledum and Tweedledee would have been nowhere in it in deciding who was the real owner of this nice new *Marie* (*sic*) *Celeste* rattle. But, many years before his lamented death, Mr. Linforth was a director of the Amalgamated Press founded by Alfred Harmsworth, later Lord Northcliffe. It is also said that Alfred Harmsworth, had himself been educated in a Hampstead academy. Why, then, Mr. Linforth did not remember that charity begins at home, and so sell this story to one of the numerous magazines of his *own* combine is a little riddle that could best have been answered by Mr. Linforth.

In 1930, the author of this book received a postcard from a gentleman who was then living in a pleasant village near Southampton, England. The postcard professed to throw light on the identity of this shy, and true—in later years—rather sanctimonious shellback and retired mariner, who buttled or valeted (if he did!) for the Linforth family. He, whose identity the late Mr. Linforth had such delicacy in revealing to an editor, who had classed the story as "Very interesting, but fiction:"

"*Re* your article *Mary Celeste* in the London *Quarterly Review* of John Murray:

"I have always understood that my agent, Smith, cousin of the late vicar of Shorwell, Isle of Wight, a friend of mine, and, after, P.O. agent, etc., received the *Mary Celeste* all standing. There were three on the bathing-stage—one survived. He served two years in the Mediterranean, and eventually fetched up as boots (?) at Mr. Howard Linforth's, Hampstead Road, London—a good middle-class school. I believe the survivor's box on decease, was opened under advice, concerning the *Mary Celeste* by H. Linforth."

J. S. *HALL*, Roadstead, Hamble, Hants., England.
12 March, 1930."

We have now a deceased vicar dragged into the legend. Another dead man who could tell no tales!

Fosdyk, *alias* Smith, had considerable literary gifts, by the way. Here is a poem of his which Mr. Linforth found in the last box of the deceased—which box he opened *first*:

"*I pray thee, Lord, that when my race is run*
I be not left behind to linger on,
With failing power and waning light
To curse the slowness of the night
That will not fall altho' the day be done."

It had been set to music, and Mr. Linforth added that there are other poems and stories by Fosdyk in his possession. My reader is, I imagine, quite able to say whether this *"Mary Celeste"* hoax of Fosdyk *alias* Smith, the Shorwell vicar's cousin, is or is not to be classed among the other works of imagination.

I suspect Fosdyk *alias* Smith had seen the *New York Herald* of 22 January, 1911, wherein, commenting on the mystery, a writer says that Maine sailormen have always been interested in the ship, because her mate, Albert Richardson, was a Stockton, Me., man. He cites a log which no man can find today—as we noted above it seems to have been sent to the U.S. consul at Genoa in 1872, and then vanished. The *New York Herald* writer cites alleged extracts from this lost log in which occur identical references to mysterious rumblings below decks, mentioned so artfully by Fosdyk. Fosdyk's story appeared in the London *Strand Magazine* in 1913, two years later.

It seems strange that these extracts from the *Mary Celeste*'s log, were not mentioned in the Admiralty Court, at Gibraltar; and, surely, it augurs clever selective powers on the part of Fosdyk, *alias* Smith that he did not also mention the other alleged extract from the same log, which is also cited in this same issue of the *New York Herald*:

"In the mate's cabin (on the derelict *Celeste*) his log slate bore a record of temperature, weather etc., and, at the end: 'Fanny, my dear wife. . . .'"

Neither was this last extract mentioned in Court, where its evidential value would surely not have been lost on Solly Flood, Esq., or the Judge, Sir James Cochrane!

Fosdyk had also seen another extract from Lloyd's British and Foreign Shipping List, dated 12 December, 1872, and very ingenious and thrilling use did he make of it. (I here cite it again):

"The *Ebenezer* of Arendal (master) Birketvedt, sailed from New York on or about 22 August last, with maize, bound to Queenstown or Falmouth for orders, and has not since been heard of."

He cleverly changed the place-name of Arendal, which is a town on the Skager-Rak of southern Norway, to Bristol, England, and in his story the *Ebenezer* figures as follows:

"In mid-Atlantic, we sighted a boat which had turned turtle, and through our glasses we saw three on it. When we got out a boat from the *Marie Celeste*, and rowed across, we found one man decomposed, a second and third man dead, and a fourth just alive. This man died after the captain's wife (Mrs. Briggs) heard him say: 'EBENEZER, Bristol.'"

Bully for you, Master Fosdyk-Smith! "Ain't no flies on you or Linforth," at this faking of salted sea yarns!

Other legends say that the mate, Albert Richardson, "charged with theft and murder" on the high seas, died (year 1877) in "hiding in the West Indies." San Francisco newspapers, in 1897, published what purported to be the death-bed confession of one, Jacob Hamel, said to be the mate of the brig *Dei Gratia*. (Needless to say no such man was known to the Court at Gibraltar!). Hamel was dying in Iquique—where, like Callao, no extradition was allowed—and he put forth a "last confession" in which, said he:

"The brig was boarded by me on the high seas. I found the crew of the *Mary Celeste* all dead of small-pox, except the cook, the captain and Mrs. Briggs. The mate, Richardson had a big sum of money with which he was going to business in Africa. I threw the three survivors overboard, and took $8,000 in cash. Then I went back to the *Dei Gratia* with the information that the *Mary Celeste* had been abandoned."

(It is a Cocos Island night kind of fiction-story.)

The *New York Herald* queried this story, on the ground that there had been no sickness on the ship . . .

"which was evident from the fact that nothing had been used from the medicine chest. The bottles had not been touched."

The latest yarn about the *Mary Celeste* appeared in a London newspaper, in May, 1937, when it was said the Lloyd's underwriters were about to hear and discuss the claim of one, Captain Arthur Cocker, a greybearded skipper of a Hull barge, *Humber Lady*. He was, it was said, claiming salvage money for the brig *Mary Celeste*. One is told that Captain Cocker, then a cabin boy aboard the ship *Kentishman* went aboard the *Mary Celeste* and, "today, has undisclosed documents and letters" about the famous derelict:

"The documents were taken from the cabin of the *Mary Celeste*. Never shall I forget coming across her. Her sails were set, everything on board was in good order; except that there was evidence she had been hurriedly left—and there was a blood-stained hatchet buried in the mainmast. I believe someone on board went berserk and killed three of the crew, before he himself was killed. Then the remainder of the crew became frightened and took to the boats when they saw other boats (*sic*) on the horizon."

Why on earth, or in heaven, or the other place, Cap'n Cocker imagined that Lloyd's o' London would award him good and easy money, for the salvage of an American ship, already paid to the rightful, or wrongful British salvors, he alone knows. Where had he been all these years, since 1872? I should like to see those documents from the cabin of the *Mary Celeste?* Do they, by any chance, include faked document No. 139 about the non-existent mate, Henry Bilson? What old shellback passed these fakes on Cap'n Cocker, as though he might have been Cap'n Ben Cutlett, the old master mariner friend of the late Will Hay, whose deep water experience had all been acquired as skipper on a canal-barge?*

I applied to the British Admiralty in Whitehall, for information about alleged transcripts, made by the Department's officials, from documents in the archives of the Supreme Court at Gibraltar. I here cite the letter to me, written by the late Sir Charles Walker, K.C.B., deputy Secretary:

"Admiralty, S.W.1.
24 September, 1931.

"Sir,

In reply to your further letter, concerning the salvage of the derelict brigantine *Mary Celeste*, I am commanded by My Lords Commissioners of the Admiralty to inform you that the records of this Department have been fully searched and that there is no information therein which would be helpful to yourself in this connection.

I, am, Sir
Your obedient Servant
CHARLES WALKER."

To:
Harold T. Wilkins Esq."

---

*Needless to say, no such ship as the *Kentishman* appears by name in any of Lloyd's Registers of British and Foreign Shipping, between 1872-3, and 1875. Some old salt, who had kittled up his wits with one drink over the twelfth, had fobbed this yarn on to a local correspondent, who proceeded to foist it on to the News Editor of the London newspaper, which paid out good easy money for nonsense.

Of late years, we read no more death-bed stories about the mystery of the *Mary Celeste*. It has now become the pseudo-mystic appanage of wild-eyed—mostly U.S.—ladies and gentlemen, who concoct yarns alleging that Cap'n Ben Tarpowling of Nantucket, did, in the year 1872, month of December, together with Sam Cutlett, his mate, see, in mid-Atlantic a thing like a submarine taking off the officers and crew of a fore-and-aft brig, to wit, the *Mary Celeste* or *Marie Celeste*, after which, diving into the bosom of the ocean, they were all *in corpore vili* translated to a large flying saucer, or space ship waiting above a cloud. This story is backed up by citations from New England newspapers defunct in 1830, and calling in aid the august *National Geographic Magazine* of Washington, D.C., to "prove" that Cap'n Tarpowling was a regular contributor to that distinguished magazine. Needless to say; the editor of this well known journal told a public librarian, who had noted that a New England newspaper, which became defunct in 1830, had been cited by the woman writer, faking the story, as one to which Tarpowling first told his yarn, in 1899, that no such man had ever contributed to the *National Geographic Magazine*, at any time. One *would* like to hear the comments of the hard-boiled U.S. linotype or monotype operators, who are called on to set up these impudent and absurd forgeries for the "astounding story" journal whose editor accepted it. Yes, *sir!*

What is a possible solution of this famous mystery of the North Atlantic? (In advancing it, the author of this book is far from supposing that he, thereby, has settled a controversy which has now been going on for not far off ninety years).

Out of the mass of evidence a pointer dramatically emerges. One cannot help saying that, to a modern police scientist and trained criminologist—which is not necessarily the same thing as a writer of detective stories or pseudo-occult shockers and thrillers—it seems strange, today, why the British authorities at Gibraltar, in 1872-3, did not set in motion legal machinery which would have led to the arrest, on more than mere suspicion, of the captain, the mate and the crew of the British brig, *Dei Gratia*. It is likely that in the hands of a skilled cross-examiner at the Old Bailey in London, acting for the counterpart of a Public Prosecutor, or the Crown legal authorities, in 1873, Deveau the mate, might have been forced to tell the truth, which might have solved the mystery and put the police on the trail of the criminals who may have made away with the captain, Briggs, his wife and daughter, and the officers and crew of the *Mary Celeste*.

Why, for example, should a *respectable* seafaring man need to *sail under an alias?* The captain of the *Dei Gratia,* Morehouse, was called "Boyce" by the part-owner of the *Mary Celeste,* James H. Winchester of New York. It is, too, decidedly curious that the same "mistake" was made by one, Captain Parsons, former President of the New York Maritime Exchange Office. Parsons, in the New York *Maritime Exchange Bulletin,* in August, 1913, said that he had a chat, "a year or two later than 1872," with Captain D. R. Morehouse, master of the *Dei Gratia,* whom he met "at the Havana, in Cuba," *and whom he called "Boyce!"* Again, what nigger in this woodpile lay behind the mystery man who appears, in that spurious "Document 139," as "Henry Bilson?"

We may also ask this: why did Oliver Deveau, mate of the *Dei Gratia,* twice destroy what may have been important evidence, which he found in the *Mary Celeste?* There was the mysterious "vessel" he found and destroyed and for which he was severely censured by Sir James Cochrane, the Judge at Gibraltar. In the second place, Deveau evidently cleaned with lemon juice the supposed blood marks on the very picturesque and unusual sword, in its scabbard, found lying on the floor of Captain Brigg's cabin. These do *not* look like the actions of a seafaring man quite innocent or totally ignorant of the requirements of a court of law and justice. They look very much like the actions of a guilty man, deliberately destroying essential evidence.

Then, again, he told the Court at Gibraltar, that the *Dei Gratia* left the port of New York on 15 November 1872, or eight days *after* the departure of the *Mary Celeste.* Lloyd's List says she left New York on 2 October.

I, at this place, cite a remarkable letter written to me in summer 1931, by the then still surviving sister of the mate of the *Mary Celeste,* Mrs. Priscilla Richardson Shelton; and, as will be seen, this letter flatly controverts Deveau's statements in Court at Gibraltar. (This letter is in my own files):

"Dear Mr. Wilkins,

I am the sister of Albert G. Richardson, first mate of the *Mary Celeste,* at the time of the abandonment of that vessel, and the only blood relation of any of the crew, as far as I know; although my brother's widow still lives, today, at the age of 84. The last entry in the log of the *Mary Celeste* was on 24 November, 1872, and the weather was fair, and no premonition of any trouble was mentioned. Where the log is now I am unable to say.

"The mystery will never be solved, as the only people who could throw any light on the tragedy were the crew of the *Dei Gratia*, and they have long since disappeared.

"Did it ever occur to you *that they were responsible?* My late brother, Captain Lyman Richardson, agreed with me that they were. The *Dei Gratia* lay alongside the *Mary Celeste* in the harbour of New York. They sailed *ten days before the Mary Celeste;* yet they were waiting for her and towed her to Gibraltar, claiming salvage money. Where had the *Dei Gratia* been to all that time? The weather had been fair, according to her own log, and she should have been far ahead.

"The crew of the *Mary Celeste* were foully murdered by some means. They were decoyed to the other vessel, or part of them, and then the extermination of the rest was easy, as they carried no fire-arms for protection. I am firmly convinced that this is the true solution of the mystery. Captain Briggs and my brother were first-class sailors and would never have left their ship unless compelled by force. If they took to the boat and saw their error,* some of them would have returned. Albert Richardson was a wonderful swimmer, and if some of the crew of the *Dei Gratia* could board the *Mary Celeste,* so could the crew of the *Celeste*.

(Signed(: (Mrs.) Priscilla Richardson Shelton."

I wrote to Mrs. Shelton asking her—her letter sounded almost like a voice from the dead—if she cared to explain the apparent discrepancy in the dates given of the respective sailing times of the two ships; but I never again heard from her. I also wrote to the wife of the mate Albert Richardson, stated, even in 1931, to be still alive; but again, had no reply.

Lloyd's British and Foreign Shipping List, for 1872, recorded that the *Dei Gratia* put to sea from New York on 2 October, and did not clear till 11 November, 1872. *Her actual sailing-date was not reported.* It is suggested that she may have remained in port for several days after that. Anyway, Lloyd's List records that she was spoken in 41 N. lat., 66 W. long., on 19 November. The *Mary Celeste* is stated to have sailed from New York on 7 November, 1872. My own theory that there is a criminological aspect of this mystery of

---

*This refers to the conjecture, which is unsupported by any evidence of fire, that the explosion of alcoholic gas from the barrels in the derelict's hold, scared the officers and crew into hastily abandoning her, and that they were unable to return to her.

the sea, the most famous of all in the nineteenth century, is based on the general tendency and trend of the evidence given in the proceedings in the Vice-Admiralty Court, at Gibraltar. I also had two letters from Dr. Oliver Cobb, of Easthampton, Mass., who is related to the Briggs family. He points out that the New York Customs House records are that the *Mary Celeste* left port on 7 November, 1872. He explains the cuts and gashes on the rail and bow of the derelict as being caused by the sudden snapping of a tow-rope, connecting the boat of the *Mary Celeste*, in which the Captain had placed his wife, baby and crew and officers, with the peak-halliards, or rope extensions, with a gaff at the upper outer corner of the sail.

But this theory takes for granted that the officers and crew left the ship as suggested. *Why* they left the ship is the core of the unsolved mystery.

Here are other suggestions of Cobb:

"The sword . . . was picked up by Captain Briggs, some years before, when he visited a battle-field somewhere about the head of the Adriatic Sea. He carried this sword as a souvenir, not as a weapon . . . I do not know what became of the log of the *Mary Celeste* . . . Even Captain Morehouse, after he had left the sea, used to sit at home for long intervals with his head in his hands, evidently going over this case in his mind. Then he would say: 'Poor Briggs, I wonder what *did* become of him? They must have rowed like mad in that boat' . . . The peak halliards on the *Celeste* were found broken and gone."

It must be said however, that this sorrowful distress was *not* in evidence at Gibraltar, where Morehouse showed himself mightily keen on looking after the salvage money. His conduct in seeing that the crew and Deveau cleared off from Gibraltar to Genoa while he remained behind was *obstructive,* being marked by none of this hypocritical "sorrow;" but by an evident desire, as Sir James Cochrane, the Judge commented severely, to frustrate the proceedings of justice. This shady man well knew what he was doing in removing Deveau from the witness-box while the proceedings were *still fresh,* and the memories of the witnesses.

Cobb added some more of what one may call by the French word *blague,* when he said: "To my mind, there is nothing sinister about the disaster," although he also admits:

"There is something a little shady about some of the witnesses' evidence given before the Court at Gibraltar. Possibly, there was a bit of window-dressing, and that may have been the reason why Captain Morehouse was kept off the witness-stand. . . . An attorney was making a claim for salvage. . . . There is something a bit strange about the name 'Boyce' being confounded with Morehouse."

Very strange! Especially when the "confounding" was done by the part-owner of the *Mary Celeste* and another New Yorker sea captain, who implies that "Boyce" was the name by which both knew Morehouse, one of them years after the event. It was the deliberate *alias* of Morehouse himself, and must have been evidence of a guilty conscience, and, too, of consciousness that mariners who knew him, Morehouse, were whispering that there was something nefarious in Morehouse's *alias* Boyce's conduct in the affair of the *Mary Celeste*.

One may well wonder what reason, consonant with reputability, Morehouse had for using this *alias* of "Boyce," prior to the year 1872? Clearly, there was far more than met the eye in this strange affair, something which the necessity for making a "good" plea for salvage money does *not* satisfactorily explain.

There must have been more than one reason why Morehouse *alias* Boyce, kept off the "witness stand" in the Court at Gibraltar. He must have feared a skilled cross-examination, and there may well have loomed before him the shadow of the dock in the Court of Old Bailey, in London. Had his delicate reluctance any connexion with the evidential exhibits so carefully, even artfully destroyed by another very respectable mariner, one Oliver Deveau, Morehouse's *alias* Boyce's mate in the British brig *Dei Gratia*?

While Mrs. Richardson Shelton's *full* facts may—equally they may *not*—have been a little in error, but *intuitions* and that of her brother, Captain Lyman Richardson, who was also brother of the mate, Albert Richardson, of the *Mary Celeste*, about the fate of the crew, officers, and Captain and Mrs. Briggs, and the baby daughter, were in all likelihood by no means wide of the mark.

Author's Note: My attention has been courteously drawn by the Principal Librarian, of a well known public library in a New England port, to a publication, by the Dartmouth Historical Society Incorporated, U.S.A., of a brochure which is titled: "No. 74, Old Dartmouth Historical Sketches." I note, in its foreword, that a man of Liverpool, England, who is a fruit and vegetable merchant, is therein credited with "rescuing from oblivion the stenographic notes of the Vice-Admiralty Court at Gibraltar," relating to the case of the

Made in the USA
Columbia, SC
20 January 2025